HEINRICH SCHENKER

Routledge Music Bibliographies

SERIES EDITOR: BRAD EDEN

COMPOSERS

Isaac Albéniz (1998)
Walter A. Clark

C. P. E. Bach (2002)
Doris Bosworth Powers

Samuel Barber (2001)
Wayne C. Wentzel

Béla Bartók, 2e (1997)
Elliott Antokoletz

Vincenzo Bellini (2002)
Stephen A. Willier

Alban Berg (1996)
Bryan R. Simms

Leonard Bernstein (2001)
Paul F. Laird

Johannes Brahms (2003)
Heather Platt

Benjamin Britten (1996)
Peter J. Hodgson

Elliott Carter (2000)
John L. Link

Carlos Chávez (1998)
Robert Parker

Frédéric Chopin (1999)
William Smialek

Aaron Copland (2001)
Marta Robertson and
Robin Armstrong

Gaetano Donizetti (2000)
James P. Cassaro

Edward Elgar (1993)
Chrostopher Kent

Gabriel Fauré (1999)
Edward R. Phillips

Christoph Willibald Gluck, 2e (2003)
Patricia Howard

Charles Ives (2002)
Gayle Sherwood

Scott Joplin (1998)
Nancy R. Ping-Robbins

Zoltán Kodály (1998)
Michael Houlahan and Philip Tacka

Franz Liszt, 2e (2003)
Michael Saffle

Guillaume de Machaut (1995)
Lawrence Earp

Felix Mendelssohn Bartholdy (2001)
John Michael Cooper

Giovanni Pierluigi da Palestrina
(2001)
Clara Marvin

Giacomo Puccini (1999)
Linda B. Fairtile

Maurice Ravel (2003)
Stephen Zank

Gioachino Rossini (2002)
Denise P. Gallo

Alessandro and Domenico Scarlatti
(1993)
Carole F. Vidali

Camille Saint-Saens (2003)
Timothy Flynn

Heinrich Schenker (2003)
Benjamin Ayotte

Jean Sibelius (1998)
Glenda D. Goss

Giuseppe Verdi (1998)
Gregory Harwood

Tomás Luis de Victoria (1998)
Eugene Casjen Cramer

Richard Wagner (2002)
Michael Saffle

Adrian Willaert (2003)
David Michael Kidger

GENRES

Central European Folk Music (1996)
Philip V. Bohlman

Chamber Music (2002)
John H. Baron

Choral Music (2001)
Avery T. Sharp and James Michael
Floyd

Jazz Research and Performance
Materials, 2e (1995)
Eddie S. Meadows

Music in Canada (1997)
Carl Morey

North American Indian Music (1997)
Richard Keeling

Opera, 2e (2001) by Guy Marco

The Recorder, 2e (2003)
Richard Griscom and David Lasocki

Serial Music and Serialism (2001)
John D. Vander Weg

HEINRICH SCHENKER
A GUIDE TO RESEARCH

BENJAMIN MCKAY AYOTTE

ROUTLEDGE MUSIC BIBLIOGRAPHIES
ROUTLEDGE
NEW YORK AND LONDON

Published in 2004 by
Routledge
29 West 35th Street
New York, NY 10001
www.routledge-ny.com

Published in Great Britain by
Routledge
11 New Fetter Lane
London, EC4P 4EE
www.routledge.co.uk

10 9 8 7 6 5 4 3 2 1

Library of Congress Cataloging-in-Publication Data
Ayotte, Benjamin McKay.
   Heinrich Schenker : a guide to research / Benjamin McKay Ayotte.
      p. cm.—(Routledge music bibliographies)
Includes bibliographical references (p.   ) and indexes.
   ISBN 0-415-94071-0 (hardback : alk. paper)
1. Schenker, Heinrich, 1868–1935—Bibliography. I. Title. II. Series:
Routledge musical bibliographies.
   ML134.S25A95   2003
   016.78′092—dc21

                                                            2003008616

Dedicated to Professor Sylvan S. Kalib

Contents

Introduction   xi

Acknowledgments   xiii

Abbreviations   xv

List of Periodicals Cited   xvii

1 Sources of Biographical Information   1

2 Works of Heinrich Schenker   5
   Original Musical Compositions (C); Schenker's Articles, Editions and
   Arrangements, and Theoretical Works (S); and Translations and Reprints (T)

3 Articles on Schenker and His Approach   61

4 Books on Schenker and His Approach   191

5 Dissertations and Theses on Schenker and His Approach   217

6 Electronic Schenker Resources   259

Appendix A: Schenker Symposia   265

Appendix B: Chronology of Schenker's Life and Works   271

Glossary of Schenkerian Terms   277

Bibliography   281

Author Index   283

Topical Index   295

Composer Index   299

Introduction

The influence of Heinrich Schenker on professional musical discourse cannot be overstated. It is now nearly seventy years since Schenker passed away; his approach to musical hearing and musical analysis has grown steadily in influence since the posthumous publication of *Der freie Satz* in 1935. Witnesses to this are the burgeoning secondary literature and reprints of his principal theoretical works. His ideas have made their way from the outer fringes into the mainstream of music-theoretical discourse. In a 1988 article, Allen Forte remarked, "It is difficult to pick up a recent professional journal or book without finding an article which has musical illustrations that contain Schenkerian beams, slurs, and other notational apparatus" (Forte 1988). Six years later, David Gagné summed up the situation this way:

> Since Schenker's death some sixty years ago, many principles and ways of thinking that he first introduced have become an integral part of musical discourse. Concepts such as prolongation and the notion of structural levels are now frequently taught to music students, and analytical graphs are commonplace in theory journals. At the same time, the field of Schenkerian analysis has expanded and diversified in the last three decades. Studies of pre-Baroque and twentieth-century works have explored structure from a Schenkerian perspective in repertoires that Schenker himself did not address. Current research is expanding the consideration of rhythm, texture, orchestration, form, and other compositional features in relation to structure. As new ideas are being developed in teaching and research, a reexamination of established paradigms is also taking place. (Gagné 1994: 21)

The proliferation of the secondary literature informed by Schenker's approach to musical hearing and analysis is clearly a testimony to his influence on music theory and pedagogy.

The present volume consists of more than fifteen hundred citations to both primary sources (Schenker's works themselves and the three major archives) and the extensive secondary literature, annotated and subdivided by category (archival/biographical information, articles, books, dissertations and theses, and

electronic resources). The list is supplemented with an index of the pieces analyzed in the entries, as well as a selective classification index. Reviews of many
of the books are cited, and discussions stemming from certain articles are included. Entries are classified into twelve categories: (1) introductions, surveys,
and explanations; (2) analytical studies; (3) repertoire outside Schenker's sphere
of inquiry; (4) criticism and/or revision; (5) rhythm and meter; (6) historical,
philosophical, and epistemological studies; (7) motivic relationships and form;
(8) analysis and performance; (9) pedagogy; (10) computer applications; (11) relationships between Schenker and others/comparative analyses; and (12) interdisciplinary approaches. A multilingual glossary of Schenkerian terms and index
of authors concludes the volume.

The proliferation of scholarly Schenkerian literature makes the compilation
of such a bibliography as this a daunting task at best, but one that has been eased
somewhat by the excellent and beautifully annotated bibliographies prepared by
David Beach (1969/1975, 1985, and 1989) and the Bibliography and Guide prepared by David Damschroder and David Russell Williams (1990). When cataloging a field so vast, there are bound to be inadvertent oversights and
omissions, and I as author bear full responsibility and would appreciate hearing
of overlooked sources. In the selection of items for inclusion, I have tried to be
as comprehensive as possible, including minor and tangentially related sources
in addition to the stronger ones.

Acknowledgments

A project such as this is not brought to fruition without the help of many individuals and organizations. I particularly want to thank Sidney Berger and Darian Daries of the Special Collections Library at the University of California, Riverside, for their allowing me unrestricted access to the Oswald Jonas Memorial Collection collection, and Sheryl Davis and Melissa Conway for their permission to reproduce the musical quotations used in chapter 2. For permission to reproduce copyrighted prose or musical materials, I thank Rose Robinson of the University of California Press, Barbara Mackenzie of the RILM abstracts, Karin Gabel of Breitkopf und Härtel, Ingrid Meder of Josef Weinberger Verlag, and Christine Prindl of Ludwig Doblinger Verlag. For financial assistance, I wish to thank the Graduate College of Bowling Green State University and the Pro Musica foundation, which supplied grants allowing me to travel to California to study source materials, and the Society for Music Theory for underwriting some of the costs incurred in the preparation of this book with a publication subvention.

Many in the scholarly community both in the United States and abroad have supported this project by putting me in contact with sources that I might not have been able to obtain through the usual reference sources, and I apologize in advance for any omissions. I wish to offer particular thanks to Amy Chung, Irene Deliège, Boris Plotnikov, Marc Rigaudière, and Lubomír Spurný, who have graciously sent me materials, and to Gordon McQuere, Anna Celenza, and Amy Yeung for their assistance in the translation of some Russian, German, and Chinese texts, respectively. My thanks also to Chi-Jen Chang, Christopher Cipkin, Annie Coeurdevey, Andrew Davis, Jonathan Dunsby, Yosef Goldenberg, Edward Hoyenski, Chung-Kun Hung, Christoph Hust, Michael Klein, William Lake, Stephen Lindeman, Ken Moore, Edward Pearsall, Jeff Perry, Jay Rahn, William Renwick, Mathieu Schneider, PoWei Wang, Yuh-Wen Wang, and Robert Wason, all of whom who have supplied material, suggestions, or citations. To Robert Byrne and Richard Carlin for their support and expert editing of the current volume, I also express my gratitude. Last, but certainly not least, I wish to thank my wife, Sara, and daughter, Victoria, for their unyielding patience and understanding in dealing with their often absent and preoccupied husband and father during the time it took to compile this book.

Abbreviations

A	Article (chapter 3)
B	Book (chapter 4)
Bio	Biographical sources (chapter 1)
C	Musical composition of Schenker's (chapter 2)
D	Dissertation or thesis (chapter 5)
E	Electronic resource (chapter 6)
HAM	In the composer index, the *Historical Anthology of Music*, Vol. I, edited by Willi Apel and Archibald Davidson (Harvard: 1946)
JC	The Oswald Jonas Memorial Collection (JC I: 1–1 = Jonas Collection, box 1, folio 1, item 1)
LU	In the composer index, the *Liber Usualus*
OC	The Ernst Oster Collection (OC I: 1 = Oster Collection, file 1, item 1)
R	In the author index, R following an index number indicates a response to an article or a review of a book
S	Schenker's writings (chapter 2)
T	Translation of Schenker's work (chapter 2)
T	In the author index, T following an index number refers to a translation of a book or article
WTC	In the composer index, J. S. Bach's Well-Tempered Clavier

In addition, standard catalog numbers will be used for composer's works (e.g., BWV, K, Hob., etc.) in the composer index. The items will be referred to throughout the indices by their catalog number (e.g., "D1" instead of "Traut 2002"). The following system of octave identification will be used:

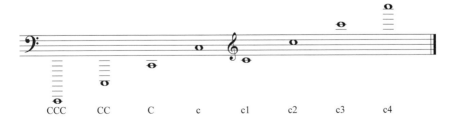

List of Periodicals Cited

Acta Musicologica (ISSN: 0001-6241)
Allgemeine Musik Zeitung
Allgemeine musikalische Zeitung
American Brahms Society Newsletter, The
American Journal of Semiotics (ISSN: 0277-7126)
Analyse Musicale (ISSN: 0295-3722)
Anbruch
Annual Review of Jazz Studies (ISSN: 0731-0641)
Archiv für Musikwissenschaft (ISSN: 0003-9292)
The Art of Music: Journal of the Shanghai Conservatory of Music (ISSN: 1000-4270)
Art: Revista da Escola de Musica e Artes Cenicas da UFBA (ISSN: 0102-3357)
Bach-Jahrbuch (ISSN: 0084-7682)
Balgarsko muzikoznanie (ISSN: 0204-823X)
Beethoven Journal (ISSN: 0898-6185)
Beethoven Studies
Beethoven-Jahrbuch
Beiträge zur Musikwissenschaft (ISSN: 0005-8106)
Canadian University Music Review (ISSN: 0710-0353)
Cardozo Law Review
Cashiers Franz Schubert
Chopin-Jahrbuch
College Music Symposium (ISSN: 0069-5696)
Composer (ISSN: 0010-4337)
Computational Musicology Newsletter
Computer Music Journal (ISSN: 0148-9267)
Contemporary Music Review (ISSN: 0749-4467)
Current Musicology (ISSN: 0011-3735)
Der Merker
Deutsche Journal für Musikwissenschaft
Die Musikantgilde

Dreiklang, Der
Dreiundzwanzig
Diastema
Fermata (ISSN: 1201-6624)
Freie Schulgemeinde, Die
Gamut (ISSN: 0713-3545)
Georgia Review, The (ISSN: 0016-8386)
Hindemith-Jahrbuch (ISSN: 0172-956X)
Hudebni Veda (ISSN: 0018-7003)
Illinois State Teacher's Association
In Theory Only (ISSN: 0360-4365)
Indiana Theory Review (ISSN: 0271-8022)
Intégral (1073–6913)
International Journal of Man-Machine Studies
International Journal of Musicology (ISSN: 0941-9535)
International Review of the Aesthetics and Sociology of Music (ISSN: 0351-
    5796)
Israel Studies in Musicology (ISSN: 0334-2026)
Jahrbuch des Österreichischen Volksliedwerkes (ISSN: 0473-8624)
Journal of Research in Music Education
Journal of Music Theory (ISSN: 0891-7639)
Journal of Music Theory Pedagogy (ISSN: 0891-7639)
Journal of Musicological Research (ISSN: 0141-1896)
Journal of Musicology (ISSN: 0277-9269)
Journal of the American Musicological Society (ISSN: 0003-0139)
Journal of the Arnold Schoenberg Institute (ISSN: 0146-5856)
Journal of the Central Conservatory of Music (ISSN 1001-9871)
Journal of the Royal Music Association (ISSN: 0269-0403)
Konservative Monatschrift
Miscellanea Musicologica (ISSN: 0076-9355)
Modern Music
Moore School of Electrical Engineering Music Report
Mozart-Jahrbuch (ISSN: 0077-1805)
Music Analysis (ISSN: 0262-5245)
Music and Letters (ISSN: 0027-4224)
Music Forum, The
Music Perception (ISSN: 0730-7829)
Music Review, The (ISSN: 0027-4445)
Music Theory Spectrum (ISSN: 0195-6167)
Musica
Musica e investigacion (ISSN: 0329-224X)
Musicae Scientae
Musical America (ISSN: 0735-777X)

Musical Mercury, The
Musical Quarterly, The (ISSN: 0027-4631)
Musical Times, The (ISSN: 0027-4666)
Musiikki (ISSN: 0355-1059)
Musik and Ästhetik (ISSN: 1432-9425)
Musik and Forskning (ISSN: 0903-188X)
Musik, Die
Musikerziehung
Musikforschung, Die (ISSN: 0027-4801)
Musiktheorie (ISSN: 0177-4182)
Musurgia: Analyse et pratique musicales (ISSN: 1257-7537)
Muzikološki Zbornik (ISSN: 0580-373X)
Muzyka
Muzykal'naja Akademij (ISSN: 0869-4516)
Nassarre: Revista aragonesa de musicología (ISSN: 0213-7305)
Neue Zeitschrift für Musik (ISSN: 0170-8791)
Nineteenth-Century Music (ISSN: 0148-2076)
Das Orchester (ISSN: 0030-4468)
Österreichische Musikzeitschrift (ISSN: 0029-9316)
Österreichische Musikzeitung
Österreichische Zeitung für Musikwissenschaft
Pauta: Cuadernos de teoria y critica musical
Periodical of Theory-Composition,
Perspectives of New Music (ISSN: 0031-6016)
Proceedings of the Royal Musical Association
Psychology of Music (ISSN: 0305-7356)
Quodlibet: Revista de especialización musical (ISSN: 1134-8615)
Revista di musicologia
Revue Belge de Musicologie (ISSN: 0771-6788)
Schweizer Jahrbuch für Musikwissenschaft
Schweizerliche Musikzeitung
SIGLASH Newsletter
Sonus
Soundings
Sovetskaia Muzyka
Theory and Practice (ISSN: 0741-6156)
Tijdschrift voor muziektheorie (ISSN: 1385-3066)
Verdi Newsletter
Von Neuer Musik
Zeitschrift für Musik
Zenetudományi dolgozatok (ISSN: 0139-0732)
Zvuk (ISSN: 0044-555X)

Chapter 1

Sources of Biographical Information

PART 1: ARCHIVES

Bio1 *The Oswald Jonas Memorial Collection*, University of California, Riverside.

The Oswald Jonas Memorial Collection (henceforth JC) was established in 1978. It is comprised of four collections, the Heinrich Schenker Archive, the Oswald Jonas Papers, the Moriz Violin Papers, and the First and Early Editions. The collections contains a wealth of biographical information, chiefly Schenker's diaries (boxes 1–4), most of his personal correspondence (boxes 5–15), his critical and analytical works (boxes 16–21), his compositional manuscripts (boxes 22–23), his research and teaching materials (boxes 24–34), and various family documents (box 35), as well as photographs (box 72). Jonas received the Schenker *Nachlaß* from Erwin Ratz, who had received it from Schenker's widow around 1945. See the bibliography (Lang 1994) for the finding list.

Bio2 *The Ernst Oster Collection*, New York Public Library.

The Oster Collection (henceforth OC) consists of the portion of the Schenker *Nachlaß* bequeathed to Oster in 1938, when he left Vienna for New York. It was established at the New York Public Library in 1977 and consists of correspondence (mostly with his publishers, files 1, 18, 52, 54, and B), Schenker's scrapbook and lesson books (files 2–3), draft material for *Der Tonwille* and *Der freie Satz* (files 20–24, 35–38, 76, 79), many pages of analyses (arranged by composer), articles by himself and others, and many scores. For the finding list, see the bibliography (Kosovsky 1990). See also Kosovsky's article in *Schenker Studies II (A43)*.

Bio3 *The Rheinhard Oppel Collection*, University of North Texas.
Dr. Timothy Jackson established the Oppel Collection at the University of North
Texas in 2000 upon the donation of the papers by Kurt Oppel in 1999. The collection consists of fifteen boxes of manuscripts (Oppel's music and analyses),
correspondence, memorabilia, and photographs, in addition to about fifty books
from Oppel's library. The collection contains, among other things, a German
translation of Fux's *Gradus ad Parnassum* dating from 1742 and Marpurg's
Handbuch bey dem Generalbasse from 1757.

PART 2: ENTRIES IN MUSICAL ENCYCLOPEDIAS

Bio4 2002 Drabkin, William. "Heinrich Schenker." In *The Cambridge History of Western Music Theory*, ed. by Thomas Christensen. Cambridge: Cambridge University Press: 812–43.

Bio5 2001 Snarrenberg, Robert. "Heinrich Schenker." In *The New Grove Dictionary of Music and Musicians*, ed. by Stanley Sadie. New York: Macmillan.

Bio6 1984 Forte, Allen. "Heinrich Schenker." In *The New Grove Dictionary of Music and Musicians,* ed. by Stanley Sadie. New York: Macmillan.

Bio7 1982 Federhofer, Helmut. "Schenker, Heinrich." In *Das Grosse Lexikon der Musik*. Vol. 7, ed. by Marc Honegger and Günther Massenkeil. Freiburg: Breisgau: 238–9.

Bio8 1963 Jonas, Oswald. "Schenker, Heinrich." In *Die Musik in Geschichte und Gegenwart*, Vol. 11, ed. by Friedrich Blume. Basel: Bärenreiter Kassel: 1670–2.

Bio9 1957 Eppstein, Hans. "Heinrich Schenker." In *Tonkonsten Internationellt Musiklexikon*. Stockholm: Ab Nordiska Uppalagböcker.

Bio10 1955 Moser, Hans Joachim "Heinrich Schenker." In *Moser's Musik Lexicon*. Hamburg: Hans Sikorski.

Bio11 1952 "Schenker, Heinrich." In *Musik-Lexicon,* ed. by Hans Joachim Moser. Hamburg: Musik-Verlag Hans Sikorski: 1018.

Bio12 1946 "Schenker, Heinrich." In *The International Cyclopedia of Music and Musicians,* ed. by Oscar Thompson. New York: Dodd, Mead and Company: 1630.

Bio13 1946 Tschierpe, Rudolph. "Schenker, Heinrich." In *Kleines Musiklexicon*. Hamburg: Hoffman and Campe Verlag: 270.

Bio14 1944 Geiringer, Karl. "Schenker, Heinrich." In *Grove's Dictionary of Music and Musicians*, Supplementary Volume, ed. by H. C. Colles: 566–7.

Bio15 1938 "Schenker, Heinrich." In *The Macmillan Encyclopedia of Music and Musicians*, ed. by Albert E. Wier. New York: Macmillan: 1660.

Bio16 1930 "Schenker, Heinrich." In *Jüdisches Lexicon: Ein enzyklopädischen Handbuch des Jüdischen Wissens*, Vol. 4, ed. by Georg Herlitz and Bruno Kirschner. Berlin: Jüdischer Verlag: 191–2.

Bio17 1929 "Schenker, Heinrich." In *Riemanns Musik-Lexicon*, 11th Ed. Berlin: Max Hesse Verlag: 1611.

Bio18 1924 "Schenker, Heinrich." In *The New Encyclopedia of Music and Musicians*, ed. by Waldo Selden Pratt. London: Macmillan: 724.

PART 3: OBITUARIES

Bio19 1935 "Dr. Heinrich Schenker." *New York Times,* 23 January: 17 (OC II).

Bio20 1935 "The Late Heinrich Schenker." *New York Times,* 3 February: Section 8, page 7.

Bio21 1935 "Heinrich Schenker Gestorben." *Der Wiener Tag*, 15 January (OC II: 89).

Bio22 1935 Bamberger, Carl. "Zum Tode Heinrich Schenker." *Wiener Musik-Zeitung*, April (OC II: 91).

Bio23 1935 Hoboken, Anthony van. "Heinrich Schenker gestorven re Weenen 14 Januari 1935." *Nieuwe Rotterdamsche Courant*, 8 February (OC II: 90).

Bio24 1935 Violin, Moriz. "Zur Erinnerung Heinrich Schenker." *Neue Freie Presse*, 31 January (OC II: 91).

Chapter 2

Works of Heinrich Schenker

PART 1: ORIGINAL MUSICAL COMPOSITIONS

Group A: The Published Compositions

C1   Zwei Clavierstücke op. 1; published by Ludwig Doblinger (Vienna) [n.d.]. Plate D. 1740 dedicated to Julius Epstein.

No 1: Etude: *Allegretto*, G minor; 3 pp. (numbered 3–5).

No. 2: Capriccio, *Appassionato*, A-flat major; 4 pp. (numbered 6–9)

aus **Heinrich Schenker**, *Zwei Clavierstücke, op. 1*
© 1982 by Ludwig Doblinger (Bernhard Herzmansky) KG., Wien
Abdruck erfolgt mit freundlicher Genehmigung des Verlages

C2   Fantasie op. 2. Breitkopf & Härtel's Klavier-Bibliothek. Leipzig: Breitkopf & Härtel, © 1898. Plate Klav. Bibl. 22290. 37 pp. At head of title: "An F. Busoni." Seinem liebsten treuen 'Floritz' H. Schenker (rev. Fr. W. Höhne). [Part I] *Movimento solene, non troppo lento. A modo di leggenda*, E-flat Major, 19 pp. (numbered 3–21). [Part II] *Preludio. Con moto solene. Thema. Moderato e cantando*, C minor; 16 pp. (numbered 22–37).

C3   Sechs Lieder für eine Singstimme mit Begleitung des Pianoforte op. 3 (Deutscher Liederverlag). Leipzig, Brussels, London, New York: Breitkopf & Härtel, © 1898, 1901. Plate no. D.L.-V. 4760. With ms. notes in Schenker's hand. Pictorial cover title, 31 pp. Series title, p. 1: Werke von Heinrich Schenker.

> Op. 3, No. 1:   Versteckte Jasminen (Detlev von Liliencron, 1844–1909). *Sehr geschwind und schalkhaft vorzutragen*, E minor, six-eight time; 6 pp. (numbered 2–7). Range: b—f^2 (g^2).

> Op. 3, No. 2:   Wiegenlied (Detlev von Liliencron) *Zart [Andante alla breve]*, G major, *alla breve*; 5 pp. (numbered 8–13). Range: d^1—e^2.

Vor der Thü - re   schläft der Baum,   durch den Gar - tem

Op. 3, No. 3:   Vogel im Busch (Detlev von Liliencron, 1844–1909). *Heiter und zierlich*, A major, two-four time; 5 pp. (numbered 13–17). Range: c—f². Showing m. 6ff (vocal entry).

Klei-ner   Vo-gel in den   Zwei-gen, bleib hübsch   sit-zen, sin-ge   wei-ter, sin-ge

Op. 3, No. 4:   Ausklang (Ludwig Jacobowski, 1868–1900). *Gehalten,* F-sharp minor, common time; 2 pp. (numbered 18–19). Range: c¹(f-sharp)—d².

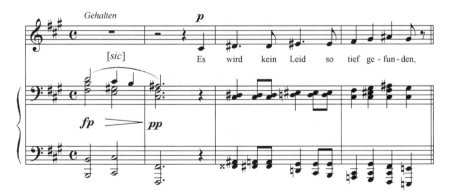

Es   wird   kein   Leid   so   tief ge - fun - den,

Op. 3, No. 5:   Allein (Ludwig Jacobowski, 1868–1900). *In langsam gehender Bewegung, wehmütig*, E-flat minor, two-four time; 4 pp. (numbered 20–23). Range: c—d-flat².

Op. 3, No. 6:   Einkleidung (Wilhelm Müller, 1794–1827). *Anmutig bewegt*, A major; 8 pp. (numbered 24–31). Range: e¹—f-sharp².

© by Breitkopf & Härtel, Wiesbaden
Used with kind permission

C4   Fünf Klavierstücke op. 4. Breitkopf & Härtel's Klavier-Bibliothek. Leipzig: Breitkopf & Härtel © 1898. Plate Klav. Bibl. 22055. 18 pp. (numbered 2–19).
A review in *The Musical Times* 41 (1900): 175 says that "[the pieces] form excellent studies for development of independence between that hands, a feature of pianoforte playing which does not always receive the attention it deserves."

Op. 4, No. 1:   *Andante*, C minor, common time; 2 pp. (numbered 2–3).

Op. 4, No. 2:   *Allegretto grazioso*, G major, two-four time; 4 pp. (numbered 4–7).

Op. 4, No. 3:   *Andante con moto e rubato*, B-flat minor, common time; 3 pp. (numbered 8–10).

Op. 4, No. 4:   *Allegretto poco agitato e rubato*, E-flat major, two-four time; 4 pp. (numbered 11–14).

Op. 4, No. 5:   *Quasi allegretto*, D major, *alla-breve*; 5 pp. (numbered 15–19).

C5   Zweistimmige Inventionen op. 5. Breitkopf & Härtel's Klavier-Bibliothek. Leipzig: Breitkopf & Härtel © 1898, 1901. Plate Klav. Bibl. 23266. 11 pp. At head of title: "Frau Irene Mayerhofer gewidmet."

  Op. 5, No. 1:   *Allegro amabile*, G major, three-eight time; 3 pp (numbered 3–5).

  Op. 5, No. 2:   *Con moto appassionato e con molto sentimento*, F-sharp minor, four-two time; 2 pp. (numbered 6–7).

  Op. 5, No. 3:   *Vivace, quasi presto*, D minor, three-eight time; 2 pp. (numbered 8–9).

  Op. 5, No. 4:   *Allegro deciso*, A major, six-eight time; 2 pp. (numbered 10–11).

C6 *Vorüber* op. 7, no. 3. Text by Johanna Ambrosius (1854–1938) from *Lieder der Liebe*. Photocopy of four printed pp. numbered 151–154 (from a published collection?). Four-voice *a cappella* (SATB). *Andante non lento*, E minor, common time. Ranges: S: d-sharp^1—g^2; A: a-flat^1—c-sharp^2; T: d—a^1; B: E—e^1.

C7 Ländler op. 10. *Ländler für Pianoforte* von Heinrich Schenker. *Op. 10.* Berlin: N. Simrock © 1899. Plate 11163. Cover title, 11, [1] pp. At head of title: "Herrn Wilhelm Kux." *Tempo Giusto*, G major, three-four time. Interior sections pass through C major, A major, E major, G-sharp minor, C major, F major, B-flat minor, B-flat major, C major, and G major.

C8 Syrische Tänze für Pianoforte zu 4 Händen (originally titled "Tänze der Chassidim"). Wien, Leipzig, Paris: Josef Weinberger [n.d.]. At head of title: "Alphons frh. v. Rothschild zugeeignet." Heft I, No. 1, 2. Plate J.W. 1092a. Cover: green ink on tan paper. 21 pp. Heft II, No. 1, 2. Plate J.W. 1092b. Cover: green ink on tan paper. 15 pp.

> Heft 1, No. 1: *Andante espressivo, Allegro scherzando,* D minor, two-four time; 8 pp. (numbered 2–9).

Heft 1, No. 2: *Allegro con fuoco*, C minor, three-eight time; 12 pp. (numbered 10–21). Showing m. 8ff; work begins with an eight-measure ostinato in secondo.

Heft 2, No. 1: *Allegretto* [*dolcissimo*], G minor, three-eight time; 8 pp. (numbered 2–9). Showing m. 4ff; work begins with a four-measure ostinato in secondo.

Heft 2, No. 2. *Allegro molto passionate*, D major, two-four time; 6 pp. (numbered 10–15).

Used by kind permission of Josef Weinberger Ges. M. B. H.

Group B: The Unpublished Works with Opus Numbers

The following measures of music are used with the permission of the Special Collections, Thomas Rivera Library, University of Califorina, Riverside.

C9   Mondnacht (Richard Dehmel, 1863–1920), op. 3, Heft I, No. 1. Four-voice (SATB) with piano accompaniment. Two ms. leaves (i.e., 4 pp.), ink, in the hand of a copyist, with pencil revisions in Schenker's hand. Open score. *Träumerisch und leise*, D minor, common time. JC XXII: 2. Ranges: S: c-sharp[1]—g[2]; A: g—e[2]; T: d—g[1]; B: G—d[1].

C10   Drei gesänge für ein tiefere Stimme mit Pianoforte Begleitung, op. 6.
Nine ms. leaves (i.e., 14 pp.). Nos. 1–2 in ink, largely in the hand of a
copyist, with pencil revisions and notes in Schenker's hand. No. 3, ink, in
Schenker's hand. Cover title, ink, in Schenker's hand. JC XXII: 3.

Op. 6, No. 1:   "Heimat" (Richard Dehmel, 1863–1920). Solo with
piano accompaniment. Two ms. leaves (i.e., 4 pp.),
ink, in the hand of a copyist, with ink and pencil revisions in Schenker's hand. Marked "Gärtner." *Unruhig
(fast im Allabreve) jadoch nicht hurtig,* C minor–E
major, common time. Range: c¹—f-sharp.

Op. 6, No. 2:   "Nachtgruß" (J. v. Eichendorff). Solo voice with piano
accompaniment. Three ms. leaves (i.e., 5 pp.), ink, in
Schenker's hand, with pencil revisions. *Leise mit Aus-
druck,* B-flat major. Range: c¹—f².

Op. 6, No. 3:   "Wanderers Nachtlied" (Johann Wolfgang von
Goethe, 1749–1832). Solo voice with piano accompa-
niment. two ms. leaves (i.e., 3 pp.), ink, in the hand of
a copyist, with pedal markings in ink in another hand
(Schenker's?). *Feierlich, nicht zu langsam,* D-flat
Major, *alla breve.* Range: g—d¹

Op. 6, No. 3a: "Meeresstille" (Johann Wolfgang von Goethe, 1748–1832). Solo voice with piano accompaniment. One ms. leaf (i.e., 2pp.). Ink, in Schenker's hand. *Sehr Langsam*. G major, three-four time. Range: a-flat—f².

C11 [Three songs for mixed chorus, unaccompanied, op. 7]. JC XXII: 7–9.

Op. 7, No. 1: "Was ich liebe?" (Johanna Ambrosius Voigt, 1854–1938). Two ms. leaves (i.e., 4 pp.), ink, in Schenker's hand. Four-voice *a cappella* (SATB). *Poco allegro*, D major, common time. Ranges: S: e¹—a²; A: b—d²; T: f-sharp—g¹; B: A—e¹.

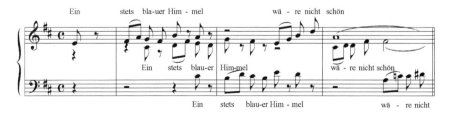

Op. 7, No. 2:   "Die Nachtigall" (Theodore Storm, 1817–88). Two
ms. leaves (i.e., 4 pp.), ink, in Schenker's hand. Four-
voice *a cappella* (SATB). *Grazioso*, E major, two-four
time. Ranges: S: e^1—f-flat^2; A: b—d^1; T: f-sharp—a^1;
B: E—c^1.

Op. 7, No. 3:   "Vorüber," see C6 above.

C12   "Drei Gesänge für Frauenstimmen a cappella." Heinrich Schenker. Op. 8.
Four-voice (SSAA). JC XXII: 10.

Op. 8, No. 1:   "Agnes" (Friedrich Mörike, 1804–1875). *Andante*, A
minor, three-four time. Ranges: S^1: g-sharp^1—g^2; S^2:
d^1—e^2; A^1: b—d^1; A^2: e—a^1.

Op. 8, No. 2:   "Im Rosenbusch der Liebe Schlief" (Hoffmann von Fallersleben, 1798–1874). *Zart und ziemlich schnell,* B-flat major, *alla breve.* Ranges: S¹: d¹—g²; S²: d¹—e²; A¹: b-flat—c²; A²: f—b-flat¹.

Op. 8, No. 3:   "Der Traum" (Ludwig Uhland, 1787–1862). *Träumerisch langsam,* B major, common time. Ranges: S¹: g-sharp¹—g²; S²: c-sharp¹—d-sharp²; A¹: g—e²; A²: e—c².

Op. 8, No. 4:   "Tausend schöne goldne Sterne" (Ludwig, Uhland, 1787–1862). *Allegretto,* E major. Two ms. leaves, conjugate, the second leaf blank, ink, in Schenker's hand; opus numbering added in pencil in another hand (Jonas's?). Four-voice *a cappella* (SSAA). JC XXII: 13. Ranges: S^1: g-sharp^1—g-sharp^2; S^2: e^1—c-sharp^2; A^1: d-sharp^1—b^1; A^2: e—g^1.

Group C: The Unpublished Vocal Music without Opus Numbers

C13   "Der Abschied" (unknown poet). *Allegro risoluto.* D-sharp minor, common time. Solo voice with piano accompaniment. JC XXII: 14. Range: c—e-flat^2.

C14   "Blumengruß" (Johann Wolfgang von Goethe, 1749–1842). Solo voice with piano accompaniment. JC XXII: 15. Range: c^1—e-flat^2. Showing m. 8ff (vocal entry).

C15 "Die Braut" (Wilhelm Müller, 1794–1827). *Bewegt und klagend*, F minor, *alla breve*. Signed: H. Schenker; dated (Schenker's hand) 14. V. 1898. JC XXII: 16. Range: d-flat[1]—g[2].

C16 "Drunten auf der Gassen. Ein Mädchenlied" (Paul Heyse, 1830–1914). Solo voice with piano accompaniment. *Bewegt*, G minor, two-four time. JC XXII: 17. Range: f-sharp[1]—g[2].

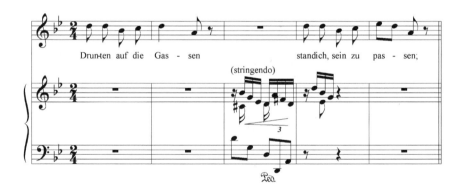

C17 "Eros rüffelt mich wieder. Ode" (Sappho, ca. 66 BC). Solo voice with piano accompaniment. *Allegro moderato*, three-four time. Range: c[1]—e[2]. JC XXII: 18.

C18   "Der Gang von Wittow nach Jasmund" (Wilhelm Müller, 1794–1827). Solo voice with piano accompaniment. Version 1: B-flat minor, two-four time. Range: b-flat—f^2. Version 2: D minor, *alla breve, allegro agitato*. JC XXII: 19a–b.

   Version 1:

   Version 2:

C19 "Harfenspieler" (Johann Wolfgang von Goethe, 1749–1832). F-sharp minor, two-four time. *Andante*. Four-voice *a cappella* (SATB). Dated 10. VII. 1897. Ranges: S: f-sharp-a¹; A: a—d¹; T: d—g¹; B: G—d¹. JC XXII: 20.

C20 "Ich hör im Himmel Rosse traben." Solo voice with piano accompaniment. *Allegretto*, C-sharp major, *alla breve*. Range: C-sharp¹—F-sharp². JC XXII: 21.

C21 "Der Lindenbaum" (H. Meyerhofer). Solo voice with piano accompaniment. *Ziemlich langsam,* G minor, three-four time. Range: c¹—g². Signed: H. Schenker. JC XXII: 22.

C22   "Mädchenlied, No. 1" ("Auf die Nacht in der Spinnstub'n") (Paul Heyse,
1830–1914) Solo voice with piano accompaniment. *Legato*, G minor,
three-eight time. Range: d[1]—f-sharp[2]. JC: XXII: 23.

C23   "Mädchenlied" ("Der Himmel hat Keine Sterne so klar") (Paul Heyse,
1830–1914). Solo voice with piano accompaniment. D major. Range:
d[1]—f-sharp[2]. JC XXII: 24

C24   "Ich bin bei dir gewesen. Mädchenlied" (Johanna Ambrosius, 1854–
1938). Solo voice with piano accompaniment. *Langsam, jedoch neigend
und leidenschaftslich*. D-sharp minor, common time. Signed: H. Schenker.
JC XXII: 25. Range: b-sharp—f[2].

C25 "Mädchenlied" ("Mir träumte von einem Myrthenbaum") (Paul Heyse, 1830–1914). Solo voice with piano accompaniment. Version 1: *Innisch gekehrt*, F minor, common time. Range: e¹—a-flat². Version 2: *Langsam, leise*, D minor, common time. Range c-sharp¹—d². JC XXII: 26.
Version 1:

Version 2:

C26 "Mailied" ("Zwischen Weizen und Korn") (Johann Wolfgang von Goethe, 1749–1832). Solo voice with piano accompaniment. JC XXII: 27. D-flat major, *non-legato*, two-four time. Range: d-flat¹—f²

C27   "Mei' Schatz hat mir 'n Kuß geb'n." Solo voice with piano accompaniment. A compilation of fragments. JC XXII: 28.

C28   "Mein Freund" (Johanna Ambrosius, 1854–1938). Solo voice with piano accompaniment. Signed: H. Schenker. F-sharp minor, *Maestoso*, *alla breve*. Range: c-sharp[1]—d[2]. JC XXII: 29.

C29   "Die Nachtigallen" (Joseph Freiherr von Eichendorff, 1788–1857). Solo voice with piano accompaniment. One ms. leaf (i.e., 2 pp.), ink, in Schenker's hand; recto has corrections on pasteover. Dated 19, VI. 1897. JC XXII: 30.

C30 "O mein einsam, einsam, einsam Kissen" (George Gordon Noël Byron, 1788–1824). Solo voice with piano accompaniment. "(Klagelied von Byron, übersetzt von O.Gildemeister)." Signed: H. Schenker op. 8 n. [number missing]. OC XXII: 31.

C31 "Rosenzeit." Solo voice with piano accompaniment, D major, common time. Range: d^1—e^2. JC XXII: 32.

C32 "Das Sträusschen. Altböhmisch" (Johann Wolfgang von Goethe, 1749–1832). Five mixed voices *a cappella* with soprano solo. E minor, six-eight time, *Mäßig bewegt*. Ranges: S: g¹—b-flat²; A: g—e²; T: d—g¹; B: e—d¹. Dated 23. VI. 1897. JC XXII: 33.

C33 "Wiegenlied" ("Bienchen, Bienchen wiegt sich in Sonnenschein") (Richard Dehmel, 1863–1920). Solo voice with piano accompaniment, G major, *Andantino semplice, mit zartezester Empfindung*. Range: d¹—g². JC XXII: 34.

C34 Music for *Hamlet*. Orchestra and voices. Includes, all in Schenker's hand, JC XXII: 36:

   C34a: "Eintrag der Schauspieler." Piano score. One ms. leaf (i.e., 2 pp.), ink, title in pencil [Act 3, scene 2]. E-flat major, common time.

C34b: "Lied der Ophelia, Act 4, scene 5." Four ms. leaves (i.e., 8 pp.), voice and orchestra. Three songs numbered in pencil:

C34b1 No. 5: "Wie erkenn' ich." Pencil with ink additions, followed by "ein Todtenmarsch [*sic*] Act 5, scene 2." Pencil and ink. C minor, common time.

C34b2 No. 6: "Auf Morgen ist Sanct Valentins Tag." Pencil and ink. D major, common time.

C34b3 No. 7: "Sie trugen ihn auf der Bahre bloß." Pencil and ink.
B-flat minor, common time.

C34c: "Trauermarsch." Piano score. Two ms. leaves (i.e., 4 pp.), ink
with pencil additions [for Ophelia, Act 5, scene 1]. C minor,
common time.

C34d: "Hamlets Tod" [Act 5, scene 2]. Fragments:
Piano score: One ms. leaf (i.e., 2 pp.), ink, title in pencil.

Orchestral score: Two ms. leaves (i.e., 4 pp.), ink with pencil additions.

C34e: "Zwischenaktsmusik":

    C34e1 1–2 Akt: Orchestral score. Two ms. leaves (i.e., 3 pp.), pencil and ink. G minor, common time.

C34e2 2–3 Akt: Orchestral score. Four ms. leaves (i.e., 8 pp.), pencil and ink. A minor, common time.

C34e3 4–5 Akt: Orchestral score. Two ms. leaves (i.e., 4 pp.), pencil. E-flat minor, common time.

Group D: The Unpublished Instrumental Compositions without Opus Numbers

Piano Compositions

C35   "Monolog." For piano. Two ms. versions: [untitled], two ms. leaves (i.e., 3 pp.), ink and pencil in Schenker's hand. "Monolog," two ms. leaves (i.e., 4 pp.), ink, in a copyist's hand. A-flat major, two-four time. JC XXIII: 6.

C36   "V. Träumerisch bewegt." Two ms. versions: Two ms. leaves (i.e., four pp.), ink and blue pencil, numerous corrections, some of which do not appear in the other versions; all in Schenker's hand. Two ms. leaves (i.e.,

4 pp.), ink, in a copyist's hand; dated in pencil 1893. D minor, common time. JC XXIII: 7.

String Trios

C37 [Trio (violin, viola, piano)] "Allegro moderato" ["moderato" crossed out]. Six ms. leaves (i.e., 12 pp.), ink with a few pencil additions, all in Schenker's hand. C minor, three-four time. JC XXIII: 17.

C38 [Trio (violin, viola, piano)] "II. Allegretto." Seven ms. leaves (i.e., 13 pp., numbered in pencil 7–19). Ink, in a copyist's hand; blue and black pencil revisions in Schenker's hand. Earlier pages missing. JC XXIII: 18.

C39   [Trio (violin, viola, piano)] "Andante." Three ms. leaves (i.e., 5 pp.), ink,
in Schenker's hand. Dated (without year) 4. IV. JC XXIII: 19.

C40   [Trio (violin, viola [*sic*], piano)] "Scherzo." Two ms. leaves (i.e., 4 pp.),
pencil, in Schenker's hand. JC XXIII: 20.

C41 [Trio (violin, cello [*sic*], piano)] "Finale." Nine ms. leaves (17 [i.e., 18] pp., the last page entirely crossed through), ink with pencil revisions, in Schenker's hand. JC XXIII: 21.

C42 [Trio (violin, viola, piano)] Two ms. fragments: Two ms. leaves (i.e., 4 pp.), ink with pencil revisions, Schenker's hand. One ms. leaf (i.e., 1 p.) of revisions, ink, in Schenker's hand. JC XXIII: 22.

[IDENTICAL TO JC XXIII: 18]

C43 [Trio (violin, viola, piano)] Three ms. fragments: Three ms. leaves (i.e., 6 pp.), ink with pencil revisions, in Schenker's hand. Two ms. leaves (i.e., 4 pp.), ink, blue and black pencil, in Schenker's hand. JC XXIII: 23.
    First fragment:

Second fragment:

C44 "Streichtrio" [for violin, viola, cello]. Four ms. leaves (i.e., 7 pp.), ink and black and blue pencil; probably in copyist's hand, with revisions and title in Schenker's hand. Also one ms. leaf, sketch of two measures headed "S.3," ink, in Schenker's hand. JC XXIII: 24.

String Quartets
The following four items may form the movements of a complete quartet, the possible order being folios 27, 28, 26, 25. JC XXIII: 25–28.

C45 "Aria." Six ms. leaves (i.e., 10 pp., the last leaf blank), ink with pencil revisions, in Schenker's hand. *Allegretto (quasi allegro) con sentimento*, C
major. JC XXIII: 25.

C46 "Scherzo. III." Two ms. leaves (i.e., 4 pp.), ink with pencil revisions, in
Schenker's hand. Autograph inscription "Marburg a/d Lahn." *Prestis-
simo e caprissioso*, G minor. JC XXIII: 26.

C47   "Largo." Four ms. leaves (i.e., 8 pp.), ink with revisions in black and green pencil, in Schenker's hand. A minor, three-four time. JC XXIII: 27.

C48   Sketches for string quartet ("Scene"). Four ms. leaves (i.e., 7 pp.), ink and pencil, in Schenker's hand. *Allegro moderato*, C minor. JC XXIII: 28.

Other Instrumental Works

C49   "Serenade für Horn und Clavier von Heinrich Schenker" [horn in F and piano]. Two ms. leaves (i.e., 4 numbered pp.), ink, black and blue pencil, in Schenker's hand. Autograph inscription at head of title: "An seinen lieben Freund Louis Savant." A major, two-four time (showing m. 10ff: horn entrance). JC XXIII: 29.

PART 2: JOURNAL ARTICLES, INCLUDING THOSE PUBLISHED POSTHUMOUSLY

Lists of these journal articles appear in many places, such as Rast 1988, Feder-hofer 1990, Meeùs 1993, as well as Lang 1994, and a partial list in Beach 1969. The numbers following the entry (e.g., F. 2–8) correspond to the pages on which the text of the article appears in Hellmut Federhofer's edition (**B39**). Studies of these early writings may be found in **A143**, **A188**, **A381**, **D7**, and **D132**.

S1   1891   "Johannes Brahms: Fünf Lieder für eine Singstimme mit Pi-anoforte, Op. 107." *Musikalisches Wochenblatt* 22 (1 November): 514–7. F. 2–8.

S2   1892   "Hermann Gradener: Quintet No. 2, C moll, für Pianoforte, zwei Violinen, Viola und Violoncell, Op. 19." *Musikalisches Wochen-blatt* 23: 214–6. F. 8–13.

S3   1892   "Johannes Brahms: Fünf Gesänge für gemischten Chor a capella, Op. 104." *Musikalisches Wochenblatt* 23 (18, 25 August, 1 Sep-tember): 409–12, 425–56, F. 14–26.

S4   1892   "Mascagni in Wien." *Die Zukunft* 1 (15 October): 137–9. F. 26–30. Italian translation in **T40**.

S5   1892   "Eine jung-italienische Schule?" *Die Zukunft* 1 (3 December): 460–2. F. 31–4. Italian translation in **T41.**

S6   1893   "Mascagnis *Rantzau*." *Die Zukunft* 2 (11 February): 280–4. F. 35–40. Italian translation in **T42**.

S7   1893   "Anton Bruckner: Psalm 150 für Chor, Soli und Orchester."
              Musikalisches Wochenblatt 24 (19 March): 159–60. F. 41–2.
              Reprinted in *Der Dreiklang* 9 (October 1937): 173–4.

S8   1893   "Ein Gruss an Johannes Brahms. Zu seinem 60. Geburtstag. 7.
              Mai 1893." *Die Zukunft* 3 (6 May): 279. F. 43–4.

S9   1893   "Notizen zu Verdi's *Falstaff*." *Die Zukunft* 3 (3 June): 474–6. F.
              44–8. Reprinted in *Der Dreiklang* 4/5 (July/August 1937): 126–7.
              Italian translation in **T43**.

S10   1893   "Friedric Smenata." *Die Zukunft* 4 (1 July): 37–40. F. 48–54.
              Reprinted in *Der Dreiklang* 4/5 (July/August 1937): 121–3.
              Czech translation in **T58**.

S11   1893   "Der Sonzongo-Markt in Wien." *Die Zukunft* 4 (5 August):
              282–3. F. 54–7. Italian translation in **T44**.

S12   1893   "Anton Bruckner." *Die Zukunft* 5 (21 October): 135–7. F. 57–61.
              Reprinted in *Der Dreiklang* 9 (October 1937): 172–3. Czech
              translation in **T58**.

S13   1894   "Die Musik von heute." *Neue Revue* 5/1 (3 January): 87–8. F.
              62–4. English translation in **T26**.

S14   1894   "Johannes Brahms: Phantasien für Pianoforte, Op. 116."
              Musikalisches Wochenblatt 25 (18 January): 37–8. F. 64–6.

S15   1894   "Ruggiero Leoncavallo." *Die Zukunft* 6 (20 January): 138–40. F.
              66–70. Italian translation in **T45**.

S16   1894   "Ondeicek–Popper–Door." *Neue Revue* 5/9 (14 February):
              278–80. F. 270–3.

S17   1894   "Im Wiener Conservatorium . . ." *Neue Revue* 5/11 (28 Febru-
              ary): 318.

S18   1894   "Smetena's *Kuß* (zur ersten Aufführung in der Hofoper)." *Neue
              Revue* 5/11 (28 February): 347–50. F. 70–5.

S19   1894   "Hofoper." *Neue Revue* 5/1 (28 February): 375. F. 274–5.

S20   1894   "Anton Rubenstein." *Neue Revue* 5/18 (18 April): 566–7. F. 82–4.

S21   1894   "Konzertdirigenten." *Die Zukunft* 7 (14 April): 88–92. F. 75–82.

S22   1894   "Verdi's *Falstaff*." *Die Zukunft* 7 (May 1894): 230–3. F. 85–9.
              Reprinted in *Der Dreiklang* 4/5 (July/August 1937): 123–6. Ital-
              ian translation in **T46**.

S23 1894 "Zum Jubiläum der Hofoper." *Neue Revue* 5/24 (30 May): 754–6. F. 90–2.

S24 1894 "Tantiemen für Instrumental komponisten?" *Die Zukunft* 7 (9 June): 477–9. F. 92–6.

S25 1894 "Das Hören in der Musik." *Neue Revue* 5/32: 115–21 (25 July). F. 96–103.

S26 1894 "Anton Rubenstein." *Die Zukunft* 8 (18 August): 326–9. F. 103–9.

S27 1894 "Aus dem Leben Smetena's. (Ein besuch bei fr. Smetena's Witwe)." *Neues Wiener Tagblatt*, 6: 28/245. F. 109–14.

S28 1894 "Eine Lebenskizze: Eugen d'Albert." *Die Zukunft* 9 (6 October): 33–6. F. 115–21.

S29 1894 "Theater an der Wien." *Neue Revue* 5/2: 377. F. 275–6.

S30 1894 "Hofoperntheater." *Neue Revue* 5/2: 475–6. F. 276–8.

S31 1894 "Volksmusik in Wien." *Neue Revue* 5/45 (24 October): 516–21. F. 121–8.

S32 1895 "Deutsch-Österrichischer Musikverkehr." *Die Zukunft* 11 (27 April): 182–5. F. 129–34.

S33 1895 "Der Geist der musikalischen Technik." *Musikalisches Wochenblatt* 26/19–26 (2, 9, 16, 23, 30 May, 13, 20 June): 245–6, 257–9, 273–4, 285–6, 297–8, 309–10, and 325–6. F. 135–54. English translation in **T29**. German reprint in **T20**.

S34 1895 "Rubenstein-Preis." *Die Zeit* 4/49 (7 September): 157. F. 278–80.

S35 1895 "Eduard Hanslick. 70. Geburtstag." *Die Zeit* 4/50 (14 September): 174. F. 280–1.

S36 1895 "Zur musikalische Erziehung." *Die Zeit* 4/51–2 (21, 28 September): 185–6. F. 154–66.

S37 1895 "*Le Comte de Chambrun et Stanislas Legis*: Wagner, Paris 1895." *Die Zeit* 4: F. 282–3.

S38 1895 "Hofoperntheater—Jules Massenet *Das Mädchen von Navarra*." *Die Zeit* 5/53 (5 October): 14. F. 283–5.

S39 1895 "H. Berté. Ballet *Amor auf Reisen*." *Die Zeit* 5/53 (5 October): 14. F. 286–8

S40   1895   "Arthur Prüfer—Johann Hermann Schein, Leipzig 1895." *Die Zeit* 5/54 (12 October): 30. F. 286–8.

S41   1895   "Hofoperntheater—Heinrich Marschner, *Der Templer und die Jüdin.*" *Die Zeit* 5/54 (19 October): 44. F. 288–9.

S42   1895   "Ludwig Hartmann, Richard Wagners *Tannhäuser*, Dresden 1895." *Die Zeit* 5/55 (19 October): 44. F. 289–90.

S43   1895   "Eine neue Haydn-Oper." *Die Zeit* 5/54 (9 November): 90–1. F. 167–71.

S44   1895   "B. Todt, Vadmecum durch die bach'schen Cantaten mit Hinweisen auf ihre Verwendbarkeit auch für Schülerchöre." *Die Zeit* 5/58 (9 November): 94. F. 290–1.

S45   1895   "Gesellschaft der Musikfreunde in Wien—Gesellschaftsconcert, Ben Davies-Quartett Rosé." *Die Zeit* 5/59 (16 November): 108. F. 291–4.

S46   1895   "Hofoperntheater—François Adrien Boieldieu. *Rotkäppchen.*" *Die Zeit* 5/60 (23 November): 108. F. 294–5.

S47   1895   "Philharmonisches Konzert—Hans Richter." *Die Zeit* 5/60 (23 November): 126. F. 295–6.

S48   1895   "Kammermusik—Das böhmische Streichquartett." *Die Zeit* 5/61 (30 November): 142. F. 296–7.

S49   1895   "Theater an der Wien—Johann Strauß, Waldmeister." *Die Zeit* 5/62 (7 December): 157. F. 298–9.

S50   1895   "Zweites Philharmonisches Konzert—Antonin Dvorák, Othello-Ouverture." *Die Zeit* 5/63 (14 December): 173. F. 300–1.

S51   1895   "J. S. Bach, *Weihnachtsoratorium*, Eugen Gura, Eugen d'Albert *Soirée des böhmischen Streichquartetts*—drittes philharmonisches Konzert." *Die Zeit* 5/64 (21 December): 186–7. F. 301–5.

S52   1896   "Bülow—Weingartner." *Musikalisches Wochenblatt* 26/48 (21 November): 610–1. F. 171–5.

S53   1896   "Viertes philharmonisches Konzert—Peter Iljitsch Tschaikowsky, *Symphonie Nr. 6.*" *Die Zeit* 6/66 (4 January): 13. F. 306–7.

S54   1896   "Wilhelm Kienzl, *Der Evangelimann*—Erstaufführung in Wien." *Die Zeit* 6/68 (18 January): 44–5. F. 307–11.

S55 1896 "Fünftes philharmonisches Konzert—Zweites Konzert der Gesellschaft der Musikfreunde in Wien." *Die Zeit* 6/69 (25 January): 46. F. 311–2.

S56 1896 "Die Jungen Dirigenten." *Die Zeit* 6/69 (25 January): 57–8. F. 175–81.

S57 1896 "Lilian Bailey (Henschel)." *Die Zeit* 6/70 (1 February): 78. F. 313–5.

S58 1896 "Böhmisches Streichquartett; Karel Bendl, Rosé Quartett, Giovanni Sgambati, Johann Nepomuk Hummel, Alfred Grünfeld." *Die Zeit* 6/71 (8 February): 94. F. 315–7.

S59 1896 "Drittes Konzert der Gesellschaft für Musikfreunde in Wien— Jules Massenet, *Mystère Eve*—Liederabend Johannes Messchaert, Julius Töntgen." *Die Zeit* 6/72 (15 February): 113. F. 317–9.

S60 1896 "Damen-Streichquartett Soldat Roeger—Böhmisches Streichquartett, Alexander Borodin, Robert Hausmann, Bronislaw Hubermann." *Die Zeit* 6/73 (22 February): 130. F. 319–22.

S61 1896 "Vianna da Motta, *Nachtrag zu Studien bei Hans von Bülow* von Theodor Pfeiffer, Berlin-Leipzig, 1896." *Die Zeit* 6/74 (29 February): 146. F. 323.

S62 1896 "Zweiter Liederabend Johannes Messchaert, Julius Röntgen— Sechstes und siebentes philharmonisches Konzert." *Die Zeit* 6/75 (7 March): 158–9. F. 323–31.

S63 1896 "Albert Kauder, *Walther von der Vogelweide*." *Die Zeit* 6/75 (7 March): 160. F. 331.

S64 1896 "Holländisches Terzett." *Die Zeit* 6/75 (7 March): 161. F. 332.

S65 1896 "Carl Reinecke." *Die Zeit* 6/76 (14 March): 178. F. 332–4.

S66 1896 "Gaëtano Donizetti: *Lucia di Lammermoor*." *Die Zeit* 6/77 (21 March): 193. F. 334–5.

S67 1896 "Bronislaw Huberman—Damen-Streichquartett Soldat-Roeger— Richard Mühlfeld—Felix Weingartmer." *Die Zeit* 6/77 (21 March): 194. F. 335–7.

S68 1896 "Carl Goldmark, *Das Heimchen am Herd*—Erstaufführung in Wien." *Die Zeit* 6/78 (28 March): 207–8. F. 337–41.

S69 1896 "Siegfried Wagner." *Die Zukunft* 15: 132–4. F. 181–5.

S70   1896   *"Das Heimchen am Herd."* *Die Zukunft* 15 (18 April): 132–4. F. 185–8.

S71   1896   "Der Chor des Laibacher Musikvereins Blasbena Matica (Leitung Matej Hubad)—Richard Strauss, *Till Eulenspiegels lustige Streiche*—Feiedrich Kiel, *Christus.*" *Die Zeit* 7/80 (11 April): 26–7. F. 342–6.

S72   1896   "Zur Mozartfeier." *Die Zeit* 7/82 (25 April): 60. F. 189–91.

S73   1896   "Giuseppe Verdi, *Aïda.*" *Die Zeit* 7/82 (25 April): 62. F. 346–7.

S74   1896   "Oper. (Ein Vorschlag zur Inscenierung des Gluck'schen *Orpheus*)." *Die Zeit* 7/84 (9 May): 91–2. F. 191–7.

S75   1896   "Marie Lehmann." *Die Zeit* 7: 93–4. F. 347.

S76   1896   "Francesco d'Andrade." *Die Zeit* 7: 109–10. F. 348–9.

S77   1896   "Ehrenzeichen für Johannes Brahms." *Die Zeit* 7: 110. F. 349. Reprinted in *Der Dreiklang* 2 (May 1937): 61.

S78   1896   "Anton Bruckner." *Die Zeit* 7/90 (20 June): 184–6. F. 197–205. Reprinted in *Der Dreiklang* 9 (October 1937): 166–72.

S79   1896   "Routine in der Musik." *Neue Revue* 7/45 (4 November): 555–8. F. 205–9.

S80   1896   "Carl Reinecke, Die Beethoven'schen Clavier-Sonaten, Leipzig 1896." *Die Zeit* 8: 14–5. F. 349–50.

S81   1896   "Ernst Possart, *Über die neueinstudierung und Neuinscenierung des Mozart'schen Don Giovanni (Don Juan) auf dem kgl. Residenztheater zu München*, München 1986." *Die Zeit* 8: 78. F. 351–2. Reprinted in *Der Dreiklang* 4/5 (July/August 1937): 120–1. Czech translation in **T59**.

S82   1896   "Daniel Françoise Esprit Auber, *Fra Diavalo-Pietro*, Mascagni, *Zanetto.*" *Die Zeit* 8:157. F. 352–4. Italian translation in **T47**.

S83   1897   "Ein Epilog zur Schubertfeier." *Neue Revue* 8/1: 211–6. F. 209–16.

S84   1897   "Konzert Carl Reinecke." *Neue Revue* 8/14 (12 April): 438–9. F. 354–6.

S85   1897   "Unpersönliche Musik." *Neue Revue* 8/15 (9 April) (1897): 464–8. F. 216–21. English translation in **T27**.

S86   1897   "Die Berliner 'Philharmoniker.'" *Neue Revue* 8/16 (16 April): 495–7. F. 222–4.

S87 1897 "Johannes Brahms." *Neue Revue* 8/17 (23 April): 516–20. F. 224–30.

S88 1897 "Johannes Brahms." *Die Zukunft* 19 (8 May): 261–5. F. 230–6. English translation in **T32**. Czech translation in **T60**.

S89 1897 "Theater an der Wien: Engelbert Humperdinck, *Königskinder.*" *Neue Revue* 8/1: 646. F. 356–7.

S90 1897 "Capellmeister-Regisseure." *Neue Revue* 8/22 (28 May): 669–72. F. 236–40.

S91 1897 "Musikalische Reisebetachtungen." *Neue Revue* 8/26 (25 June): 788–93. F. 240–8.

S92 1897 "Mehr Kunst!" *Neue Revue* 8/40 (1 October): 409–12. F. 248–52.

S93 1897 "Hofoper—Friedrich Smetena, *Dalibor*, Erstaufführung in Wien unter Gustav Mahler." *Neue Revue* 8/2: 448–9. F. 357–8.

S94 1897 "Theater an der Wien—Giacomo Puccini, *La Bohème*, Erstaufführung in Wien." *Neue Revue* 8/2: 473–4. F. 359–60. Italian translation in **T48**.

S95 1897 "Hoferntheater—P. I. Tschaikowski, *Eugene Onegin*, Erstaufführung in Wien." *Neue Revue* 8/2: 654–5. F. 360–2.

S96 1897 "Ein Wort zur Mozartrenaissance." *Neue Revue* 8/49 (3 December): 685–8. F. 252–6.

S97 1897 "Hoferntheater—Richard Heuberger, Ballet *Stuwwelpeter.*" *Neue Revue* 9/1: 82. F. 362–3.

S98 1898 "Hoferntheater—Georges Bizet, *Djamileh*, Erstaufführung in Wien unter Gustav Mahler." *Neue Revue* 9/1: 143–4. F. 363–4.

S99 1898 "Hoferntheater—Ruggiero Leoncavallo, *La Bohème*, Erstaufführung in Wien unter Gustav Mahler." *Neue Revue* 9/1: 292. F. 364–5. Italian translation in **T49**.

S100 1898 "Componisten und Dirigenten." *Neue Revue* 9/12 (20 March): 349–50. F. 256–9. English translation in **T28**.

S101 1901 "Beethoven 'Retouche.' " *Wiener Abendpost* (9 January): 6–7. F. 259–68.

S102 1916 "Heinrich Schenkers Beethoven Ausgaben." *Der Merker* 7/3: 6–7.

S103 1922 "Joh. Seb. Bach: Wohltemperiertes Klavier, Band I, Präludium c-moll." *Die Musik* 15/9: 641–51.

S104 1923 "Die Urlinie." *Die Musikanten Gilde* (1 July): 77–80 [reprinted from *Der Tonwille* I].

S105 1925 "Franz Schubert." *Moderne Welt* (1 December): 20.

S106 1927 "Beethoven und seine Nachfahren." *General-Anzeiger für Bonn und Umgegend* (26 March): 3–4.

S107 1929 "Eine Rettung der kllassischen Musik-Texte: Das Archiv für Photogrammen der National-Bibliothek, Wien." *Der Kunstwart* 42 (March): 222–30.

S108 1931 "Gedanken über Kultur, Kunst, und Musik." *Der Kunstwart* 44 (January): 222–30.

S109 1931 "Ein verschollener Brief von Mozart und das Gehemnis seines Schaffens." *Der Kunstwart* 44 (July): 660–6.

S110 1932 "Eine Anzeige und eine Selbstanzeige." *Der Kunstwart* 46 (December): 194–96.

S111 1933 "Erinnerung an Brahms." *Deutsche Zeitschrift* 46 (May): 475–82.

S112 1933 "Was wird aus der Musik." *Basler National-Zeitung* (28 May): 1.

S113 1937 "Vom Hintergrund in der Musik." *Der Dreiklang* 1 (April): 12–3 [posth].

S114 1937 "Von der stimmführung im Generalbass." *Der Dreiklang* 3 (June): 75–81 [posth].

S115 1937 "Von der Diminution." *Der Dreiklang* 4/5 (July/August): 75–81 [posth].

S116 1937 "Urlninetafel zu Haydns *Chorale St. Antoni*." *Der Dreiklang* 6 (September): 138–9 [posth].

S117 1937 "Ein Kommentar zu Schindler, Beethovens Spiel betreffend." *Der Dreiklang* 8/9 (November 1937/February 1938): 190–9 [posth].

PART 3: SCHENKER'S EDITIONS
AND ARRANGEMENTS OF MUSIC BY OTHERS

S118 1902 Bach, Carl Philipp Emanuel. *Klavierwerke vol. 1 and 2*. Vienna: Universal Edition. U.-E. 548a and 548b.

S119 [1902] Bach, Johann Sebastian. *Ich will den Kreuzstab gern tragen für Baßstimme*. Unpublished manuscript, ink, in a copyist's hand with pencil annotations in Schenker's hand; nineteen ms. leaves (JC XXV: 5). The finding list (Lang 1994) erroneously indicates folio 4.

S120 1904 Händel, Georg Friedrich. *Sechs Orgelkonzerte für vier Hände bearbeitet.* Vienna: Universal Edition. U.-E. 936. Reprinted by International Music Company as the first volume in a two-volume set (No. 1081).
Contains Händel's first set of organ concerti, HWV 289–94.

S121 [1911] Bach, Johann Sebastian. *Selig ist der Mann. Cantate No. 57 für Sopran und Bass.* Unpublished manuscript, ink, in a copyist's hand with pencil annotations in Schenker's hand and another; twenty ms. leaves (JC XXV: 7).
The finding list (Lang 1994) erroneously indicates folio 6.

S122 1921 Beethoven, Ludwig von. *Sonate op. 27/2, mit drei Skizzenblättern der Meisters, herausgegeben in Faksimile-Reproduktion.* Vienna: Universal Edition. U.-E. 7000.

S123 1928 Beethoven, Ludwig von. *Samtliche Klaviersonaten,* 2 vols. Vienna: Universal Edition. U.-E. 4010 and 4011. Reprint ed. with a forward by Carl Schachter. New York: Dover. ISBN 0-486-23134-8 and 0-486-23135-6.
Review: 1978 *In Theory Only* 4/1: 37–47 (C. Smith).

PART 4: SCHENKER'S THEORETICAL WORKS

S124 1904 *Ein Beitrag zur Ornamentik, als Einführung zu Ph. Em. Bachs Klavierwerken, mitumfassend auch die Ornamentik Haydns, Mozarts und Beethoven, etc.* Vienna: Universal Edition. U.-E. 812. English translation in **T9,** Japanese translation in **T11.**
Reviews: 1908 *Der Merker* 17 (E. Wellesz), OC II: 21.
[n.d.] *Neues Wiener Abendblatt* 1 December, OC II: 21.

S125 1906 *Neue musikalische Theorien und Phantasien I: Harmonielehre.* Berlin and Stuttgart: J. G. Cotta Verlag. Reprinted by Universal Edition, 1978. U.-E. 6886. English translation in **T2,** Spanish translation in **T31.**
Reviews: [n.d.] *Rheinische Musik-und-Theater-Zeitung* (H. Wetzel) OC II: 22.
1907 *Allgemeine Musik Zeitung* 20 November (M. Burkhardt),OC II: 20.
1907 *Schwäbische Kronik* 18 December (K. G.), OC II: 20.

1908   *Neues Wiener Tageblatt* 18 May, OC II: 20.

1911   *Österr.-ungar. Musiker-Zeitung* 12 March, OC II: 24.

1915   *Heimgarten* March, OC II: 47.

1979   *Music and Letters* 60/3: 332–3 (D. Puffett).

1979   *Musical Times* 120/1636: 485–6 (W. Drabkin).

1980   *Hi-Fi-Stereophonie* 19/6: 713 (U. Dibelius).

1980   *Musikerziehung* 33: 239–40 (F. Eibner).

1980   *Musikforschung* 33/3: 374–75 (D. de la Motte).

1980   *Neue Zeitschrift für Musik* 141/1: 65–6 (E. Karkoschka).

S126 1908   *Instrumentationstabelle* (under the pseudonym Arthur Niloff). Vienna: Universal Edition. Reprinted as U.-E. 1999.

Review: 1988   *Brass Bulletin* 61: 124 (C. Gottfried).

S127 1910   Bach, Johann Sebastian. *Chromatische Phantasie und Fuge D-moll*. Vienna: Universal Edition. Rev. ed., 1969. ISBN 0-287-3240-5. English translation in **T16**.

Reviews: [n.d.] *Wiener Mode* XXIV, OC II: 21.

1910   *Neues Wiener Journal* 27 November (Else Bienenfeld), OC II: 21.

1910   *Neues Wiener Abendblatt* 1 December, OC II: 21.

1913   *Neue Preussische Zeitung* 15 July (D. S.), OC II: 37.

S128 1910   *Neue musikalische Theorien und Phantasien II, 1: Kontrapunkt I: Cantus firmus und zweistimmiger Satz.* Berlin, Stuttgart: J. G. Cotta. Also, Universal Edition. U.-E. 6867. Reprint ed., 1978. Also, reprinted by Georg Olms Verlag, 1991. ISBN 3-487-09520-3. English translations in **T1, T13, T15,** and **T23**.

Reviews: 1910   *Sonn- und Montags Zeitung* 24 October, OC II: 21.

1911   *Norddeutsche Allgemeine Zeitung* 26 January, OC II: 23.

1911   *Österreichische Musikerzeitung* 11 March, OC II: 23.

1911   *Allgemeine Musik Zeitung* 7 April (R. v. Mojsisovics), OC II: 24.

1911   *Frankfurter Zeitung* 6 August (H. Wetzel), OC II: 27.

[1911] *Rheinische Musik-und-Theater-Zeitung* (H. Wetzel), OC II: 24.

[1911] *Neue Freie Presse* n.d., OC II: 26.

[1911] *Die Musik* 18 (H. Wetzel), OC II: 26.

1912   *Öster.-ungar. Musikerzeitung* 16 March, OC II: 27.

1979   *Music and Letters* 60/3: 332–3 (D. Puffett)

1979   *Österreichische Musikzeitschrift* 34/11: 578–80 (H. Kratochwill).

1980   *Musical Times* 120/1636: 485–6 (W. Drabkin).

1980   *Hi-Fi-Stereophonie* 19/6: 713 (U. Dibelius).
1980   *Muzikerziehung* 33: 239–40 (F. Eibner).
1980   *Musikforschung* 33/3: 374–5 (D. de la Motte).
1980   *Neue Zeitschrift für Musik* 141/1: 65–6 (E. Karkoschka).

S129 1911   *Die Kunst des Vortrags.* Unpublished.

S130 1912   *Beethovens Neunte Sinfonie: Eine Darstellung der musikalischen Inhaltes unter fortlaufender Berücksichtung auch des Vortrags und der Literatur.* Vienna: Universal Edition. U.-E. 3499.
Reviews: [n.d.] Unidentified periodical (P. O.), OC II: 51.
1912   *Musikpädagogische Zeitschrift* 7 (F. S.), OC II: 29.
1913   *Die Zeit am Montag* 25 March (B. Schrader), OC II: 29.
1913   *Neues Wiener Tageblatt* 7 April, OC II: 29.
1913   *Die Zeit* 27 April (M. Graf), OC II: 29.
1913   *Musicpädagogische Zeitchrift*, June, OC II: 37.
1913   *Musicpädagogische Zeitschrift* 1 August, OC II: 37.
1914   [Unidentified] 7 June (J. V. Da Motta), OC II: 39.
1914   *Heimgarten* September (B. Paumgartner), OC II: 45.

S131 1913   Beethoven, Ludwig von. *Die letzten fünf Sonaten von Beethoven, Kritische Ausgabe mit Einführung und Erläuterung. Sonate E dur, op. 109.* Vienna: Universal Edition. Rev. ed. edited by Oswald Jonas, 1971 as U.-E. 3976.

S132 1914   Beethoven, Ludwig von. *Die letzten fünf Sonaten von Beethoven, Kritische Ausgabe mit Einführung und Erläuterung. Sonate As dur, op. 110.* Vienna: Universal Edition. Rev. ed. edited by Oswald Jonas 1972 as U.-E. 3977.

S133 1915   Beethoven, Ludwig von. *Die letzten fünf Sonaten von Beethoven, Kritische Ausgabe mit Einführung und Erläuterung. Sonate C moll, op. 111.* Vienna: Universal Edition. Rev. ed. edited by Oswald Jonas 1971 as U.-E. 3978.

S134 1920   Beethoven, Ludwig von. *Die letzten fünf Sonaten von Beethoven, Kritische Ausgabe mit Einführung und Erläuterung. Sonate A dur, op. 101.* Vienna: Universal Edition. Rev. ed. edited by Oswald Jonas,1972 as U.-E. 3974. English translation in **T37**.
Reviews: 1914 *Rheinische Musik-und-Theater-Zeitung* 28 February, OC II: 39.
1914   *Die Zeit* 8 March (M. Graf), OC II: 39.
1914   *Die Musik* 13/12 15 March, (H. Wetzel), OC II: 40.
1922   *Musikblätter des Anbruch* February, OC II: 60.

1925   *Rivista Musicale Italiana* 32/4: 658–60 (A. E.), OC II:
        68.
1971   *Österreichische Musikzeitung* 26/5–6: 334 (R. Klein).
1973   *Neue Zeitschrift für Musik* 134/7: 465 (R. Stephan).
1973   *Perspectives of New Music* 12/1–2: 319–30 (W.
        Drabkin).
1974   *Musikforschung* 27/3: 383 (H. Federhofer).

S135–143 *Der Tonwille. Flugblätter [Vierteljahrschaft] zum Zeugnis unwandelbarer Gesetze der Tonkunst einer neuen Jugend dargebracht.* Vienna: "Tonwille Flugblätterverlag," i.e., Universal Edition, 1921–4. Reprinted by Georg Olms Verlag as ten volumes bound in one, 1990. ISBN 3-487-09357-X. English translations in **T8, T10, T18, T24, T25, T39, T55**, and **T62**. Italian translation in **T30**. Czech translation in **T61**.

S135 Heft 1 (1921): *Von der Sendung des Deutschen Genies (3–21), Die Urlinie (eine Vorbemerkung) (22–26), Beethoven: V. Sinfonie I (27–37), J. S. Bach: Präludium Es-Moll (WTC I) (38–45), Schubert: Ihr Bild (46–50), Vermischtes.*

S136 Heft 2 (1922): *Gesetze der Tonkunst (3–4), Geschichte der Tonkunst (4), Noch ein Wort zur Urlinie 4–6), Mozart: Sonata A-Moll, K. 310 (7–24), Beethoven: Sonate op. 2, nr. 1 (25–48).*

S137 Heft 3 (1922): *Haydn: Sonate Es-Dur (3–21), Die Kunst zu Hören (22–25), Vermischtes (26–38).*

S138 Heft 4 (1923): *J. S. Bach: 12 kleine Präludien, nr. 1 & 2 (3–7), Händel: Allemande (XIV. Suite) (8–9), Ph. Em. Bach: Kürze und leichte Klavierstücke, nr. 1, Ph. Em. Bach: Sonate C-Dur, Haydn: Sonate C-Dur, Mozart, Sonate C-Dur, Beethoven: Sonate op. 49, nr. 2, Vermischtes.*

S139 Heft 5 (1923): *J. S. Bach: 12 kleine Präludien, nr. 3, 4, & 5, Beethoven: V. Sinfonie (Fortsetzung), Vermischtes.*

S140 Heft 6 (1923): *Schubert: Gretchen am Spinnrad, Beethoven: V. Sinfonie (Schluß), Der wahre Vortrag, Vermischtes.*

S141 Heft 7 (1924): *Beethoven: Sonate op. 57, J. S. Bach: Matthäuspaßion, Revitativ "Erbarm uns*

Gott," *Beethoven zu seinem op. 127, Ver-*
mischtes.
S142 Heft 8/9 (1924): *Brahms: variationen und Fuge über ein*
Thema von Händel op. 24, Wirkung und
Effekt, Erläuterungen, Vermischtes.
S143 Heft 10 (1924): *J. S. Bach: Matthäuspaßion Einleitung-*
schor; Haydn: Österreichische Volk-
shymne; Schubert: Quatre Impromptu op.
90, nr. 3; Schubert: Impromptu F-Moll,
op. 94, nr. 6; Mendelssohn: Venezianis-
ches Gondellied op. 30, nr. 6; Mendels-
sohn, Lieder ohne Worte op. 67, nr. 6;
Schumann, Kinderszenen, nr. 1 u. 15, Er-
läuterungen, Vermischtes.
Reviews: 1921 *Das Deutsche Tageblatt* 16 September (W. Altmann),
OC II: 59.
1924 *Roseggers Heimgarten* 4. Heft (B. Paumgartner), OC
II: 62.
1925 *Die Musik* 10, July (W. Kahl), OC II: 67.
1992 *Music and Letters* 73/1: 141 (N. Marston).
2000 *Music Analysis* 19: 10–28 (C. Wintle).

S144 1922 *Neue musikalische Theorien und Phantasien II, 2: Kontra-*
punkt 2: Drei- und mehrstimmiger Satz: Übergänge zur freier
Satz. Vienna: Universal Edition, 1922. U.-E. 6868. Reprinted
by Georg Olms Verlag, 1991. ISBN 3-487-09521-1.

S145 1925 *Beethovens Fünfte Sinfonie: Darstellung des musikalischen*
Inhaltes nach der Handschrift unter fortlaufender Berücksich-
tigung des Vortrages und der Literatur. Vienna: A. Gutman
Verlag, 1925. Reprinted from *Der Tonwille* 1, 5, and 6. Reprint
ed., 1969.
Review: 1924 *Unidentified periodical*, 14 October (P. v. Klenau), OC
II: 65.

S146–148 *Das Meisterwerk in der Musik: Ein Jahrbuch.* Munich, Vienna,
Berlin: Drei Masken Verlag, 1925, 1926, and 1930. Reprinted by
Georg Olms Verlag as three volumes in one, 1974. ISBN 3-487-
05274-1. English translations in **T4, T5, T6, T7, T8, T17, T21, T33,**
T36, T50, and **T51**. German reprints in **T19** and **T22**.
S146 Jahrbuch I (1925): *Die kunst der Improvatsation. Weg*
mit dem Phrasierungsbogen. Joh. S.
Bach: Sechs Sonaten für Violine:
Sonate III, Largo, Partita III (E-Dur)

Präludio. Joh. S. Bach: Zwölf kleine
Präludien: nr. 6, 7, 12. Domenico
Scarlatti: Sonate für Klavier, D-Moll,
G-Dur. Chopin: Etude op. 10, nr. 5–6.
Noch einmal zur Beethovens op. 110.
Fortsetzung der Urlinie-Betrachtun-
gen. Erläuterungen. Vermischtes.

S147 Jahrbuch II (1926): *Fortzetzung der Urlinie-Betrachtun-*
gen. Vom Organischen der Sonaten-
form. Das Organische der Fuge. Joh.
S. Bach: Suite III für Violoncello,
Sarabande. Mozart: Sinfonie, G
Moll. Haydn: Die Schöpfung, Die
Vorstellung des Chaos. Ein Gegen-
beispiel: Max Reger, op. 81, Varia-
tionen und Fuge über ein Thema von
Joh. S. Bach für Klavier. Erläuterun-
gen. Vermischtes.

S148 Jahrbuch III (1930): *Rameau oder Beethoven: Erstarrung*
oder Geistiges leben in der Musik?
Beethovens Dritte Sinfonie zum er-
stenmal in ihrem wahren Inhalt
dargestellt. Eine von Beethovens re-
verte Abschrift. Vortrag. Literatur.
Vermischtes.

Reviews: 1926 *Der Abend* 16 December, OC II: 71.
1926 *Allgemeine Musik Zeitung* 24 December (W. Dahms), OC II: 72.
1927 *Zeitschrift für Musik* May (J. H. Wetzel), OC II: 78.
1928 *Allgemeine Musik Zeitung* 3 February, (W. Dahms), OC II: 75.
1928 *Neue Musik-Zeitung* Heft 18 (O. Vrieslander), OC II: 77.
1930 *Deutsche Tonkünstler-Zeitung* 11 (F. v. Cube), OC II: 80.
1931 *Music and Letters* 12/3: 306–7 (E. Walker).
1931 *Der Auftakt* February (T. Veidl), OC II: 82.
1931 *Der Kunstwart*, January, (O. Vrieslander), OC II: 81.
1931 *Die Musik* June (C. Perl), OC II: 83.
1931 *National-Zeitung* 3 October (M.), OC II: 85.
1932 *Zeitschrift für Musikwissenschaft* 15/2: 92–4 (O. Jonas).

S149 1932   *Fünf Urlinie-Tafeln.* Vienna: Universal Edition. Reprint ed.,
New York: Dover, 1969. ISBN 0-486-22294-2.

Reviews: 1971   *Musical Times* 112/1536: 140 (E. Sams).
1971   *New York Review of Books* 16/11: 32–4 (C. Rosen).

S150   1933   *Johannes Brahms: Oktaven und Quinten u[nd] A[nderes]. Aus dem Nachlass herausgegeben und erläutert.* Vienna: Universal Edition. U.-E. 10.508. English translation in **T14**.

S151   1935   *Neue musikalische Theorien und Phantasien III: Der Freie Satz,* ed. by Oswald Jonas. Vienna: Universal Edition [posth]. U.-E. 6869. Rev. ed. published 1969. English translations in **T3**, **T12**, and **T38**. French translation in **T35**, Chinese translation in **T52**, Polish translations in **T54**, Russian translation in **T63**.
Reviews: 1939   *Modern Music* 15/3: 192–7. (R. Sessions).
1959   *Musikforschung* 12/4: 523–5 (C. Dalhaus).
1959   *Schweizer musikpädagogische Blätter* 47 (F. Eibner).

PART 5: TRANSLATIONS AND REPRINTS

T1   [?]   Dunn, John Petrie. *Counterpoint*, part I. University of Edinburgh. [Although cited in several sources, I have not been able to verify its existence.]

T2   1954   Borgese, Elizabeth. *Harmony*, ed. by Oswald Jonas. Chicago: University of Chicago Press. Reprint ed., 1980. ISBN 0-226-73734-9.
Reviews: 1955   *Musical Quarterly* 41/2: 256–60 (W. Mitchell).
1956   *Chicago Review* 9/1: 132–5 (R. Bloch).
1956   *Music and Letters* 37/2: 180–2 (H. K. Andrews).
1956   *Notes* 13/1: 53–6 (C. Seeger).
1957   *The Music Review* 18/3: 249–51.
1975   *Music Educator's Journal* 61/9: 92.
1976   *The School Musician* 47/9: 24.

T3   1960   Krueger, Theodore Howard. "*Der Freie Satz* by Heinrich Schenker: A Complete Translation and Re-Editing. Vol. I: The Complete Text. Vol. II: Supplement of Musical Examples." Ph.D. diss., University of Iowa, 1960.

T4   1968   Grossman, Orin. "Organic Structure in Sonata Form." *Journal of Music Theory* 12/2: 164–83.

T5   1973   Siegel, Heidi. "The *Sarabande* of J. S. Bach's Suite No. 3 for Unaccompanied Violoncello [BWV 1009]." *The Music Forum* 2: 274–82.

T6   1973   Kalib, Sylvan Sol. "Thirteen Essays from the Three Yearbooks *Das Meisterwerk in der Musik*: An Annotated Translation," 3 vols. Ph.D. diss., Northwestern University. UMI Number 7330626.
Includes, from Yearbook I, translations of "The Art of Improvisation," "Let's Do Away with the Phrasing Slur," "J. S. Bach: Six Sonatas for Unaccompanied Violin: Sonata III, Largo," "Chopin, Etude in G-flat Major, Op. 10, No. 5," "Resumption of *Urlinie* Considerations," and "Clarifications." From Yearbook II, translations of "Resumption of *Urlinie* Considerations," "The Organic Aspect of Sonata Form," "The Organic Aspect of the Fugue," "Mozart, Symphony in G Minor," "Haydn: The Representation of Chaos," and "A Negative-Example: Max Reger, Op. 81." And from Yearbook III, a translation of "Rameau or Beethoven: Paralytic Standstill or Ingenious Life in Music?"

T7   1976   Rothgeb, John. "The Largo of J. S. Bach's Sonata No. 3 for Unaccompanied Violin." *The Music Forum* 4: 141–59. Reprinted in *Approaches to Tonal Analysis*. Garland Library of the History of Western Music, Vol. 14. New York: Garland, 1985: 259–8. ISBN 0-824-7463-7.

T8   1976   Rothstein, William. "Mozart: Sonata in A Minor, K. 310." Unpublished typescript, "For: Readings in Schenker / Allen Forte / December."

T9   1976   Siegel, Heidi. "A Contribution to the Study of Ornamentation." *The Music Forum* IV 1–139.

T10   1977   Forbes, Elliott, and F. John Adams Jr. "Beethoven: Fifth Symphony, First Movement." In *Beethoven: Symphony #5*, Norton Critical Scores, Vol. 9. New York: Norton. From *Der Tonwille* I [excerpt].

T11   1979   Noro, Aiko, and Akiko Tamamoto. *Koten piano soshokuon soho*. Japan: Ingaku nu tomo.

T12   1979   Oster, Ernst. *Free Composition*. New York: Longman. ISBN 0-028-72332-5. Reprinted by Pendragon Press, 2001. ISBN 1-57647-074-1 (Vol. 1), 1-57647075-X (Vol. 2).
           Reviews: 1980   *Choice* 17/3: 398.
                     1980   *RCMM* 78/2: 199–201 (R. B. Swanson).
                     1980   *TLS* 79/4042: 1046 (C. Wintle)
                     1980   *Musical Times* 121/1651: 560–62 (A. Whittall).
                     1980   *RMARC* 16: 140–8 (J. Dunsby).

1980   *Notes* 36: 879–81 (G. Proctor).
1981   *Journal of Music Theory* 25/1: 115–42 (C. Schachter).
1981   *Journal of Music Theory* 25/1: 143–53 (D. Epstein).
1981   *Journal of Music Theory* 25/1: 155–73 (W. Benjamin).
1981   *Musical Quarterly* 67/1: 113–18 (R. Kamien).
1981   *Music Theory Spectrum* 3: 158–84 (E. Laufer).
1981   *Tempo* 136: 37–38 (R. Evans).
1982   *Music Analysis* 1/1: 101–7 (M. Musgrave).
1985   *Musicology* 8: 51–5 (C. Ayrey).

T13   1980   Gould, Murray. "Translations from Schenker's *Kontrapunkt* 1 and 2." In "Species Counterpoint and Tonal Structure." Ph.D. diss., New York University: 134–78. UMI Number 7401984.
Contains, from Vol. 1, "Verbot des chromatischen Genges," "Vom Verbot auch der Mischungs intervalle im C. f.," "Warum die Quart in der vertikalen Richtung verboten wird," "Der dreie Zugang au den unvollkomenen Konsonanzen," "Über das eventuelle Verbot einer Folge zweier grossen Terzen," "Von der Modulation und vom Querstand," and "Die sogen. Nota cambiata (Wechselnote)." Contains, from Vol. 2, "Von der Folge zweier grosser Terzen," "Übergänge zum freien Satz: Einleitendes," and "Von der Ellipse einer Stimme als Brücks zum freien Satz."

T14   1980   Mast, Paul. "Johannes Brahms: Octaves and Fifths." *The Music Forum* V 1–196.

T15   1983   Stewart, James. "Heinrich Schenker's *Kontrapunkt* I and II: A Translation and Commentary." Ph.D. diss., Ohio State University. UMI Number 8403579.

T16   1984   J. S. Bach's Chromatic Fantasy and Fugue. trans. by Heidi Siegel. New York: Longman. ISBN 0-582-28330-2.
Reviews: 1984   *Choice* 22/2: 280 (J. E. Johnson).
1985   *Music Theory Spectrum* 7: 203–7 (W. Rothstein).
1985   *Music Analysis* 7/2: 225–33 (J. Rink).

T17   1985   "Organic Structure in Sonata Form." Reprinted in *Classic Music*, Garland Library of the History of Western Music, vol. 7 New York: Garland. ISBN 0-824-07456-4

T18   1985   Pastille, William, "Franz Schubert: Ihr Bild." *Sonus* 6/2: 31–37.

T19   1985   "*Die Vorstellung des Chaos* aus der Schöpfung." Reprinted in *Musik-Konzepte* 45: 15–23.

T20   1986   "Der Geist der musikalischen Technik." Reprinted in *Musiktheorie* 1988: 237.

T21 1986 Bent, Ian. "Essays from *Das Meisterwerk in der Musik*, Vol. 1 (1925)." *Mus Analysis* 5/2–3: 151–91.

T22 1986 "Zwei Sonaten Domeinco Scarlattis." *Musik-Konzepte* 46: 40–56.

T23 1987 Rothgeb, John, and Jürgen Thym. *Counterpoint: A Translation of* Kontrapunkt *by Heinrich Schenker*. New York: Schirmer, 1987. ISBN 0-02-873221-9 (2-vol. set), ISBN 0-02-873222-7 (Vol. 2). Reprinted by Musicalia Press, 2001. ISBN 0-967-80990-8 (2-vol. set) ISBN 0-967-80992-4 (Vol. 1) ISBN 0-967-80992-4 (Vol. 2).
Reviews: 1988 *Brio* 25/1: 36–7 (C. Bartlett).
1988 *Choice* 25/5: 778 (R. Stahura).
1988 *Musical Times* 129/1748: 524–9 (C. Schachter).
1988 *Theoria* 3: 161–9 (W. Pastille).
1989 *Music Theory Spectrum* 11/2: 232–9 (M. Bowen and R. Wason).
1989 *Music Analysis* 8/1–2: 197–204 (W. Drabkin).
1989 *Intégral* 3: 201–25 (P. McCreless).
1994 *Indiana Theory Review* 15/1: 35–52 (S. Larson).

T24 1988 Petty, Wayne. "Haydn: Sonata in E-flat Major," *Theoria* 3: 105–60.

T25 1988 Larson, Steve. "C. P. E. Bach: *Kurze und leichte Klavierstücke mit veränderten Reprisen* (1766), No. 1, Allegro." *In Theory Only* 10/4: 5–10.

T26 1988 Dunsby, Johnathan. "The Music of Today" in "Three Essays from *Neue Revue* (1894–97)." *Musical Analysis* 7/2: 133–4.

T27 1988 Loeschmann, Horsch B. "Impersonal Music" in "Three Essays from *Neue Revue* (1894–97)." *Musical Analysis* 7/2: 135–8.

T28 1988 Loeschmann, Horsch B. "Conductor-Directors" in "Three Essays from *Neue Revue* (1894–97)." *Musical Analysis* 7/2: 138–41.

T29 1988 Pastille, William. "The Spirit of Musical Technique." *Theoria* 3: 86–104.

T30 1989 Annibaldi, Claudio. "J. S. Bach, Zwölf kleine Präludien: il Preludio n. 1." In Drabkin, William. "'Bisogna leggere Schenker'": Sull'analisi del preludio in do maggiore BWV 924 di Bach." *Rivista italiana di musicologia* 24/1: 60–6.

T31 1990 Barce, Ramón. *Tratado de armonía*. Madrid: Real Musical.

Reviews: 1992 *Musica y educacion* 5/2: 122.

T32 1991 Pastille, William. "Johannes Brahms." From *Die Zukunft* 19, *The American Brahms Society Newsletter* 9/1: 1–3.

T33 1991 Temperley, Nicholas. "Heinrich Schenker (1926)." In *Haydn: The Creation.* Cambridge: Cambridge University Press: 100–2. [excerpt].

T34 1992 Rothgeb, John. *Beethoven's Ninth Symphony.* New Haven: Yale University Press. ISBN 0-300-0545-9.
Reviews: 1994 *Music Theory Spectrum* 16/1: 139–43 (M. Broyles). 1993 *Notes* 50/4: 1426–8 (K. Korsyn).

T35 1993 Meeùs, Nicholas. *L'écriture Libre.* Liège: Mardaga. ISBN 2-870-09559-7 (Vol. I) and 2–870–09508–2 (Vol. II).
Review: 1996 *Revue de Musicologie* 82: 376–7 (S. Gut).

T36 1994 *The Masterwork in Music I*, Cambridge Studies in Music Theory and Analysis 5, ed. by William Drabkin, trans. by Ian Bent, William Drabkin, Richard Kramer, John Rothgeb, and Heidi Siegel. Cambridge: Cambridge University Press. ISBN 0-521-45541-3.
Review: 1994 *Musicology Australia* 18: 61–2.

T37 1994 Weiner, Brien. "Notes from the Middleground: The Convergence of *Ur-Idee* and *Urlinie* in Schenker's *Erläuterungsausgabe* of Beethoven's Op. 101." Ph.D. diss., Yale University. UMI Number 9523249.

T38 1994 "Introduction to *Free Composition.*" Reprinted in *German Essays on Music*, ed. by Jost Hermand and Michael Gilbert. New York: Continuum.

T39 1995 Lubben, Ralph. "Analytic Practice and Ideology in Schenker's *Der Tonwille,*" Ph.D. diss., Brandeis University 1995.
Includes, from Pamphlet I, translations of "The Urlinie," "J. S. Bach: Prelude in E-flat Minor from the Well-Tempered Clavier," from Pamphlet II, "Yet Another Word about the Urlinie," from Pamphlet IV, "J. S. Bach: Twelve Little Preludes, Number One," "J. S. Bach: Twelve Little Preludes, Number Two," "Händel: Allemande," "Mozart: Sonata [in C Major] K. 545." From Pamphlet V, "J. S. Bach: Twelve Little Preludes, Number Five," "Urlinie and Voice-Leading." From Pamphlet X, "Haydn: Austrian National Hymn," "Schumann: Kinderszenen, Number One," and "Schumann: Kinderszenen, Number Nine."

T40 1995 Sanguinetti, Giorgio. "Mascagni a Vienna" in "L'opera italiana nella critica musicale di Heinrich Schenker." *Nuova Rivista musicale italiana* 29/3: 445–8.

T41 1995 Sanguinetti, Giorgio. "Una giogane scuola italiana?" in "L'opera italiana nella critica musicale di Heinrich Schenker." *Nuova Rivista musicale italiana* 29/3: 448–50.

T42 1995 Sanguinetti, Giorgio. "*I Rantzau* di Mascagni" in "L'opera italiana nella critica musicale di Heinrich Schenker." *Nuova Rivista musicale italiana* 29/3: 450–3.

T43 1995 Sanguinetti, Giorgio. "Appunti sul *Falstaff* di Verdi" in "L'opera italiana nella critica musicale di Heinrich Schenker." *Nuova Rivista musicale italiana* 29/3: 453–6.

T44 1995 Sanguinetti, Giorgio. "La fiera Sonzogno a Vienna" in "L'opera italiana nella critica musicale di Heinrich Schenker." *Nuova Rivista musicale italiana* 29/3: 456–8.

T45 1995 Sanguinetti, Giorgio. "Ruggiero leoncavallo" in "L'opera italiana nella critica musicale di Heinrich Schenker." *Nuova Rivista musicale italiana* 29/3: 458–61.

T46 1995 Sanguinetti, Giorgio. "Il *Falstaff* di Verdi" in "L'opera italiana nella critica musicale di Heinrich Schenker." *Nuova Rivista musicale italiana* 29/3: 461–5.

T47 1995 Sanguinetti, Giorgio. "Arte e vita: *Zanetto* di Mascagni" in "L'opera italiana nella critica musicale di Heinrich Schenker." *Nuova Rivista musicale italiana* 29/3: 465–6.

T48 1995 Sanguinetti, Giorgio. "*Bohème* di Puccini" in "L'opera italiana nella critica musicale di Heinrich Schenker." *Nuova Rivista musicale italiana* 29/3: 466–7.

T49 1995 Sanguinetti, Giorgio. "*Bohème* di Leoncavallo" in "L'opera italiana nella critica musicale di Heinrich Schenker." *Nuova Rivista musicale italiana* 29/3: 467.

T50 1996 *The Masterwork in Music II*, Cambridge Studies in Music Theory and Analysis 8, ed. by William Drabkin, trans. by Ian Bent, William Drabkin, John Rothgeb, and Heidi Siegel. Cambridge: Cambridge University Press. ISBN 0-521-45542-1.

    Reviews: 1996 *Music Analysis* 15/2–3: 301–42 (R. Snarrenberg).
               1996 *Canadian University Music Review* 17/1: 111–14 (W. Renwick).

1996   *The Musical Times* 137/1843: 13–21 (D. Puffett).
1996   *Music and Letters* 77/2: 291–3 (N. Marston).

T51   1997   *The Masterwork in Music III*, Cambridge Studies in Music Theory and Analysis 10, ed. by William Drabkin, trans. by Ian Bent, Alfred Clayton, and Derrick Puffett. Cambridge: Cambridge University Press. ISBN 0-521-45543-X.
Reviews: 1997   *Musicology Australia* 20: 110–1.
1999   *Journal of the American Musicological Society* 52: 647–52. (R. Lubben).

T52   1997   ⌈世賓. 自由 作曲. 北京 : 人民 音樂 出版社.

[1997   Chen, Shi-Ben. *Free Composition*. Beijing: People's Music Publications. ISBN 7-103-01431-0.]

T53   1998   Williams, H. "Analyse du Moment musical D. 780/3." *Ostinato Rigore* 11/12: 255–62. ISBN: 2-85893-492-4.

T54   1998   Mazur, Krzysztof. "O praosnowie i jej formach." *Muzyka* 43/1: 79–92.

T55   2000   Wintle, Christopher. "Ihr Bild." *Music Analysis* 19: 3–9.

T56   2000   Scott, Irene Schreier. *The Art of Performance*, ed. by Heribert Eiser. Oxford: Oxford University Press, 2000. ISBN 0-19-512254-2.
Reviews: 2001   *Notes* 57/4: 933–4 (P. Burstein).
2000   *Musical Times* 141/1873: 74–5.

T57   2000   Spurný, Lubomír. "Anton Bruckner." In *Heinrich Schenker—dávný neznámý*: 133–6.

T58   2000   Spurný, Lubomír. "Smetena, Prodaná nevĕsta." In *Heinrich Schenker—dávný neznámý*: 136–7.

T59   2000   Spurný, Lubomír. "Mozartův Don Juan." In *Heinrich Schenker—dávný neznámý*: 138–9.

T60   2000   Spurný, Lubomír. "Johannes Brahms." In *Heinrich Schenker—dávný neznámý*: 139–43.

T61   2000   Spurný, Lubomír. "Felix Mendelssohn-Bartholdy: Lieder ohne Worte op. 67/6." In *Heinrich Schenker—dávný neznámý*: 144–50.

T62   2002   *Der Tonwille: Pamphlets in Witness to the Immutable Laws of Music*, ed. by William Drabkin, trans. by Ian Bent, Robert

Snarrenberg, Robert Lubben, et al. Oxford: Oxford University Press. ISBN 0-19-5122-372.

T63	2003	Плотников, Борис. *Свободное сочинение.* Красноярск: Красноярская Академия Музьіки и Театра.

[2003	Plotnikov, Boris. *Free Composition.* Krasnoyarsk: Krasnoyarsk Academy of Music and Theatre]

Chapter 3

Articles on Schenker and His Approach

A1 2002 DeBellis, Mark. "Musical Analysis as Articulation." *Journal of Aesthetics and Art Criticism* 60/2: 119–35.

"Examines the relation between perceptions of, and judgments about, musical structure, and asks whether Schenkerian structures function like theoretical entities in science and whether Schenkerian theory can be reconciled with a model of musical composition and reception as communication." (RILM; used by permission)

A2 2001 Borio, Gianmario. "Schenker versus Schoenberg versus Schenker: The Difficulties of a Reconciliation." *Journal of the Royal Music Association* 126: 250–74.

"[Compares] Schenker's analyses [of Beethoven's sonatas op. 2 no. 1, op. 10 no. 1, and op. 57] in *Der Tonwille* and *Der freie Satz* with those of Schoenberg, Webern, Rufer and Ratz; [shows] that the disagreement principally concerns musical form and the functions of its components. The differences can finally be traced back to two opposite paradigms: music as nature and music as language." (274)

A3 2001 Ellison, Paul M. "Beethoven and Schenker: Unraveling Those Graphs, with an Explanation of Schenker's Analysis of the Ode to Joy." *Beethoven Journal* 16/2: 69–73.

Contains a discussion of Schenker's analysis of the piece; includes an introduction to Schenker's ideas.

A4 2001 Jackson, Timothy. "Heinrich Schenker as Composition Teacher: The Schenker-Oppel Exchange." *Music Analysis* 20/1: 1–115.

Examines in detail Oppel's arrangements of three of Händel's solo cantatas (HWV 108, 102, and 115) in the context of his correspondence with Heinrich

Schenker. Contains translations of the texts of the cantatas and the relevant correspondence between Schenker and Oppel. Includes copies of twenty-nine manuscript pages in Oppel's hand in addition to a valuable comparison of Oppel's passages with Schenker's suggestions below.

A5   2001   Maas, Hans. "Schenkeranalyse en onbegeleide melodie." *Tijdschrift voor muziektheorie* 6/3:175–87.
"[M]akes an attempt to pin down criteria [for analytical decisions], after discussing examples of analysis of monophonic fragments in the works of Schenker. Finally, the implications of the results for the analysis of polyphonic music is shown in an analysis of Bach's Invention in F." (175)

A6   2001   Meeùs, Nicholas. "Teaching Schenker at the Sorbonne." *Tijdschrift voor muziektheorie* 6/3:171–4.
Describes the conception of the first Schenker course at the Sorbonne and its results, noting that heretofore, "the only systematic reference to Schenker in the Sorbonne curriculum had been included in a course on the history of analytical methodology." (171)

A7   2001   Moreno, Jairo. "Schenker's Parallelisms, Schoenberg's Motive, and Referential Motives: Notes on Pluralistic Analysis." *College Music Symposium* 41: 91–111.
"[Stresses] the pedagogical need for broader, more comprehensive analyses of motivic content and [offers] an account of the difficulties and notational revisions necessary to carry this out; demonstrates the insufficiency of single analytical strategies to provide a comprehensive reading of motivic relations." (92)

A8   2001   Schachter, Carl. "Elephants, Crocodiles, and Beethoven: Schenker's Politics and the Pedagogy of Schenkerian Analysis." *Theory and Practice* 26: 1–20.
"[Surveys] Schenker's political views and attempt[s] to place them in historical context; consider[s] whether the musical and political ideas are necessarily bound together for Schenker's readers today," and speculates "whether the teaching of his approach nowadays needs to incorporate references to his political ideology." (4)

A9   2001   Schachter, Carl. "Taking Care of the Sense: A Schenkerian Pedagogy for Performers." *Tijdschrift voor muziektheorie* 6/3:159–70.
Discussion of Schenkerian concepts from the performer's perspective; notes that "the performer's perspective and the analyst's should provide mutual reinforcement" and not be "exclusively intellectual." (159)

A10   2001   Schwab-Felisch, Oliver. "Functions of the Unclear: Chromaticism in Beethoven's String Quartet in E-flat Major, op. 74." *Tijdschrift voor muziektheorie* 6/3: 188–94.

Using the theories of Schenker, Rothstein, Meyer, and Narmour, the author suggests that the work's "aesthetic quality . . . [is] supported by a strong temporary incongruence between perceived and analytically discovered features, and . . . that its goal-directedness is created not only by harmony and voice leading, but also by a subtle interaction of manifest and extrapolated meanings." (188)

A11 2001 Traut, Donald. "Displancment and Its Role in Schenkerian Theory." *Theory and Practice* 26: 99–116.
Extension of the idea of rhythmic displacement and normalization based on Rothstein's dissertation; discusses Schenker's use of diagonal lines, "which are used to connect displaced tones that are simultaneous at some higher level." (99)

A12 2001 Tuchowski, Andrzej. "The Integrative Role of Motion Patterns in Lutosławski's Mature Symphonic Works: A Comparison of *Livre pour orchestre* and the Symphony No. 4." In *Lutosławski Studies*, ed. by Zbigniew Skowron. Oxford: Oxford University Press: 287–304.
Establishes a "broad compromise position" taking into account ideas of Kurth, Schenker, Mersmann, Meyer, Asafiev, and others. Suggests that "the concept of temporal perspective affecting the perception of motion corresponds to the Schenkerian ideas of structural levels." Although the idea of structural levels originates with Schenker, the graphic analyses are completely foreign. (288)

A13 2001 Wen, Eric. "Stripped of the G String: Bach's Air from the Suite No. 3 in D." *Theory and Practice* 26: 117–40.
A voice-leading graph with commentary, "[showing] how the melody in the opening section presents a model which is echoed throughout the entire piece." (118)

A14 2000 Drabkin, William. "Chopin, Schenker, and 'Musical Form.' " *Ostinato Rigore* 15: 173–86 ISBN 2-85893-604-8.
After discussing Schenker's published analyses of Chopin's Waltz op. 34/1 and Nocturne op. 15/2, Drabkin discusses the unpublished analyses of Chopin's Prelude p. 28/2 and the Mazurka op. 24/2 that serve to "demonstrate Schenker's principal concern as an analyst: to explain how, whatever novelties or difficulties it may present, a well-composed piece can ultimately be understood as a complete and hence perfect harmonic-contrapuntal structure." (179)

A15 2000 Fessel, Pablo. "La concepcion kantiana del tiempo y la anterioridad de lo tonal en la teoria de Heinrich Schenker." *Musica e investigacion* 3/6: 127–34.
Questions "Schenker's rejection of the traditional concept of harmonic modulation, [and takes issue with] the derived character of meter and rhythm with respect to the tonal dimension. In agreement with Kant's conception of time, as formulated in his *Kritik der reinen Vernunft* (1781), a connection between the two objections is reached, which would turn up to be a consequence of a single

principle, namely, the tonal organicism of the musical composition." (RILM; used by permission)

A16 2000 Jarzebska, Alicja. "Amerkanskie metody sformalizowanej analizy muzycznej." *Muzyka*: 87–112.
Examines the analytical approaches of Forte (set theory), Van den Toorn, Straus (transformational and associational voice leading), and Martha Hyde (twelve-tone harmony and meter). Notes that "[t]he scientific character of American music theory and the formalized language of the methods of analysis developed by Milton Babbitt and Allen Forte and their disciples have been criticized in recent years, giving rise to theoretical orientations open to the percipient and cultural, historical, and philosophical contexts of music." (RILM; used by permission)

A17 2000 Krims, Adam. "Music Theory as Productivity ('Redistribution' of Meaning of Texts: Schubert's *Impromptu in G Flat*; Schenker's *Free Composition*; Schoenberg's *Theory of Harmony*)." *Canadian University Music Review* 20/2: 16–30.
    Responses: 2000 *Canadian University Music Review* 20: 31–44 (W. Renwick).
                 2000 *Canadian University Music Review* 20/2: 42–4 (A. Krims).
Examines Schubert's D. 899 in light of Schenkerian and Schoenbergian theory intending "to exemplify the notion that readings of texts—both theoretical and musical—may generally enter into relations of productivity." (18)

A18 2000 Medina, Cedilia, and Juan Pablo Medina. "Entrevista a Carl Schachter." *Pauta* 74: 18–24.
An interview with Carl Schachter, focusing on his application of Schenkerian ideas to rhythm and meter.

A19 2000 Plenckers, Leo. "Drie Schenkeranalyses van Bachs Inventio 8." *Tijdschrift voor muziektheorie* 5/1: 16–25.
    Response: 2000 *Tijdschrift voor muziektheorie* 5/2: 130–3 (P. Scheepers).
Examines two analyses by Felix-Eberhard von Cube and Allen Forte/Steven Gilbert; offers a third interpretation that "does better justice to the musical text." (16)

A20 2000 Plotnikov, Boris. "On Blending Schenkerian Techniques with Traditional Foreground Analysis." *Tijdschrift voor muziektheorie* 5/2: 124–9.
Analyzes Nicolay Metener's *Märchen* op. 26/3 according to "integral" analysis (survey of thematic contents; extramusical associations) and from a Schenkerian perspective, concluding that "the ultimate goal [of studying and producing

graphs] consists in teaching students to *graph in imagination*, to trace lines that can be heard and produced by individuals on their instruments." (124)

A21 2000 Rothstein, William. "Chopin and the B-Major Complex: A Study of the Psychology of Composition." *Ostinato Rigore* 15: 149–72.
Discusses most of Chopin's B-major works, presenting graphs and commentary, particularly noting "the use of D-sharp, especially d-sharp^2, as a focal melodic pitch; the prevalence of neighboring motion to D-sharp, with special emphasis on the upper neighbor, E; prominent outlining of the major sixth between d-sharp^2 and f-sharp^1; and the coupling of d-sharp^2 and d-sharp^1," which he terms the B-Major Complex. (157)

A22 2000 Schachter, Carl. "Counterpoint and Chromaticism in Chopin's Mazurka in C-sharp Minor, Op. 50/3." *Ostinato Rigore* 15: 121–34.
A graphic analysis with commentary; notes that the Mazurka in question is a "remarkable example of a dance piece which contains passages that hint at a fugal exposition." (121)

A23 2000 Scheepers, Paul. "Schenker in de praktijk." *Tijdschrift voor muziektheorie* 5/2: 101–14.
"This article urges a more prominent place for Schenkerian analysis in the [European] music theory curricula. The Schenkerian approach enables valuable insights into musical structure that are not, or are far less directly, obtainable with other analytical methods. [The author] suggests ways of introducing a quasi-Schenkerian approach to analysis, harmony and counterpoint into the earlier years of [study]." (101)

A24 2000 Sly, Gordon. "Schubert's Innovations in Sonata Form: Compositional Logic and Structural Interpretation." *Journal of Music Theory* 45/2: 119–50.
Discusses Schubert's "well-known propensity for preserving in the recapitulation the broad modulation scheme of the exposition," where "the tonic serves as goal rather than as source, of the tonal motion." Focuses on recapitulations that begin away from the tonic. (1–2)

A25 2000 Smith, Peter. "Outer-Voice Conflicts: Their Analytical Challenges and Artistic Consequences." *Journal of Music Theory* 44/1: 1–44.
Discusses the difficulties involved in making analytical decisions (specifically in determining the structural upper voice). Based on Schachter's ideas of "either/or" and "both/and," Smith shows how passages may be interpreted more than one way. The outer-voice conflict occurs when "melody and bass seem to work at cross-purposes whereas the outer voices of a prolonged dissonant sonority are usually congruent." (3)

A26   2000   Teboul, Jean-Claude. "Les trois etudes ecrites pour la Methode des methods de Moscheles et Fétis: Approche Schenkerienne." *Ostinato Rigore* 15: 249–63.

Presents analyses of the *trios nouvelles etudes* of Chopin, showing formal divisions and voice-leading graphs.

A27   2000   Traut, Donald. "Revisitng Stravinsky's Concerto." *Theory and Practice* 25: 65–86.

Discusses Schenker's analysis of an excerpt from Stravinsky's Piano Concerto from *Das Meisterwerk* II, citing responses by Robert Morgan, Joseph Straus, and Milton Babbitt. The author then offers his own analysis of the work, using Schenker's graph as a starting point.

A28   2000   Wintle, Christopher. "Franz Schubert, *Ihr Bild* (1828): A Response to Schenker's Essay in *Der Tonwille*, Vol. I." *Music Analysis* 19/1: 10–28.

Taking Schenker's analysis from *Der Tonwille* as a starting point, Wintle offers his own reading based on Schenker's mature theories, exploring particularly "the principle of transference across levels—from foreground to deep middleground—of configurations which [Schenker] rightly hesitates to call motives." (10)

A29   1999   Alpern, Wayne. "Music Theory as a Mode of Law: The Case of Heinrich Schenker, Esq." *Cardozo Law Review* 205–6: 1459–511.

Documents Schenker's law studies, noting that "he placed great value upon the breadth of his education outside of music"; focuses on his studies with Georg Jellinek and how the latter's legal philosophy influenced Schenker's musical thinking. Includes a transcription of Schenker's *Meldungsbuch* (course of study). (1459)

A30   1999   Benjamin, William. "Schenker's Theory and Virgil's Construction of the World." *Theory and Practice* 24: 107–16.

Speculates that "the life philosophy that is articulated in the *Aeneid* has striking parallels with Schenker's view of tonal music, parallels which lead to a deeper understanding of the problems that people face who grapple with Schenker's ideas"; discusses the difficulties faced by "music students encountering Schenker for the first time, and by their teachers trying to explain his ideas." (107)

A31   1999   Божцкоба, Мцлена. "Методът на Редукция на Хайнрих Шенкер по Примери от Българската Музика." *Българската музикознанце* 23/2: 79–82.

[1999 Bozikova, Milena. "The Analytical Method of Heinrich Schenker [applied to] Examples of Bulgarian Music." *Balgarsko muzikoznanie* 23/2: 79–82.]

Discusses the applicability of Schenker's method to Bulgarian music. Examines the applicability of Schenker's ideas to post-tonal music, citing literature by Salzer, Travis, Straus, and Baker.

A32 1999 Broman, Per. "Touching Up the Paint or a Complete Vinyl Residing? Reflections Over Meta-Scientific Problems in Music Theory." *Perspectives of New Music* 37/1: 5–25.
Uses architectural metaphors to describe the (Schenkerian) analytic process; notes that "[m]usic theory, as represented by Schenkerian analysis, is thus concerned with showing similarities as well as differences between art works." Questions whether this constitutes "scientific work." (7–8)

A33 1999 Burstein, L. Poundie. "Comedy and structure in Haydn's Symphonies." In *Schenker Studies II*. Cambridge: Cambridge University Press: 67–81.
After examining humor in general, focusing on the juxtaposition of incongruities, Burstein examines excerpts from six symphonies of Haydn, stating that "structural analysis does not counteract appreciation of oddities or quirks, but rather highlights them by contextualizing them." (81)

A34 1999 Cadwallader, Allen, and William Pastille. "Schenker's Unpublished Work with the Music of Johannes Brahms." In *Schenker Studies II*. Cambridge: Cambridge University Press: 26–48.
Speculates on the relationship between Schenker and Brahms, noting that "the apparent neglect of Brahms's music is somewhat inconsistent with the notion that the composer had been a formative influence on Schenker and his work." Provides sketches and transcriptions from the "Brahms Folder" of the Oster Collection, focusing on the two intermezzi op. 119/1–2. (26)

A35 1999 Cadwallader, Allen, trans. by Jean-Claude Teboul. "Les analyses non publiees faites par Schenker des intermezzi op. 119 No. 1 et 2 de Brahms." *Ostinato Rigore* 13: 97–112.
French translation of above.

A36 1999 Clark, Suzannah. "Schenker's Mysterious Five." *Nineteenth-Century Music* 23/1: 84–102.
"[Schenker] continually spotted the number five in the derivation of tonality, and its recurrence lent it credibility. Thinking it nevertheless had some kind of otherworldly presence, he went so far as to call it the Mysterious Five (*geheimnisvolle Fünfzahl*) and in so doing instilled in it the quality of being an inexplicable, enigmatic or, at the very least, non controvertible structuring force. Characteristically, he gave the impression that it is an observed and not an invented property. It is, as he tried to indicate, not humanly derived." (87)

A37 1999 Cook, Nicholas. "At the Borders of Musical Identity: Schenker, Corelli and the Graces." *Music Analysis* 18/2: 179–233.

Discusses the questions of authenticity vis-à-vis ornamented versions of Corelli's op. 5 violin sonatas, accepting them as authentic for purposes of his argument; speculates that Schenker may have "derived . . . [his] idea of the tonal archetype [from Corelli's music]." Questions whether Schenker's method of analysis "can be usefully applied to Corelli's graces." (180, 181)

A38   1999   Cook, Nicholas. "Heinrich Schenker, Modernist: Detail, Difference, and Analysis." *Theory and Practice* 24: 91–106.
Discusses Schenker's works in light of the cultural artomsphere of fin-de-siècle Vienna, noting that "one of [fin-de-siècle Vienna's] central features, and a particularly controversial one, was a preoccupation with the role and nature of the decorative arts." (91–2)

A39   1999   Eybl, Martin. "Archäologie der Tonkinst: Mozart-Analysen Heinrich Schenkers." *Mozartanalyse im 19. und frühen 20. Jahrhundert: Bericht über die Tagung Salzburg 1996.* Laaber: Laaber-Verlag: 119–32.
An analysis of the piano sonata K. 310, showing Mozart's "ability to link melodic diversity at the surface level with latent motivic [connections]"; refutes the idea that Mozart indulged in "formulaic passage work" and "insufficiently grounded motivic and thematic work." (RILM; used by permission)

A40   1999   Gagné, David. "'Symphonic Breadth': Structural Style in Mozart's Symphonies." In *Schenker Studies II*. Cambridge: Cambridge University Press: 82–108.
Discusses the "structural style" of the opening movements of four Mozart symphonies (K. 338, K. 385, and K. 504) and the quartet K. 387. By "structural style," the author refers to "the characteristics of a work's harmonic and voice-leading structure, in conjunction with rhythm and with design features (texture, orchestration, dynamics)." (82)

A41   1999   Jackson, Timothy. "Diachronic Transformation in a Schenkerian Context: Brahms's *Haydn Variations*." In *Schenker Studies II*. Cambridge: Cambridge University Press: 239–75.
"[P]roposes that Saussure's distinction between synchronic and diachronic 'facts of a different order' [from his *Cours de linguistic génerale*] can illuminate the entelechy of musical structure as viewed from a Schenkerian perspective. A musical work may embody in its endstate a conceptually prior state, which has become the endstate through a diachronic transformation. From a synchronic perspective, the endstate is a 'distortion' of the 'previous' state and vice versa. Diachronic transformation is essentially different from voice-leading transformation. Voice-leading transformation assumes structure to be in a steady state, all structural levels embodied and undistorted in the endstate." (239)

A42 1999 Jackson, Timothy L. "Diachronische Transformation im Schenkerschen Kontext: Brahms' *Haydn-Variationen.*" In *Johannes Brahms: Quellen-Text-Rezeption-Interpretation: Internationaler Brahms-Kongress, Hamburg 1997*, ed. by Friedhelm Krummacher and Michael Struck. Munich: Henle Verlag: 453–94. ISBN 3-873-28098-1.

German translation of Jackson's preceding article.

A43 1999 Kosovsky, Robert. "Levels of Understanding: An Introduction to Schenker's Nachlass." In *Schenker Studies II*. Cambridge: Cambridge University Press: 3–11.

An overview of the Oster Collection, with suggestions for use and acknowledgment of the difficulties contained therein, such as Schenker's "barely-ledgible" handwriting and the organization of the collection. "In defining such problems and suggesting solutions, this article hopes to serve as a preliminary guide to source studies involving Schenker and his papers." (3)

A44 1999 Larson, Steve. "Swing and Motive in Three Performances by Oscar Peterson." *Journal of Music Theory* 43/2: 283–314.

Analyzes three performances by Oscar Peterson of Cole Porter's *Night and Day*, "demonstrating how these performances swing on a variety of levels." Examines Peterson's use of motives in his performances. (283)

A45 1999 Laufer, Edward. "On the First Movement of Sibelius's Fourth Symphony: A Schenkerian View." In *Schenker Studies II*. Cambridge: Cambridge University Press: 127–59.

Contains graphic analyses and commentary, focusing on compositional techniques such as, "in the melodic sphere, motivic transformation and developing transition and, in the harmonic sphere, elision (as omission of notes that are due), oblique relationship (in which certain notes are to be understood as belonging together but are not aligned rhythmically with each other), and anticipation (in the sense of overlapping, whereby one or more notes are stated before the sonority to which they belong)." (127)

A46 1999 Lewin, David. "*Auf dem Flüße*: Image Poetique et structure musicale profonde dans un lied de Schubert." *Cashiers F. Schubert: Bulletin de la Societe Franz Schubert et Revue des etudes schubertienes* 12: 7–35.

French translation of Lewin's 1982 *Nineteenth-Century Music* article (see **A582** below)

A47 1999 Maisel, Arthur. "Voice-Leading as Drama in *Wozzeck*." In *Schenker Studies II*. Cambridge: Cambridge University Press: 160–91.

Asserts that "much of the musical expression of the drama in *Wozzeck* takes place in the voice leading; [shows] that the voice leading itself derives from these symbols [i.e., extramusical associations applied to certain constructs of the opera] and allows them to enact basic elements of the drama in musical terms." (160)

A48   1999   McKee, Eric. "Influences of the Early Eighteenth Century Social Minuet on the Minuets from J. S. Bach's French Suites, BWV 812–17." *Music Analysis* 18/2: 235–60.

Examines minuets from four of the French Suites (BWV 812, 814, 815, and 817); speculates that "Bach's progressive approach to phrase structure in his minuets is directly related to a conscious effort on his part to establish and maintain a prominent two-bar hypermeter." (236)

A49   1999   McKee, Eric. "Alternative Meanings in the First Movement of Beethoven's String Quartet in E-flat Major, Op. 127." *Theory and Practice* 24: 1–27.

Provides graphic analysis with commentary, focusing on "[interpreting] Beethoven's use of the term *Maestoso* . . . by asking the questions: what did *Maestoso* mean in Beethoven's time, what does it mean in Beethoven's works, and what does it mean in particular for op. 127?" (2)

A50   1999   Pastille, William. "Music and Life: Some Lessons." *Theory and Practice* 24: 117–9.

Discusses the benefits of the Schenkerian viewpoint in general musical pedagogy and in life situations, such as "self-discovery, deep engagement, and responsible judgment." (118–9)

A51   1999   Petty, Wayne. "Chopin and the Ghost of Beethoven." *Nineteenth-Century Music* 22/3: 281–99.

Examines Chopin's Sonata, op. 35, noting Chopin's "absorbtion" or "resistance" to Beethoven's influence. Suggests that the funeral march "[enacts] a symbolic death ritual whereby Chopin puts Beethoven to rest, affirming his own identity against Beethoven's." (282)

A52   1999   Petty, Wayne. "C. P. E. Bach and the Fine Art of Transposition." In *Schenker Studies II*. Cambridge: Cambridge University Press: 67–81.

Examines the recapitulations in three pieces of C. P. E. Bach, showing that Bach often used the recapitulation to "make new connections between earlier passages, [making] concealed relationships explicit" and "[continuing to develop] the tonal issues around which the other sections evolve, thereby recalling, summarizing, and resolving the tonal tensions at the end." (50–1)

A53   1999   Petty, Wayne. "Koch, Schenker, and the Development Section of Sonata Forms by C. P. E. Bach." *Music Theory Spectrum* 21/2: 151–173.

Examines the development section of three sonata movements according to Koch's and Schenker's approaches, revealing them "to use a variety of harmonic and voice-leading structures that one would not suspect from either Koch's or Schenker's work alone. These tonal structures reflect the individual style and character of each movement, often in ingenious ways." (173)

A54 1999 Renwick, William. "Analysis: Schenkerian." In *The Reader's Guide to Music*. Chicago and London: Fitzroy Dearborn Publishers: 24–25. ISBN 1-579-5843-9.
A brief explanation of Schenker's analytic method, with a survey of contributions by Forte and Gilbert, Jonas, Salzer, and Snarrenberg.

A55 1999 Renwick, William. "Chemins mystérieux de la fugue: Un point de vie schenkérien sur la fugue en fa majeur de la 2e suite de Händel." *Musurgia* 4: 12–24.
French translation of Renwick's 1995 *Music Analysis* article (see **A184** below).

A56 1999 Rink, John. "'Structural Momentum' and Closure in Chopin's Nocturne Op. 9, No. 2." In *Schenker Studies II*. Cambridge: Cambridge University Press: 109–26.
"This essay will review the studies of several authors and on the basis of these define a consensus view of the Nocturne's structure. I will then offer an analytical alternative and will consider how the work relates to other early compositions by Chopin, noting similarities which explain its more unusual characteristics, and differences which can perhaps be understood only by comparison with Field's Nocturnes Nos. 1 and 9, both in E Flat major." (109)

A57 1999 Samarotto, Frank. "Strange Dimensions: Regularity and Irregularity in Deep Levels of Rhythmic Reduction." In *Schenker Studies II*. Cambridge: Cambridge University Press: 222–38.
Uses Schachter's idea of durational reduction "in order to demonstrate how the technique of rhythmic reduction can absorb—or express—some particularly significant irregular features in order to explore not *whether* but *how* models of deeper rhythmic levels can be related to the surface." (223)

A58 1999 Schachter, Carl. "Structure as Foreground: 'Das Drama des Ursatzes.'" In *Schenker Studies II*. Cambridge: Cambridge University Press: 298–314.
Explores "a few of the varied ways in which the projection of an implicit background forms part of the explicit compositional discourse"; shows how background elements are "foregrounded" and "participate in the most striking events of the foreground and are integral to its tonal conflicts, its unexpected twists, and its climaxes." (298–9)

A59 1999 Shaftel, Matthew. "From Inspiration to Archive: Cole Porter's *Night and Day*." *Journal of Music Theory* 43/2: 315–47.

Emphasizes Porter's musical training; holds that Schenkerian analysis of *Night and Day* "demonstrates the intricate sophistication of Cole Porter's compositional style and highlights his nearly perfect unification of music and lyrics." (315)

A60 1999 Siegel, Heidi. "When *Freier Satz* Was Part of *Kontrapunkt*: A Preliminary Report." *Schenker Studies II*. Cambridge: Cambridge University Press: 12–25.

Taking as its impetus a letter of January 1920 from Schenker to August Halm, the essay describes the unpublished draft material preserved in the Oster Collection and speculates on the ordering of chapters and creative process involved in his working out of the "relation between scale degree and voice leading in free composition." (24)

A61 1999 Smyth, David. "Schenker's Octave Lines Reconsidered." *Journal of Music Theory* 43/1: 101–33.

Examines Schenker's discussion of octave lines followed by later theorists' objections; argues that octave lines are "entirely appropriate for deep structural levels, while at the same time they engender strikingly diverse surface designs." Pleads for the reconsideration of octave lines as a viable *Urlinie* form. (101)

A62 1999 Suurpää, Lauri. "Continuous Exposition and Tonal Structure in Three Late Haydn Works." *Music Theory Spectrum* 21/1: 174–99.

Examines the "interaction of voice-leading structure and tonal organization" in the expositions of three Haydn works; suggests that, since the secondary key area is postponed until the end of the exposition, the form of the three works examined is "better described as continuous than as two-part." (174)

A63 1999 Suurpää, Lauri. "Programmatic Aspects of the Second Sonata of Haydn's *Seven Last Words*." *Theory and Practice* 24: 29–55.

A programmatic study of the motto preceding the second sonata of the *Seven Last Words* examining (1) basic narrative tensions, (2) how these tensions may be interpreted as being mirrored in the form and the deep-level voice-leading structure of the sonata, (3) motivic elements that support the programmatic aspects created by the form and the deep-level voice leading, and (4) how the musical factors creating the programmatic quality of the sonata are related to the compositional theory and practice of the eighteenth century. (30)

A64 1999 Wagner, Naphtali. "KV 614: Schock und Struktur in der Wiener Klassik." *Musik and Ästhetik* 3/10: 28–46.

Examines Mozart's K. 614 quartet from the viewpoints of Schenker and Adorno, emphasizing how each approach treats the dissonances. Schenker views them as integrated into the structure, while Adorno interprets them as "a shock that destroys the structure." (RILM; used by permission)

A65 1999 Wen, Eric. "Bass-Line Articulations of the *Urlinie*." In *Schenker Studies II*. Cambridge: Cambridge University Press: 276–97.

Explores the technique of "shifting of the top-voice structure into the bass so that a linear continuity bridges the registral gap between the highest and lowest sounds." Examines several pieces (see appendix B), noting register transfers of the *Urlinie* into the lower voice. (276)

A66 1999 Willner, Channan. "Sequential Expansion and Hendelian Phrase Rhythm." In *Schenker Studies II*. Cambridge: Cambridge University Press: 192–221.
Analyzes the *Allemande* from Mozart's Suite in C, K. 399, examining his gradual expanding of a sequential passage that results in hidden motivic repetitions. Also presents an analysis of Handel's op. 6/2 *concerto grosso*.

A67 1998 Agawu, V. Kofi. "Musical Analysis Versus Musical Hermeneutics." *American Journal of Semiotics* 13/1–4: 9–24.
Uses Kretzschmar's *Anregungen zur Forderung musikalischer Hermeneutik* as "a springboard for reflecting on some of the dilemmas that face today's music analysts." Discusses the "interface between hermeneutics and . . . theory-based analysis," considering the former the "more fruitful" of the two. (9)

A68 1998 Baroni, Mario, with Rossana Dalmonte and Egidio Pozzi. "Quand une analyse schenkerienne est-elle utile aux interprètes?" *Revue Belge de Musicologie* 52: 321–45.
Presents a graphic analysis, with commentary, of Liszt's *La Marquise de Blocqueville*; shows how Schenkerian analysis may aid interpretation.

A69 1998 Beach, David. "An Analysis of Schubert's *Der Neugierige*: A Tribute to Greta Kraus." *Canadian University Music Review* 19/1: 69–80.
The harpsichordist and pianist Greta Kraus (1907–98) taught for many years at the University of Toronto. An analysis of *Der Neugierige* from Schubert's *Die schöne Mullerin* follows the linear approach developed by Schenker, with whom Kraus studied in Vienna. Throughout her teaching career, Kraus remained interested in Schenker's ideas, which she applied practically to performance-related issues. (RILM; used by permission)

A70 1998 Brown, Matthew. "Rothstein's Paradox and Neumeyer's Fallacies." *Intégral* 12: 95–132.
       Response: 1998 *Intégral* 12: 133–5 (D. Neumeyer).
Explains the "nature and testability" of the *Ursatz* concept; responds to Neumeyer's idea that "[we must] wither abandon the *Ursatz* or abandon the notion that Schenker's method constitutes a theory." Also responds to Richard Cohn's supposition that, since Schenker's analytic methods can be detached from his *Weltanschauung,* they may also be detached from "some other music-theoretic tenets" (i.e., the *Ursatz*). (96)

A71   1998   Burstein, L. Poundie. "Surprising Returns: The VII# in Beethoven's
              Op. 18 No. 3, and Its Antecedents in Haydn." *Music Analysis* 17/3:
              295–312.

Examines the development section, in which "the sudden reinterpretation of the
C-sharp [from V of F-sharp to VII# of D] creates a type of tonal crisis which has
deep structural ramifications for the entire movement." (295)

A72   1998   Clark, Suzannah, trans. by Thomas Aigner. "Terzverwandtschaft
              in der 'Unvollendeten' von Schubert und der 'Waldstein-Sonate'
              von Beethoven." *Schubert durch die Brille: Internationales
              Franz Schubert Institut Mitteilungen* 20: 123–30.

Examines third-relations in Schubert's Eighth Symphony and Beethoven's
Sonata op. 53.

A73   1998   Forte, Allen. "A Schenkerian Reading of an Excerpt from Tristan
              und Isolde." *Musicae Scientae* [2/1a] (special issue).

Examines the English horn solo from Act III of *Tristan*, noting that "[t]hrough-
out the excerpt, the instantiation of such paradigms as middleground linear progressions and foreground unfoldings leads to the conclusion that Schenker's
approach to analysis illuminates the music in effective ways and suggests that
Wagner's oeuvre may be more amenable to that approach than has previously
been thought to be the case." (15)

A74   1998   Forte, Allen. "Paul Hindemith's Contribution to Music Theory in
              the United States." *Journal of Music Theory* 42/1: 1–14.

Documents the reception of Hindemith's theories in the United States and
describes his tenure at Yale University, leading, ultimately, to the institution
of the first Ph.D. program in music theory. Forte also discusses the influences of
Schenker and Babbitt, which served to effectively undermine the influence
of Hindemith's ideas.

A75   1998   Hilgendorf, Simone. "Die Analyse des 'Phrase Rhythm' von
              William Rothstein: Ein Amerikanische Modell zum Verständnis
              tonaler Musik." *Musik als Text*: Bericht uber den Internationalen
              Kongress der Gesellschaft fur Musikforschung, Vol. 2, ed. by
              Hermann Danuser and Tobias Plebuch. Kassel: Bärenreiter:
              123–9. ISBN 3-7618-1402-X.

A discussion of Rothstein's concept of phrase rhythm, as outlined in his *phrase
rhythm in tonal music* (see **B42** below).

A76   1998   Hinton, Stephen. "Die Musiktheorie Heinrich Schenkers und ihre
              Übertragung ins Englische." *Musik als Text*: Bericht uber den In-
              ternationalen Kongress der Gesellschaft fur Musikforschung, Vol.
              1, ed. by Hermann Danuser and Tobias Plebuch. Kassel: Bärenre-
              iter: 185–9. ISBN 3-7618-1401-1.

A discussion of the English translations of Schenker's writings, particularly noting the suppression of Schenker's political ideas.

A77   1998   Kamien, Roger. "Non-tonic settings of the primary tone in Beethoven Piano Sonatas." *Journal of Musicology* 16: 379–93.
Examines three Beethoven sonatas (opp. 10/3, 31/2, and 31/3), showing how the "dramatic effect" of the primary tone is heightened by its being supported by a non-tonic harmony. (379)

A78   1998   Lerdahl, Fred. "Prolonging the Inevitable." *Revue Belge de Musicologie* 52: 305–9.
Explains atonal prolongational theory as a "logical extension of GTTM's prolongational structure." Discusses ways in which atonal music can be heard as hierarchical based on auditory "streaming," the "anchoring principle," and "psychoacoustic consonance/dissonance." (305)

A79   1998   Lerdahl, Fred. "Prolongational Structure and Schematic Form in Tristan's 'Alte Weise.'" *Musicae Scientae* [2/1a] (special issue).
Presents a time-span reduction with commentary, based on the techniques outlined in Lerdahl/Jackendoff, of the English horn solo from *Tristan*; relates this excerpt to other passages in the opera.

A80   1998   Littlefield, Richard, and David Neumeyer. "Rewriting Schenker: Narrative–History–Ideology." In *Music and Ideology: Resisting the Aesthetic,* ed. by Adam Krims. New York: Routledge: 113–55. ISBN 9-057-01321-5.
Reprint of the 1992 *Music Theory Spectrum* article (see **A271** below).

A81   1998   London, Justin, and Ronald Rodman. "Musical Genre and Schenkerian Analysis." *Journal of Music Theory* 42/1: 101–24.
Examines Chopin's prelude op. 28/4, citing analyses by Schenker (an unpublished sketch) and Schachter; discuss the concentions of the prelude in the nineteenth century, and presents the idea of a "gapped" *Urlinie,* e.g., $\hat{5}$-$\hat{4}$-$\hat{2}$-$\hat{1}$.

A82   1998   Meeùs, Nicholas. "La direction de la ligne fondamentale schenkerienne." *Revue Belge de Musicologie* 52: 311–20.
Examines the concept of the *Urlinie,* especially its descending direction. Discusses three aspects of the *Urlinie*: its being composed of passing tones, its cadential properties, and its suggestion of the I-V-I harmonic progression.

A83   1998   Mesnage, Marcel. "Emplois compositionnels de la notion de register." *Revue Belge de Musicologie* 52: 299–304.
Examines the general compositional importance of register, including discussions of Schenker's concepts of octave coupling and register transfer.

A84   1998   Rosen, Charles. "Concealed Structures: Heinrich Schenker, Ferdinand de Saussure, Roman Jakobson." In *Romantic Poets, Critics, and other Madmen*. Cambridge, Mass: Harvard University Press: 182–211. ISBN 0-674-77951-7.
Describes the ideas of Schenker, Saussure, and Jakobson in separate sections, showing how each emphasizes hidden meaning in music, structural linguistics, and literary criticism, respectively. Rosen remains critical of Schenker's ideas.

A85   1998   Schneider, Mathieu. "Les *Metamorphoses* de Richard Strauss éraint-elles à l'origine de forme lied?" *Cashires Franz Schubert: Revue de musique classique et romantique* 13: 17–38.
Based on the author's dissertation (see **D31** below).

A86   1998   Smith, Peter. "Brahms and the Neapolitan Complex: flat-II and flat-VII and Their Multiple Functions in the First Movement of the F-Minor Clarinet Sonata." *Brahms Studies* 2: 169–208.
Discusses hidden motivic repetition and Brahms's use of chromatic key relationships. Examines "the relationship of thematic design, key succession, and middleground voice leading" in addition to the motivic processes. (169)

A87   1998   Stefanija, Leon. "Glasbeno-analiticni nastavki: Med idejo in strukturo." *Muzikoloski zbornik* 34: 147–54.
Discusses the understandings of compositional structures from ancient Greek mathematical ratios to language-based theories of music. Examines Schenker's writings in conjunction with Koch, Forkel, and various musical treatises from the tenth through the twentieth centuries.

A88   1998   Suurpää, Lauri. "Viisi näkökulmaa Brahmsin lauluun *Der Tod dasist die kühle Nacht*, op. 96/1: Schenkeriläinen näkökulma" *Musiikki* 28/1: 68–80.
A contribution, illustrating the Schenkerian approach, to an analysis symposium on the Brahms song. Other approaches in the symposium were hermeneutic (semiotic), motivic, and historical.

A89   1998   Larson, Steve. "Schenkerian Analysis of Modern Jazz: Questions about Method." *Music Theory Spectrum* 20: 209–41.
Examines three questions: (1) Is it appropriate to apply to improvised music a method of analysis developed for the study of composed music? (2) Can features of jazz harmony (ninths, elevenths, and thirteenths) not appearing in the music Schenker analyzed be accounted for by Schenkerian analysis? (3) Do improvising musicians really intend to create the complex structures shown in Schenkerian analyses? (210)

A90   1998   Lerdahl, Fred. "Atonal Prolongational Structure" *Contemporary Music Review* 3/2: 65–87.

Selects structural over embellishing events by prioritizing salience (registral placement, dynamics, duration, and timbre) over stability; essentially an extension of his and Jackendoff's theory (explained in **B59**) to encompass the atonal repertoire.

A91 1998 Плотников, Борис. "Интерпретационныье Возможности Аналит, ической Методики Г. Шенкера (на примере зтюда Шонена соч. 10 No. 3)." In *Культура, Искусство, Образование*. Красноярск: Красноярская Академия Музыки и Театра: 97–109.

[1998 Plotnikov, Boris. "Interpretive Possibilities of the Analytical Method of H. Schenker (exemplified by Chopin's Etude Op. 10/3." In *Culture, Art, Education*. Krasnoyarsk: Krasnoyarsk Academy of Music and Theatre: 97–109.

An examination of Chopin's Etude in E Major, op. 10/1, showing rhythmic displacement in the first phrase; also contains a sketch of the deep middleground.

A92 1998 White, John. "Liszt and Schenker." In *Liszt and His World*, ed. by Michael Staffle. Analecta Lisztiana, Stuyvesant: Pendragon: 353–64. ISBN 0-945193-34-3.

After speculating on reasons for Schenker's neglect of the music of Liszt, deciding that "Schenker's judgment of tonal music was clouded by his biases," the author provides a voice leading graph, with commentary, of Liszt's *Chasse-Niege*. (354)

A93 1998 Williams, Alastair. "Torn Halves: Structure and Subjectivity in Analysis." *Music Analysis* 17/3: 281–93.

Discusses Adorno's approach to musical analysis; examines his criticism of Schenkerian analysis and the Darmstadt composers.

A94 1998 Williamson, Richard. "Comparing Pitch Hierarchies in Schenkerian and Koch-Based Analyses: Rationale, Method, and Correlations." *Gamut* 8: 31–51.

Analyzes Mozart's *Beatus Vir* (from K. 339) from the points of view of Schenker and Koch. Concludes that "the structure of (tonal) music is hierarchical [but] there is no isomorphic correlation between Koch's formal units and Schenker's structural levels." He further concludes that "both theorists agree in terms of which material is most essential." (50–1)

A95 1997 Agawu, Kofi. "Prolonged Counterpoint in Mahler." In *Mahler Studies*, ed. by Stephen Hefling. Cambridge: Cambridge University Press: 217–47.

Through brief excerpts, Agawu "[studies] aspects of Maler's harmony and voice-leading . . . to identify common procedures in his music as well as their similarity or dissimilarity to eighteenth- and nineteenth-century norms." (217) Presents an analysis of "Der Abschied" from *Das Lied von der Erde*.

A96   1997   Акопян, Левон. "Теория Музыки в Поисках Научности: Ме
одология и Философия 'Структурного Слышания' в Музык
оведении Последних Десятилетий." *Муыкалъная академия*
1: 181–9/2: 110–23.

[1997   Akopian, Levon. "Music Theory in Search of a Scientific Basis:
The Methodology and Philosophy of 'Structural Hearing' in
Musicology's Last Decade." *Muzykal'naia Akademiia* 1: 181–9/2:
110–23.]

Uses the term *structural hearing* as a category encompassing a wide range of theoretical ideas (both Western and Russian) that he places under the category of "formal approaches" that show "conceptual clarity" and "generalization." Schenkerian
theory only appears in part 2. Based largely on the work of Felix Salzer, but cites
Schenker and others as well. Discusses extensions of and responses to Schenkerian
theory, including the work of Epstein, Narmour, and Lerdahl/Jackendoff.

A97   1997   Beach, David. "The Submediant as Third Divider: Its Representation at Different Structural Levels." In *Music Theory in Concept
and Practice*. New York: University of Rochester Press: 309–36.
ISBN 1-878822-79-9

Examines several examples of the I-VI-IV-II-V-I progression in which "the function of the submediant is potentially ambiguous, or the progression itself occurs
only at some deeper level of structure and thus may not be easily recognized."
Discusses Bach's Prelude in B Major, BWV 868. (309)

A98   1997   Botstein, Leon. "Music and the Critique of Culture: Arnold
Schoenberg, Heinrich Schenker, and the Emergence of Mod-
ernism in Fin de Siècle Vienna." In *Constructive Dissonance:
Arnold Schoenberg and the Transformations of Twentieth-Century
Cultutre*, ed. by Julianne Brand and Christopher Hailey. Berkeley:
University of California Press: 3–22. ISBN 0-520-20314-3.

Discusses the "correspondence" of the early writings of Schenker and Schoenberg, especially in light of their cultural milieu; notes their views of the Viennese
musical establishment and their "shared conviction that music, although independent of words, operated by laws that were analogous to those of linguistic
grammar." (17)

A99   1997   Brown, Matthew. " 'Little Wing': A Study in Musical Cognition."
In *Understanding Rock: Essays in Musical Analysis*, ed. by John
Covach and Graeme M. Boone. New York: Oxford University
Press: 155–69. ISBN 0-195-10004-2.

Consists of two parts: (1) "considers problem solving in detail and focuses on
the so-called information processing model . . . [and] examines how Schenkerian theory . . . [represents] the model analytically"; and (2) uses the model "in

conjunction with Schenkerian theory . . . [to demonstrate] how Hendrix solved various problems of tonal and motivic organization." (156)

A100 1997 Brown, Matthew, Douglas Dempster, and Dave Headlam. "The #IV (flat-V) hypothesis: Testing the limits of Schenker's theory of tonality." *Music Theory Spectrum* 19/2: 155–183.

Posits a hypothesis to "[test the boundaries] of the applicability of the theory." The hypothesis is "based on Schenkerian theory's predication that if sharp-IV/flat-V sonorities appear in a tonal context, they are always *indirectly* related to the tonic; thus, whenever sharp-IV/flat-V *Stufen* are interpreted as being *directly* related to the tonic or are not explainable in a convincing way as indirectly related, either the analysis is incorrect, or the work must be deemed non-tonal." (183)

A101 1997 Burns, Lori. "'Joanie' Get Angry: k. d. lang's Feminist Revision." In *Understanding Rock: Essays in Musical Analysis*, ed. by John Covach and Graeme M. Boone. New York: Oxford University Press: 93–112. ISBN 0-195-10004-2.

The title parodies Joanie Sommers's 1962 *Johnny Get Angry.* Burns "analyzes text/music relations . . . in order to consider how the 'feminine' and the 'masculine' are constructed within the musical discourse of the song." Includes a transcription and analytic sketch. (93)

A102 1997 Cadwallader, Allen. "Une analyse graphique non publiee faite par Schenker de l'intermezzo op. 117 no. 2 de Brahms: Structure tonale et repetition motivique cachée." *Ostiato Rigore* 10: 55–71.

French translation of Cadwallader's 1984 *Music Theory Spectrum* article (see **A506** below).

A103 1997 Covach, John. "We Won't Get Fooled Again: Rock Music and Musical Analysis." *In Theory Only* 13/1–4: 117–42.

Discusses why the study of rock music can make a positive contribution within the music-theoretical discourse, and how the analysis of popular music can make a significant contribution to the field of popular-music studies. (117)

A104 1997 Everett, Walter. "Swallowed by a Song: Paul Simon's Crisis of Chromaticism." In *Understanding Rock: Essays in Musical Analysis*, ed. by John Covach and Graeme M. Boone. New York: Oxford University Press: 113–53. ISBN 0-195-10004-2.

Examines three songs of Simon, *Still Crazy After All These Years*, *I Do It for Your Love*, and *Jonah*, each of which contain tonal structures "that are quite atypical of rock music." Provides transcriptions and voice-leading graphs. (113)

A105 1997 Federhofer, Helmut. "Zur Demokratisierung von Heinrich Schenkers Musikanschauung." In *Festschrift Christoph-Hellmut Mahling zum 65. Geburtstag,* ed. by Axel Beer and Kristina Pfarr. Tutzing: Schneider: 331–39.

Essentially a rebuttal to Richard Littlefield and David Neumeyer's "Rewriting Schenker" (see **A80** above or **A271** below); discusses Schenker's sketch of Schumann's *Träumerei* from *Tonwille* 10.

A106 1997 Foulkes-Levy, Laurdella. "Tonal Markers, Melodic Patterns, and Musicianship Training I: Rhythmic Reduction." *Journal of Music Theory Pedagogy* 11: 1–25.

Uses the basic melodic configurations of Schenker's theory, combined with the rhythmic reduction of Lerdahl/Jackendoff as the basis for aural skills pedagogy; presents exercises to "develop musical memory, ear training, sight singing, improvisation, and dictation skills." (1)

A107 1997 Gilbert, Steven. "Reflections on a Few Good Tunes: Linear Progressions and Intervallic Patterns in Popular Song and Jazz." In *Music Theory in Concept and Practice*. New York: University of Rochester Press: 377–92. ISBN 1-878822-79-9.

Exploring the question of "why songs such as [those examined] have been attractive to improvisers, as opposed to the question of what may have accounted for their initial attractiveness as songs," Gilbert examines linear progressions in several popular songs, noting that "richness in linear progression is a major indication of melodic eloquence." (378)

A108 1997 Hefling, Stephen E. " '*Ihm in die Lieder zu blicken*': Mahler's Seventh Symphony Sketchbook." In *Mahler Studies*, ed. by Stephen Hefling. Cambridge: Cambridge University Press: 169–216.

Uses Schenkerian graphic techniques to compare the sketches of the Seventh Symphony with the finished project.

A109 1997 Jackson, Timothy. "Bruckner's *Oktaven*." *Music and Letters* 78/ 3: 391–410.

Examines Bruckner's analysis of parallel octaves in Mozart's Requiem and Beethoven's Third Symphony. "Bruckner's study, like Brahms's compendium of *Oktaven und Quinten,* reveals that not all consecutives are intrinsically evil, and that both composers were prepared to allow 'forbidden' consecutives in practice, even when they could not rationalize them." (391)

A110 1997 Jackson, Timothy. "The Finale of Bruckner's Seventh Symphony and the Tragic Reversed Sonata Form." In *Bruckner Studies*, ed. by Timothy Jackson. New York: Cambridge University Press: 209–55. ISBN 0-521-57041-X.

The reversed recapitulation occurs "when the recapitulation opens with the second or third group, the recapitulated material being recomposed so that the tonic due at the beginning of the recapitulation is either suppressed or devalued." Examines several pieces, in addition to Bruckner's, where the second group is situated over

(1) a dominant prolongation; (2) a passing tone; (3) a submediant prolongation; (4) a 5–6 exchange; and (5) the upper third of a fundamental harmony. (143)

A111 1997 Larson, Steve. "Triple Play: Bill Evans's Three-Piano Performance of Victor Young's *Stella by Starlight*." *Annual Review of Jazz Studies* 9: 45–56.

Examines the layered polyrhythms preceeding the recapitulation of the main theme in said performance; shows how these passages relate motivically, and in terms of voice leading, to the whole.

A112 1997–8 Larson, Steve. "Musical Forces and Melodic Patterns." *Theory and Practice* 22–3: 55–72.

An examination of musical patterns underlying fugue expositions (based on Renwick's 1995 book see B27 below) and the various melodic patterns put forth by Schenker; discusses the role of metaphor in musical discourse. Includes a bibliography of literature on hidden repetition.

A113 1997 Larson, Steve. "The Problem of Prolongation in Tonal Music: Terminology, Perception, and Expressive Meaning." *Journal of Music Theory* 41: 101–36.

Responses: 1997 *Journal of Music Theory* 41: 137–40 (J. Straus).

1997 *Journal of Music Theory* 41: 141–56 (F. Lerdahl).

Building on ideas from art history, artificial intelligence, and gestalt psychology, Larson discusses the concept of prolongation from the viewpoint of cognitive psychology, seeking "to understand the *experience* of music" that "allows it to suggest . . . feelings, actions, or motion." (101)

A114 1997 Laufer, Edward. "Some Aspects of Prolongation Procedures in the Ninth Symphony (Scherzo and Allegro)." In *Bruckner Studies*, ed. by Timothy Jackson. New York: Cambridge University Press: 209–55. ISBN 0-521-57041-X.

Considers "some of Bruckner's distinctive, individual procedures [seeking] to understand why they were problematic, as far as Schenker was concerned. In particular [considers] the question of organic, large-scale prolongations in the second and third movements of the Ninth Symphony and [tries] to suggest certain typical Brucknerian procedures." (211)

A115 1997 Legrand, Raphäelle. "Quelques aspects de l'analyse de le musique baroque." *Musurgia* 4/2: 7–11.

Presents a survey of various analytical techniques amenable to baroque music, of which Schenker's approach is one.

A116 1997 Marston, Nicholas. "Notes to an Heroic Analysis: A Translation of Schenker's Unpublished Study of Beethoven's Piano Variations, Op. 35." In *Nineteenth-Century Piano Music: Essays in*

Performance and Analysis. New York: Garland: 15–52. ISBN 0-8153-1502-3.

Presents Schenker's unpublished study, noting his treatment of variation form and comparing it to his study of the *Eroica* in *Das Meisterwerk in der Musik*, Vol. III.

A117   1997   Morgan, Robert. "Chasing the Scent: Tonality in Lizst's *Blume und Duft*." In *Music Theory in Concept and Practice*. Rochester: University of Rochester Press: 361–76.

Taking Forte's 1987 article emphasizing octatonic structures (see **A437** below) as his starting point, Morgan notes that the piece, taken as a whole, is "equally resistant" to a tonal reading as to an octatonic one.

A118   1997   Neumeyer, David. "Synthesis and Association, Structure, and Design in Multi-Movement Compositions." In *Music Theory in Concept and Practice*. Rochester: University of Rochester Press: 197–216.

Surveys literature on synthesis in multimovement compositions, and explains Schenkerian mechanisms for "joining together independent pieces or movements." Proposes his own model "consistent with Schenkerian theory." (197)

A119   1997   Peles, Stephen. "An Introduction to Westergaard's Tonal Theory." *In Theory Only* 13/1–4: 73–94.

An introductory sketch of Westergaard's theoretical ideas, culled from his articles and his book (*An Introduction to Tonal Theory*), which is Schenker-influenced.

A120   1997   Perry, Jeffrey. "Beethoven and the Romantic Unique Subject: The Dialectic of Affect and Form in the *Marcia Funebre sulla morte d'un eroe*, Op. 26/III." *Indiana Theory Review* 18/2: 47–73.

Explores Schenker's analysis of the piece in *Der freie Satz* in light of Lawrence Kramer's idea of the "Romantic unique subject." Attempts to reconcile the approaches of structuralism and hermeneutics.

A121   1997   Rothgeb, John. "Salient Features." In *Music Theory in Concept and Practice*. Rochester: University of Rochester Press: 181–96.

Discusses the concept of "salience," noting that "the most readily apparent characteristics are not the primary conveyors of musical content" and that "the criteria for musical salience . . . have far less to do with immediate noticeability than is commonly supposed." (181)

A122   1997   Rothstein, William. "The Form of Chopin's *Polonaise-Fantasy*." In *Music Theory in Concept and Practice*. Rochester: University of Rochester Press: 337–60.

Surveys some of the analytical literature on the piece, argues that "multiple formal paradigms are invoked in op. 61 . . . [that] are far from equal in their significance for the work's large-scale shape." Explores the connection with the op. 53 polonaise. (338)

A123 1997–8 Saslaw, Janna. "Life Forces: Conceptual Structures in Schenker's *Free Composition* and Schoenberg's *The Musical Idea*." *Theory and Practice* 22–3: 17–34.

Compares the two texts, noting the similarity of metaphors with regard to the concept of musical organicism; notes that "both authors often employ specifically biological terms, referring to life forces at play within musical works." Examines the influence of these metaphors on their respective analytical techniques. (18)

A124 1997 Schmalfeldt, Janet. "Coming to Terms: Speaking of Phrase, Cadence, and Form." *In Theory Only* 13/1–3: 95–116.
Discusses the concepts of phrase, cadence, and form as used in Westergaard's *Introduction to Tonal Theory*; discusses theories of Schenker, Sessions, and Rothstein in light of Westergaard's.

A125 1997 Straus, Joseph. "Voice-Leading in Atonal Music." In *Music Theory in Concept and Practice*. Rochester: University of Rochester Press: 237–74.
Describes and applies three models for atonal voice leading: prolongational, associational, and transformation, the first of which has its basis in Schenker's approach. Feels that, "If one cannot distinguish the structural from the nonstructural tones or determine the means by which the nonstructural tones embellish the structural tones, then one cannot produce convincing prolongational analyses," and suggests "that prolongation may not be a reliable basis for sustained analytic inquiry, or for structural levels beyond the immediate musical surface." (241)

A126 1997 Suppan, Wolfgang, and Victor Zuckerkandl. *"Musik der Menge:* 'Volk' und 'Volksmusik' in den Schriften Heinrich Schenkers und seines Schülers Viktor Zuckerkandl. Mit einem Anhang: Viktor Zuckerkandls bisher ungedruckter Aufsatz über *Das Staunen. Verhältnis von Mensch und Musik.*" In *Festschrift Christoph-Hellmut Mahling zum 65. Geburtstag*, ed. by Axel Beer and Kristina Pfarr: 471–91. ISBN 3-7952-0900-5.
Describes Zuckerkandl's association with Schenker, noting their philosophical differences (regarding ethnographic research and folk music, for example). Considers Zuckerkandl's ideas in light of the philosophies of Wittgenstein and Heidigger.

A127 1997 Van Beek, Johan. "Der zweite Takt des Rezitativs in Beethovens Klaviersonate As-Dur opus 110." *Musiktheorie* 12/3: 235–54.

Examines the second measure of Beethoven's op. 110, describing Beethoven's sketches and commenting on his manner of notation. Discusses Schenker's comments from his edition of op. 110.

A128 1997 Williamson, John Gordon. "Dissonance and Middleground Prolongations in Mahler's Late Music." In *Mahler Studies*, ed. by Stephen Hefling. New York: Cambridge University Press: 248–70. ISBN 0-521-47165-6.

Examines the Sixth and Seventh Symphonies and "Von der Jugend" from *Das Lied von der Erde*. Suggests that "what deviates from the Schenkerian paradigm in Mahler [may actually constitute] a Mahlerian norm, resulting in special forms of dissonant prolongations and incomplete structures at the middleground (and more tentatively, background) level." (249)

A129 1997 Witten, David. "Stemless Noteheads, Flying Frisbees, and Other Analytic Tools." In *Nineteenth-Century Piano Music: Essays in Performance and Analysis*. New York: Garland: 3–14. ISBN 0-8153-1502-3.

Bemoans the state of music theory, in which "an embarrassing number of theory professors continue to teach tedious chord-labeling with no mention of harmonic priority, levels of tension and resolution, or the presence of 'up'-bars and 'down'-bars." Calls for a theory curriculum more cognizant of recent developments. (3)

A130 1996 Almén, Byron. "Prophets of the Decline: The Worldviews of Heinrich Schenker and Oswald Spengler." *Indiana Theory Review* 17/1: 1–24.

Notes that Spengler and Schenker shared the views that "(1) The cultural and artistic development of the West is in decline, due to the fact that the, 'creative disposition' of that culture no longer exists; and that (2) there are no more geniuses." Examines these questions to provide a "clearer sense of how Schenker's theories were influenced by the period in which he lived." (3)

A131 1996 Anson-Cartwright, Mark. "Chord as Motive: The Augmented-Triad Matrix in Wagner's Siegfried Idyll." *Music Analysis* 15: 57–71.

Suggests that Schenker's idea of hidden repetitions be extended to include chords; cites the *Siegfried Idyll*'s structural use of the augmented triad as both a foreground sonority and as a key scheme.

A132 1996 Benjamin, William. "Tonal Dualism in Bruckner's Eighth Symphony." In *The Second Practice of Nineteenth-Century Tonality*, ed. by William Kinderman and Harald Krebs. Lincoln: University of Nebraska Press: 237–58.

Suggests that directional tonality has more to do with "semiotic context" than with "tonal coherence"; presents a bass-line sketch of the first movement.

A133 1996 Божцкоба, Мцлена. "Хайнрих Шенкер и Диагозата му за Муз/ икално Съвършенство." *Българската музцкознание* 20/3: 23–55.

[1996 Bozikova, Milena. "Heinrich Schenker and His Diagnosis for Musical Perfection." *Balgarsko muzikoznanie* 20/3: 23–55.]

Discusses the Schenkerian theory and applies it to the music of Vassil Kasandiev (two voice-leading graphs appear at the end of the article). Discusses the extensions of Schenker's ideas by Leonard B. Meyer and Lerdahl and Jachendoff as well as the work of Jean-Jacques Nattiez.

A134 1996 Cavanaugh, Lynn. "The Integration of Harmonic Idiom and Tonal Design in Schoenberg's String Quartet op. 7." *Fermata* 2: 1–24.

Describes three principles of foreground chromaticism and their middleground integration with the tonal design: chord cycles derived from the leading-tone diminished seventh chord; chromatic projections and double-neighbor chords; and chromaticism resulting from mixture. Under each heading, tonal design is considered from one or more of the following points of view: (1) the key scheme within separate movements of the quartet; (2) the key scheme of the collected movements; and (3) the key scheme of the one-movement sonata form that is superimposed on the four movements. (RILM 12751; used by permission)

A135 1996 Chiang, Yu-Ring. "Heinrich Schenkers Wiener Gedenkstätten: Gedanken zu seinem sechzigsten Todesjahr." *Mitteilungen der österreichischen Gesellschaft für Musikwissenschaft* 30: 41–51.

Provides a chronological list of Schenker's residences, along with a description of each.

A136 1996 Don, Gary. "Goethe, Boretz, and the 'Sensuous Idea.' " *Perspectives of New Music* 34/1: 124–39.

Examines Goethe's conception of the *Urpflänze*, developed over his lifetime, noting that it "bears strong resemblance to Schenker's *Ursatz*, [but] more closely resembles Benjamin Boretz's semantic fusion, in which the mental image transforms and is transformed by the object under consideration." (124)

A137 1996 Drabkin, William. "Schenker, the Consonant Passing Note, and the First-Movement Theme of Beethoven's Sonata Op. 26." *Music Analysis* 15/2–3: 149–89.

Discusses Schenker's use of the subdominant harmony and examines Beethoven's op. 26, providing graphs and commentary.

A138 1996 Eybl, Martin. "Zweckbestimmung und historische Voraussetzungen der Analytik Heinrich Schenkers." In *Zur Geschichte der* *musikalischen Analyse*, Schriften zur musikalischen Hermeneutik, Vol. 5, ed. by Gernot Grüber. Laaber, Germany: Laaber-Verlag: 145–56. ISBN 3-89007-316-6.

Examines Schenker's analysis of Beethoven's op. 101, comparing it to the approach of Sechter and Hauptmann; contains examples drawn from Schenker.

A139 1996 Federhofer, Hellmut. "Das Verhältnis von Guido Adler und Heinrich Schenker zur musikalischen Analyse." In *Musik und Geschichte: Aufsätze aus nichtmusikalischen Zeitschriften.* Hildesheim: Georg Olms Verlag: 546–54 ISBN: 3-487-10199-8. Reprinted in *Zur Geschichte der musikalischen Analyse*, Schriften zur musikalischen Hermeneutik, Vol. 5, ed. by Gernot Grüber (Laaber, Germany: Laaber-Verlag): 145–56. ISBN 3-89007-316-6.

Discusses the relationship of Adler and Schenker, noting that, while their writings contained "covert attacks" and neither agreed with the other's approach, the approaches may be reconciled.

A140 1996 Gut, Serge. "Schenker et la 'Schenkeromanie': Essai d'appreciation d'une methode d'analyse musicale." *Revista di musicologia* 82/2: 344–56.

Discusses the state of Schenkerian theory in France, suggesting that its usefulness is limited to eighteenth-century music; proposes that a hybrid method of analysis, including Schenkerian approach, would be more useful for a complete analytical system.

A141 1996 Hill, David. "The Time of the Sign: *O Haupt voll Blut und Wunden* in Bach's *St. Matthew Passion.*" *Journal of Musicology* 14/4: 514–53.

Examines, through voice-leading graphs and commentary, Bach's five settings of *O Haupt voll Blut und Wunden* from the *St. Matthew Passion.*

A142 1996 Kalisch, Volker. "Zum Verhältnis von Analyse und Musiktheorie zu Beginn des 20. Jahrhunderts." In *Zur Geschichte der musikalischen Analyse*, Schriften zur musikalischen Hermeneutik, Vol. 5, ed. by Gernot Grüber (Laaber, Germany: Laaber-Verlag): 119–30. ISBN 3-89007-316-6.

Discusses the relationship of music theory to composition noting that, for Riemann, Schoenberg, and Schenker, music obeyed certain natural laws, a view abandoned by Sigfrid Karg-Elert and Hugo Leichtenschritt.

A143 1996 Keiler, Allan. "Melody and Motive in Schenker's Earliest Writings." In *Critica Musica: Essays in Honor of Paul Brainard*, ed. by John Knowles. Amsterdam: Gordon and Breach. ISBN 9-056-99522-7.

Considers Schenker's concepts of melody and motive, as expressed in *Der Geist der musikalischen Technik* and his early writings on Brahms in light of other writers such as Hegel, Hoffmann, Hausegger, and Ambros.

A144 1996 Keller, Wilhelm. "Heinrich Schenker's *Harmonielehre*." In *Beiträge zur Musiktheorie des 19. Jahrhunderts*, ed. by Martin Vogel. Regensburg: Gustav Boße Verlag: 203–33.

A review-essay of Schenker's *Harmonielehre* of 1906. Keller discusses Schenker's ideas on harmony, motive, the overtone series, the minor mode, the church modes, mixture, intervals, the *Stufe* and its role in counterpoint, seventh chords, form, higher-order lines, chromaticism and tonicization, and modulation.

A145 1996 Williamson, John. "Wolf's Dissonant Prolongations." In *The Second Practice of Nineteenth-Century Tonality*, ed. by William Kinderman and Harald Krebs. Lincoln: University of Nebraska Press: 215–36.

Examines three songs of Wolf: (1) *Seufzer;* (2) *Herr, was trägt der Boden hier?;* and (3) *Sonne der Schlummerlosen.* Presents graphic analysis and commentary describing Wolf's use of tonality and prolongations of dissonant sonorities.

A146 1996 Köhler, Rafael. "Linie und Urlinie: Zur Methodendiskussion in der energetischen Musiktheorie." In *Zur Geschichte der musikalischen Analyse*, Schriften zur musikalischen Hermeneutik, Vol. 5, ed. by Gernot Grüber (Laaber, Germany: Laaber-Verlag): 157–75. ISBN 3-89007-316-6.

Discusses analyses and discussions of Beethoven's music from Schenker's *Tonwille* and Halms's theory of "musical energetics" from his *Form und Sinn in der Musik*; concludes that for Halm, "music analysis offers a new aesthetic experience of the music and new insight, whereas for Schenker, analysis is there to confirm his theory of the Urlinie." (RILM; used by permission)

A147 1996 Korsyn, Kevin. "Directional Tonality and Intertextuality: Brahms's Quintet Op. 88 and Chopin's Ballade Op. 38." In *The Second Practice of Nineteenth-Century Tonality*, ed. by William Kinderman and Harald Krebs. Lincoln: University of Nebraska Press: 45–83.

Suggests that Brahms modeled his work after Chopin's; contains graphic analyses of both works, and discusses use of tonality; the ideas of literary critics Bloom and Bakhtin figure prominently.

A148 1996 Krebs, Harald. "Some Early Examples of Tonal Pairing: Schubert's *Meeres Stille* and *Der Wanderer*." In *The Second Practice of Nineteenth-Century Tonality*, ed. William Kinderman and Harald Krebs. Lincoln: University of Nebraska Press: 17–33.

As the two songs present two seemingly structurally important key areas, Krebs presents alternate readings of the two, each taking one of the keys as primary.

A149 1996 Laitz, Steven. "The Submediant Complex: Its Musical and Poetic Roles in Schubert's Songs." *Theory and Practice* 21: 123–66.
The article "focuses on the issue of chromatic pitch class and its interaction with scale-degree relationships," centering on Schubert's use of flat melodically and as a key area. Discusses the use of $\hat{5}$-flat $\hat{6}$-natural $\hat{6}$ as a motive. (123–4)

A150 1996 Larson, Steve. "A Strict Use of Analytic Notation." *Journal of Music Theory Pedagogy* 10: 37–77.
Proposes a method of Schenker pedagogy that limits the use of analytic notation to stages, much as the discipline of species counterpoint limits rhythm and dissonance; his reasons are to (1) "lead the ear of the serious student into the infinite world of fundamental analytic questions"; (2) "progress in small steps, [explaining] more complex analytic representations as extensions [of those learned]"; and (3) "separate [strict use] from Schenkerian analysis if the ideas and practical verities of both are to be fully developed." (39)

A151 1996 Larson, Steve. "The Art of Charlie Parker's Rhetoric." *Annual Review of Jazz Studies* 8 (special edition on jazz theory): 63–115. ISBN 0-8108-3199-6.
Presents a transcription and analysis of Parker's 1946 performance of "Oh, Lady Be Good." Shows how Parker paraphrases the "arpeggiated gestire of the original melody, turning it into a blues-inflected forward-directed fifth-progression that supplies the thematic material for his improvisation and forecasts its fundamental structure." (141)

A152 1996 Mathis, Michael. "Arnold Schoenberg's *Grundgestalt* and Gustav Mahler's *Urlicht*." *International Journal of Musicology* 5: 239–59.
Suggests that the Schenkerian approach to analysis, as it stands, does not work for Mahler's music. Therefore, Mathis combines it with Schoenberg's *Grundgestalt* concept to analyze the *Urlicht* movement from Mahler's Second Symphony.

A153 1996 McCreless, Patrick. "An Evolutionary Perspective in Nineteenth-Century Semitonal Relations." In *The Second Practice of Nineteenth-Century Tonality*, ed. by William Kinderman and Harald Krebs. Lincoln: University of Nebraska Press: 87–113.
Discusses the idea of substitution, whereby a chromatic inflection or a key a semitone away may substitute for an expected diatonic degree; cites Boss's analysis of a Shostakovich march where D-flat, the Neapolitan II, substitutes in the middle section for C, the tonic.

A154 1996 McKee, Eric. "Auxiliary Progressions as a Source of Conflict between Tonal Structure and Phrase Structure." *Music Theory Spectrum* 18/1: 51–76.
Notes two sources of conflict between inner and outer form (i.e., between voice-leading structure and phrase structure): (1) "a beginning boundary in outer form may not agree with an articulation in inner form"; or (2) changing of grouping boundaries "as a result of rhythmic displacement or normalization." (51)

A155 1996 Murtomäki, Veijo. "Fisztin *Faust-konsertto*: Semanttinen analyysi." *Musiikki* 4: 469–88.
A "semantic" analysis of Liszt's *Faust* concerto (i.e., his first piano concerto); provides a voice-leading graph of the work, showing linkage between movements and key motivic ideas. Discusses Liszt's use of concerto form.

A156 1996 Pearsall, Edward. "Multiple Hierarchies: Another Perspective on Prolongation." *Indiana Theory Review* 17/1: 37–66.
Based on the Lerdahl/Jackendoff theory, in which "pitches manifest their prominence or 'subordinance' only with regard to the schema they are associated with." After a review of literature on prolongation (including Schenker), Pearsall "[discusses] trees and schemas as separate analytical representations of music cognition and finally [suggests] a way to illustrate multiple hierarchies by combining trees with schemas." (38)

A157 1996 Pople, Anthony. "Misleading Voices: Contrasts and Continuities in Stravinsky Studies." In *Analytical Strategies and Musical Interpretation: Essays on Nineteenth- and Twentieth-Century Music*, ed. by Craig Ayrey and Mark Everist. New York: Cambridge University Press: 271–87. ISBN 0-521-46249-5.
Analyzes Stravinsky's *The Dove Descending* from the viewpoints of Whittall, Van Den Toorn, Forte, Straus, Taruskin, Abraham, Asafiev, Cone, and Schenker.

A158 1996 Popovic, Linda. "Liszt's Harmonic Polymorphism: Tonal and Non-Tonal Aspects in *Héroïde funèbre*." *Music Analysis* 15: 41–55.
Combines Schenkerian techniques with pitch-class set theory to show how tonal and nontonal relationships are operative in the work.

A159 1996 Redmann, Bernd. "Zum (Schein-)Antipodentum von Hugo Riemann und Heinrich Schenker." In *Zur Geschichte der musikalischen Analyse*. Schriften zur musikalischen Hermeneutik, Vol. 5, ed. by Gernot Grüber (Laaber, Germany: Laaber-Verlag): 131–44. ISBN 3-89007-316-6.
Combines the analytical approaches of Riemann and Schenker, and applies them to Beethoven's op. 53 sonata; contains a Riemannian chart of harmonic layers and a Schenkerian voice-leading graph of excerpts from the sonata.

A160 1996 Russ, Michael. "Be Bored: Reading a Mussorgsky Song." *Nineteenth-Century Music* 20/1: 27–45.

A study of the song *Skucay* from *Bez solnca* that combines a study of the poetry, the musical structure, and documentary evidence; emphasizes the satirical nature of the song.

A161 1996 Schachter, Carl. "Idiosyncratic Features of Four Mozart Slow Movements: The Piano Concertos K. 449, K. 453, and K. 467." In *Mozart's Piano Concertos: Text, Context, and Interpretation*, ed. by Neal Zaslaw. Ann Arbor: University of Michigan Press: 315–33.

Examination of the four movements, providing graphs and commentary. Notes that "all of the movements incorporate important features of the classical sonata style; but none of them resembles anyone's idea of a 'textbook' sonata, and only K. 453 has a tonal plan typical of a classical sonata movement." (315–6)

A162 1996 Scheepers, Paul. "*Geistiges Leben oder Erstarrung in der Musik? De verwording van Schenkers methode tot dogma.*" *Tijdschrift voor muziektheorie* 1/1: 4–17.

Examines Schenker's view of Rameau as expressed in the title essay, which led to the "paralysis" in musical analysis. Scheepers questions whether Schenker himself is also a victim of "paralysis." (4)

A163 1996 Smith, Charles J. "Musical Form and Fundamental Structure: An Investigation of Schenker's *Formenlehre*." *Music Analysis* 15/2–3: 191–297.

After a survey of literature on Schenker's *Formleher* (the last section of *Der freie Satz*), Smith examines the work in detail, answering the questions, "Do we need to make only minor adjustments to get a comprehensive and insightful approach to musical form? Or will a systematic attempt to characterize form from a strict Schenkerian-structural perspective inevitably fail?" (192)

A164 1996 Spicer, Mark. "Root versus Linear Analysis of Chromaticism: A Comparative Study of Selected Excerpts from the Oeuvres of Chopin." *College Music Symposium* 36: 138–47.

Examines three excerpts from Chopin's opp. 28/2, 10/3, and 61 in terms of root-based analysis, proposing to offer an alternative to linear analysis.

A165 1996 Steffen, Ralph. "Text and Form in Schubert's *Die Schöne Müllerin, Wohin?*: A Schenkerian Perspective." *Music Research Forum* 11/2: 44–59.

Discusses both the Schenkerian and a more traditional motivic approach to the Schubert song.

A166 1996 Strunk, Steven. "Linear Intervallic Patterns in Jazz Repertory." *Annual Review of Jazz Studies* 8 (special edition on jazz theory): 63–115. ISBN 0-8108-3199-6.
Examines linear intervallic patterns, based on Forte/Gilbert, as applied to melodies from *The Real Book*, a collection of melodies with chord symbols representing harmonies.

A167 1996 Suurpää, Lauri. "Schumann, Heine, and Romantic Irony: Music and Poems in the First Five Songs of *Dichterliebe.*" *Intégral* 10: 93–123.
Examines the relationships between the music and text, providing Schenkerian graphs of the musical structure and describing the narrative arch of the texts, drawing on Schumann's writings as well as ideas of romantic irony.

A168 1996 Todd, R. Larry. "Franz Liszt, Carl Friedrich Weitzmann, and the Augmented Triad." In *The Second Practice of Nineteenth-Century Tonality*, ed. by William Kinderman and Harald Krebs. Lincoln: University of Nebraska Press: 153–77.
Discusses Liszt's structural use of the augmented triad; contains a graph of eleven measures of the *Faust* symphony.

A169 1996 Van den Toorn, Pieter. "What's in a Motive? Schoenberg and Schenker Reconsidered." *Journal of Musicology* 14/3: 370–99.
Discusses the changing view of motive in Schenker's writings from *Harmonielehre* through *Der freie Satz*; notes similarities with Schoenberg's ideas, particularly involving the relationships of part to whole.

A170 1995 Beach, David. "Phrase Expansion: Three Analytical Studies." *Music Analysis* 14/1: 27–47.
Examines the concept of phrase expansion (as transmitted from Schenker through Schachter and Rothstein) as a means of heightening the musical tension by delaying the expected tonal goal. Discusses works of Schubert (D. 956 and 667) and Beethoven (op. 7), providing graphs and commentary.

A171 1995 Beeson, Roger, trans. by Luis Gago. "Fondo y modelo." *Quodlibet: Revista de especialización musical* 1: 51–65
Spanish translation of Beeson's 1971 *Music Review* article (see **A704** below).

A172 1995 Cook, Nicholas. "The Conductor and the Theorist: Furtwängler, Schenker, and Beethoven's Ninth." In *Studies in Musical Interpretation*, ed. by John Rink. Cambridge: Cambridge University Press: 105–25. ISBN 0-521-45274-7.
　　　Review:　　　1996 *Indiana Theory Review* 17/1: 87–117 (R. Hatten).
Analyzes Furtwängler's 1951 and 1953 performances of Beethoven's Ninth via computer processes, based on Furtwängler's statement that "a score cannot give

the slightest clue as to the intensity of a *forte* or a *piano* or exactly how fast a tempo should be; . . . the dynamics are quite deliberately not literal but symbolic, not with a practical meaning for each individual instrument but of broad significance, added with a solid sense of the work as a whole in mind." (107)

A173 1995 Cook, Nicholas. "Schenker, Polemicist: A Reading of the *Symphony #9* Monograph" *Music Analysis* 14/1: 89–105.
Aims "to evaluate [Schenker's] claim that [he is 'concerned only with the illumination of truth'] by exploring the contexts of some of [his] most virulent polemics, and in particular those directed against the figure whom Schenker saw as the most formidable of all his opponents: Richard Wagner." (90)

A174 1995 Galand, Joel. "Form, Genre, and Style in the Eighteenth-Century Rondo." *Music Theory Spectrum* 17/1: 27–52.
Employs "Schenkerian analysis in order to shed light on rondo-form problems in the eighteenth and nineteenth centuries," exploring Schenker's own analyses of rondo forms and providing his own analyses of several pieces, focusing on the "interaction of ritornello patterns with binary structural divisions." (28)

A175 1995 Gerling, Cristina. "Schenker e seus discípulos na América: Os ortodoxos." *Art: Revista da Escola de Música e Artes Cênicas da UFBA* 23: 81–7.
Discusses the "orthodox" Schenkerian movement in the United States.

A176 1995 Goldwurm, Giuliano. "L'analisi Schenkeriana a la forma sonata." *Rivista Italiana di musicologia* 30/1: 135–69.
Examines the Schenkerian interpretation of sonata form based on the writings of Oster, Salzer, Forte/Gilbert, Beach, Schmalfeldt, and Adrian; applies these to Mozart's K. 545 sonata.

A177 1995 Jackson, Timothy L. "Aspects of Sexuality and Structure in the Later Symphonies of Tchaikovsky." *Music Analysis* 14/1: 3–26.
Examines the finales of the Fourth, Fifth, and Sixth Symphonies of Tchaikovsky, speculating that "the unorthodox tritonal deformation of diatonic structural harmony becomes a metaphor for the homosexual departure from heterosexual norms." (13)

A178 1995 Lacerda, Marcos. "Breve resenha das contribuiçoes de Schenker e Schoenberg para a análise musical." *Art: Revista da Escola de Música e Artes Cênicas da UFBA* 23: 65–79.
Provides overviews of each analytical approach in separate sections; not a comparative study. Reproduces Schenker's analysis of *Ich Bin's, ich sollte büßen* from his *Fünf Urlinie-Tafeln*.

A179 1995 Lester, Joel. "Performance and Analysis: Interaction and Interpretation." In *The Practice of Performance: Studies in Musical Inter-*

pretation, ed. by John Rink. Cambridge: Cambridge University Press: 197–216. ISBN 0-521-45374-7

Views performance as "projecting implicit analyses"; considers approaches to analysis and performance taken by Cone, Rothstein, Schenker, Schachter, and Westergaard.

A180 1995 Marion, Gregory. "Inciting Transformational Insights." *Intégral* 9: 1–32.

Acknowledging the limitation of any one analytical approach to account for all features of a work, Marion approaches Beethoven's op. 53 from the Schenkerian and Lewinian points of view, coupling harmonic reduction and transformational networks.

A181 1995 Moore, Allan. "The So-Called 'Flattened Seventh' in Rock." *Popular Music* 14/2: 185–201.

Discusses rock music's use of the mixolydian seventh to avoid a sense of finality; speculates that, because of generic conventions (e.g., VII-I cadences, modulations with no return to the tonic), Schenkerian analysis is not helpful in understanding the structure of rock music.

A182 1995 Pastille, William. "The God of Abraham, Aquinas, and Schenker: Art as Faith in an Age of Unbelief." *Indiana Theory Review* 16: 105–44.

A collection of fifty-five quotations from diverse sources (Schenker, Nietzsche, Aquinas, Freud, the Bible, Goethe, the Baal Shem Tov, Shelley, Wordsworth, and Emily Dickinson to name a few) on the subjects of faith and art. The article is divided into five sections: Unbelief (§1–14), Substitutions (§15–25), Revelations (§26–34), Creations (§35–47), and Faith (§48–55).

A183 1995 Renoldi, Marco. "Eventi ingannevoli del livello eterno: Livelli strutturali ed elaborazione compositiva." *Rivista Italiana di Musicologia* 30/2: 385–418.

Discusses Schenker's idea of structural levels and compositional elaboration; draws examples from Schenker's works.

A184 1995 Renwick, William. "Hidden Fugal Paths: A Schenkerian View of Handel's F Major Fugue (Suite II)." *Music Analysis* 14/1: 49–67.

Examines Händel's fugal technique, exemplified in his Suite in F. Regarding the designation "hidden fugal paths," Renwick states that, "in terms of Schenker's own way of thinking about music, hidden paths must be understood primarily as voice-leading paths. Thus, we could say that Handel's fugues follow even more unusual and convoluted voice-leading progressions than Bach's." (50)

A185 1995 Rink, John. "Ballady Chopina i dialektyka metod analitycznych." *Rocznik chopinowski* 21: 45–66.

A survey of literature on Chopin's ballades in light of various analytical approaches; presents possible directions for future research on improvisation, aesthetics, and contemporaneous theory.

A186 1995 Rothstein, William. "Beethoven mit und ohne Kunstgesprang: Metrical Ambiguity Reconsidered." *Beethoven Forum* 4: 165–93.
Discusses hypermeter in Beethoven's op. 10/2 sonata, particularly noting the presence of conflicting hypermeters. Examines the theories of Tovey, Schenker, Imbrie, and Kamien.

A187 1995 Sabourin, Carmen. "Vers une approche critique de la theorie schenkerienne." *Revista de Musique des Universites Canadiennes* 15/1: 1–43.
Suggests that "only a recourse to interpretive models developed in the fields of social science and cultural anthropology will allow for critical revisions of Schenkerian discourse."

A188 1995 Sanguinetti, Giorgio. "L'opera italiana nella critica musicale di Heinrich Schenker." *Nuova Rivista musicale italiana* 29/3: 431–67.
Comments on ten of Schenker's essays on Italian opera and Italian composers that Schenker wrote between 1891 and 1901, focusing on Schenker's criticism of Verdi's *Falstaff*. Provides translations (see **T40–49** above).

A189 1995 Schachter, Carl. "The Triad as Place and Action." *Music Theory Spectrum* 17/2:149–69. Reprinted in *Unfoldings: Essays in Schenkerian Theory and Analysis,* ed. by Joseph N. Straus. Oxford: Oxford University Press, 1999: 161–83.
        Translations: Boris Plotnikov, "Трезвучие как место и Действие." In *Очеки иЗтюдьι по Методологии Музыкального Анализа*: 264–70 (excerpts).
Examines Chopin's E Minor Prelude, the Fourth Movement from Beethoven's Sixth Symphony, and Mendelssohn's op. 62/1, discussing "static and kinetic" properties of the composed-out chords. (161)

A190 1995 Sly, Gordon. "The Architecture of Key and Motive in a Schubert Sonata." *Intégral* 9: 67–89.
Discusses Schubert's large-scale tonal structure as seen in two violin sonatas and his Fourth Symphony, commenting on his use of the three-key exposition and the tonal plan of the recapitulations, which often begin off tonic.

A191 1995 Smith, Peter. "Structural Tonic or Apparent Tonic?: Parametric Conflict, Temporal Perspective, and a Continuum of Articulative Possibilities." *Journal of Music Theory* 39/2: 245–83.
Examines the use of the tonic *Stufe* from the points of view of Schenker and Lewin; states that the tonic may have multiple functions.

A192 1995 Teboul, Jean-Claude. "Comment analyser le neuvième interlude en si-flat du Ludus tonalis de Paul Hindemith? (Hindemith ou Schenker?)." *Ostinato Rigore* 6/7: 215–32.
Surveys Hindemith's and Schenker's theoretical ideas; discusses the applicability of Schenker's method of analysis (as expounded by Salzer) to Hindemith's music.

A193 1995 Van den Toorn, Pieter. "Schenker and His Critics" and "In Defense of Music Theory and Analysis." In *Music, Politics, and the Academy*. Berkeley: University of California Press: 75–100. ISBN 0-520-20115-9.
Discusses Treitler's reactions to Schenker's analysis of Beethoven's Ninth (and Schenker in general) and the problems of music-theoretical writings being less accessible to the public than musicological writings.

A194 1995 Wagner, Naphtali. "No Crossing Branches? The Overlapping Technique in Schenkerian Analysis." *Theory and Practice* 20: 149–76.
Examines theoretical ideas of Schachter, Berry, and Benjamin, focusing on the issue of segmentation. Applies them to works of Bach, Mozart, Haydn, and Beethoven, illustrating harmonic and melodic relationships with "tree notation" derived from Lerdahl/Jackendoff. (RILM; used by permission)

A195 1995 Yan-Di, Yang. "A Critical Survey of Analytical Theories in Twentieth-Century Musicology (2): Schenkerian Analysis." *The Art of Music: Journal of the Shanghai Conservatory of Music* 61: 42–52
A discussion of Schenker's basic concepts; cites his analysis of Bach's Prelude no. 1 in C Major (WTC I).

A196 1995 Yan-Di, Yang. "A Critical Survey of Analytical Theories in Twentieth-Century Musicology (3): The Expansion and Modification of Schenkerian Analysis." *The Art of Music: Journal of the Shanghai Conservatory of Music* 62: 54–62.
Discusses the application of Schenker's ideas to pre- and post-tonal music, citing the writings of Novack and Salzer.

A197 1994 Beach, David. "The Influence of Harmonic Thinking on the Teaching of Simple Counterpoint in the Latter Half of the Eighteenth Century." in *Eighteenth-Century Music in Theory and Practice: Essays in Honor of Alfred Mann*, Festschrift Series, Vol. 13, ed. by Mary Ann Parker. Stuyvesant: Pendragon: 159–85. ISBN 0-945193-11-4.
Discusses Schenker's use the species approach to counterpoint; examines the writings of Kirnberger, Daube, and Koch, who considered the study of harmony a prerequisite to the study of counterpoint—the reverse of Schenker's approach.

A198 1994   Beach, David. "The Initial Movements of Mozart's Piano Sonatas
              K. 280 and K. 332: Some Striking Similarities." *Intégral* 8: 126–45.
Beach notes similarities between the two works, such as "(1) the sharing of similar motives, (2) the sharing of similar voice-leading patterns, and (3) similar
manipulation of registers." He also notes "the similarities in voice-leading patterns at equivalent places in the formal design—e.g., the extended and chromati-
cally elaborated voice-exchange in the bridge to the second key area." (126–7)

A199 1994   Bernard, Jonathan. "Voice-Leading as a Spatial Function in the
              Music of Ligeti." *Music Analysis* 13/2–3: 227–53.
Examines Ligeti's music, explaining that, while not strictly hierarchical, voice
leading plays an important role; notes that structural levels in Ligeti "are defined
by the differences between local, note-to-note structures and large-scale resultant structures." (227)

A200 1994   Boss, Jack. "Schoenberg on Ornamentation and Structural Lev-
              els." *Journal of Music Theory* 38/2: 187–216.
Examines the op. 22 *Lieder* of Schoenberg using the ideas of Straus and Lester
devised for the prolongation analysis of atonal music; acknowledges three categories for strategies of discriminating between structural and ornamental tones:
"1) the use of contextual criteria, 2) limiting the acceptable structures, and 3)
limiting the acceptable ornament types." (189)

A201 1994   Burns, Lori. "Modal Identity and Irregular Endings in Two Har-
              monizations by J. S. Bach." *Journal of Music Theory* 38/1:
              43–77.
Studies two Bach chorales, *Christ, unser Herr, zum Jordan kam* and *Durch
Adams Fall ist ganz verderbt*, providing dual analyses of the chorales (both Do-
rian and Aeolian interpretations).

A202 1994   Cinnamon, Howard. "E Major Tonality as Dominant or Mediant
              in Chopin's Op. 10/1: Schenker's Graphs from *Free Composition*
              Reconsidered." *Indiana Theory Review* 15/1.
Explains the "local disturbance" of real versus apparent tonics at the beginning
of the development section, intending to establish "a coherent and correspondent
view of musical form in general and the sonata form in particular." (3)

A203 1994   Federhofer, Hellmut. "Heinrich Schenker (1868–1935) und
              Arnold Schönberg (1874–1951) als Musiktheoretiker." In *Studien
              zur Musikwissenschaft*, Vol. 43. Tutzing: Schneider: 319–40.
Discusses the relationship of Schenker and Schoenberg, focusing on their theoretical differences, and examines the influence of Sechter on both.

A204 1994   Gagné, David. "The Place of Schenkerian Analysis in the Under-
              graduate and Graduate Curricula." *Indiana Theory Review* 15/1:
              21–33.

Ponders the appropriateness of introducing Schenkerian ideas in the early years of study. Because of the subtlety and complexity of Schenker's ideas, Gagné argues, it is beneficial to introduce general concepts as early as possible.

A205 1994　Elliker, Calvin. "Classification Schemes for Scores: Analysis of Structural Levels." *Notes* 50/4: 1269–320.
Studies several classification schemes; constructs synoptic tables "[demonstrating] that the classification structures tend to organize scores by medium of performance in the background, by forms and genres in the middleground, and by aspects of musical character in the foreground." (1269)

A206 1994　Komar, Arthur. "Ruminating about Schenker." In *Musical Transformation and Musical Intuition: Eleven Essays in Honor of David Lewin*, ed. by Raphael Atlas and Michael Cherlin. Dedham, Mass.: Ovenbird Press: 23–39 ISBN 1-886-46400-6.
A critical essay; contains discussions of the Prelude no. 1 in C from WTC I and Beethoven's op. 13 in reaction to Schenker's analyses, as well as reminiscences of the author's association with David Lewin.

A207 1994　Larson, Steve. "Musical Forces, Step Collections, Tonal Pitch Space, and Melodic Expectation." *Report of the Third International Congress on Musical Perception:* 277–89.
A discussion of cognitive processes involved in the perception of tonal music; examines such concepts as gravity, magnetism, and inertia, to be developed more fully in his 1997 article (see **A112** above). Cites the work of Schenker, Lerdahl, Deutsch/Feroe, Lake, and Povel.

A208 1994　Levenson, Irene. "Smooth Moves: Schubert and Theories of Modulation in the Nineteenth Century." *In Theory Only* 7/5–6: 35–52.
A survey of theoretical ideas on modulation, including Reicha, Marx, Fétis, Hauptmann, and Louis/Thuille; examines several Schubert excerpts from the Schenkerian point of view.

A209 1994　Montgomery, Kip. "Schenker and Schoenberg on Harmonic Tonality." *Indiana Theory Review* 15/1: 53–68.
Examines the *Harmonielehren* of Schenker (1906) and Schoenberg (1911), noting that they are both "principally concerned with the relationship between harmonic tonality and musical coherence. In their approaches, both men attempt to account for tradition, but from different angles: Schenker seeks origins, the laws that stand behind the works, and Schoenberg seeks in the works of the past an explanation for the present." (53–4)

A210 1994　Petty, Wayne. "Cyclic Integration in Haydn's E-flat Piano Sonata Hob. XVI: 38." *Theory and Practice* 19: 31–56.

Discusses the integrative structure of the sonata, examining temporal ordering, links, and resemblances between the movements. Shows how closure is undermined in the first movement in order that it may occur in the finale. (RILM; used by permission)

A211 1994 Pierce, Alexandra. "Developing Schenkerian Hearing and Performing." *Intégral* 8: 54–123.

Suggests that the process of producing graphic analysis has little relation to performance; that in most Schenkerian studies, "listening and playing are generally ignored or taken for granted." Further suggests that "written graphs can impede the development of Schenkerian hearing." (51–3)

A212 1994 Platt, Heather. "Dramatic Turning Points in Brahms Lieder." *Indiana Theory Review* 15/1: 69–104.

Examines two Brahms songs, *Von ewiger Liebe* and *Vorschneller Schwur,* tying the delayed entrance of the first *Urlinie* tone to a dramatic turning point in the text; notes that this is also underscored musically by other foreground changes (such as in dynamics or accompanimental figuration).

A213 1994 Rodman, Ronald. "Retrospection and Reduction: Modal Middlegrounds and Foreground Elaborations in Telemann's *Zwanzig kleine Fugen.*" *Indiana Theory Review* 15/1: 105–37.

Discusses the table of modes that Telemann constructed for his *20 kleine Fugen* of 1731, showing his modal outline of the principal voice as well as chord progressions to be elaborated during the course of the works. Compares the process to Schenker's analytic ideas.

A214 1994 Rothstein, William. "Ambiguity in the Themes of Chopin's First, Second, and Fourth Ballades." *Intégral* 8: 1–49.

Examines Chopin's ballades, observing that "in the second Ballade, the degree of thematic contrast is moderate, [and it is] less sonata-like than the others." He examines the three ballades from a Schenkerian viewpoint, concentrating on thematic properties. (125)

A215 1994 Sabourin, Carmen. "Methodologie schenkerienne et apprentissage de l'analyse musicale." *Canadian University Music Review* 14: 98–145.

Provides an analysis of Bach's Invention no. 12; examines the Schenkerian analytical approach from a pedagogical perspective, noting the absence of a Schenker text in the French language.

A216 1994 Samson, Jim. "Chopin Reception: Theory, History, Analysis." In *Chopin Studies II,* ed. by Jim Samson. Cambridge: Cambridge University Press: 1–17.

A general discussion of Chopin's reception. Mentions Schenker's acceptance of Chopin into his select canon, noting that "for the profundity with which Nature has endowed him, Chopin belongs more to Germany than to Poland." Mentions that Schenker likely would not have approved of American "Schenkerian analysis." (7)

A217 1994 Schachter, Carl. "Chopin's Prelude, Op. 28/5: Analysis and Performance." *Journal of Music Theory Pedagogy* 8: 27–45.
Offers voice-leading analyses with commentary of the prelude, providing suggestions for effective performance of hidden repetitions and voice-leading effects.

A218 1994 Schachter, Carl. "The Sketches for Beethoven's Piano and Violin Sonata Op. 24." In *Beethoven Forum 3,* ed. by Christopher Reynolds. Lincoln: University of Nebraska Press: 107–25.
Examines the sketches for the first movement, providing graphic analyses of the sketches and discussing similarities between the sketches especially with regard to hidden motivic repetitions.

A219 1994 Schachter, Carl. "Chopin's Prelude, Op. 28, No. 4: Autograph Sources and Interpretation." In *Chopin Studies II,* ed. by Jim Samson. Cambridge: Cambridge University Press: 161–82.
Discusses the autographs of op. 28/4 and op. 41/1, comparing the toal structure of the published works with the manuscripts and pointing out motivic relationships. Considers idiosyncrasies of notation in the autograph scores.

A220 1994 Schachter, Carl. "The Prelude from Bach's Suite No. 4 for Violoncello Solo: The Submerged Urlinie." *Current Musicology* 56: 54–71.
Analyzes the work employing graphic analysis and commentary, highlighting motivic repetition. The subtitle refers to the *Urlinie* being in the middle of the texture rather than in the upper voice. Describes the linear "strands" iniated by the covering tones $\hat{8}$ and $\hat{5}$ and their interaction.

A221 1994 Smith, Peter. "Liquidation, Augmentation and Brahms's Recapitulatory Overlaps." *Nineteenth-Century Music* 17/3: 237–61.
Discusses the first movements of three works of Brahms, opp. 51/1, 98, and 99, noting that "these movements provide a context for reflections on the debate between Schenkerians and Schoenbergians regarding the priority of middleground tonal structures vs. foreground motivic process in the articulation of musical form." (237)

A222 1994 Smith, Peter. "Brahms and Schenker: A Mutual Response to Sonata Form." *Music Theory Spectrum* 16/1: 77–103.
Describes how Brahms and Schenker were both "concerned with the perpetuation of traditional compositional procedures at a time in which ultratraditional approaches to composition were gaining status in musical circles." Makes mention of the association between Schenker and Brahms. (77)

A223 1994   Snarrenberg, Robert. "Competing Myths: The American Aban-
                donment of Schenker's Organicism." In *Theory, Analysis, and
                Meaning in Music*, ed. by Anthony Pople. Cambridge: Cambridge
                University Press: 29–56. ISBN 0-521-45236-8.

Comments on the trend of English translations of Schenker to replace his biological and poetic metaphors with scientific and architectural terms, and to downplay the metaphysical aspects of his writing.

A224 1994   Wick, Norman. "Shifted Downbeats in Classic and Romantic
                Music." *Indiana Theory Review* 15/2: 73–87.

Examines passages from the works of Mozart, Mendelssohn, Chopin, and
Brahms in which the notated downbeat and perceived downbeat differ. Ad-
dresses four compositional techniques "(1) written-out *fermata*, (2) written-out
ritardando, (3) unspecified change of meter, and (4) elision (i.e., overlap) of less
than one measure of material." (74)

A225 1993   Beach, David. "Schubert's Experiments with Sonata Form: Formal-
                Tonal design versus Underlying Structure." *Music Theory Spec-
                trum* 15/1: 1–18.

Considers what effect Schubert's predilection for beginning recapitulations off
tonic has on the overall structure of a work.

A226 1993   Brown, Matthew. "Tonality and Form in Debussy's *Prélude à
                l'Après-midi d'un faune*." *Music Theory Spectrum* 15: 127–43.

Examines the work from a Schenkerian vantage point, citing literature by Salzer
and Katz that apply Schenker's ideas to Debussy's music.

A227 1993   Burkholder, Peter. "Music Theory and Musicology." *Journal of
                Musicology* 11/1: 11–23.

Notes the relationships between the two disciplines, and discusses Schenker's
theory as a historical "problem" (i.e., a question to be considered).

A228 1993   Burnham, Scott. "Musical and Intellectual Values: Interpreting
                the History of Tonal Theory." *Current Musicology* 53: 76–88.

A hermeneutic approach to the history of music theory, "[attempting] to understand how seemingly counterintuitive elements of an earlier theory's conceptual-
ization of music may be indispensable to that theory"; presents vignettes on
Schenker and Rameau. (76)

A229 1993   Burns, Lori. "J. S. Bach's Mixolydian Chorale Harmonizations."
                Music Theory Spectrum 15/2: 144–72.

Constructs a theoretical model for the examination of Bach's modal chorales
based on Schenker's ideas; examines *Gelobet seist du, Jesu Christ* and *Dies sind
die heil'gen zehn Gebot.*

A230 1993 Cinnamon, Howard. "Tonal Elements and Unfolding Nontriadic Harmonies in the Second of Schoenberg's Drei Klavierstücke, Op. 11." *Theory and Practice* 18: 127–70.

Demonstrates how, in Schoenberg's Op. 11, "[pitch-class set] operations serve as foreground substitutes for conventional tonal procedures to enlarge the harmonic vocabulary in the context of underlying (i.e., middleground) structures that remain fundamentally tonal." (136)

A231 1993 Cook, Nicholas. "Heinrich Schenker: Anti-Historicist." *Rivista Italiana di musicologia*: 24–36. Reprinted in *Culturas musicales del Mediterraneo y sus ramificaciones*, ed. by Alfonso de Vicente Delgado (Madrid: 1992).

Discusses Schenker's views on music history, holding that "Schenker's overriding aim is to abolish history, to abolish subjectivity, and so to recapture the objective and authentic voice of Music, as it spoke through the genius-composers of the past," and that his reductive method of analysis is the instrument through which this "abolition" would be accomplished. (26)

A232 1993 Coeurdevey, Annie. "L'analyse schenkerienne et ses frontières." *Revue de Musicologie* 79/1: 5–30.

Discusses the basic ideas of Schenkerian analysis, considering its chronological boundaries, represented by Bach's modal chorales (the transition between modes and keys) and Wagner's *Tristan und Isolde* (moving away from common practice tonality).

A233 1993 Cohn, Richard, trans. by Piero Marconi. "Le theoria Schenker, la theoria schenkeriana: Unità pura o conflitto constructivo?" *Analitica* 4/12: 3–12.

Italian translation of Cohn's 1992 article (see **A263** below).

A234 1993 Dale, Catherine. "Schoenberg's Concept o Variation Form: A Paradigmatic Analysis o *Litanei* from the Second String Quartet, Op. 10." *Journal of the Royal Musical Association* 118/1: 94–120.

Uses Schenkerian analysis to explore motivic relationships in the work; shows the work in light of Schoenberg's movement from tonality to atonality.

A235 1993 Damiani, Giovanni. "La necessita della variazione nel pensiero Viennese progressista." *Studi musicali* 22/2: 447–65.

Examines the artistic and aesthetic positions of the second Viennese school, with regard to musical unity, from the perspectives of Réti, Adorno, Busoni, Schenker, and others.

A236 1993 Federhofer, Hellmut. "Die Verhältnis von Intervall und Akkord zum strengen und freien Satz." *Musiktheorie* 8/3: 211–5.

Considers the relationship of intervals and chords in strict counterpoint and free composition through a discussion of texts of Schenker and Bernard.

A237 1993 Federhofer, Helmut. "Johann Joseph Fux (1660–1741) und die Kontrapunktlehre." *Die Musikforschung* 46/2: 157–70.
Discusses Fux's counterpoint treatise as the basis for instruction in counterpoint, leading to free composition; discusses Schenker's uniting of the disciplines of harmony and counterpoint in his theoretical writings.

A238 1993 Gibeau, Peter. "An Introduction to the Theories of Heinrich Schenker." *Journal of the Conductors' Guild* 14/2: 77–90 [part 1] and 15/1: 31–45 [part 2].
A general introduction; states concepts and applies them progressively from nursery tunes to symphonic excerpts; contains a short bibliography.

A239 1993 Grunsqeig, Werner. "Vom 'Schenkerismus' zum 'Dahlhaus-Projekt': Einflusse deutschsprachiger Musiker und Musikwissenschaftler in den Vereinigten Staaten—Anfänge und Ausblick." *Österreichische Musikzeitschrift* 48/3–4: 161–70.
Describes the career of Hans Weisse, one of the first proponents of Schenker's theories in the United States; contrasts this with Carl Dahlhaus's views.

A240 1993 Hendersonellers, Brian. "Has Classical-Music a Fractal Nature? A Reanalysis."*Computers in the Humanities* 27/4: 277–284.
Concludes that there is no inherent fractal nature in classical music; however, it is feasible to use fractal ideas to compose musical pieces; uses Bach's Invention no. 1 as an example.

A241 1993 Korsyn, Kevin. "Schenker's Organicism Re-examined." *Intégral* 7: 82–118.
Examine's Schenker's *Der geist der musikalischen Technik* in light of Pastille's 1984 article and Keiler's response (1989). Suggests that Schenker's essay was influenced by Nietzsche's aesthetics, possibly a "covert debate with Wagner," and by the antimetaphysics of Ernst Mach. (83)

A242 1993 Lai, Eric. "Toward a Theory of Pitch Organization: The Early Music of Chou Wen-Chung." *Asian Music* 25/1–2: 177–207.
Combines Chinese modal theory with Schenker's methods and pitch-class set theory to examine three of Chou's compositions, *And the Fallen Petals*, *The Willows Are New*, and *Soliloquy of a Bhiksuni*.

A243 1993 Larson, Steve. "Dave McKenna's performance of *Have You Met Miss Jones*." *American Music* 11/3: 283–315.
Examines McKenna's improvisation, noting especially his use of rhythm and register; includes transcriptions and analytical graphs.

A244 1993 Lubben, Joseph. "Schenker the Progressive: Analytic Practice in Der Tonwille." *Music Theory Spectrum* 15/1: 59–75.

Examines *Der Tonwille* as an early application of Schenker's blossoming ideas to "illustrate the degree to which an integrative approach enriched Schenker's method [and] bring forward his effective and engaging interpretations of musical events that lie beyond the narrow domain of a single harmonic-contrapuntal background." (61)

A245 1993 Meeùs, Nicholas. "Du bon usage de l'analyse schenkerienne." *Analyse Musicale* 30: 21–24.
Noting that Schenkerian theory is "ignored" in France, Meeùs discusses a Schubert waltz (D. 365), contrasting a "traditional" approach and a Schenkerian approach.

A246 1993 Rink, John. "Schenker and Improvisation." *Journal of Music Theory* 37/1: 1–54.
"Investigates Schenker's theoretical notion of improvisation and asseses its historical context, [and] contains three analytical case studies designed to evaluate Schenker's ideas on this subject." (1)

A247 1993 Russ, Michael. "On Schenkerism: A Closed Circle of Elite Listeners?" *Music Analysis* 12/2: 266–85.
A review-essay on the contents of *Schenker Studies* and *Trends in Schenkerian Research*; discusses each essay in turn, interspersed with commentary.

A248 1993 Sharpe, R. A. "What Is the Object of Musical Analysis?" *Music Review* 54/1: 63–72.
Surveys writings of Schenker, Epstein, Narmour, Lerdahl, and others; suggests that analysis is concerned with interpretation and "highlighting features" of music rather than describing facts, compositional method, or listener competence. (RILM; used by permission)

A249 1993 Smyth, David H. "Balanced Interruption and the Formal Repeat." *Music Theory Spectrum* 15/1: 76–88.
Examines sonata form from the Schenkerian perspective.

A250 1993 Suurpää, Lauri. "Äänenkuljetus ja koherenssi: Johdatus Schenker-analyysiin." *Musiikki* 23/3–4: 45–78.
A thorough introduction to Schenker's ideas, presenting explanations of his graphic notation and the techniques of *Auskomponierung*. Examines several excerpts from the repertoire, focusing on Schumann and Mozart, to illustrate these techniques.

A251 1993 Stock, Jonathan. "The Applications of Schenkerian Analysis to Ethnomusicology: Problems and Possibilities." *Music Analysis* 12/2: 215–40.
Begins with a brief summary of the aims of ethnomusicological inquiry, focusing on those studies that use reductive analysis; considers the applicability of Schenkerian analysis to world music; contains three sample analyses.

A252 1993   Viljoen, Martina, and Nicol Viljoen. "Schenker's Analytical Concepts and Their Relation to Aesthetic Experience." *South African
Journal of Musicology* 13: 81–8.
Discusses the interrelation of analysis and aesthetics; examine's Schenker's use
of the organic metaphor.

A253 1992   Agawu, V. Kofi. "Theory and Practice in the Analysis of the
Nineteenth-Century Lied." *Music Analysis* 11/1: 3–36.
Discusses questions of analysis and interpretation; explores various analytical
models for *Lieder* analysis.

A254 1992   Bent, Ian. "History of Music Theory: Margin or Center?" *Theoria*
6: 1–21.
Discusses the issues involved in studying the history of music theory, as it does
not quite belong to music theory (with its emphasis on "compositional theory"
and "analytical practice") or music history (emphasizing "music itself as the
central concern of music history"); examines "its place within the various disciplines that have music as their object." (2–3)

A255 1992   Burnham, Scott. "The Criticism of Analysis and the Analysis of
Criticism." *Nineteenth-Century Music* 16/1: 70–6.
A response to Kramer's 1992 article (see **A270** below), considering the relation-
ship of analysis and criticism.

A256 1992   Cadwallader, Allen, and William Pastille. "Schenker's High-
Level Motives." *Journal of Music Theory* 36/1: 119–48.
Explores two questions: "How did Schenker arrive at such a radical reversal in
his thinking [regarding 'motive' as a middleground line rather than a foreground
succession of tones]? And what, precisely, did Schenker come to accept as an alternative to conventional motivic analysis?" (119)

A257 1992   Cadwallader, Allen. "More on Scale-Degree Three and the Cadential Six-Four." *Journal of Music Theory* 36/1: 187–98.
Response to Beach's 1990 article; adds to Beach's article by contributing to the
"theoretically driven" solution involving "preexisting rules and definitions" (see
A324) (45)

A258 1992   Cinnamon, Howard. "New Observations on Voice Leading,
Hemiola, and Their Roles in Tonal and Rhythmic Structures in
Chopin's Prelude in B Minor, Op. 28 No. 6." *Intégral* 6: 66–106.
Examines the prelude using durational reduction and hypermetric analysis; cites
an analysis by Burkhart.

A259 1992   Cinnamon, Howard. "Third-Related Harmonies as Elements of
Contrapuntal Prolongation in Some Works by Franz Liszt." *In
Theory Only* 12/5–6: 1–30.

Studies Liszt's *Blume und Duft* and *Faust* symphony from the Schenkerian perspective, concentrating on the composer's use of third-related harmonies at all structural levels.

A260 1993 Coeurdevey, Annie. "La 'Gigue en sol' K. 574. Une approche schenkerienne." *Ostinato Rigore* 1/2: 29–44. ISBN 2-858-93198-4.
Discusses the models for Mozart's works, including Händel (gigue from the Keyboard Suite No. 8) and possibly Bach. Includes voice-leading graphs.

A261 1992 Cohn, Richard. "The Autonomy of Motives in Schenkerian Accounts of Tonal Music." *Music Theory Spectrum* 14/2: 150–70.
Examines "two different kinds of unity, based on association and derivation respectively, and sketching their relationship as it evolved in Schenker's writing." Believes that "the standard Schenkerian account of the relationship between motives and 'structure' is insufficient to account for the complex analytic practices of most Schenkerians." (151)

A262 1992 Cohn, Richard, and Douglas J. Dempster. "Hierarchical Unity, Plural Unities: Toward a Reconciliation." In *Disciplining Music: Musicology and Its Canons*, ed. by Katherine Bergon and Philip Bohlman. Chicago: University of Chicago Press: 156–81.
Discusses the notion of "underlying simplicity" in music; proposes to "clarify the formal nature of hierarchies, to spectate three different ontological types of hierarchies, and to raise a question of scope with respect to the claim that music is hierarchical." Examines the work of Meyer and Narmour, "[considering] how their view encourages relocating musical unity on the compositional 'surface' itself, rather than in some 'underlying simplicity.' " (157)

A263 1992 Cohn, Richard. "Schenker's Theory, Schenkerian Theory: Pure Unity or Constructive Conflict?" *Indiana Theory Review* 13/1: 1–19.
Examines writings of Cook, Beach, Schachter, Rothgeb, and Rothstein, noting their appeal to a "constructive conflict paradigm." Conctructive conflicts occurs when, "some significant compositional feature is incompatible with the 'structure' of the composition." (2)

A264 1992 Cohn, Richard. "Metric and Hypermetric Dissonance in the *Menuetto* of Mozart's Symphony in G Minor, K. 550." *Intégral* 6/2: 1–33.
Examines the interrelatedness of pitch and rhythm, relying on mathematical formulae for defining metrical *consonance* and *dissonance*. Discusses the role played by hemiola at the hypermetric level.

A265 1992 Gołąb, Maciej. "Akkord und Stimmführung in den chromatischen Fakturen bei Chopin." In *Secondo Convegno Europeo di Analisi Musicale*, Vol. 2, ed. by Rossanna Dalmonte and Mario

Baroni. Trento: Universitá degli Studi di Trento: 643–6. ISBN 88-86135-09-2.

Studies Chopin's op. 28/8 and 68; combines traditional functional analysis with Schenkerian ideas.

A266 1992 Gołąb, Maciej. "Анализ н Произвдение." *Муыкалъная ак, адемця* 3: 221.

[1992 Gołąb, Maciej. "Analysis and Work." *Muzykali'naja Akademiia* 3: 221.]

Russian translation of an excerpt of Gołąb's 1986 *Muzyka* article (see **A466** below).

A267 1992 Hanson, John. "Cantus Firmi for Species Counterpoint: Catalog and Characteristics." *Journal of Music Theory Pedagogy* 6: 43–81.

A catalog of 191 cantus firmi from eight counterpoint books analyzed in terms of the properties found in Salzer/Schachter 1969 (see **B82** below).

A268 1992 Jackson, Timothy. "Current Issues in Schenkerian Analysis." *Musical Quarterly* 76/2: 242–63.

Provides directions to Schenker's grave and describes the history of the Schenker *Nachlass*; concludes with a review-essay of *Schenker Studies* (see **B40** below) and *Trends in Schenkerian Research* (see **B38** below).

A269 1992 Jan, Steven. "X Marks the Spot: Schenkerian Perspectives on the Minor-Key Classical Development Section." *Music Analysis* 11/1: 37–54.

Discusses the Schenerian interpretation of the development section base on readings of G-minor compositions of Mozart.

A270 1992 Kramer, Lawrence. "Haydn's Chaos, Schenker's Order: or, Hermeneutics and Musical Analysis: Can They Mix?" *Nineteenth-Century Music* 16/1: 3–17.

Attempts to bridge the gap between analysis and criticism by reexamining Schenker's analysis of Haydn's *Vorstellung des Chaos* in light of hermeneutic approaches drawn from literary theory and Schenker's linear analysis.

A271 1992 Littlefield, Richard, and David Neumeyer. "Rewriting Schenker: Narrative–History–Ideology." *Music Theory Spectrum* 14/1: 38–65.

Describes Schenker's narrative technique as an amalgam of the genres of drama and epic and "advance[s] an historicist interpretation which interrogates those genres in terms of their semantic and logical conditions." (114)

A272 1992 Marston, Nicholas. "Beethoven's 'Anti-Organicism'? The Origins of the Slow Movement of the Ninth Symphony." In *The Creative Process*, Studies in the History of Music, Vol. 3. New York: Broude; 1992: 169–200. ISBN 0-8540-7403-2.

Suggests that the most appropriate analysis of the slow movement should downplay the importance of organic connection based on Beethoven's sketches and Schenker's comments in *Beethovens Neunte Sinfonie*.

A273 1992 Modena, Elena. "Il concetto di coerenza organica secondo la teoria schenkeriana. Appunti per una verifica analitica." *Diastema* 3: 17–21.

A discussion of the ideas of diminution and linear progressions, using Mozart's Double Piano sonata K. 448 as an example. Available online at www.ensemble900.it/Diastema/Rivista/ Vecchia%20serie/03/Modena.pdf.

A274 1992 Неклюдов, Юрий. "Заметки о Шенкеризме." *Муыкалъная академия* 3: 213–6.

[1992 Nekljudov, Yurii. "Remarks on Schenkerism." *Muzykal'naja Akademija* 3: 213–6.]

Describes Schenker's importance to music theory in general and to Réti and Keller in particular.

A275 1992 Nattiez, Jean-Jacques. "Existe-t-il des relations entre les diverses methods d'analyse?" Trento, Italy: U. degli Studi Dipartimento di Storia della Civilta: 537–66.

Describes two types of analysis, semantic and "structural-immanent," the latter of which is subdivided into taxonomic, parametric, and linear categories. Studying each method for relationships to the other, Nattiez analyzes the theme from Mozart's G Minor Symphony, K. 540.

A276 1992 Renwick, William. "Modality, Imitation, and Structural Levels: Bach's *Manualiter Kyries* from *Clavierübung* III." *Music Analysis* 11/1: 55–74.

Analyzes the three compositions, tracing their unusual tonal structure to their basis in chant as well as the techniques of imitation employed by Bach.

A277 1992 Renwick, William, and David Walker. "*CD-Brahms*: An Interactive Multimedia Program in Music Analysis." *Computers in Music Research* 4: 45–76.

A republishing of Schenker's *Tonwille* essay in CD-ROM format, featuring a recording of the work, cross-references among structural levels, and the score of Händel's original work. Also includes a glossary of Schenkerian terms.

A278 1992 Scarpellini Pancrazi, Franco. "Introduzione all' Analisi schenkeriana: Principi teorico-practici." *Diastema* 2: 25–31.

An introduction to Schenker's methodology.

A279 1992   Schmalfeldt, Janet. "Cadential Processes: The Evaded Cadence
                and the 'One More Time' Technique." *Journal of Musicological
                Research* 12/1–2: 1–52.
By "one more time" technique, Schmalfeldt refers to the practice of repeating
the approach to a final cadence. Works of Mozart, Verdi, Beethoven, D. Scarlatti,
and C. P. E. Bach are analyzed according to Schenkerian principles.

A280 1992   Snarrenberg, Robert. "Schenker's Theories of Concealment."
                Theoria 6: 97–133.
Explores "the sense of concealment in Schenker's musical psychology and its
connections with 'illusion' and 'mystery,' his assessment of the psychological
state of his culture, and examines two issues that are affected by Schenker's different senses of concealment: his conflicting views on the nature of the listener's
activity and the effect of his cultural critique on his pedagogical mission." (98)

A281 1992   Webster, James. "The Form of the Finale of Beethoven's Ninth
                Symphony." In *Beethoven Forum 1*: 23–62. Lincoln: University
                of Nebraska Press.
English translation of Webster's 1992 article (see **A358** below).

A282 1991   Adrian, John. "The Function of the Apparent Tonic at the Begin-
                ning of Development Sections." *Intégral* 5: 1–53.
Apparent tonics do not disrupt the long-term unfolding of a sonata form, except
on a local level. "It is this 'local disturbance' which must be explained if a coherent and correspondent view of musical form in general and the sonata form in
particular is to be realized." (2)

A283 1991   Babbitt, Milton. "A Composer's View." In *Harvard Library
                Bulletin* 2/1. Cambridge, Mass.: Harvard University Library:
                123–32.
Discusses Babbitt's views on writings of Schenker, Oppel, Kurth, Halm, and Erpf.

A284 1991   Babbitt, Milton. "A Life of Learning: The Charles Homer Hask-
                ins Lectures." American Council of Learned Societies, Occa-
                sional Paper #17.
Contains anecdotal material on Schenker drawn from Eduard Steuermann; discusses the influence of both Schenker and Schoenberg on contemporary musical
theory.

A285 1991   Barcaba, Peter. "The Artistic and Scientific Aspect of Schenker-
                ian Theory." In *Analyse musicale*: Proceedings of the 1st Euro-
                pean Congress on Musical Analysis (Colmar, 26–28 October
                1989): 39–41.
Discusses the two aspects of Schenkerian analysis.

A286 1991 Bent, Ian, and Claudio Annibaldi. "Heinrich Schenker e la missione del genio germanico." *Rivista italiana di musicologia* 26/1: 3–34.
Examines Schenker's essay "von den Sendung Deutschen Genies" from *Der Tonwille* 1 and his nationalistic tendencies; comments on some of his analyses from *Der freie Satz*.

A287 1991 Burkhart, Charles. "How Rhythm Tells the Story in *La ci darem la mano.*" *Theory and Practice* 16: 21–38.
Discusses programmatic implications of bar lengths; contains voice-leading graphs detailing hidden motivic repetition.

A288 1991 Cook, Nicholas. "The Editor and the Virtuoso; or, Schenker versus Bülow." *Journal of the Royal Music Association* 116/1: 78–95.
Examines both Schenker's and Bülow's editions of C. P. E. Bach's keyboard music; noting their conflicting aims (Bülow's to adapt the music to nineteenth-century practice versus Schenker's to reproduce Bach's original music as he conceived it).

A289 1991 Cook, Nicholas. "Heinrich Schenker and the Authority of the Urtext." In *Tradition and Its Future in Music*, ed. by Yoshihiko Tokumaru, et al. Osaka: Mita: 27–33.
Discusses the ideas behind the "Urtext" editions as being "a reaction against the interpretive editions perpetrated by nineteenth-century virtuosi like von Bülow." Examines problems associated with attempting to divine composers' intentions through autograph study. (27)

A290 1991 Chew, Geoffrey. "Ernst Kurth, Music as Psychic Motion and *Tristan und Isolde*: Towards a Model for Analysing Musical Instability." *Music Analysis* 10/1–2: 171–93.
Discusses the similarities between Kurth's musical theory and Schenker's.

A291 1991 Dale, Catherine. "Foreground Motif as a Determinant of Formal and Tonal Structure in the First Movement of Schoenberg's Second String Quartet." *The Music Review* 52/1: 52–63.
Approaches the work from a Schenkerian vantage point, pointing out that the need for the second subject to "confirm the tonic key rather than challenge it" poses problems for Schenker's conception of sonata form. (52)

A292 1991 Deutsch, Walter. "Anmerkungen zur Melodientypologie." *Jahrbuch für Volksliedforschung* 36: 18–28.
An examination of folk melodies, analyzing them using Schenkerian techniques; shows examples of a $\hat{3}$-line and a $\hat{5}$-line.

A293 1991 Edwards, G. "The Nonsense of an Ending: Closure in Haydn's String Quartets." *Musical Quarterly* 75: 227–54.

Examines the popular conception of Haydn as a "trivial" composer as well as his comparative neglect by musical scholars.

A294 1991 Everett, Walter Tripp. "Voice Leading, Register, and Self-Discipline in Mozart's *Die Zauberflöte.*" *Theory and Practice* 16: 103–26.

Examines excerpts from *Die Zauberflöte*, concentrating on register and voice-leading relationships between the inner voices and the *Urlinie*; argues that the "reductionist" approach allows for better understanding of character development.

A295 1991 Folio, Cynthia. "Analysis and Performance of the Flute Sonatas of J. S. Bach: A Sample Lesson Plan." *Journal of Music Theory Pedagogy* 5/2: 133–60.

Discusses ways to strengthen the relationship of analysis to performance in the classroom; provides a sample lesson plan and bibliography.

A296 1991 Greer, Taylor. "Modal Sensibility in Gabriel Fauré's Harmonic Language." *Theory and Practice* 16: 127–42.

Analyzes three songs of Fauré, showing his use of the flat mediant as both a coloristic sonority, and a structural harmony, as well as for programmatic purposes.

A297 1991 Hubbs, Nadine. "Schenker's Organicism." *Theory and Practice* 16: 143–62.

Surveys the literature on organicism; examines the "organic" nature of Schenker's thought; examines the "attributes" (primary and secondary) of organicism.

A298 1991 Jost, Peter. "Heinrich Schenker und Mozart." *Mozart-Jahrbuch*: 606–12.

Outlines Schenker's basic approach and surveys his analyses of Mozart's music.

A299 1991 Johns, Donald. "Aimez-vous Brahms?: Ein Hindemith-Schenker Briefwechsel." *Hindemith Jahrbuch* 20: 141–51. Reprinted in *Über Hindemith: Aufsätze zu Werk, Ästhetik und Interpretation.* Mainz: Schott: 283–93. ISBN 3-7957-0285-2.

Describes a correspondence between Schenker and Hindemith in October–November 1926; provides transcriptions of two letters with commentary.

A300 1991 Krebs, Harald Manfred. "Tonal and Formal Dualism in Chopin's Scherzo, Op. 31." *Music Theory Spectrum* 13/1: 48–60.

Examines the work, emphasizing the dual key scheme of B-flat minor and D-flat major; notes that "not all [tonally] deviating works of the early nineteenth century surrender their secrets when they are analysed with respect to only one tonic; their intricacy and ingenuity can be fully revealed only by listening to and analyzing them from more than one tonal angle." (49)

A301 1991 Laufer, Edward. "Voice-Leading Procedures in Development Sections." *Studies in Music from the University of Western Ontario* 13: 69–120.

Describes the techniques used in the development sections through a series of twelve voice-leading paradigms, showing how these paradigms underlie the development sections of Beethoven, Mozart, Schubert, Haydn, Schumann, and Brahms. Examines twenty-seven works in all.

A302 1991 McCreless, Patrick. "The Hermeneutic Sentence and Other Literary Models for Tonal Closure." *Indiana Theory Review* 12/1–2: 35–74.

Draws on the writing of Roland Barthes, noting similarities between his concept of the "hermeneutic sentence" and Schenker's *Ursatz*.

A303 1991 McCreless, Patrick. "Syntagmatics and Paradigmatics: Some Implications for the Analysis of Chromaticism in Tonal Music." *Music Theory Spectrum* 13/2: 147–78.

Using Saussure's Syntagmatic and Paradigmatic relations, McCreless argues that "[these concepts] can illuminate certain problematic areas of analysis, notably the chromaticism in the music of the later eighteenth and nineteenth centuries." (178)

A304 1991 Miller, Patrick. "The Published Music of Heinrich Schenker: An Historical-Archival Introduction." *Journal of Musicological Research* 10: 177–97.

An examination of the published music, drawing commentary from Schenker's letters and diary. Contains musical examples.

A305 1991 Morrison, Charles. "Prolongation in the Final Movement of Bartók's String Quartet No. 4." *Music Theory Spectrum* 13: 179–96.

Surveys some of the literature on prolongation in post-tonal music; applies methodology to said work.

A306 1991 Pearsall, E. R. "Harmonic Progressions and Prolongation in Post-Tonal Music." *Music Analysis* 10/3: 344–55.

A survey of available literature on post-tonal prolongation.

A307 1991 Renwick, William. "Structural Patterns in Fugue Subjects and Fugal Expositions." *Music Theory Spectrum* 13/2: 197–218.

"[Proposes] that Baroque fugue subjects can be classified into a small number of structural paradigms and explores the implications of those paradigms for formal structure and style, revealing their impact on the structures of fugal answers and countersubjects, and the disposition of voices in fugal expositions." (197)

A308 1991 Rothstein, William. "On Implied Tones." *Music Analysis* 10/3: 189–328.

Explores the idea of implied tones through the analysis of various excerpts.

A309 1991 Schachter, Carl. "20th-Century Analysis and Mozart Performance." *Early Music* 19/4: 620–4.

Examines several Mozart pieces, focusing on slur markings and the meanings that they convey; relates Schenkerian analysis to performace practice.

A310 1991 Schachter, Carl. "Mozart's Last and Beethoven's First: Echoes of K. 551 in the First Movement of Op. 21." In *Mozart Studies,* ed. by Cliff Eisen. Oxford: Oxford University Press: 227–51.

Describes similarities in the two works, focusing on the modulation scheme as well as some melodic gestures.

A311 1991 Schachter, Carl. "The Adventures of an F-sharp: Tonal Narration and Exhortation in Donna Anna's First-Act Recitative and Aria." *Theory and Practice* 16: 5–20. Reprinted in *Unfoldings: Essays in Schenkerian Theory and Analysis,* ed. by Joseph N. Straus. Oxford: Oxford University Press, 1999: 221–38.

Traces the significance of F-sharp (G-flat) in the unfolding of the recitative and aria; shows a large-scale 5–6 exchange as the basis for the recitative.

A312 1991 Schmalfeldt, Janet. "Towards a Reconciliation of Schenkerian Concepts with Traditional and Recent Theories of Form." *Music Analysis* 10/3: 233–88.

Examines the difference in Schoenberg's and Schenker's thinking regarding the concept of musical form.

A313 1991 Schubert, Giselher. "Ludwig Rottenberg über Schenker: Zwei Dokumente." *Hindemith-Jahrbuch* 20: 152–8.

Quotes a letter from Rottenberg to Karl Holl mentioning Schenker, as well as a review of Schenker's *Das Meisterwerk in der Musik* III. Also quotes a brief passage from Schenker's diary indicating Rottenberg's desire that Schenker take on Hindemith as a student.

A314 1991 Snyder, John. "Schenker and the First Movement of Mozart's Sonata K. 545: An Uninterrupted Sonata Form?" *Theory and Practice* 16: 51–78.

Surveys definitions of sonata form; presents contrasting analyses of K. 545.

A315 1991 Viljoen, Nicol. "The Motivic, Structural, and Formal Implications of Mixture for Chopin's Mazurka Op. 30/3." *South African Journal of Musicology* 11: 143–52.

Examines how chromaticism operates at various structural levels in the work; speculates on its effect on the motivic, structural, and formal unity of the music.

A316 1991 Wick, Norman. "Transformations of Middleground Hypermeasures in Selected Mozart Keyboard Sonatas." *Theory and Practice* 16: 79–102.
Discusses the idea of "asymmetry within symmetry"; specifically, hypermetrical asymmetry at the middleground level.

A317 1991 Willner, Channan. "The Two-Length Bar Revisited: Händel and the Hemiola." *Göttinger Händel-Beiträge* 4: 208–31.
Using tonal and durational reduction, Willner categorizes three types of hemiola in Händel's works: (1) cadential hemiolas, which do not affect the metrical structure; (2) expansion hemiolas, which allow two bars to occupy the span of one; and (3) contraction hemiolas, which let two bars occupy the span of three.

A318 1990 Adrian, John. "The Ternary-Sonata Form." *Journal of Music Theory* 34/1: 57–80.
Proposes to "define the structural problems created by the tonic chord at the beginning of the development section and to offer two solutions." The term *ternary sonata form* refers to the "three-fold placement of the tonic scale-step"; includes an analysis of Brahms's clarinet sonata op. 120/2 focusing on the conflict between the dominant of the second tonal area and the dominant that concludes the development section. (57)

A319 1990 Baker, James. "Voice-Leading in Post-Tonal Music: Suggestions for Extending Schenker's Theory." *Music Analysis* 9/2: 177–200.
Examines Schoenberg's op. 19 piano pieces, considering Schoenberg's comments on the work and then applying Schenker's analytical method. Speculates on how the Schenker method may be applied to atonal music in general.

A320 1990 Barcaba, Peter. "Domenico Scarlatti oder die Geburtsstunde der klassischen Sonate." *Österreichische Musikzeitschrift* 43/7–8: 382–90.
Examines some of Scarlatti's keyboard sonatas from the Schenkerian perspective, and discusses his role in the development of the classical sonata.

A321 1990 Beach, David. "The Cadential Six-Four as Support for Scale-Degree Three of the Fundamental Line." *Journal of Music Theory* 34/1: 81–99.
Demonstrates that the "[elimination of] the six-four as legitimate support for $\hat{3}$ of the fundamental line can lead to interpretations that are both illogical in view of the musical evidence and inconsistent with what we hear." Examines five excerpts from Mozart's sonatas. (82)

A322 1990 Burkhart, Charles. "Departures from the Norm in Two Songs from Schumann's *Liederkreis*." In *Schenker Studies*, ed. by Heidi Siegel. Cambridge: Cambridge University Press: 146–64.

Discusses the idea of the auxiliary cadence in general, and examines two songs from the *Liederkreis* (*Schöne Fremde* and *Mondnacht*) that are based, at the background level, on the auxiliary cadences.

A323 1990 Cadwallader, Allen. "Form and Tonal Process: The Design of Different Structural Levels." in *Trends in Schenkerian Research*, ed. by Allen Cadwallader. New York: Schirmer: 1–22.

Elaborates on Schenker's essay on form from *Der freie Satz*, noting that Schenker's essay "is based initially on a single premise that leads him to elaborate only the most basic formal patterns [and] does not develop and redefine traditional formal principles in light of the central issue in his system, the notion of structural levels." (1)

A324 1990 Christensen, Thomas. "Hudební teorie v programu americké muzikologie." *Hudební veda* 27/3: 245–252.

Discusses the theories of Babbitt, Perle, and Schenker as representative of American musical theory; includes a bibliography of recent works.

A325 1990 Cummings, Naomi Helen. "Metaphors of Space and Motion in the Linear Analysis of Melody." *Miscellanea Musicologica* 17: 143–66.

Discusses "problems related to the use of visual or graphic lines to symbolize aspects of melodic structure." Discusses Roger Scruton's ideas on melody as well as the theories of Schenker and Meyer. (143)

A326 1990 Damschroder, David, and David Russell Williams. "Heinrich Schenker." In *Music Theory from Zarlino to Schenker: A Bibliography and a Guide,* Harmonologia no. 4. Stuyvesant: Pendragon: 203–314. ISBN 0-918728-99-1.

Contains, after an introductory essay, an extensive bibliography of primary and secondary sources.

A327 1990 Darcy, Warren. "A Wagnerian *Ursatz*; or, Was Wagner a Background Composer After All?" *Intégral* 4: 1–35.

Examines the first tonal episode of *Das Rheingold* (mm. 137–431), showing "a clear 3̂-line *Ursatz*," and demonstrating how Wagner "[employs] complex diminutions and deep-level motives" in his *Auskomponierung* process. (4)

A328 1990 Don, Gary W. "Thoughts on Geertz's Local Knowledge." *In Theory Only* 11/6: 15–7.

"A meditation on Clifford Geertz's treatment of culture as frames of local awareness (New York: Basic, 1983) and its relevance to music theory, including Schenker's precepts." (16)

A329 1990 Dubiel, Joseph. "Three Essays on Milton Babbitt." *Perspectives of New Music* 28/2: 216–61.

Discusses points of convergence between Babbitt and Schenker in Babbitt's twelve-tone theory.

A330 1990 Dubiel, Joseph. "When You Are Beethoven: Kinds of Rules in Schenker's Counterpoint." *Journal of Music Theory* 34/2: 291–340.

Explores remarks of Schenker's in *Counterpoint* discussing the relationship of counterpoint and harmony and the misunderstanding of that relationship by previous writers.

A331 1990 Dunsby, Jonathan. "Schenkerian Theory in Great Britain: Developments and Responses." In *Schenker Studies*, ed. by Heidi Siegel. Cambridge: Cambridge University Press: 182–90.

Discusses the emergence of Schenkerian theory in Britain, from Salzer's *Structural Hearing* through the founding of *Music Analysis*; concludes with a bibliography of recent British writings.

A332 1990 Everett, Walter. "Grief in Winterreise: A Schenkerian Perspective." *Music Analysis* 9/2: 157–76.

Explains how "the various textual references to grief are given a consistent motivic treatment in the music." Shows that the cycle is unified through the use of the $\hat{5}$-flat $\hat{6}$ neighbor-note motive. Studies *Einsamkeit* and *Der Wegweiser* in detail. (157)

A333 1990 Gagné, David. "The Compositional Use of Register in Three Piano Sonatas by Mozart." In *Trends in Schenkerian Research*, ed. by Allen Cadwallader. New York: Schirmer: 23–40.

Considers structure, form, and melodic and motivic elements as well as texture and dynamics in his study of Mozart's use of register; discusses Oster's 1961 article (see **A741** below).

A334 1990 Hinton, Stephen. "'Natürliche Übergänge': Heinrich Schenker's Begriff von der Sonatenform." *Musiktheorie* 5/2: 101–16.

Discusses Schenker's concept of sonata form, drawing examples from his early writings: Beethoven's opp. 109, 101, and 110, and his Fifth Symphony; traces the development of his thought from the Kantian-influenced anti-organicism through the embrace of organicism.

A335 1990 Kamien, Roger. "Aspects of the Neapolitain Sixth Chord in Mozart's Music." In *Schenker Studies*, ed. by Heidi Siegel. Cambridge: Cambridge University Press: 94–106.

"[Focuses] on the use of the Neapolitan sixth in conjunction with a melodic contrast in the top voice between the natural and lowered second scale degrees (natural-$\hat{2}$ and flat-$\hat{2}$)." (94)

A336 1990 Laskowski, Larry. "Voice Leading and Meter: An Unusual Mozart Autograph." In *Trends in Schenkerian Research*, ed. by Allen Cadwallader. New York: Schirmer: 41–50.
Examines the barring of two manuscript versions of "Bei Männern, welche Liebe fühlen" from *Die Zauberflöte*; discusses voice-leading considerations that would favor one over the other.

A337 1990 Laskowski, Larry. "J. S. Bach's 'Binary' Dance Movements: Form and Voice-Leading." In *Schenker Studies*, ed. by Heidi Siegel. Cambridge: Cambridge University Press: 84–93.
Discusses the minuet and sarabande from Bach's E Major French Suite in terms of voice leading and "the relationship between tonal and formal structures." (85)

A338 1990 Loeb, David. "Dual-Key Movements." In *Schenker Studies*, ed. by Heidi Siegel. Cambridge: Cambridge University Press: 76–83.
Discusses pieces and movements that begin and end in different keys, such as the second movement of the Sixth Brandenburg Concerto and the recitative/arioso "und siehe da . . . Mein Herz, indem die ganze Welt" from the *St. Matthew Passion*.

A339 1990 London, Justin. "Phrase Structure in 18th- and 19th-Century Theory: An Overview." *Music Research Forum* 5: 13–50.
Provides an overview of literature pertaining to phrase structure. Cites the writings of Kirnberger, Koch, Weber, Riemann, Schenker, and others.

A340 1990 Maisel, Arthur. "Talent and Technique: George Gershwin's *Rhapsody in Blue*." In *Trends in Schenkerian Research*, ed. by Allen Cadwallader. New York: Schirmer: 51–70.
Discusses problems of popular music analysis and the role of improvisation in eighteenth- and nineteenth-century art music as well as in popular music; shows tonal coherence in the *Rhapsody*.

A341 1990 McCreless, Patrick. "Schenker and Chromatic Tonicization: a Reappraisal." In *Schenker Studies*, ed. by Heidi Siegel. Cambridge: Cambridge University Press: 125–45.
Compares Treitler's approach to Schenker's; discusses chromaticism as it relates to motives. Examines Beethoven's *Leonore Overture* no. 3 and Schubert's *Pause* in terms of the compromise he is advocating between linear analysis and harmonic cross-reference.

A342 1990 Meeùs, Nicolas. "Schumann: Quatre *Lieder* du *Dichterliebe* Op. 48." *Analyse Musicale* 21: 23–36.
Examines four songs (nos. 1, 2, 7, and 9) in terms of underlying voice leading as well as surface-level motivic analysis and musical-textual associations.

A343 1990 Nogueira, Ilza. "Arnold Schoenberg *Mein Herz, das ist ein tiefer Schacht*: Uma abordagem schenkeriana." *Art: Revista da Escola de Música e Artes Cênicas da UFBA* 17: 39–62.
Applies Schenkerian analytical techniques to Schoenberg's song.

A344 1990 Novack, Saul. "Foreground, Middleground, and Background: their Significance in the History of Tonality." In *Schenker Studies*, ed. by Heidi Siegel. Cambridge: Cambridge University Press: 60–75.
Traces the significance of the concept of structural levels through the development of tonality; seeks to understand why Schenker limited his sphere of inquiry.

A345 1990 Pastille, William. "The Development of the *Ursatz* in Schenker's Published Works." In *Trends in Schenkerian Research*, ed. by Allen Cadwallader. New York: Schirmer: 71–86.
Traces the *Ursatz* concept from its inception to its definitive formulation in *Der freie Satz*; discusses the metaphors and language associated with it: Schenker's biological metaphors versus the scientific metaphors frequently encountered in the literature.

A346 1990 Pastille, William. "Music and Morphonogy: Goethe's Influence on Schenker's Thought." In *Schenker Studies*, ed. by Heidi Siegel. Cambridge: Cambridge University Press: 29–44.
Demonstrates Schenker's assimilation of Goethe's scientific methodology and epistemology; suggests that "a Goethean interpretation of Schenker's musical ontology can help to explain some puzzling aspects of his thought." (29)

A347 1990 Puffett, Derrick. "A Graphic Analysis of Mussorgsky's *Catacombs*." *Music Analysis* 9/1: 67–77.
Presents an analysis of the *Catacombae* movement from *Pictures at an Exhibition*; discusses the "incompleteness" of the movement and the resolution of its harmonic tension in the following movement.

A348 1990 Rink, John. "A Select Bibliography of Literature Related to Schenker by British Authors or in British Publications Since 1980." In *Schenker Studies*, ed. by Heidi Siegel. Cambridge: Cambridge University Press: 190–192.
A representative bibliography of British Schenker scholarship.

A349 1990 Rothgeb, John. "Schenkerian Theory and Manuscript Studies: Modes of Interaction." In *Schenker Studies*, ed. by Heidi Siegel. Cambridge: Cambridge University Press: 4–14.
Examines the work of Schenker and Jonas in the field of manuscript study (considering both autographs of finished compositions as well as sketches); discusses the importance of these sources for Schenker.

A350 1990 Rothstein, William. "Rhythmic Displacement and Rhythmic Normalization." In *Trends in Schenkerian Research*, ed. by Allen Cadwallader. New York: Schirmer: 87–114.

Outlines the concepts of displacement and normalization in terms of an enlargement of the suspension concept; discusses the rules of simultaneity, arpeggiation, and the primary tone. Applies the concepts to excerpts from Mozart's K. 333 and Chopin's op. 40/1.

A351 1990 Russ, Michael. "The Mysterious Thread in Mussorgsky's Nursery." *Music Analysis* 9/1: 47–65.

Produces and discusses two graphic analyses of the song that employ symbols and methodology from Schenker, Schoenberg, and Forte. Discusses the musical-textual relationship.

A352 1990 Schachter, Carl. "Either/Or." In *Schenker Studies*, ed. by Heidi Siegel. Cambridge: Cambridge University Press: 165–81. Reprinted in *Unfoldings: Essays in Schenkerian Theory and Analysis,* ed. by Joseph N. Straus. Oxford: Oxford University Press, 1999: 121–33.

Discusses the different meanings musical events may seem to have upon first hearing, the true meaning of which becomes apparent once the context is understood.

A353 1990 Schulenberg, David. "Expression and Authenticity in the Harpsichord Music of J. S. Bach." *Journal of Musicology* 8/4: 449–76.

Discusses the question of musical authenticity. Examines the writings of Gottsched, Scheibe, Mattheson, Schenker, Taruskin, and others in his discussion. Examines BWV 903 and 830.

A354 1990 Siegel, Heidi. "A Source for Schenker's Study of Thorough Bass: His Annotated Copy of J. S. Bach's Generalbaßbüchlein." In *Schenker Studies*, ed. by Heidi Siegel. Cambridge: Cambridge University Press: 15–28.

Discusses Schenker's tripartite plan of musical instruction (strict counterpoint, thoroughbass, and free composition), noting that he never published his ideas on thoroughbass instruction. Examines his unpublished manuscript entitled *Von der Stimmführung des Generalbasses* as well as his annotated copy of Bach's *Generalbaßbüchlein* in order to show how this second stage is implemented.

A355 1990 Solomon, Larry. "Graphic Analysis: An Algorithm." *Musicus: Computer Applications in Music* 2/1: 19–38. Available online as "Schenkerian Primer" (see **E42** below).

The author "attempts to develop a consistent and logical series of steps for carrying out [a Schenkerian-style] analysis" using Bach's C Major Prelude (WTC I) as an example. Compares his own analysis with Schenker's. Includes a glossary of Schenkerian symbols.

A356 1990 Stern, David. "Hidden Uses of Chorale Melodies of Bach's Cantatas." In *Trends in Schenkerian Research*, ed. by Allen Cadwallader. New York: Schirmer: 115–34.

Discusses Bach's use of the chorale tune in his cantatas, from simple melodic (usually ornamented) quotation to using the chorale tune's structure (e.g., motives), without direct quotation.

A357 1990 Stern, David. "Schenkerian Theory and the Analysis of Renaissance Music." In *Schenker Studies*, ed. by Heidi Siegel. Cambridge: Cambridge University Press: 45–59.

Discusses Schenker's views on music history, noting that the analytical method may help elucidate "structure, voice leading, and motivic organization in Renaissance music." (45)

A358 1990 Webster, James. "Zur Form des Finales von Beethovens 9. Symphonie." In *Probleme der symphonischen Tradition im 19. Jahrhundert*. Tutzing: Schneider: 157–86.

A response to Schenker's and Tovey's analyses; notes that the finale, representative of Elysium, avoids closure until the final two sections (see **A281** above for an English translation).

A359 1990 Wen, Eric. "Illusory Cadences and Apparent Tonics: the Effect of Motivic Enlargement Upon Phrase Structure." In *Trends in Schenkerian Research*, ed. by Allen Cadwallader. New York: Schirmer: 133–44.

Examines passages in Mozart's instrumental works in which the tonic ending the consequent phrase, when part of a motivic enlargement, does not constitute the true end of a phrase. Rather, it is the motivic expansion that determines phrase length.

A360 1990 Wen, Eric. "Enharmonic Transformation in the First Movement of Mozart's Piano Concerto in C Minor, K. 491." In *Schenker Studies*, ed. by Heidi Siegel. Cambridge: Cambridge University Press: 107–24.

Discusses the "two second themes" of the first movement of K. 491, exploring motivic relationships within the work.

A361 1990 Wick, Norman. "An Historical Approach to Six-Four Chords." *Theoria* 5: 61–73.

Presents an overview of the treatment of the six-four chord in the writings of Kirnberger, C. P. E. Bach, Riemann, Schenker, and Schoenberg.

A362 1989 Agawu, V. Kofi. "Schenkerian Notation in Theory and Practice." *Music Analysis* 8/3: 275–301.

Critiques current application of Schenkerian notation to post-tonal music, suggesting that over-reliance on Schenker-based notation may mask "inadequate analytical thinking." Describes various uses of analytical reduction. (276)

A363 1989   Agawu, V. Kofi. "Stravinsky's 'Mass' and Stravinsky Analysis." *Music Theory Spectrum* 11/2: 139–63.

Discusses the differing analytical approaches of Forte and Taruskin; examines the *Kyrie* movement of Stravinsky's mass, stressing "Schenker's idea of 'connection,' manifest in three conventional categories, cadence, diminution, and prolongation." Shows the tonal conflict of Stravinsky's large-scale tonal strategy. (141)

A364 1989   Barcaba, Peter. "L'analyse schenkérienne et interprétation musicale: Pour une lecture artistique de l'oeuvre de H. Schenker." *Analyse musicale* 17: 91–104.

Discusses the benefits of studying Schenkerian analysis for performers; suggests that the performer will be better able to project the musical content of the work.

A365 1989   Beach, David. "The Analytic Process—a Practical Demonstration: The Opening Theme from Beethoven's Op. 26." *Journal of Music Theory Pedagogy* 3: 25–46.

Discusses analysis as a three-stage process involving considerations of formal design (including large-scale harmonic motions), details of the individual parts (e.g., harmony, motives, rhythm), and examination of the contrapuntal structure of the work (metric reduction, graph of the deep structure). Examines the opening theme of Beethoven's op. 26 in light of this approach.

A366 1989   Blume, Jürgen. "Analyse als Beispiel musiktheoretischer Probleme: Auf der Suche nach der angemessenen Beschreibung chromatischer Harmonik in romantischer Musik." *Musiktheorie* 4/1: 37–51.

Examines Chopin's Prelude op. 28/4 and Schubert's *Der Wegweiser* from three points of view: *Stufentheorie* (Oliver Podszus), *Funktionstheorie* (Alexander von Edlinger), and *Schichtenlehre* (Schenker).

A367 1989   Brown, Matthew, and Douglas Dempster. "The Scientific Image of Music Theory." *Journal of Music Theory* 33/1: 65–106.

Response: 1989   *Journal of Music Theory* 33/1: 143–54 (J. Rahn).

Examines the claims for and against a scientifically based music theory. Suggests that "if theorists adopt scientific standards of explanation, then they must be prepared to abandon all hope of explaining what is unique about particular compositions." (66)

A368 1989   Chew, Geoffrey. "The Perfections of Modern Music: Consecutive Fifths and Tonal Coherence in Monteverdi." *Music Analysis* 8/3: 247–73.

Discusses Monteverdi's *O Mirtillo* (from book V of Monteverdi's madrigals), showing the tonal structure to be independent of the text setting.

A369 1989 Clark, William. "Intelligibility in Music: Heinrich Schenker's Theory of Musical Coherence." *Aristos: The Journal of Esthetics* 4/5: 1–5.
A nontechnical introduction in which Clark contrasts traditional music theory (harmonic and formal analysis) with Schenker's ideas of the unified masterwork, noting that Schenker "delighted in showing the structure behind modulations that drove conventional theorists into embarrassed silence." (4)

A370 1989 Clarke, David. "Structural, Cognitive and Semiotic Aspects of the Musical Present." *Contemporary Music Review* 3/1: 111–32.
Discusses temporal perception and tonal hierarchy; also draws from the ideas of Saussure.

A371 1989 Clarke, Eric F., and Simon Emmerson. "Music, Mind and Structure." *Contemporary Music Review* 3/1: 235
Constructs a cognitive theory of musical analysis using Mozart's K. 331; surveys the writings of Schenker, Narmour, Lerdahl/Jackendoff, Schachter, Cooper/Meyer, and Sloboda.

A372 1989 Clarke, Eric F. "Mind the Gap: Formal Structures and Psychological Processes in Music." *Contemporary Music Review* 3/1: 1–13.
Discusses the differences between structural musical analysis and cognitive psychology, as well as the "conceptual leakage" between the two approaches. (1)

A373 1989 Cook, Nicholas John. "Schenker's Theory of Music as Ethics." *The Journal of Musicology* 7/4: 415–39.
Suggests that divorcing Schenker's analytical method from his philosophy and polemics profoundly impoverishes it, as they are "a matter of substance and not just of style." Discusses Schenker's polemics and his "frequent excursions into metaphysics, religion, and politics" throughout his writings. (415–6)

A374 1989 Cook, Nicholas. "Music Theory and 'Good Comparison': A Viennese Perspective." *Journal of Music Theory* 33/1: 117–41.
Suggests that an important aspect of a musical theory is how it relates to the listener's perceptions; discusses the writings of Lerdahl/Jackendoff and Schenker in this regard.

A375 1989 Drabkin, William, trans. by Claudio Annibaldi. "'Bisogna leggere Schenker'" Sull'analisi del preludio in do maggiore BWV 924 di Bach." *Rivista italiana di musicologia* 24/1: 48–66.
Discusses Schenker's analysis from *Der Tonwille* 4; presents a translation of the essay.

A376 1989 Dunsby, Jonathan. "Performance and Analysis of Music." *Music Analysis* 8/1–2: 5–20.
Discusses both Schenkerian and Schoenbergian approaches to performance, as well as the notion of "authentic historicist performance practice." Examines semiotic and linguistic approaches as well. (5)

A377 1989 Federhofer, Hellmut. "Methoden der Analyse im Vergleich." *Musiktheorie* 4/1: 61–9.
Discusses the theories of Riemann and Schenker applied to an excerpt from Beethoven's op. 2/1.

A378 1989 Gerling, Cristina Capparelli. "A teoria de Heinrich Schenker: Una breve introducao." *Em pauta* 1/1: 22–34.
A brief introduction to Schenker and his ideas.

A379 1989 Gligo, Niksa. "O problemu glazbene analize." *Zvuk* 3: 29–40.
Croation translation of Adorno's "On the Problem of Musical Analysis" (see **A563** below)

A380 1989 Graybill, Roger. "Phenomenal Accent and Meter in the Species Exercise." *In Theory Only* 11/1–2: 11–44.
Responses: 1990 *In Theory Only* 11/5: 27–31 (J. Rothgeb).
1990 *In Theory Only* 11/5: 33–36 (R. Graybill).
Discusses rhythm in species counterpoint, focusing on phenomenal accent (as defined by Lerdahl/Jackendoff) and the interaction of accent and meter.

A381 1989 Keiler, Allan. "The Origins of Schenker's Thought: How Man is Musical." *Journal of Music Theory* 33/2: 273–98.
Examines Schenker's earlier writings in the context of contemporaneous musical thought; notes connections between his early and later writings. Focuses specifically on *Der Geist der musikalischen Technik*.

A382 1989 Marston, Nicholas. "Analysing Variations: The Finale of Beethoven's String Quartet Op. 74." *Music Analysis* 8/3: 303–24.
Discusses the problems of analyzing variations from a Schenkerian viewpoint.

A383 1989 McCreless, Patrick Phillip. "Schenker and the Norns." In *Analyzing Opera:Verdi and Wagner*, California studies in 19th-Century music, Vol. 6, ed. by Roger Parker and Carolyn Abbate. Los Angeles: University of California Press: ISBN: 0-520-06157-8.
Discusses the opening scene of *Götterdämmerung*, showing where Schenker's approach and Wagner's converge and diverge.

A384 1989 Riggins, H. Lee, and Gregory Proctor. "A Schenker Pedagogy." *Journal of Music Theory Pedagogy* 3/1: 1–24.
Comments: 1990 *Journal of Music Theory Pedagogy* 4/2: 295–300 (W. Rothstein).

Designs a pedagogy of Schenkerian analysis for undergraduate and graduate students.

A385 1989 Schachter, Carl. "Mozart's *Das Veilchen*: An Analysis of the Music." *Musical Times* 130: 149–55. Reprinted in *Ostinato Rigore* 1–2: 164–73. ISBN 2-85893-198-4.
The second part of the article, the first part being a discussion of the autograph by John Arthus. Analyzes Mozart's song, focusing on the repetition of hidden motives.

A386 1989 Street, A. "Superior Myths, Dogmatic Allegories: The Resistance to Musical Unity." *Music Analysis* 8: 77.
Discusses ideas of unity in music, citing Schoenberg, Webern, and Schenker.

A387 1989 于蘇賢. "论兴德米特'调性游戏'中的调性." 中央音乐学院学报 2: 3–13.

[1989 Su-xian, Yu. "The Tonalities in Hindemith's *Ludus Tonalis*." *Journal of the Central Conservatory of Music* 2: 3–13.]
Gives an overview of the tonalities in the whole set; focuses analysis on the Fugue in C.

A388 1988 Bass, Richard. "Prokofiev's Technique of Chromatic Displacement." *Music Analysis* 7/2: 197–214.
Describes the technique, in Prokofiev's music, whereby an expected diatonic pitch is "displaced" by a chromatic infection thereof, which is treated as if it were the expected diatonic pitch. Bass proceeds to show "how the seemingly foreign elements assume both a tonal and a motivic role." (200)

A389 1988 Bass, Richard. "The Second-Theme Problem and Other Issues in Mozart's Sonata K. 457." *Indiana Theory Review* 9/1: 2–22.
Discusses varying views of sonata form; traces Mozart's structural use of motive in the work.

A390 1988 Breslauer, Peter. "Diminutional Rhythm and Melodic Structure." *Journal of Music Theory* 32: 1–21.
Discusses the concept of diminution in general and the rhythms created by diminutions.

A391 1988 Cadwallader, Allen. "Echoes and Recollections: Brahms's Op. 76, No. 6." *Theory and Practice* 13: 65–78.
Discusses motivic resemblance between Brahms's op. 76/6 and op. 118/2, suggesting that "one is tempted to view the later piece as a recomposition of the first." Provides comparative graphs.

A392 1988 Cadwallader, Allen. "Foreground Motivic Ambiguity: Its Clarification at the Middleground Levels in Selected Late Piano Pieces of Johannes Brahms." *Music Analysis* 7/1: 59–91.

Traces ambiguous motivic patterns that appear "incongruous or indistinct in the prevailing harmonic/linear context") in three pieces. Op. 117, op. 118/2, and op. 119/2 show how the ambiguity is clarified at the middleground level. (59)

A393 1988 Cadwallader, Allen. "Prolegomena to a General Description of Motivic Relationships in Tonal Music." *Intégral* 2: 1–35.
Begins to establish a theory of motive within Schenker's system, hoping to "elucidate how motives and their associations interact with tonal processes at all structural levels." (3)

A394 1988 Carpenter, Patricia. "A Problem in Organic Form: Schoenberg's Tonal Body." *Theory and Practice* 13: 31–64.
Discusses Schoenberg's conception of musical form; examines Brahms's *Intermezzo*.

A395 1988 Cavett-Dunsby, Esther. "Mozart's Codas." *Music Analysis* 7/1: 31–51.
Because there is no "consistent theoretical approach to finding a coda," Cavett-Dunsby examines the "formal codas" in Mozart, i.e., those designated with a double-bar line. (32)

A396 1988 Cavett-Dunsby, Esther. "Mozart's 'Haydn' Quartets: Composing Up and Down Without Rules." *Journal of the Royal Musical Association* 113/1: 57–80.
Examines the quartets of Mozart, discussing the second thematic group of the recapitulation, noting that there seems to be no consistency whether Mozart transposed the melodic line up or down.

A397 1988 Cherlin, Michael. "Hauptmann and Schenker: Two Adaptations of Hegelian Dialectics." *Theory and Practice* 13: 115–31.
Discusses Hegel's ideas on music and examines his influence on Riemann, Schenker, and Hauptmann; contrasts the ideas of Hauptmann and Schenker, examining the use of "dialectical organicism" in their theoretical writings.

A398 1988 Cook, Nicholas. "De l'ambigüité de la notion de thème pour l'analyse musicale." *Analyse musicale* 13: 30–6.
Discusses sonata-form analysis in the nineteenth and twentieth centuries; describes *theme* as the "articulation of the relationship between [the foreground and the underlying structure]." (30)

A399 1988 Don, Gary. "Goethe and Schenker." *In Theory Only* 10/8: 1–14.
Examines the relationship between Schenker's and Goethe's ideas on organicism, based on Goethe's theory of the *Urphänopmen* (archetype) and plant metamorphosis.

A400 1988 Federhofer, Hellmut. "Anton Bruckner im Briefwechsel von August Halm (1869–1929) und Heinrich Schenker (1868–1935)." In

Anton Bruckner: Studien zu Werk und Wirkung. Mainzer Studien zur Musikwissenschaft, Vol. 20, ed. by Christoph-Hellmut Mahling. Tutzing: Schneider: 33–40. ISBN 3-7952-0525-5.
Examines Schenker's correspondence with Halm, focusing on their respective views of Bruckner. Also contains Schenker's comments on Beethoven's op. 109 expressed in a letter to Halm.

A401 1988 Forte, Allen. "New Approaches to the Linear Analysis of Music." *Journal of the American Musicological Society* 41: 315–48.
Discusses the "advantages as well as shortcomings" of the application of linear analysis to music; surveys some current applications, and suggests a method of analysis combining pitch-class set theory and linear analysis. (315)

A402 1988 Gołąb, Maciej. "Analyse und Werk: Zu den Polemiken über Heinrich Schenkers Theorie." *International Review of The Aesthetics and Sociology of Music* 19/2: 197–215.
German translation of Gołąb's 1986 *Muzyka* article (see **A466** below).

A403 1988 Graybill, Roger. "Harmonic Circularity in Brahms's F Major Cello Sonata: An Alternative to Schenker's Reading in *Free Composition*." *Music Theory Spectrum* 10: 43–55.
Discusses Brahms's "experimentation" with sonata form, explores an anomaly in the tonal plan of the exposition of op. 99, and proposes an alternate reading to "stand alongside" Schenker's. (43)

A404 1988 Helman, Zofia. "Von Heinrich Schenkers Analytischer Methode bis zur generativen Theorie der tonalen Musik." *International Review of The Aesthetics and Sociology of Music* 19/2: 181–95.
German translation of Helman's 1986 *Muzyka* article (see **A470** below)

A405 1988 Hinton, Stephen. "Musikwissenschaft und Musiktheorie; oder, Die Frage nach der phänomenologischen Jungfräulichkeit." *Musiktheorie* 3/3: 195–204.
Discusses the debate between Forte and Taruskin regarding the place of music theory as a discipline. Considers Schenker's early works and the idea of organicism.

A406 1988 Irving, Howard, and H. Lee Riggins. "Advanced Uses of Mode Mixture in Haydn's Late Instrumental Works." *Canadian University Music Review* 9/1: 104–35.
Discusses modal mixture in the writings of Schenker and Kollmann; studies Haydn's use of mixture and third-relations.

A407 1988 Kinderman, William. "Directional Tonality in Chopin." In *Chopin Studies*, ed. by Jim Samson. Cambridge: Cambridge University Press: 195–220.

Discusses the nineteenth-century practice of directional tonality, where the tonic key is the goal, but not the originator, of tonal motion. Examines opp. 31, 38, and 49, demonstrating "how the modulatory structures of these works are integrated with the basic thematic material and reflected in harmonic and melodic detail." (196)

A408 1988 Komar, Arthur. "Pedagogically Speaking: The Pedagogy of Tonal
            Hierarchy." *In Theory Only* 10/5: 23–8.
      Responses: 1989 *In Theory Only* 11/3: 31–5 (C. Brower).
                     1988 *In Theory Only* 10/7: 31–5 (K. Mooney).
Using the Lerdahl/Jackendoff definition of *hierarchy* as "an organization composed of discrete elements or regions related in such a way that one element or region subsumes or contains other elements or regions," Komar discusses how such ideas are implemented in the theory classroom. (23)

A409 1988 Korsyn, Kevin. "Schenker and Kantian Epistemology." *Theoria*
            3: 1–58.
Discusses Schenker's use of the terms *Synthese* and *Kausalität*, in light of the role that the concepts play Kant's epistemology. Notes that Schenker's texts "gain new depth when [Kant's] influence is traced." (2)

A410 1988 Krebs, Harald. "Schenker's Changing View of Rameau: A Comparison of Remarks in *Harmony*, *Counterpoint*, and *Rameau or
            Beethoven*." *Theoria* 3: 59–72.
Discusses the "untold damages" that Rameau's theory has wrought on musical composition and theory, specifically in the separation of voice leading and harmony into separate disciplines. Discusses Schenker's view of Rameau throughout his writings. (59)

A411 1988 Lerdahl, Fred. "Tonal Pitch Space." *Music Perception* 5: 315–49.
"Introduces a [model of pitch space] that (1) treats pitches, chords, and regions within one framework, (2) correlates with the experimental data, and (3) connects in interesting ways with a variety of music theories." (315)

A412 1988 Laufer, Edward. "On the Fantasy." *Intégral* 2: 99–133.
Suggests that the procedure of the fantasy may be "expressed through a kind of motto, or middleground motive, which, restated and transformed, is the carrier of the musical denouement." Examines four works according to this view.

A413 1988 Lewis, Christopher. "Beginning Harmony: The Post-Schenkerian
            Dilemma." *Canadian University Music Review* 9/1: 136–56.
Discusses the problems of teaching Schenkerian analysis to undergraduates, drawing examples from Haydn, Beethoven, Schubert, and Schumann.

A414 1988 McCreless, Patrick Phillip. "Roland Barthes's *S/Z* From Musical
            Point of View." *In Theory Only* 10/7: 1–29.

Describes Barthes's career and thought vis-à-vis *S/Z* and its five "narrative codes" for understanding literary texts; discusses "certain intriguing parallels between Barthes's view of classic literary narratives . . . and current theoretical views, particularly those of Schenker." (1)

A415　1988　Pastille, William. "Strict Counterpoint and Free Composition." *Theoria* 3: 161–9.

Discusses Schenker's tripartite plan of study (counterpoint, thoroughbass, and free composition), anticipating Siegel's translation of the *Generalbaßbüchlein* (see above).

A416　1988　Plum, Karl-Otto, and William Drabkin. "Towards a Methodology for Schenkerian Analysis." *Music Analysis* 7/2: 143–64.

Discusses two ways of approaching a piece of music: moving from foreground to background or background to foreground, noting that Schenker's analyses take the latter path. Examines Salzer's analogy of deductive and inductive philosophical methods, respectively.

A417　1988　Proctor, Gregory A., and Herbert Lee Riggins. "Levels and the Reordering of Chapters in Schenker's *Free composition*." *Music Theory Spectrum* 10: 101–26.

Suggests that Schenker's theory is "incomplete in subtle ways, and is communicated through imperfect instruments." Discusses a foreground theory called "replacement figures" and the boundaries between the structural levels. (103)

A418　1988　Rast, Nicholas. "A Checklist of Essays and Reviews by Heinrich Schenker." *Music Analysis* 7/2: 121–32.

Contains a list of Schenker's early writings, including the articles published posthumously in *Der Dreiklang*. He includes call numbers from the Austrian National Library. Mentions, in a footnote, a forthcoming catalog of Schenker's original compostions, which is as yet unavailable.

A419　1988　Renwick, William. "Brackets and Beams in Schenker's Graphic Notation." *Theoria* 3: 73–85.

Discusses Schenker's analytical notation, especially his use of brackets and beams, noting the consistency with which he used symbols.

A420　1988　Rigaudière, Marc. "Les conceptions théoretiques de Heinrich Schenker et leur application à l'analyse musicale." Unpublished paper, University of Paris IV-Sorbonne.

Summarizes the status of Schenkerian research, comparing the influence of Schenkerian ideas in the United States and Europe. Presents an overview of Schenker's ideas and guidelines for application. Contains a discussion of Schenker's analysis of Chopin's op. 10/12. Examines possibilities of deviating from "Schenkerian orthodoxy."

A421 1988   Rink, John. "The Barcarolle: Auskomponierung and Apotheosis."
                In *Chopin Studies*, ed. by Jim Samson. Cambridge: Cambridge
                University Press: 195–220.

Discusses Chopin's practice of rarely "[expressing] an idea more than once in
the same manner," employing the "principle of variety." Suggests that *"Auskomponierung* . . . acts in conjunction with other agents of synthesis to define the
'essence' of the work, [enhancing] unity through the elaboration of an all-
embracing harmonic plan and [overcoming] the sense of thematic concatenation
implicit in the Barcarolle's form." (196)

A422 1988   Rothstein, William. "Phrase Rhythm in Chopin's Nocturnes and
                Mazurkas." In *Chopin Studies*, ed. by Jim Samson. Cambridge:
                Cambridge University Press: 115–41.

Discusses hypermeter in the nocturnes and mazurkas, addressing the "rhythm
problem," the "tyranny of the four-bar phrase." Discusses Chopin's rhythmic
style.

A423 1988   Samson, Jim. "The Composition-Draft of the Polonaise-Fantasy:
                The Issue of Tonality." In *Chopin Studies*, ed. by Jm Samson.
                Cambridge: Cambridge University Press: 41–58.

Examines the genesis and the tonal structure of Chopin's op. 61, citing previous
analyses by Nowik and Kalber.

A424 1988   Schachter, Carl. "Chopin's Fantasy Op. 49: The Two-Key
                Scheme." In *Chopin Studies*, ed. by Jim Samson. Cambridge:
                Cambridge University Press: 221–53. Reprinted in *Unfoldings:
                Essays in Schenkerian Theory and Analysis*, ed. by Joseph N.
                Straus. Oxford: Oxford University Press, 1999: 260–88.

Discusses directional tonality in the context of Schenker's analytical theories,
asking four questions: "1) is the piece tonally unified? can one understand it in
terms of a single governing tonal center, or does it flesh out a progression from
an initial center to a closing one of equal status? 2) If there is a single primary
tonic, which one is it? 3) How does the composer establish its primacy? and 4)
What is the artistic purpose of the two-key scheme; how does it influence the
piece's larger structure, its details, and its expressive character?" (260)

A425 1988   Siegel, Heidi, and Arthur Maisel. "Heinrich Schenker: Graphic
                Analysis of Brahms's *Auf dem Kirchhofe*, Op. 105, No. 4." *Theory and Practice* 13: 1–14.

Presents Schenker's analysis of Brahms's *Auf dem Kirchhofe* that was prepared
by William Mitchell and Felix Salzer.

A426 1988   Tepping, Susan. "A Lesson in Analysis: An Account of the Study
                of Bach's E Major Invention with Felix-Eberhard von Cube." *Indiana Theory Review* 9/1: 63–74.

A companion piece to her interview transcript; discusses the analytical work in detail.

A427 1988 Willner, Channan. "Chromaticism and the Mediant in Four Late Haydn Works." *Theory and Practice* 13: 79–114.
Discusses the use of the mediant key in the development sections of Piano Sonata in C (Hob. XVI: 50), the finale of Symphony no. 98, the first movement of Symphony no. 101, and the finale of Symphony no. 104. Speculates on the extent to which the mediant is a principal harmonic goal.

A428 1987 Agawu, V. Kofi. "The First Movement of Beethoven's Opus 132 and the Classical Style." *College Music Symposium* 27: 30–45.
Examines how Beethoven "retains both the procedural premises and material sources of the classical style [while he] calls into question one of its fundamental assumptions" thus delineating the "limits of the Classical style." Using Schenkerian techniques, proposes to present a new analytical method. (31)

A429 1987 Beach, David. "Motivic Repetition in Beethoven's Piano Sonata Op. 110." *Intégral* 1: 1–29 and 2: 75–98.
Shows how op. 110 can be regarded as the working out of a single motivic idea, and how "the motivic derivation of the Adagio and Arioso [stems from] the initial phrase of the first movement." Examines Beethoven's use of register in the work. (2)

A430 1987 Beach, David. "The First Movement of Mozart's Piano Sonata in A Minor, K. 310: Some Thoughts on Structure and Performance." *Journal of Musicological Research* 7: 157–86.
Discusses ideas on the relationship of analysis to performance; examines the work, focusing on "1) phrase structure and metric organization; 2) important repetitions of ideas and their articulation; 3) long- and short-term goals; and finally 4) motivic repetitions, both obvious and concealed." (157)

A431 1987 Cook, Nicholas. "Musical Form and the Listener." *Journal of Aesthetics and Art Critisism* 46/1: 23–9.
Discusses the cognition of musical form, citing the theories of Schenker and Schoenberg. Also examines the issue of unity of parts to whole and large-scale perception of closure.

A432 1987 Cook, Nicholas. "The Perception of Large-Scale Tonal Closure." *Music Perception* 5/2: 197–205.
Details an experiment in which "listeners were required to evaluate a number of compositions in two versions, one of which was in each case tonally closed while the other was not." Suggests that music theory "is more usefully regarded as a means of understanding such organization than as a means of making empirically verifiable predictions regarding the effects of music upon listeners." (197)

A433 1987 Damschroder, David. "Structural Levels: A Key to Liszt's Chromatic Art." *College Music Symposium* 27: 46–58.
Suggests that the music of Liszt is "of critical importance in the careful reassessment of chromatic practice." Analyzes five excerpts according to Schenker's theory of levels. (46)

A434 1987 Dunsby, Jonathan. "The Formal Repeat." *Journal of the Royal Musical Association* 112/2: 196–207.
Examines the work of Schenker and Cone, suggesting that the repeat at the end of a sonata exposition is an integral part of the structure of eighteenth-century music, while used much less frequently in the twentieth century. Examines the "formal repeat" in works of Beethoven.

A435 1987 Everett, Walter. "Text-Painting in the Foreground and Middleground of Paul McCartney's Beatle Song 'She's Leaving Home': A Musical Study of Psychological Conflict." *In Theory Only* 9/7: 5–21.
A detailed study of the text and a Schenkerian approach to the musical structure combine to indicate how text painting works at levels below the surface to characterize a family's set of blurred perceptions of each other in McCartney's "She's Leaving Home," from the Beatles' album *Sgt. Pepper's Lonely Hearts Club Band*. (RILM; used by permission)

A436 1987 Federhofer, Hellmut, trans. by Stanisław Spulskizy. "Dzieła Chopina jako przykłady w podręcznikach zakresu teorii muzyki." *Rocznik chopinowski* 19: 151–62.
Examines examples from Chopin's works in the writings of Riemann, Lissa, Stohr, Leichtentritt, Chominski, and Schenker.

A437 1987 Forte, Allen. "Liszt's Experimental Idiom and Music of the Early Twentieth Century." *Nineteenth-Century Music* 10: 209–28.
Examines Liszt's "experimental" music, in which he, in his use of similar structural aspects to Bartók, Scriabin, and Schoenberg, "anticipated a significant historical development." (210)

A438 1987 Gagné, David. "Monteverdi's *Ohimé dov'é il mio ben* and the Romanesca." *The Music Forum* VI/1. New York: Columbia University Press: 61–92.
Outlines the origins and development of the Romanesca; analyzes Monteverdi's madrigal according to Schenkerian ideas.

A439 1987 Hefling, Stephen. "'Of the Manner of Playing the Adagio': Structural Levels and Performance Practice in Quantz's *Versuch*." *Journal of Music Theory* 31.2: 205–23.

Discusses the section on ornamentation from Quantz's treatise, noting especially his treatment of dynamics. Traces, through Schenkerian techniques, the musical significance of Quantz's dynamic markings.

A440 1987 Kurth, Ulrich. "Alte Musik im Werk Heinrich Schenkers und Felix Salzers." In *Alte Musik als asthetische Gegenwart: Bericht über den internationalen musikwissenschaftlichen Kongreß Stuttgart 1985*, vol. 2, ed. by Dietrich Burke and Dorthee Hanemann. Kassel: Bärenreiter: 337–42.

Examines Schenker's writings from "Der Geist" through *Das Meisterwerk* II, providing an overview of Schenker's aesthetics. Cites the work of Salzer (*Sinn und Wesen* and *Structural Hearing*); discusses the "amerikalischen Reformschenkerismus" movement founded by Weisse, Katz, Salzer, and Mitchell. (340)

A441 1987 Larson, Steve. "A Tonal Model of an 'Atonal' Piece: Schoenberg's Op. 15/2." *Perspectives of New Music* 25/1–2: 418–33.

Describes the song as having tonal underpinnings, over which atonal and tonally ambiguous passages are superposed. Discusses levels of meaning in the text, also.

A442 1987 Martin, Henry. "Syntax in Music and Drama." *In Theory Only* 10/1–2: 65–78.

Examines the correlation between Chomsky's deep structure and Schenker's *Ursatz*—and the problems of such comparisons. Discusses the playwriting theory of Bernard Grebanler, which is "strikingly similar to Schenker's theory of tonal music." Explores the analogies among the approaches. (66)

A443 1987 Marsden, Alan. "A Study of Cognitive Demands in Listening to Mozart's Quintet for Piano and Wind Instruments K. 452." *Psychology of Music* 15/1: 30–57.

Discusses the work using the theories of Komar and Schenker to model the cognitive processes of listeners.

A444 1987 Neumann, Frederick. "Conflicting Binary and Ternary Rhythms: From the Theory of Mensural Notation to the Music of J. S. Bach." *The Music Forum* VI/1. New York: Columbia University Press: 93–128.

Discusses the performance problems inherent in simultaneous binary and ternary rhythms from their roots in mensuration theory through the usage of Bach.

A445 1987 Neumeyer, David. "The Urlinie from $\hat{8}$ as a Middleground Phenomenon." *In Theory Only* 9/5–6: 3–25.
Responses: 1989 *In Theory Only* 11/3: 13–30 (D. Neumeyer).
1990 *In Theory Only* 11/5: 9–17 (D. Beach).
1990 *In Theory Only* 11/5: 19–22 (D. Neumeyer).

Surveys writings of Schenker, Schachter, Salze, and Forte regarding the status of
the *Urlinie* from $\hat{8}$. Suggests that it is better understood as a middleground line
than as a background structure; based partly on von Cube's ideas.

A446 1987   Neumeyer, David. "The Ascending Urlinie." *Journal of Music
Theory* 31/2: 275–303.
     Response: 1988   *Journal of Music Theory* 32/2: 271–94 (D. Beach).
Based partly on Zuckerkandl's ideas; surveys Schenker's early works, noting his
gradual preference for descending lines. Suggests that, for some pieces, an ascending line presents "a closer correspondence between the motivic and thematic materials of the surface of the music." (301)

A447 1987   Neumeyer, David. "The Three-Part Ursatz." *In Theory Only*
19/1–2: 3–29.
     Response: 1987   *In Theory Only* 10/4: 11–31 (S. Larson).
Suggests a three-voiced model of the *Ursatz*, including a structural alto, that "is
useful when one is uncertain whether the first tone of the *Urlinie* is $\hat{3}$ or $\hat{5}$." This
model is also useful in amelioratring the "confusion between [ascertaining] the
roles of structural soprano and cover tone." (4–5)

A448 1987   Pastille, William. "Schenker's Brahms." *The American Brahms
Society Newsletter* 5/2: 1–2.
Discusses the role Brahms played for Schenker, noting the profound impression
that their conversations had for him.

A449 1987   Rink, John. "Chopin i Schenker: Improwizacja a struktura."
Rocznik chopinowski 19: 163–76.
Examines the Polonaise-Fantasy of Chopin, op. 61; discusses the relationship of
improvisation and tonal structure.

A450 1987   Roth, Lynette. "Kirnberger's Concept of Musical Reduction." *In
Theory Only* 9/8: 21–6.
Examines Kirnberger's theoretical writings, commenting on his use of reductive
analysis. Discusses the insights gained therefrom regarding eighteenth-century
ornamentation; notes his foreshadowing of Schenker's analytical techniques.

A451 1987   Schachter, Carl. "Rhythm and Linear Analysis: Aspects of
Meter." *The Music Forum* VI/1. New York: Columbia University
Press: 1–60. Reprinted in *Unfoldings: Essays in Schenkerian
Theory and Analysis,* ed. by Joseph N. Straus. Oxford: Oxford
University Press, 1999: 79–121.
Discusses perceived rhythm and meter, such as situations where the "time signa-
ture seems not to correspond to the actual meter of a passage" and "conflicts be-
tween the metrical and the tonal or durational emphases of a passage." (80)

A452 1987 Schachter, Carl. "The Gavotte en Rondeaux from J. S. Bach's Partita in E Major for Unaccompanied Violin." *Israel Studies in Musicology* 4: 7–26.
Discusses the relationships between poetry and music with regard to the rondeau. Contains a graphic analysis of the work.

A453 1987 Schachter, Carl. "Analysis by Key: Another Look at Modulation." *Music Analysis* 6/3: 289–318. Reprinted in *Unfoldings: Essays in Schenkerian Theory and Analysis,* ed. by Joseph N. Straus. Oxford: Oxford University Press, 1999: 134–60.
Suggests that "a deep and intense hearing of music cannot be only from a moment-by-moment perspective, and existing concepts of modulation have surely not done justice to the piece of music as a "com-position"—something put together to form a unity." (135)

A454 1987 Straus, Joseph. "The Problem of Prolongation in Post-tonal Music." *Journal of Music Theory* 31/1: 1–21.
Notes that, after an initial period of activity, "theorists have virtually ceased to produce prolongational analyses of post-tonal music" because the approach seems to have failed. Discusses four conditions of traditional tonal prolongation that post-tonal music does not meet, and proposes a "more defensible approach to the middleground organization of post-tonal music." (1)

A455 1987 Sobaskie, James William. "Associative Harmony: The Reciprocity of Ideas in Musical Space." *In Theory Only* 10/1–2: 31–64.
Proposes a theory of associative harmony, which is "pitch collections that express secondary referential constructs, which are abstract partitionings of the pitch-class domain that serve as generative compositional ideas in some tonal works." (31)

A456 1987 Travis, Roy. "The Recurrent Figure in the Britten/Piper Opera *Death in Venice*." *The Music Forum* VI/1 (New York: Columbia University Press): 129–246.
Questions the motivation for having one singer represent seven characters in *Death in Venice*. Discusses the characters in turn and the music associated with them, noting relationships that lie below the surface.

A457 1987 Wagner, Naphtali. "Tonic References in Non-tonic Key Areas." *Israel Studies in Musicology* 24: 59–72.
Discusses references to the tonic as the "IV of V" in major or "VI of III" in minor, which are "reminders" of the tonic, and not part of a tonic prolongation. Examples drawn from Mozart and Clementi.

A458 1986 Bent, Ian. "Heinrich Schenker, Chopin and Domenico Scarlatti." *Music Analysis* 5/2–3: 131–50.

Examines the position of Chopin and Scarlatti in Schenker's "aggressively Germanic scale of values." Based on his writings in *Der Tonwille* and *Das Meisterwerk in der Musik*. (132)

A459 1986 Brown, Matthew. "The Diatonic and the Chromatic in Schenker's Theory of Harmonic Relations." *Journal of Music Theory* 30/1: 1–33.

Demonstrates that (1) in the *Harmonielehre*, Schenker derived a fully chromatic tonal system from the tonic triad; (2) chromatic triads do not substitute for or elaborate diatonic chords but are generated directly from the tonic triad; and (3) Schenker used this theory in *Der freie Satz* to generate chromatic events as far back as the deep middleground. (2)

A460 1986 Cavett-Dunsby, Esther. "Schenker's Analysis of the *Eroica* Finale." *Theory and Practice* 11: 43–51.

Reacts to Schenker's analysis, suggesting that it is valuable both for its treatment of variation form and for the development of Schenker's theories.

A461 1986 Cinnamon, Howard. "Tonic Arpeggiation and Successive Equal Third Relations as Elements of Tonal Evolution in the Music of Franz Liszt." *Music Theory Spectrum* 8: 1–24.

Examines five pieces of Liszt to "demonstrate a continuity of tonal practice and development, suggesting the degree to which structural procedures found in these pieces may be characteristic of Liszt's compositional style specifically, and that of nineteenth-century music in general." (1)

A462 1986 Deliege, Célestin. "L'analyse post-Schenkerienne: Quand et pourquoi?" *Analyse musicale* 2: 12–20.

Examines *Träumerei* by Schumann according to Schenkerian reductive techniques

A463 1986 Everett, Walter. "Fantastic Remembrance in John Lennon's 'Strawberry Fields Forever' and 'Julia.' " *Musical Quarterly* 72/3: 360–93.

After examining the use of fantasy and memory in the music of the Beatles, Everett provides transcriptions and voice-leading graphs of the two works. Includes an appendix of several thematically related texts.

A464 1986 Federhofer, Hellmut. "Heinrich Schenker," trans. by Zofia Helman and Maciej Gołąb. *Muzyka* 31/4: 5–24.

Compares Schenker's system with Riemann, Rameau, and Kurth; applies Schenker's method to excerpts from Beethoven's *Waldstein* and Chopin's Nocturne in E Flat and Etude in F, op. 10/8. Presents biographical information.

A465 1986 Gjeringen, Robert O. "The Formation and Deformation of Classic/Romantic Phrase Schemata: A Theoretical Model and Historical Study." *Music Theory Spectrum* 8: 25–43.

Eighteenth- and early-nineteenth-century composers generally chose from a repertoire of stock patterns, or schemata, when crafting musical phrases. These phrase schemata were formed and subsequently altered in response to new aesthetic and cultural demands. (RILM; used by permission)

A466 1986 Gołąb, Maciej. "Analiza i dzieło: Na marginesie polemik wokół teorii Heinricha Schenkera." *Muzyka* 31/4: 25–41.
Considers (1) the relationship between theory and analysis; (2) "logical fallacies" of Schenkerian theory; (3) specific criticisms of Meyer and Narmour; and (4) the theory of Lerdahl/Jackendoff. Espouses the removal of the *Ursatz* as a condition for the acceptance of Schenkerian theory. (40–1)

A467 1986 Gołąb, Maciej. "Główne nurty badań Schenkerowskich. Bibliografia z lat 1904–1984." *Muzyka* 31/4: 67–84.
A bibliography covering eighty years (211 items) of Schenkerian research.

A468 1986 Gołąb, Maciej. "Leksykon terminologii Schenkerowskiej." *Muzyka* 31/4: 56–66.
Defines some forty terms of Schenker, in Polish and English.

A469 1986 Gut, Serge. "Analyse musicale en musicology: Le choix des methods pour l'analyse d'un lied de Hugo Wolf." *Analyse Musicale* 2: 52–8.
Suggests that no single analytical technique is suitable for "transitional" nineteenth- and early-twentieth-century works. Wolf's *Das verlassene Mägdlein* is analyzed using Schenkerian techniques.

A470 1986 Helman, Zofia. "Od metody analitycznej Heinricha Schenkera do generatywnej teorii muzyki tonalnej." *Muzyka* 31/4: 43–58.
Discusses (1) Schenker's theories in light of the development of tonal theory; and (2) current Schenkerian research. Discusses the generative theory of Lerdahl/Jackendoff and the implication-realization model of Meyer/Narmour.

A471 1986 Kamien, Roger. "Subtle Enharmonic Relationships in Mozart's Music." *Journal of Music Theory* 30/2: 169–83.
Concerns enharmonic relationships that are not readily apparent because they are "obscured by differences of rhythm and thematic material." Examines seven works, showing how "subtle enharmonic relationships are clarified by additional musical associations, such as registral connection and hidden motivic repetition." (169–70)

A472 1986 Kielian-Gilbert, Marianne. "Motive Transfer in Chopin's A-Minor Prelude." *In Theory Only* 9/1: 21–32.
Discusses three types of motivic relations: (1) the coincidence of motivic and harmonic patterns, (2) the reinforcement or doubling of prominent pitches within motives, and (3) the transfer of intervallic motives from linear to harmonic structures.

A473 1986 Lamblin, André. "L'analyse tonale selon Schenker." *International Review of The Aesthetics and Sociology of Music* 17/2: 187–202.

      Responses: 1988 *International Review of The Aesthetics and Sociology of Music* 19/1: 117–9 (J. Dunsby).

                      1988 *International Review of The Aesthetics and Sociology of Music* 19/1: 119 (A. Lambin).

An introduction to Schenker's method.

A474 1986 Marston, Nicholas. "Schenker and Forte Reconsidered: Beethoven's Sketches for the Piano Sonata in E, Op. 109." *Nineteenth-Century Music* 10/1: 24–42.

Discusses the analyses of op. 109 by Forte and Schenker vis-à-vis Beethoven's sketches for the movement, noting that the end of the third movement functions simultaneously as an ending for the first.

A475 1986 Miller, Malcolm. "Schenkerian Analysis: A Practical Introduction, at Nottingham University 21–22 September 1985." *Music Analysis* 5/1: 119–21.

Discusses the results of the first course in Schenkerian analysis offered at Nottingham by Ian Bent and Robert Pascall, consisting of the historical perspective and practical application of Schenkerian analysis.

A476 1986 Miller, Patrick. "Report: Symposium on the Life and Music of Heinrich Schenker." *Theory and Practice* 11: 5.

Reports on the conference from 26 April 1986 at the Hartt School of Music, University of Hartford, which included two speakers and a concert of Schenker's music. This concert was preserved on disc by the Musical Heritage Society, catalog number MHS 522205H.

A477 1986 Phipps, Graham. "A Response to Schenker's Analysis of Chopin's Etude Opus 10, No. 12, Using Schoenberg's *Grundgestalt* Concept." *Musical Quarterly*, 69/4: 543–69.

Considers whether the "surface of a given musical composition [is] generated by [the higher structural levels] . . . or [whether] the architecture generated by the surface." This question is brought into relief through the application of the two differing analytical approaches. (543)

A478 1986 Purroy Chicot, Pedro. "Heinrich Schenker a través de Felix Salzer, como una posible alternativa de comprensión y progreso, o la necesidad de un nuevo planteamiento." *Nassarre: Revista aragonesa de musicología* 2/1: 71–94.

A survey of different views on harmony, including those of Rameau, C. P. E. Bach, and especially Schoenberg and Schenker. Advocates the study of Schenkerian theory in music schools through Salzer's methods. (RILM; used by permission)

A479 1986 Rothfarb, Lee. "Ernst Kurth in Historical Perspective: His Intellectual Inheritance and Music-Theoretical Legacy." *Schweizer Jahrbuch für Musikwissenschaft* 6/7: 23–41.

Contrasts the "dynamicist, psychologically oriented, 'experiential-theoretical'" perspective of Kurth with the "syntactic, 'material-theoretical'" approaches of Riemann and Schenker. Notes Kurth's influence on Toch, Zuckerkandl, Westphal, and Meyer. (RILM 89–09105; used by permission)

A480 1986 Rothstein, William. "The Americanization of Heinrich Schenker." *In Theory Only* 9/1: 5–17. Reprinted in *Schenker Studies*, ed. by Heidi Siegel. Cambridge: Cambridge University Press: 193–203.

Discusses "Schenkerism in America," suggesting that, while America readily absorbs foreign ideas, these ideas must be "flexible enough to fit certain basic American preconceptions." (6)

A481 1986 Salzer, Felix. "The Significance of the Ornaments in Carl Philipp Emanuel Bach's Keyboard Works." *Theory and Practice* 11: 15–42.

Suggests that, rather than simply providing an "enlivening" effect, Bach's ornaments "actively participate in the shaping of motives, and frequently even influence the voice-leading." (16)

A482 1986 Swain, Joseph. "The Need for Limits in Hierarchical Theories of Music." *Music Perception* 4/1: 121–48.

Suggests that "any hierarchical theory should be limited because the amount of information humans are able to take in and process is limited." According to gestalt theories of perception, events are limited to four per level, which may be exceeded by grouping them into musical constituents. (121)

A483 1986 Tepping, Susan. "Sonata and Fugue: The Finale of Mozart's String Quartet in G. K. 387." *Gamut* 3: 55–77.

An examination of the quartet using Schenkerian techniques.

A484 1986 Wen, Eric. "A Tritone Key Relationship: The Bridge Sections of the Slow Movement of Mozart's 39th Symphony." *Music Analysis* 5/1: 59–84.

Examines the anomaly of the tritone relationship in the recapitulation of the movement (i.e., the second theme is transposed a tritone away from its original statement).

A485 1986 Wintle, Christopher. "'Skin and Bones': The C-Minor Prelude from J. S. Bach's Well-Tempered Clavier, Book II." *Music Analysis* 5/2–3: 85–96.

Poses a question: "[I]f it can be demonstrated that Schenker's 'background forces' are also integral to Baroque tonal music, may one not also find precedent in this earlier repertoire, not just for parallelism, but for the treatment of its temporal aspect as well?" Examines BWV 871 for the affirmative answer. (85)

A486 1986 Williamson, John. "The Structural Premises of Mahler's Introductions: Prolegomena to an Analysis of the First Movement of the Seventh Symphony." *Music Analysis* 5: 29–57.

Examines the introductions of Mahler's symphonies as structural upbeats, noting the different types of structures he employs (e.g., beginning with an auxiliary cadence).

A487 1985 Damschroder, David. "Pedagogically Speaking: Structural Levels and the College Freshman." *In Theory Only* 8/6:17–25.

"[Demonstrates] the value of separating figured-bass and Roman-numeral analyses and show how this separation fosters the development of concepts of prolongation and structural levels, thus preparing students for more advanced analytical training." (17)

A488 1985 Drabkin, William. "A Lesson in Analysis from Heinrich Schenker: The C-Major Prelude from Bach's *Well-Tempered Clavier*, Book 1." *Music Analysis* 4/3: 241–58.

Transcribes and discusses a letter from Schenker to von Cube describing the structure of BWV 846.

A489 1985 Forte, Allen. "Tonality, Symbol, and Structural Levels in Berg's *Wozzeck*." *The Musical Quarterly* 71/4: 474–99.

Examines the F-minor variation from III/I of *Wozzeck* from both a tonal (Schenkerian) perspective and an atonal perspective. Suggests that the "composer's use of tonal referents in this music is highly significant with respect to the work as a whole and that the music engages in a concise and very special manner certain general questions concerning Berg's music [regarding musical symbolism and structural levels]." (474)

A490 1985 Headlam, Dave. "A Rhythmic Study of the Exposition in the Second Movement of Beethoven's Quartet Op. 59/1." *Music Theory Spectrum* 7: 114–38.

Employs Schachter's ideas that "the interaction of [tonal and durational rhythm] creates the rhythmic life of a piece." Also utilizes rhythmic hierarchy, including hypermeter. (114)

A491 1985 Hoyt, Reed. "In Defense of Music Analysis." *Musical Quarterly* 71/1: 38–51.

Examines attacks on musical analysis by Treitler and Kerman; states what the author believes the purpose of analysis to be.

A492 1985 Hoyt, Reed. "Chopin's Prelude in A Minor Revisited: The Issue of Tonality." *In Theory Only* 8: 5–18.

Examines analyses by Schenker (voice leading), Meyer (motivic alteration), and Rodgers (rhythmic proportions). Discusses how the key of A minor is established.

A493 1985 Hoyt, Reed. "Recurring Implications and Long-Range Melodic Relationships in Beethoven's Sonata op. 31/3." *Gamut* 2: 53–82.

The organic approach to music analysis can be extended to newer methodology, both Schenkerian and post-Schenkerian. By using post-Schenkerian techniques, we can see that the outer voices of the themes of Beethoven's Sonata op. 31, no. 3, have intermovement melodic implications, which are transformed in various ways throughout the sonata but are only fully realized at the end. (RILM; used by permission)

A494 1985 Judd, Christle Collins. "Some Problems of Pre-Baroque Analysis: An Examination of Josquin's *Ave Maria . . . Virgo Serena*." *Music Analysis* 4: 201–39.

"[Explores] the applicability of existing techniques to this repertory, suggests modifications of these techniques and proposes a systematic method for the application of aspects of Renaissance theory in an analytical, as well as a descriptive, context." (201)

A495 1985 Krebs, Harald. "The Background Level in Some Tonally Deviating Works of Franz Schubert." *In Theory Only* 8/8: 5–18.

Discusses the difficulty of conceiving directionally tonal works as prolonging a single triad at the background level.

A496 1985 Mark, Christopher. "Contextually Transformed Tonality in Britten." *Music Analysis* 4: 265–87.

Examines Britten's Quartet op. 25, showing how the form is articulated by the tonal functions. (265)

A497 1985 McNamee, Ann. "The Role of the Piano Introduction in Schubert's *Lieder*." *Music Analysis* 4: 95–106.

"[Examines] the introductory passages from seven Schubert songs and identifies various melodic motives in the piano introduction which take on greater significance when they recur in the subsequent music, both in the piano and the voice and at both the foreground and middleground levels." (95)

A498 1985 Schmalfeldt, Janet. "On the Relation of Analysis to Performance: Beethoven's Bagatelles Op. 126, Nos. 2 and 5." *Journal of Music Theory* 29: 1–31.

Presents a dialogue between analyst and performer in which eclectic methods of analysis are employed.

A499 1985 Schulenberg, David. "Modes, Prolongations, and Analysis." *Journal of Musicology* 4/3: 303–29.

Discusses the problems of applying Schenker's ideas to pre-tonal music; offers a "critical review of a number of analytical approaches taken by various writers toward non-tonal music." Show that "modality . . . is a different type of system which . . . still renders comprehensible and coherent the music of styles that do not seek the same types of order . . . as tonal works." (303, 329)

A500 1985 Tanenbaum, Faun. "Tonal Identity in *Simon Boccanegra.*" *Verdi Newsletter* 13: 20–9.
Analysis of Verdi's 1881 revision to the 1857 version from a Schenkerian viewpoint. A comparison of specific foreground and middleground events reveals significant elements in Verdi's style and suggests possible reasons for the revisions.

A501 1985 Wintle, Christopher. "*Kontra-Schenker: Largo e mesto* from Beethoven's Op. 10/3." *Music Analysis* 4/1–2: 145–82.
Examines the recapitulation of op. 10/3, discussing "early 19th-c. description of key-characteristics and [examining] the affective and structural role of diminished and augumented intervals. The formulation of a counter-structure, which is shown to interact with the Schenkerian voice-leading structure, in a quasi-contrapuntal way, concludes the inquiry." (RILM 85–06089; used by permission)

A502 1984 Adrian, Jack. "Pedagocally Speaking: On Studying Species Counterpoint Before Studying Harmony." *In Theory Only* 8/2: 15–9.
Suggests that the problems encountered in writing harmony exercises would be lessened if the student were to focus on strict counterpoint first, as the student would be applying skills already learned, instead of focusing on an entirely new concept.

A503 1984 Agawu, V. Kofi. "Analytical Issues Raised by Bartók's *Improvisations for Piano* Op. 20." *Journal of Musicological Research* 5: 131–63.
Surveys analytical approaches to Bartók's music, including those of Parks (atonal), Bartók (tonal), Babbitt (a compromise between the two), and Antokoletz (emphasis on the folk music/art music dichotomy). Agawu approaches the pieces from the viewpoints of Schenker (structural levels), Forte (set theory), and Lenvai (axis system).

A504 1984 Баский, В. "О теории Х. Шенкера и 'музыке настоящего'." *Советская музіка* 1: 121–2.

[1984 Barskii, V(ictor). "The Theory of H. Schenker and 'genuine music.'" *Sovetskaia Muzyka* 1: 121–2.]
One of the few Soviet-era, Russian-language publications about Schenker; presents basic concepts in a nontechnical manner and includes a discussion about Schenker's aesthetic ideas. Mentions the work of Schachter, Epstein, Benjamin, and Yurii Kholopov (see **A631** below).

A505 1984 Beach, David. "Motive and Structure in the Andante Movement of Mozart's Piano Sonata K. 545." *Music Analysis* 3/3: 227–36. Discusses the work, concentrating on voice leading and concealed motivic structure.

A506 1984 Cadwallader, Allen. "Schenker's Unpublished Graphic Analysis of Brahms's Intermezzo Op. 117, No. 2: Tonal Structure and Concealed Motivic Repetition." *Music Theory Spectrum* 6: 1–13. "[Demonstrates] how Schenker's analysis of Brahms's B-flat minor intermezzo illuminates the progressively enlarged, hidden repetitions of a foreground motive, and [describes] how these repetitions unify the various sections and levels of the piece." (1)

A507 1984 Caplin, William. "Moritz Hauptmann and the Theory of Suspensions." *Journal of Music Theory* 28/2: 251–69. "Hauptmann appeals continually to these three dialectical components in order to distinguish between musical phenomena that are logical and comprehensible and those that violate the universal laws of nature and should thus be banned from compositional practice." (252)

A508 1984 Cinnamon, Howard. "Some Elements of Tonal and Motivic Stucture in *In diesen Wintertagen,* Op. 14, No. 2 by Arnold Schoenberg: A Schoenbergian-Schenkerian Study." *In Theory Only* 7/7–8: 23–49. Describes the song's form, tonal structure, and motivic development. Demonstrates "how a combined application of Schoenbergian and Schenkerian concepts can elucidate the tonal and motivic structure in a more complete way than either approach could achieve independently." (23)

A509 1984 Deliège, Célestin. "Some Unresolved Problems in Schenkerian Theory." In *Musical Grammars and Computer Analysis*, ed. by M. Baroni and L. Callegari. Olschiki: Firenze: 71–82. Discusses Schenkerian theory as "a starting point from which more exact proposals may be put forward." Suggests amendments to the theory, such as dispensing with the middleground and the *Ursatz.* Contains discussions of a recitative from Scarlatti's *Attilio Regolo* and Chopin's op. 28/2. (71)

A510 1984 Drabkin, William. "Felix-Eberhard von Cube and the North-German Tradition of Schenkerism." *Proceedings of the Royal Musical Association* 111: 180–207. After an introduction describing the growth of "Schenkerism," Drabkin discusses the life and works of von Cube, the principal exponent of Schenker's theories in Germany. Subjects include his studies with Schenker through 1926, the founding of the Schenker-Institut, and von Cube's *Lehrbuch.* Contains an excerpt from von Cube's Sonata in A-flat Major.

A511 1984 Dunsby, Jonathan. "A Bagatelle on Beethoven WoO 60." *Music Analysis* 3: 57–68.
Examines Beethoven's G Minor Bagatelle, exploring the issue of tonality where the reprise "is preceded by [prolongations of V, flat-VI, and III] only." (57)

A512 1984 Forte, Allen. "Middleground Motives in the *Adagietto* of Mahler's Fifth Symphony." *Nineteenth-Century Music* 8/2: 153–63.
Discusses motive as (1) fundamentally an intervallic structure; and (2) not restricted to the foreground stratum. Suggests the term *motivic counterpoint* which creates a "significant degree of analytical advantage" in examining motivic unity in a piece. (153)

A513 1984 Gilbert, Steven. "Gershwin's Art of Counterpoint." *Musical Quarterly* 70: 423–56.
Examines the *Concerto in F* and *Rhapsody in Blue*, using a "modified Schenkerian approach." (423)

A514 1984 Lerdahl, Fred, and Ray Jackendoff. "An Overview of Hierarchical Structure in Music." *Music Perception* 1/2: 229–52.
"[Presents] four kinds of hierarchical structure in music: grouping structure, metrical structure, time-span reduction, and proilongational reduction" making comparisons with Schenker's theory. (1)

A515 1984 Narmour, Eugene. "Some Major Theoretical Problems Concerning the Concept of Hierarchy in the Analysis of Tonal Music." *Music Perception* 1/2: 199–229.
Notes that the "systematic" view of level analysis does not "distinguish compositional structures from perceptual structures." Formulates a "theory that relies on the cognitive concepts of return, reversal, and continuation (i.e., similarity) as regards the parameters of melody, harmony, and duration" and applies this to Mozart's K. 331, comparing analyses of DeVoto, Lester, Schenker, and Meyer. (199)

A516 1984 Noden-Skinner, Cheryl. "Tonal Ambiguity in the Opening Measures of Selected Works by Chopin." *College Music Symposium* 24/2: 28–34.
Discusses Chopin's methods of "suspending tonality" through his use of "a series of altered chords which have no traditional harmonic function." Contains a percentage table of non-tonic openings. (28)

A517 1984 Pastille, William A. "Heinrich Schenker: Anti-Organicist." *Nineteenth-Century Music* 8/1: 28–36.
Examines the view of musical organicism presented in *Der Geist des musikalisches Technik*, noting that it "is precisely the opposite of that expressed in Schenker's later works. He firmly denies that music can be organic." Describes his embracing of the organic metaphor in *Harmonielehre* and *Der Tonwille*. (31)

A518 1984 Phipps, Graham. "Comprehending Twelve-Tone Music as an Extension of the Primary Musical Language of Tonality." *College Music Symposium* 24/2: 35–54.
Notes the conservatism of Schoenberg's approach to tonality, imparted through Sechter. Examines passages from his *Harmonielehre* (1911) that reject the concept of atonality.

A519 1984 Rothgeb, John. "Translating Texts on Music Theory: Heinrich Schenker's *Kontrapunkt.*" *Theory and Practice* 9/1–2: 71–5.
A commentary on the Rothgeb/Thym translation of *Kontrapunkt*; discusses the difficulties of translating Schenker.

A520 1984 Rothstein, William. "Heinrich Schenker as an Interpreter of Beethoven's Piano Sonatas." *Nineteenth-Century Music* 8/1: 3–27.
Based on four sources from the Oswald Jonas Memorial Collection: (1) an eighty-six-page manuscript titled *Vom Vortrag*; (2) a thirty-six-page typescript, titled *Entwuft einer 'Lehre vom Vortrag'*; (3) "numerous notes by Schenker on various sheets and scraps of paper"; and 4) a manuscript titled *Ein Kommentar zu Schindler, Beethovens Spiel betreffend.* This last item was published in *Der Dreiklang* (see B98 below). (4)

A521 1984 Walsh, Stephen. "Musical Analysis: Hearing is Believing?" *Music Perception* 2/2: 237–44.
"[Draws] attention to problems arising from the separation of the disciplines of perceptual psychology and musical analysis." Suggests that cognitive scientists are often ill informed about music and musicians often ill informed about cognitive science. (237)

A522 1984 Wagner, Aleksandra. "Na puta ka novoj teoriji muzike—Heinrich Schenker." *Zvuk* 3: 17–29.
Discusses the basic ideas of Schenker's theory; contains a discussion of Schenker's analysis of *Aus meinen Tränen spriessen.* Examines semiological and semantic approaches as well.

A523 1984 Wilson, Paul. "Concepts of Prolongation and Bartók's Opus 20." *Music Theory Spectrum* 6: 79–89.
Aims to "1) provide evidence of long-range structure within [op. 20]; 2) show some characteristic means by which Bartók set out and supported such structures; and 3) consider some issues about prolongation which these structures seem to raise quite directly." (79)

A524 1983 Baker, James. "Schenkerian Analysis and Post-Tonal Music." In *Aspects of Schenkerian Theory*, ed. by David Beach. New Haven: Yale University Press): 153–188.

Surveys and critiques applications of Schenker's ideas to post-tonal music; examines issues raised by "borderline" tonal-atonal works; and proposes an analytical approach, demonstrated on Scriabin's *Enigme*.

A525 1983 Beach, David. "A Recurring Pattern in Mozart's Music." *Journal of Music Theory* 27/1: 1–29.
Examines movements in which the mediant key, not the customary dominant, is the goal of the development section. Shows how this arpeggiation pattern is "related to the primary motivic component of that movement." Discusses K. 280, K. 332, and K. 333. (1–2)

A526 1983 Beach, David. "Schenker's Theories: A Pedagogical View." In *Aspects of Schenkerian Theory*, ed. by David Beach. New Haven: Yale University Press: 1–38.
Discusses a pedagogical plan for Schenkerian analysis: (1) counterpoint and harmony; (2) Schenkerian analysis proper, including (a) introduction, (b) principles of graphic notation, and (c) advanced studies; and (3) readings and related studies including both Schenker's writings and secondary sources. Includes a short bibliography of extensions to Schenker's theories.

A527 1983 Burkhart, Charles. "Schenker's Theory of Levels and Musical Performance." In *Aspects of Schenkerian Theory*, ed. by David Beach. New Haven: Yale University Press: 95–112.
Discusses references to performance throughout Schenker's writings; considers what bearing the "multi-level view" has on musical performance. Discusses articulating motivic parallelisms and the role of the background.

A528 1983 Burstein, L. Poundie. "A New View of *Tristan*: Tonal Unity in the Prelude and Conclusion to Act I." *Theory and Practice* 8/1: 15–41.
  Responses: 1983 *Theory and Practice* 8/2: 53–61 (A. Maisel).
                1983 *Theory and Practice* 8/2: 62–7 (B. McKinney).
Discusses the issue of directional tonality, stressing the difference between compositions that "seem to start in a key different from the background tonality and those that change keys midway." Poses three questions to ascertain the difference: "Does the tonal structure form a coherent whole? Can the separate sections be viewed independently, or do they only make sense within the larger structure? Is the final tonic, at least in retrospect, a logical outgrowth of the beginning?" (17)

A529 1983 Cadwallader, Allen. "Motivic Unity and Integration of Structural Levels in Brahms's B Minor Intermezzo, op. 119/1." *Theory and Practice* 8/2: 5–24.
Discusses "how the formal and harmonic structure of [the work] reflects the disguised repetitions of an initial foreground motive." (7)

A530 1983 Chew, Geoffrey. "The Spice of Music: Towards a Theory of the Leading Note." *Music Analysis* 2/1: 35–53.

Discusses the melodic semitone between 7̂ and 8̂, drawing from the writings of Schenker and Kurth. Shows "that the attractive force of the semitone, mentioned above, possesses fundamental importance in shaping the upper voices of tonal compositions secondary to those that carry the *Urlinie*." (35)

A531 1983 Cinnamon, Howard. "Chromaticism and Tonal Coherence in Liszt's Sonetto 104 del Petrarca." *In Theory Only* 7/3: 3–19.

Examines the work according to Schenkerian principles, to "illustrate those features which are both most original and most significant to its structural coherence." (3)

A532 1983 Dalhaus, Carl. "Im Namen Schenkers." *Die Musikforschung* 36/2: 82–7.

Responses: 1984 *Musikforschung* 37/1: 21–4 (H. Federhofer).
1984 *Musikforschung* 37/1: 24–6 (K. Plum).
1984 *Music Analysis* 3/3: 289–92: Summary of above.

Discusses Schenker's theories in general, taking issue with their application to pre- and post-tonal works. Critiques Federhofer's book *Akkord und Stimmführung*.

A533 1983 Dunsby, Jonathan. "The Multi-Piece in Brahms: *Fantasien* Op. 116." In *Brahms: Biographical, Documentary, and Analytical Studies*, ed. by R. Pascall. Cambridge: Cambridge University Press: 167–89.

Translation: Ramón Stilles. "La obra multiple en Brahms: Las fantasías op. 116." *Quodlibet: Revista de especialización musical* 9 (1997): 97–119.

Suggests how the seven pieces that comprise op. 116 may be construed as an organic whole; considers the works from a Schenkerian vantage point in showing their interrelatedness.

A534 1983 Forte, Allen. "Motivic Design and Structural Levels in the First Movement of Brahms's String Quartet in C Minor." *Musical Quarterly* 69: 471–502. Reprinted in *Brahms 2: Biographical, Documentary, and Analytical Studies*, ed. by Michael Musgrave. Cambridge: Cambridge University Press: 165–96.

Discusses form and "traditional features" of the music, as well as motivic unity. Examines the use of imitation and double counterpoint as it "relates to motivic design." Emphasizes pitches and dyads of structural importance that have a "catalytic role." (472)

A535 1983 Forte, Allen. "Foreground Rhythm in Early Twentieth-Century Music." *Music Analysis* 2/3: 239–68.

Examines the ways in which pitch and rhythmic structures interact in the non-tonal composition; examines works of Bartlók, Debussy, Schoenberg, Scriabin, Stravinsky, and Webern. Discusses "essential aspects of middleground structures using analytical representations, the proportional graph and the attack-release partition." (240)

A536 1983 Forte, Allen. "Motive and Rhythmic Contour in the Alto Rhapsody." *Journal of Music Theory* 27: 255–71. Reprinted in *Approaches to Tonal Analysis*, Garland Library of the History of Western Music, Vol. 14. New York: Garland, 1985: 23–40. ISBN 0-824-7463-7.

"Discusses several of the primary motives in the music and the ways in which they are expressed in rhythmic contours"; "presents some ideas about the significance of these motives as they occur throughout the work at various levels of structure." (255)

A537 1983 Kamien, Roger. "Analysis and Performance: Some Preliminary Observations." *Israel Studies in Musicology* 3: 156–70.

Demonstrates how analysis may be useful to performers in divining structural motives, understanding the relation of rhythm and meter, connections between themes, etc.

A538 1983 Kamien, Roger. "Aspects of Motivic Elaboration in the Opening Movement of Haydn's Piano Sonata in C-sharp Minor." In *Aspects of Schenkerian Theory*, ed. by David Beach. New Haven: Yale University Press: 77–112.

Discusses "the ways in which motives are rhythmically transformed and used on various structural levels"; shows how "a motive may be presented several times in succession, each time unfolding over a larger time span," what he calls *progressive motivic enlargement*. (77)

A539 1983 Kassler, Jamie Croy. "Heinrich Schenker's Epistemology And Philosophy of Music: An Essay on the Relations Between Evolutionary Theory and Music Theory." In *The Wider Domain of Evolutionary Thought*, ed. by D. Oldroyd and I. Langham. New York: D. Reidel: 221–60.

Discusses Schenker's ideas in the larger intellectual context; "[presents] the historical matrix which explains why Schenker adopts a particular solution to the music-theoretic problem." (222–223)

A540 1983 Keiler, Allan. "On Some Properties of Schenker's Pitch Derivations." *Music Perception* 1/2: 200–28.

"Examines aspects of Schenker's notation of pitch derivations and his concept of interruption (Unterbrechung) in order to establish some formal constraints as well as inadequacies of Schenker's analytical system from the point of view of pitch derivation." (200)

A541 1983 Larson, Steve. "On Analysis and Performance: The Contribution of Durational Reduction to the Performance of J. S. Bach's Two-Part Invention in C Major." *In Theory Only* 7/1: 31–45.
Response: 1983 *In Theory Only* 7/4: 25–35 (H. Cinnamon).
Suggests that the difficulty performers have with analysis stems from the unfamiliarity with analytic notation and their viewing of the graphing technique as a mental exercise only. Employs durational reduction to elucidate BWV 772.

A542 1983 Marcozzi, Rudy. "Deep-Level Structures in J. S. Bach's D Minor Chaccone." *Indiana Theory Review* 6/1–2: 5–16.
Examines the work from the Schenkerian viewpoint.

A543 1983 McCreless, Patrick. "Ernst Kurth and the Analysis of the Chromatic Music of the Late Nineteenth Century." *Music Theory Spectrum* 5: 56–75.
Surveys "aspects of Kurth's . . . contribution to the analysis of chromatic music," applying his approach to excerpts from *Götterdämmerung, Parsifal, and Siegfried.* (56)

A544 1983 Novack, Saul. "The Analysis of Pre-Baroque Music." In *Aspects of Schenkerian Theory*, ed. by David Beach. New Haven: Yale University Press: 113–34.
Considers criticisms of applying Schenker's ideas to pre-Baroque music; cites analyses of Salzer, and applies Schenkerian ideas to excerpts ranging from monophonic chants and rondeaux through the instrumental Canzonas of Isaac.

A545 1983 Parker, Roger, and Matthew Brown. "Motivic and Tonal Interaction in Verdi's *Un Ballo in Maschera.*" *Journal of the American Musicological Society* 36/2: 243–65. Reprinted in *Approaches to Tonal Analysis*, Garland Library of the History of Western Music, Vol. 14. New York: Garland, 1985: 363–85. ISBN 0-824-7463-7.
"[Reviews] Act I, scene I from several analytic perspectives; from this foundation we will consider certain aspects of the entire score and, ultimately, attempt to engage some general questions about the analysis of Verdi opera." (245–6)

A546 1983 Palmer, Virginia. "The Application of the Sonata Principle to Structure in *La Clemenza di Scipione* by J. C. Bach." *Indiana Theory Review* 6/1–2: 36–62.
After an introduction describing the operatic output and historical milieu of J. C. Bach, Palmer shows structural connections within the work.

A547 1983 Pople, Anthony. "Serial and Tonal Aspects of Pitch Structure in Act III of Berg's *Lulu.*" *Soundings* 10: 36–57.

Analyzes the *Konzertante Choral-Variationen* of III: 1 using Schenkerian techniques.

A548 1983   Rothgeb, John. "Thematic Content: A Schenkerian View." In *Aspects of Schenkerian Theory*, ed. by David Beach New Haven: Yale University Press: 39–60.

Presents Schenker's ideas on thematic analysis; "[illustrates] . . . the sorts of thematic features whose recognition and understanding seem . . . to be fostered by a Schenkerian view of tonal organization in general." (39)

A549 1983   Salzer, Felix. "Heinrich Schenker and Historical Research: Monteverdi's Madrigal *Oimé, se tanto amate*." in *Aspects of Schenkerian Theory*, ed. by David Beach. New Haven: Yale University Press: 135–52.

Suggests that Schenker's approach may aid in discovering "the development of tonality as tonal coherence and consequently the development of composition as a stratified organism." Presents a structural analysis, with commentary, of the madrigal. (136)

A550 1983   Samson, Jim. "Przeglad modeli analitycznych i próba ich zastosowania do analizy jezyka harmonicznego Karola Szymanowskiego." *Muzyka* 28/2: 27–36.

Surveys various analytical systems, including those of Schenker, Réti, and Lendvaï, to explain the harmonic language of Szymanowskiego.

A551 1983   Schachter, Carl. "The First Movement of Brahms's Second Symphony: The Opening Theme and Its Consequences." *Music Analysis* 2: 55–68.

Translation: 2001   Gil, Lores, and Juan Carlos. "El primer movimiento de la segunda sinfonia de Brahms: El tema inicial y sus consecuencias." *Quodlibet* 20: 90–105.

Inspired by a recollection of Gustave Jenner that, according to Brahms, "sonata form must be the necessary consequence of the themes," Schachter describes "how the motivic contents and character of the opening theme influence the structure and form of the exposition." (55)

A552 1983   Schachter, Carl. "Motive and Text in Four Schubert Songs." In *Aspects of Schenkerian Theory*, ed. by David Beach. New Haven: Yale University Press: 61–76. Reprinted in *Unfoldings: Essays in Schenkerian Theory and Analysis,* ed. by Joseph N. Straus. Oxford: Oxford University Press, 1984: 209–21.

Examines relationships "between the imagery of the poem and the motivic design of the music" in D. 300. D. 775, D. 531, and D. 827. (61)

A553 1983 [Schenker, Heinrich]. "The Opening of Beethoven's Sonata Op. 111: A Letter by Heinrich Schenker." *Theory and Practice* 7/1: 3–13.

Provides a translation of a draft of Schenker's response to an inquiry from an unnamed professor concerning Beethoven's op. 111. Explains the difference in notation in Schenker's edition (following Beethoven's manuscript) of the arpeggios in bars 2 and 4.

A554 1983 Schoffman, Nachum. "Descriptive Theory and the Standard Table of Triads." *Israel Studies in Musicology* 3: 144–55.

Examines the origins of the now-ubiquitous table of diatonic triads from Sorge's *Grosse General-Bass-Schule* of 1731 through Schoenberg's *Harmonielehre* of 1911.

A555 1983 Sharpe, Robert. "Two Forms of Unity in Music." *Music Review* 44/3–4: 274–86.

Response: *Music Review* 44/3–4: 97–102 (W. Reynolds).

Discusses "internal unity," e.g., thematic, rhythmic, and harmonic unity, versus "external unity," or "unity [that] cannot plausibly be accounted for on the basis of thematic transformation." (274)

A556 1983 Stein, Deborah. "The Expansion of the Subdominant in the Late Nineteenth Century." *Journal of Music Theory* 27/2: 153–80.

Examines the roles played by the subdominant harmony: dominant preparation, tonic prolongation (as neighbor), noting its subsidiary importance until the nineteenth century. "[Traces] the late nineteenth-century development of what had been a limited common-practice subdominant function" using examples of Wolf and the analytical approach of Schenker. (153)

A557 1983 Straus, Joseph. "The Motivic Structure of Palestrina's Music." *In Theory Only*, 7/4: 3–24.

Describes four sources of motivic unity: simple repetition, thematic varying, thematic transformation, and hidden repetitions. Uses the term *thematic transformation* when speaking of the foreground, and *repetition* to refer to "the comparison of foreground to middleground or background." (3–4)

A558 1983 Somfai, László. "Wolfgang Amadeus Mozart 4-hangos ornamense." *Zenetudományi dolgozatok:* 17–33.

Examines passages from the opening tenor aria of *Die Entführung aus dem Serail*, focusing on Mozart's placement of the turn ornament. Examines writings of Schenker, Badura-Skoda, and Frederick Neumann regarding proper performance.

A559 1983 Tepping, Susan, and John Bullard. "An Interview with Felix-Eberhard von Cube." *Indiana Theory Review* 6/1–2: 77–100.

A transcript of interviews conducted in July 1983, including "reminiscences of his career and of his studies with Heinrich Schenker as well as discussions of theoretical philosophy." (77)

A560 1983   Treibitz, C. Howard. "Substance and Function in Concepts of Musical Structure." *Musical Quarterly* 69/2: 209–26.
Discusses "means by which one concept of structure evolves from what we perceive historically as its predecessor," critiques serial theory, and "[suggests] some criteria by which judgments of the strength of structural conception within various idioms may be made." (210)

A561 1983   Viljoen, Nicol. "The Drone Bass and Its Implications for the Voice-Leading Structure in Two Selected Mazurkas by Chopin." *Indiana Theory Review* 6/1–2: 17–35.
Discusses Chopin's op. 6/2 and op. 56/2 mazurkas in terms of folk elements, e.g., modality, rhythmic characteristics, and the drone bass.

A562 1983   Wason, Robert. "Schenker's Notion of Scale-Step in Historical Perspective: Non-essential Harmonies in Viennese Fundamental Bass Theory." *Journal of Music Theory* 27/1: 49–73.
"[Discusses] the origin of the notion of non-essential or passing chords in eighteenth century German harmonic theory, to show the somewhat different form it took in Viennese fundamental bass theory of the nineteenth century, and [shows] the influence of non-essential harmonies upon German and Austrian theorists at the beginning of the twentieth century." (50)

A563 1982   Adorno, Theodor. "On the Problem of Musical Analysis." *Music Analysis* 1/2: 169–87. Transcribed and translated by Max Paddison.
Adorno's 1969 lecture contains an "extensive account of his views on analysis." Describes Schenker's system as limited, "for, in reducing music to its most generalized structures, what seems to him and to his theory to be merely casual and fortuitious is, in a certain sense, precisely that which is really the essence, the being, of the music." (174)

A564 1982   Arias, Enrique Alberto. "The Application of General System Theory to Musical Analysis." *Music Review* 43/3–4: 236–48.
Examines Ludwig von Bertalanffy's general system theory describing "relationships and coordination between parts and processes in organisms." Applies these theories, combined with ideas of Schenker and Goethe, to musical analysis.

A565 1982   Ayrey, Craig. "Berg's *Scheideweg*: Analytical Issues in Op. 2/2." *Music Analysis* 1/2 : 189–202.
Discusses interpretations of the song by Perle; examines whether the song is a "mutation of functional tonality in which features of the progenital system are perceptible or even present as a high-level structure, or a primal example of new techniques of tonal organization." (190)

A566 1982 Badura-Skoda, Paul. "Beiträge zu Haydns Ornamentik." *Musica* 36/5: 409–18.
Discusses ornamentation in Haydn based on C. P. E. Bach's *Versuch* and Heinrich Schenker's *Beitrag*.

A567 1982 Benjamin, William E. "Models of Underlying Tonal Structures: How Can They Be Abstract, and How Should They Be Abstract?" *Music Theory Spectrum* 4: 28–50.
Examines the relationship between *piece* (the level of experience "to establish the identity of the work in question") and *model* (one level in a hierarchy of elements). Outlines seven ways in which a model "may be more or less distant from the piece it represents." (28–9)

A568 1982 Christensen, Thomas. "The *Schichtenlehre* of Hugo Riemann." *In Theory Only* 6/4: 37–44.
Discusses overlappings in the theoretical ideas of Riemann and Schenker, despite the former's predilection for vertical sonorities.

A569 1982 Cinnamon, Howard. "Tonal Structure and Voice-Leading in Liszt's *Blume and Duft*." *In Theory Only* 6/3: 12–24.
Discusses Liszt's undermining of traditional tonal fifth-relationships and prioritizing third-relations.

A570 1982 Clark, William. "Heinrich Schenker on the Nature of the Seventh Chord." *Journal of Music Theory* 26/2: 221–59.
Discusses Schenker's view of the seventh chord, especially regarding the prolongation of the seventh, throughout his writings.

A571 1982 Dahlhaus, Carl. "Hindemiths Theorie des Sekundgangs und das Problem der Melodielehre." *Hindemith-Jahrbuch* 11: 114–25. Reprinted in *Über Hindemith: Aufsätze zu Werk, Ästhetik und Interpretation.* Mainz: Schott: 191–202. ISBN 3-7957-0285-2.
Discusses similarities between Hindemith and Schenker, particularly with regard to the *Urlinie* concept. Suggests that "Hindemith's concept of the *Sekundgang* is unmistakable—and indeed, so it seems, through the intercession of Herman Roth—influenced by Heinrich Schenker's theory of the *Urlinie*." (197)

A572 1982 Drabkin, William. "Characters, Key Relations, and Tonal Structure in *Il Trovatore*." *Music Analysis* 1/2: 143–53.
Examines tonality in the work, noting that often "characters are associated with certain pitches, tonalities or melodies: that a sequence of events or emotions is associated with, and even illustrated by, a chord progression or succession of keys; and that a home key, if it exists—that is, if it seems useful to identify—can provide a focal point for the unity of drama and music." (143)

A573 1982 Federhofer, Hellmut. "Heinrich Schenkers Bruckner-Verständnis."
Archiv für Musikwissenschaft 39/3: 198–217.
Examines Schenker's attitude toward Bruckner; cites excerpts from his writings
as well as substantial correspondence with Karl Grunsky.

A574 1982 Federhofer, Hellmut. "Fux's Gradus ad Parnassum as Viewed by
Heinrich Schenker," translated by Alfred Mann. *Music Theory
Spectrum* 4: 66–75.
Discusses Schenker's criticism of Fux for "identifying the study of counterpoint
with the study of composition." He desired to preserve Fux's teachings, however, because he wanted to show that "the laws of part writing do not lose their va-
lidity in free composition but always retain their fundamental importance." (69)

A575 1982 Forte, Allen. "Theory." *Musical Quarterly* 68: 161–81.
A review of the "theory" and "analysis" sections of the *New Grove*. Also exam-
ines the articles on "tonality" (citing Dahlhaus's omission of the work of
Schenker), "harmony," "continuo," "counterpoint," and on individual theorists.

A576 1982 Hantz, Edwin. "Motive and Structure in Liszt's *Blume und Duft*."
In Theory Only 6/3: 3–11.
Focuses on "the internal workings of the piece" and examines how the song
functions as a "commentary on tonality." Discusses the "pivotal role" played by
diminished seventh chords and augmented triads. (3)

A577 1982 Holland, Mark. "Schubert's Moment Musical in F Minor, Op. 94,
No. 3: An Analysis." *Theory and Practice* 7/2: 5–32.
An analysis of the work based on Schenkerian ideas, emphasizing the influence
of psychology on Schenker's ideas.

A578 1982 Hush, David. "Asynordinate Twelve-Tone Structures: Milton
Babbitt's Composition for Twelve Instruments, I." *Perspectives
of New Music* 21/1–2: 152–208.
"[Describes] the system of partitionings formed by each [of the multiple twelve-
part arrays], and then examines the structure of the surface to reveal a system of
aggregates . . . based on three contextually defined strata: background, middleground, and foreground." (152)

A579 1982 Kamien, Roger. "The *Menuetto* from Mozart's *Eine Kleine
Nachtmusik*, K. 525: An Analytic Study." *Theory and Practice*
7/1: 3–19.
"[Shows] how the highly contrasting minuet (B) and trio (B) sections are subtly in-
terrelated. It will also consider the ways in which Mozart avoids excessive segmentation within musical units that are made up of clearly articulated subunits." (3)

A580 1982 Korde, Shirish. "North Indian *Alap*: An Analytical Model." *Sonus*
2/2: 41–70.

"[Presents] an analysis of *alap* raga *Bhairavi* as performed by Ustad Ali Akbar Khan, in which the integral role of [rhythm, register design, and tone-color] is demonstrated. . . . Heinrich Schenker's theories of linked structural levels are applied with modification to illuminate the essential role of large-scale linear design." (41)

A581 1982 Larson, Steve. "Yellow Bell and a Jazz Paradigm." *In Theory Only* 6/3: 31–46.
Offers his personal responses to the piece; employs the analytical methods of Cooper/Meyer and Schenker.

A582 1982 Lewin, David. "*Auf dem Flüße*: Image and Background in a Schubert Song." *Nineteenth-Century Music* 6/1: 47–69.
"[Develops] a general critical stance toward the relation of music and text in Schubert's songs [and] offers a reading of the text [that suggests the] climactic musical events over the second half of the song . . . project the tensions experienced by the singer." (47)

A583 1982 Lubet, Alex. "Vestiges of Tonality in a Work of Arnold Schoenberg." *Indiana Theory Review* 5/3: 11–21.
Examines Schoenberg's op. 19/3 according to a linear perspective, after describing the inadequacies of set theory, Roman-numeral analysis, and the "reiterative" approach to explain the music.

A584 1982 McIrvine, Edward. "Form and Tonality in J. S. Bach's Settings of *Jesu, der du meine Seele*." *Indiana Theory Review* 5/1: 1–22.
Examines Bach's use of the chorale tune, noting three modifications: "altered pitches to overcome modal implications of the original chorale, embellishment with non-harmonic tones, and lengthened rhythmic values at cadences." Examines the structural implications of these alterations. (2)

A585 1982 Neumeyer, David. "Organic Structure and the Song Cycle: Another Look at Schumann's *Dichterliebe*." *Music Theory Spectrum* 4: 92–105.
Examines the idea of organic unity across multimovement cycles. Notes two important "assumptions": "(1) organic unity is liked to key unity (but demands closure in the fundamental line as well as harmonic closure); and (2) the harmonic-contrapuntal fundamental structure overrides any other structuring forces [i.e., the *Urlinie* requires closure; harmonic closure is insufficient]." (92)

A586 1982 Schachter, Carl. "Beethoven's Sketches for the First Movement of Op. 14, No. 1: A Study in Design." *Journal of Music Theory* 26/1: 1–21.
Examines the sketches, drawing attention to motivic relations and articulations that reveal larger structural connections.

A587 1982 Stern, David. "A Quotation from Josquin in Schenker's *Free Composition. Theory and Practice* 7/2: 33–40.

Discusses Schenker's use of an excerpt from the Credo from Josquin's *Missa Gaudeamus* to "illustrate parallel fifths that result from foreground decoration of an admissible intervallic progression." (RILM; used by permission)

A588 1982 Treitler, Leo. " 'To Worship That Celestial Sound': Motives for Analysis." *Journal of Musicology* 1/2: 153–70.

Discusses nineteenth-century analysis as having two sides: "reflection on the nature of the creative process, and the search for structural coherence in music." Examines the role of the organic metaphor and the "genius." (157)

A589 1982 Wen, Eric. "A Disguised Reminiscence in the First Movement of Mozart's G Minor Symphony." *Music Analysis* 1/1: 55–71.

Examines the exposition and corresponding passages of the recapitulation of minor key sonata forms, noting that "the thematic material in the recapitulation is often rewritten in order to bring back literally the same sequence of notes in the parallel passage of the exposition." (55)

A590 1982 Wintle, Christopher. "Corelli's Tonal Models: The Trio Sonata Op. 3/1." In *Nouvissimi studi Corelliani: Attí del terzo Congresso Internationale, Fusignano, 1980*, ed. by S. Durante and P. Petrobelli. Florence: Società Italiana di Musicologia: 29–69.

Examines the work from a Schenkerian viewpoint.

A591 1981 Dunsby, Johnathan, and John Stopford. "The Case for a Schenkerian Semiotic." *Music Theory Spectrum* 3: 49–53.

Suggests that "[organicism] is Schenker's metaphor for a semiotic equivalent— that musical structure reveals itself as significant organization. . . . Schenker seems to have made what we would now call a semiotic proposal in that he removed the musical structure to the same ontological level as its interpretant." (51)

A592 1981 Erwin, Charlotte, and Bryan Simms. "Schoenberg's Correspondence with Heinrich Schenker." *Journal of the Arnold Schoenberg Institute* 5/1: 22–43.

Provides transcriptions and translations of letters in Schoenberg to Schenker in the years 1903–7.

A593 1981 Krebs, Harald. "Alternatives to Monotonality in Early Nineteenth-Century Music." *Journal of Music Theory* 25/1: 1–16.

Examines several Schubert songs that exhibit directional tonality, discussing the problems that these pieces pose for the monotonal approach of Schenker.

A594 1981 Lester, Joel. "Simultaneity Structures and Harmonic Functions in Tonal Music." *In Theory Only* 5/5: 3–28.

Discusses the analytical process in general.

A595 1981 Lewis, Christopher. "Tonal Focus in Atonal Music: Berg's Op. 5/3." *Music Theory Spectrum* 3: 84–97.

Uses the term *tonal* according to Roy Travis's definition: "[music that] unfolds through time some particular tone, interval, or chord." Examines Berg's op. 5/3 for its "surface implications and the manner in which both [tonal and atonal] aspects of the pitch organization contribute to the structure of the piece." (85)

A596 1981 Lewin, Harold. "A Graphic Analysis of Béla Bartók's *Major Seconds Broken and Together, Mikrokosmos* V: 132." *Theory and Practice* 6/2: 40–6.

A graphic analysis, with commentary, of the work, showing a background intervallic structure of P8-A6-P8 (b^1—a-sharp^1—b^1 in the upper voice counterpointed by b—c^1—b in the bass).

A597 1981 Maxwell, John. "The Finale of Mozart's Oboe Quartet, K. 370: A Reductive Analysis." *Indiana Theory Review* 4/2: 33–50.

"[Mozart's Quartet K. 370] is in three movements: an opening sonata-allegro, a poignant slow movement in the relative minor, and a lighthearted finale in 6/8 meter, marked 'rondo,' that is the subject for analysis in this study. The virtuostic style of the solo part and the somewhat irregular rondo from of the movement should provide interesting challenges for Schenkerian analysis." (33)

A598 1981 Maisel, Arthur. "The Fourth of July by Charles Ives: Mixed Harmonic Criteria in a Twentieth-Century Classic." *Theory and Practice* 4/1: 3–32.

Suggests that *The Fourth of July*, "is built upon a structural framework involving a bass arpeggiation and an upper-voice descent in the background"; discusses "motivic references in the foreground to the long-range unfoldings." (3)

A599 1981 Neumeyer, David. "The Two Versions of J. S. Bach's A Minor Invention, BWV 784." *Indiana Theory Review* 4/2: 69–99.

Shows how "the four measures inserted in the final version demand the greatest changes in interpretation of the composition, affecting all the fundamental aspects of structure: motivic development, formal design, the 'dramatic' argument (or psychological progression), and the harmonic-contrapuntal framework." (70)

A600 1981 Phillips, Edward R. "Pitch Structures in a Selected Repertoire of Early German Chorale Melodies." *Music Theory Spectrum* 3: 98–116.

Examines 125 four-phrase chorale melodies of the years 1523—45, examining melodic structures (via Schenkerian-influenced techniques) and suggesting classification schemes; suggests possible theoretical and historical trends in pretonal music.

A601 1981 Riggins, Herbert. "Change of Register in Schenker's Late Theoretical Works." *Indiana Theory Review* 6/1–2: 63–75.

Discusses four middleground *Auskomponierung* procedures that result in registral changes: coupling (*Koppelung*), ascending register transfer (*Höherlegung*), descending register transfer (*Tieferlegung*), and reaching over (*Übergreifen*).

A602 1981 Riggins, Herbert Lee. "Neighbor Motion and Its Graphic Notation in Schenker's *Free Composition*." *In Theory Only* 6/7: 3–11.
Examines Schenker's representation of the neighbor note on the foreground and middleground levels; discusses mixture, interruption (*Unterbrechung*), and first-order linear progressions (*Züge*), also.

A603 1981 Rothgeb, John. "Schenkerian Theory: Its Implications for the Undergraduate Curriculum." *Music Theory Spectrum* 3: 142–9.
Suggests that "the traditional undergraduate curriculum stands in need of certain modifications if it is to be made fully compatible with Schenker's conception of tonal structure." Offers a program of strict counterpoint, figured bass, and harmony. (142)

A604 1981 Stern, David. "Tonal Organization in Modal Polyphony." *Theory and Practice* 6/2: 2–39.
Examines "the connections between Renaissance music and the music of the major-minor era" and investigates "the significant changes which occurred in the transition from the modal system to the major-minor system." Demonstrates underlying structures by means of Schenker's "momentous discovery" that "strict counterpoint underlies the music of the major-minor era." (5–6)

A605 1981 Tepping, Susan. "Form in the Finale of Haydn's String Quartet Op. 64, No. 5." *Indiana Theory Review* 4/2: 51–68.
Discusses Schenker's ideas on form; examines the fourth movement of the work, presenting several graphs and discussing Haydn's fugal technique.

A606 1981 Wagner, Aleksandra. "Heinrich Schenker ili kakva je zapravo *Biologija tonova*." *Zvuk* 2: 68–73.
Examines Schenker's analysis of Chopin's op. 10/8; explains basic tenets of Schenkerian theory, focusing on the biological metaphors Schenker employs. Cites criticisms of Schenker by Charles Rosen, centering on Schenker's apparent neglect of rhythm.

A607 1980 Baker, James M. "Scriabin's Implicit Tonality." *Music Theory Spectrum* 2: 1–18.
Discusses Scriabin's "extension of traditional tonality" through a linear analysis of his op. 32/2 of 1903.

A608 1980 Bergquist, Peter. "The First Movement of Mahler's Tenth Symphony: An Analysis and an Examination of the Sketches." In *The Music Forum* V. New York: Columbia University Press: 335–94.

Proposes that the linear analysis "should contribute to a better understanding of Mahler's position in the history of tonality and of his style in general, while examination of the sketches in conjunction with the analysis should indicate not only what changes were made during the process of composition but also why they were made and how they may or may not have improved the structure of the movement." (336)

A609 1980 Berry, Wallace. "On Structural Levels in Music." *Music Theory Spectrum* 2: 19–45.

Discusses the ideas of hierarchy and level in music. Discusses how "application of the concept of hierarchic level can bring about decisive and critical refinement of a theoretical idea like dissonance." (20)

A610 1980 Burkhart, Charles. "The Symmetrical Source of Webern's Op. 5, No. 4." In *The Music Forum* V. New York: Columbia University Press: 317–34.

Examines the "single symmetrical construct that functions in this piece as the source of its most crucial operations" and serves, as it were, as a background structure. (317)

A611 1980 Dunsby, Jonathan. "Schoenberg on Cadence." *Journal of the Arnold Schoenberg Institute* 4/1: 41–49.

Contrasts Schoenberg's ideas of cadence with Schenker's and Piston's; demonstrates Schoenberg's view that textbook descriptions of musical form are generally inadequate to describe the processes in actual composition.

A612 1980 Forte, Allen. "Generative Chromaticism in Mozart's Music: The Rondo in A Minor, K. 511." *Musical Quarterly* 66/4: 459–83.

Discusses "the way in which the chromatic elements, expressed in the detail of melodic lines and in their interaction, contribute to a unified and organic whole." The term *generative* refers to "the derivation of the characteristic components from a small number of kernel elements." (459)

A613 1980 Grave, Floyd. "Abbé Vogler's Theory of Reduction." *Current Musicology* 29: 41–69.

Discusses Vogler's anticipation of some of Schenker's ideas by his representation of key areas with Roman numerals and his suggestion that all tonal relationships may be understood as deriving from the I-IV-V-I pattern.

A614 1980 Hearts, Daniel. "The Great Quartet in Mozart's *Idomeneo*." In *The Music Forum* V. New York: Columbia University Press: 233–56.

Shows how Mozart's use of the tritone in *Idomeneo* at a climactic moment foreshadows the use of dissonance as a dramatic symbol in the operas of Wagner (Hagen's motive in *Götterdämmerung*) and Webern (the Wolf Glen's scene from *Der Freischütz*).

A615 1980   Meehan, J. R. "An Artificial Intelligence Approach to Tonal Music Theory." *Computer Music Journal* 4: 66–72.
Discusses the formalization of Schenkerian theory, among other approaches that may be suited to explication through computerized processes.

A616 1980   Parish, George. "Tonality: a Multi-Leveled System." *Music Review* 41/1: 52–9.
Examines Schenker's analytical system, applying it to the music of Mozart, Liszt, and Hindemith. Concludes that Schenker's system is best applied to diatonic, tonal works.

A617 1980   Rahn, John. "On Some Computational Models of Music Theory." *Computer Music Journal* 4/2: 66–72.
Mentions Schenker's "disgustingly" organic metaphors and the "idealistic [philosophy] in which his theories swarm" before making suggestions as to the formalization of the theory to make it "digestible" to a computer. Cites research in the area of computer-aided analysis. (66)

A618 1980   Riedel, Johannes. "Echoes of Political Processes in Music During the Weimar Republic." In *Germany in the Twenties: The Artist as Social Critic*, ed. by Frank Hirschbach, et al. Minneapolis: University of Minnesota: 62–73.
Discusses how music and writings on music reflects political trends, e.g., Schenker's "clinging to the heroic German past"; a "trend toward depoliticization of German youth" in the music of Hindemith, Fritz Jode, and Kurt Thomas; Kurt Weil and Hanns Eisler's "advocating the overthrow of Germany's class-structured society"; and Krenek's "satirical-intellectual assessment of the German political situation." (RILM; used by permission)

A619 1980   Rothgeb, John. "Chopin's C-Minor Nocturne, op. 48/1, First Part: Voice-Leading and Motivic Content." *Theory and Practice* 5/2: 26–31.
Discusses the form and tonal structure of the work, investigating its motivic unity.

A620 1980   Rothstein, William. "Linear Structure in the Twelve-Tone System: An Analysis of Donald Martino's *Pianississimo*." *Journal of Music Theory* 24/2: 129–65.
Discusses the work in light of Martino's theories, especially his prioritizing of the boundary notes of a "filled musical space," e.g., a complete row statement, noting parallels with Schenker's *Aussensatz*.

A621 1980   Salzer, Felix. "*The Variation Movement of Mozart's Divertimento K. 563.*" In *The Music Forum* V. New York: Columbia University Press: 257–316.

Examines the work using Schenkerian techniques to show its coherence.

A622 1980 Solie, Ruth. "The Living Work: Organisicm and Musical Analysis." *Nineteenth-Century Music* 4/2: 147–59.

Examines the theories of Schenker and Réti "as loci of two now familiar impulses in analysis, especially of music of the common-practice period, that is, both exemplify methodologies which have to some degree become 'standard.' Both reductive or layer analysis and notions of thematic unity are, in their several ways, offspring of the same metaphoric orientation in nineteenth-century aesthetics." (147–8)

A623 1980 Smoliar, Stephen. "A Computer-Aid for Schenkerian Analysis." *Computer Music Journal* 4/2: 41–59.

Uses some of Schenker's ideas "as a launching pad for a theoretical approach to music which is highly compatible with computer programming." Suggests that "is the consequence of examining Schenkerian analysis from the point of view of a computer programmer and using computer programming to make more explicit certain key insights which had been only implicitly stated in Schenker's writings." (41)

A624 1980 Tanenbaum, Faun. "The Sarabande of J. S. Bach's Suite No. 2 for Unaccompanied Violoncello, BWV 1008: Analysis and Interpretation." *Theory and Practice* 5/1: 40–56.

Examines the piece, showing the structural voice leading. Discusses the manuscript and shows how analysis and performance complement each other.

A625 1980 Thym, Jürgen. "Text-Music Relationships in Schumann's *Frühlingsfahrt*." *Theory and Practice* 5/2: 7–25.

Constructs a "detailed investigation of the text's poetic structure, imagery, and content . . . followed by a discussion of Schumann's emendations of particular words and phrases . . . complemented by a close study of the music as it relates to the poem on various levels." (7)

A626 1980 Treitler, Leo. "History, Criticism, and Beethoven's Ninth Symphony." *Nineteenth-Century music* 3/3: 193–210.

Takes issue with Schenker, suggesting that "while music analysis attempts to explain the musical object as part of an organic whole and regards the particular as exemplification of the general, music criticism seeks to illuminate the particular in itself, to highlight its uniqueness terms of style and genre." (RILM; used by permission)

A627 1979 Bashour, Frederick. "Towards a More Rigorous Methodology for the Analysis of the Pre-Tonal Repertory." *College Music Symposium* 19/2: 140–53.

"[Combines] the melodic principles of Gregorian chant theory and the contrapuntal principles of discant theory . . . with the concepts of prolongation, structural levels, and essential voice leading, as first expressed in the theories of Schenker" to elucidate the tonal structure of Medieval and Renaissance music. Contains a reduction of the motet *Trop lonc temps*. (141)

A628 1979 Burkhart, Charles. "Schenker's Motivic Parallelisms." *Journal of Music Theory* 22/2: 145–75.
Concerns motivic repetition across structural levels. The original motive (or *pattern*) and its repetition (*copy*) are subject to enlargement (*Vergrösserung*, repetition at a higher structural level) or contraction (*Verkleinerung*, repetition at a lower structural level).

A629 1979 Gauldin, Robert. "Wagner's Parody Technique: *Träume* and the *Tristan* Love Duet." *Music Theory Spectrum* 1: 35–42.
Suggests that there "exist deeper and more subtle relationships between the two works [than the foreground borrowing] which suggest a kind of parody technique." Further suggests that "harmonic and linear functions embedded within the song provice the seeds for important tonal relations which appear in expanded form later in the opera." (35)

A630 1979 Horton, Charles. "A Structural Function of Dynamics in Schumann's *Ich grolle nicht*." *In Theory Only* 4/8: 33–49.
         Response: 1979 *In Theory Only* 5/2: 15–7 (J. Rothgeb).
Discusses "the role of dynamics in articulating the recurrence of a significant pitch motive and with the notion that the structure of this piece is enhanced in performance and analysis when these expressive gestures are faithfully observed." (30)

A631 1979 Холопов, Ю. "Музыкально-эстетические взгляды Х. Шенкера." *эстетические очерки* 5: 234–53.

         [1979 Kholopov, Y(urii). "Musical-Aesthetic Views of H. Schenker." *Esteticheskie Ocherki* 5: 234–53.]
The article is in three parts: an overview of Schenker's aesthetics, basic tenets of the theory, and a summary of the merits of the approach. In the first part, Schenker's aesthetics are discussed along with ideas of Spengler and Nietszche. The second part describes Schenker's metaphysics as being inextricably linked to his analytical ideas, and the third concludes that despite his "conservative and, sometimes, utterly reactionary aesthetic-philosophical position, [Schenker's] theory seems, to a great extent, true and fruitful." (252)

A632 1979 Levy, Edward. "Analysis Applied to Performance." *College Music Symposium* 19/1: 128–38.
Examines Mozart's K. 581 quintet according to Schenkerian techniques, showing how these relate to effective performance.

A633 1979 Neumeyer, David. "Liszt's *Sonetto 104 del Petrarca:* The Romantic Spirit and Voice-Leading." *Indiana Theory Review* 2/2: 2–22.
Examines the work, describing its place in Liszt's oeuvre and providing a translation of the text; approaches the work with linear analysis.

A634 1979 Rahn, John. "Logic, Set Theory, Music Theory." *College Music Symposium* 19/1: 114–27.
Drawing on axiomatic theory, Rahn creates a theory for undergraduate students that "purports to better express precisely how a given piece is heard," and is meant to serve as an introduction to the theories of Schenker, Westergaard, Komar, and others. (114)

A635 1979 Turnstall, Patricia. "Structuralism and Musicology: An Overview." *Current Musicology* 27: 51–64.
Discusses the origins of structuralist theories, citing especially the linguistic theories of Saussure; examines the possible influence of Saussure's ideas on Schenker. Examines musical semiology and the writings of Nattiez and others.

A636 1978 Forte, Allen. "Schoenberg's Creative Evolution: The Path to Atonality." *Musical Quarterly* 64/2: 133–76.
Although the bulk of the article is a discussion of Schoenberg's atonal music utilizing the set-theoretic approach, Forte employs the Schenker approach to analyze *Lockung* op. 6/7. Describes three types of passages: "more-or-less tonal" passages, tonal passages "extended in unusual ways," and "harbingers of atonal structures." (153)

A637 1978 Frankel, Robert, Stanley J. Rosenschein, and Stephen W. Smoliar. "Schenker's Theory of Tonal Music—Its Explication through Computational Processes." *International Journal of Man-Machine Studies* 10/2: 121–38.
Transforms Schenker's ideas into a series of prolongational "rules" that are interpreted by the computer; employs the "LISP" language. A continuation and expansion of their earlier article.

A638 1978 Johnson, Douglas. "Beethoven Scholars and Beethoven's Sketches." *Nineteenth-Century Music* 2/1: 3–17.
Response: 1979 *Nineteenth-Century Music* 2/3: 270–6. (S. Brandenburg and W. Drabkin).
Discusses the recent burgeoning of sketch studies, questioning whether the "new contributions fill old scholarly needs? Or do they subvert traditional assumptions about the sketches?" Considers the history of Beethoven sketch studies.

A639 1978 Morgan, Robert. "Schenker and the Theoretical Tradition: the Concept of Musical Reduction." *College Music Symposium* 18/1: 72–96.

Discusses historical precedents for Schenker's work; aims "to reveal that his theory represents a remarkable synthesis of some of the main currents of Western Musical thought." (73)

A640 1978 Morgan, Robert. "The Theory and Analysis of Tonal Rhythm." *Musical Quarterly* 64/4: 435–73.
"[Shows] . . . that a Schenkerian approach leads to important insights into the nature of tonal rhythm." Examines the work of Cooper/Meyer, Edward Cone, and Leo Schrade.

A641 1978 Stephan, Rudolf. "Zum Thema *Schönberg* und *Bach.*" *Bach-Jahrbuch* 64: 232–44.
Examines Schenker's analysis of BWV 853 from *Der Tonwille* as well as Schoenberg's orchestration of BWV 654 and his comments on the "Royal Theme" of BWV 1079.

A642 1978 Winkler, Peter. "Toward a Theory of Popular Harmony." *In Theory Only* 4/2: 3–26.
Examines some harmonic "clichés" of jazz and popular music using Schenkerian analytical techniques.

A643 1977 Beach, David. "A Schenkerian Analysis [of Beethoven's Piano Sonata Op. 53, Introduzione]." In *Readings in Schenker Analysis and Other Approaches*, ed. by Maury Yeston. New Haven: Yale University Press: 202–16.
After discussing the manuscript, Beach demonstrates how the interdiction to Beethoven's op. 53 not only "depends upon but gives added meaning to the Rondo which follows." (204)

A644 1977 Boatwright, Howard. "A Motivic-Harmonic View [of Mozart's Meunetto K. 355]." In *Readings in Schenker Analysis and Other Approaches*, ed. by Maury Yeston. New Haven: Yale University Press: 112–20.
Suggests that the chromaticism in the work "may appear to be an anticipation of romantic (or even later) harmonic practice, [and that experimentation] was perhaps Mozart's own objective." (112)

A645 1977 Cone, Eward. "Three Ways of Reading a Detective Story—or a Brahms Intermezzo." *Georgia Music Theory Review* 31/3: 554–74. Reprinted in *Approaches to Tonal Analysis*, Garland Library of the History of Western Music, Vol. 14. New York: Garland, 1985: 2–22. ISBN 0-824-7463-7. Reprinted in *Music: A View from the Delft*, ed. by Edward T. Cone (Chicago: University of Chicago Press, 1989): 77–93.
Discusses three points of view that may be applied to the work of art being examined: (1) the "purely expeiential"; (2) the "constantly shifting back and forth

(until a 'bird's-eye view' is obtained); and (3) following a "double trajectory," i.e., being aware of the work while trying to listen/read as if for the first time. Cites analyses by Schenker and Tovey of Brahms's op. 118/1. (558)

A646 1977 Dunsby, Jonathan Mark. "Schoenberg and the Writings of Schenker." *Journal of the Arnold Schoenberg Institute* 2/1: 26–33.
Cites a letter from Schoenberg to Leichtenschritt that placed "all Heinrich Schenker's writings" on a list of "German writers on music who had interested him." Discusses Schenker's marginalia and glosses on his copies of Schenker's works. (26)

A647 1977 Hatten, Robert. "A Critical Re-examination of Schenker's Thought." *Indiana Theory Review* 1/3: 22–30.
Describes Schenker's work as "laden with inconsistencies, illogical reasoning, questionable theoretical absolutes, and inevitable traps for the would-be disciple." Suggests that the "invalidity of [Schenker's philosophical ideas] clearly infect [his analyses]." Proposes an "alternate model . . . that can help us account for style and style changes within a theoretical framework." (22–3).

A648 1977 Hughes, Matt. "A Quantitative Analysis [of Schubert's Op. 94, No. 1]." In *Readings in Schenker Analysis and Other Approaches*, ed. by Maury Yeston New Haven: Yale University Press: 144–64.
Discusses, using mathematical formulae, the prominence of some notes and their place on the circle of fifths to examine the "tonal orientation" of the work. (144)

A649 1977 Kassler, Michael. "Explication of the Middleground of Schenker's Theory of Tonality." *Miscellanea Musicologica: Adelaide Studies in Musicology* 9/1: 72–81.
Explanation of a computer program that "determines of any appropriately presented musical composition whether or not it belongs to the 'middleground' of Heinrich Schenker's theory of tonality and, if so, provides a derivation of the composition from one of the three *Ursätze*." (72)

A650 1977 Keiler, Allan. "The Syntax of Prolongation (Part I)." *In Theory Only* 3/5: 3–27.
Explains how, in Schenker's writings, the "*Stufe* . . . is explained as the mere byproduct of several layers of prolongational derivation." Cites his analysis of Bach's A Minor Prelude from *Das Meisterwerk* I. (4)

A651 1977 Lerdahl, Fred, and Ray Jackendoff. "Toward a Formal Theory of Tonal Music." *Journal of Music Theory* 21/1: 111–171.
Describes music theory as "a formal description of the musical intuitions of an educated listener." Explains their "generative" theory as having two parts: "well-formedness conditions, which specify possible structural descriptions; and preference rules, which designate, out of the possible structural descriptions, those

that correspond to the educated listener's hearing of any particular piece."
(111–3)

A652 1977 Martin, Henry. "A Structural Model for Schoenberg's *Der ver-lorne Haufen*, Op. 12/2." *In Theory Only* 3/3: 4–22.
"The first section of this paper examines the opening three bars of the piece to see if certain structural features may suggest a model which can be profitably applied to the piece as a whole. . . . The next section presents an overview of the piece in which relationships inferred from the first three measures lead to an interesting large-scale model for the piece as a whole. First of all, it will be useful to roughly determine the way the text of the poem conforms to the formal organization of the music." (4, 7)

A653 1977 Moss, Lawrence. "A Compositional Analysis." In *Readings in Schenker Analysis and Other Approaches*, ed. by Maury Yeston. New Haven: Yale University Press: 165–70.
Describes the symmetry and tonal structure of Schubert's op. 94/1; misattributes the term *tonicization* to Sessions. (165)

A654 1977 Oster, Ernst. "A Schenkerian View." In *Readings in Schenker Analysis and Other Approaches*, ed. by Maury Yeston. New Haven: Yale University Press: 121–43.
Discusses the origins of the Menuetto K. 355 and its place in Mozart's oeuvre. Graphically depicts the tonal structure and motivic unity of the work.

A655 1977 Palmer, Robert. "A Original Analytic Technique." *Readings in Schenker Analysis and Other Approaches*, ed. by MauryYeston. New Haven: Yale University Press: 217–229.
Examines the introduction of Beethoven's op. 53 through eclectic analytical approaches.

A656 1977 Rothgeb, John. "Another View on Schubert's Op. 94, No. 1." In *Readings in Schenker Analysis and Other Approaches*, ed. by Maury Yeston. New Haven: Yale University Press: 185–92.
A response to Schachter's analysis (see **A658** below).

A657 1977 Schachter, Carl. "Diversity and the Decline of Literacy in Music Theory." *College Music Symposium* 17/1: 150–53.
Discusses the overdiversifying of musical theory and the stress it places on traditional two-year curriculum.

A658 1977 Schachter, Carl. "A Schenkerian Analysis." In *Readings in Schenker Analysis and Other Approaches*, ed. by Maury Yeston. New Haven: Yale University Press: 171–84.
Contains a Schenkerian voice-leading analysis of Schubert's Op. 94/1, section by section.

A659 1977 Schachter, Carl. "More about Schubert's Op. 94, No. 1." In *Readings in Schenker Analysis and Other Approaches*, ed. by Maury Yeston. New Haven: Yale University Press: 193–201.
A response to Rothgeb's comments (see **A656** above)

A660 1977 Simms, Bryan. "New Documents in the Schoenberg-Schenker Polemic." *Perspectives of New Music* 16/1: 110–24.
Examines "recently discovered or identified documents in this debate and attempt[s] to clarify some of the theoretical and historical problems which they raise." Cites passages from Schoenberg's *Harmonielehre* and Schenker's *Erläuterungsausgabe* op. 111, marginalia by Schoenberg in his copies of Schenker's works, and an unpublished essay (by Schoenberg) titled "Warum neue Melodien schwerverständlich sind." (110)

A661 1977 Smith, Charles. "Registering Distinctions: Octave Non-equivalence in Chopin's 'Butterfly' Etude." *In Theory Only* 3/5: 32–40.
Examines op. 25, no. 9, suggesting that octave equivalence ought not to be considered as a natural law or principle, and that patterns of both pitches and pitch-classes can be heard as significant in the course of the work. Based in part on the work of William Benjamin. Contains a graphic analysis of the piece.

A662 1977 Yeston, Maury. "Rubato and the Middleground." In *Readings in Schenker Analysis and Other Approaches*, ed. by Maury Yeston. New Haven: Yale University Press: 94–111.
Explores the following questions: "To what extent does a performer's informality with regularity of tempo and prescribed durational values risk obscuring the metric structure of a piece? How much and what kind of change is permissible? And finally, should a specific meter survive through a highly distorting rubato treatment, what are the inherent structural aspects of a musical work that provide for such survival?" (94)

A663 1976 Bamberger, Jeanne. "The Musical Significance of Beethoven's Fingerings in the Piano Sonatas." In *The Music Forum* IV. New York: Columbia University Press: 237–80.
Decries the practice of editors who substitute "more 'comfortable' fingerings" in lieu of the fingerings that Beethoven provided, which are "often technically awkward," suggesting that they are "depriving students and performers of the musical insight which Beethoven's own fingering provides." (237)

A664 1976 Burdick, Michael. "Some Nineteenth-Century Precedents of the *Stufe* Concept." *Indiana Theory Review* 1/1: 23–30.
By putting the concept in a historical context, Burdick proposes that "the concept of the *Stufe*, as presented in the *Harmonielehre*, was not as original as Schenker would have us believe." Examines writings of Richter and Goetschius. (24)

A665 1976   Frankel, Robert, Stanley J. Rosenschein, and Stephen W. Smoliar.
                 "A LISP-Based System for the Study of Schenkerian Analysis."
                 Computers in the Humanities 10/1–2: 21–32.
A discussion of a program written using the EUTERPE language to "[model]
musical perception on a digital computer using the methodology of Heinrich
Schenker's theory of music." (21)

A666 1976   Gluck, Marion. "Analysis Symposium: Brahms, *Der Tod, das ist
                 die kühle Nacht*, Op. 96, No. 1." *In Theory Only* 2/6: 27–34.
A contribution to an analysis symposium on the work, illustrating the Schenkerian approach; discusses problems in determining the certain prolongations.

A667 1976   Goldschmidt, Harry, and Clemens Brenneis. "Aspekte der gegen-
                 wärtigen Beethovenforschung." *Beiträge zur Musikwissenschaft*
                 18/1: 3–38.
Examines editions of sketchbooks, letters, and analyses of Beethoven's works.
Mentions the influence of Schenker and Riemann on musical analytical trends.

A668 1976   Jonas, Oswald. "Ein Brief Bernhard Paumgartners an Heinrich
                 Schenker." *Österreichische Musikzeitschrift* 31/7–8: 371–2.
Contains excerpts from Schenker's diary as well as a transcription of a letter
from Paumgartner to Schenker (4 June 1915) praising Schenker's ideals. The
original letter is now in JC: LIX: 13.

A669 1976   Kamien, Roger. "Aspects of the Recapitulation in Beethoven's
                 Piano Sonatas." In *The Music Forum* IV. New York: Columbia
                 University Press: 195–236.
Examines the recapitulations in Beethoven's sonatas, noting especially those
that "contain (1) extended prolongations of chromatic triads, (2) new elaboration
of exposition motives, and (3) new thematic material." (196)

A670 1976   Loeb, David. "An Analytic Study of Japanese Koto Music." In
                 The Music Forum IV. New York: Columbia University Press:
                 335–94.
Discusses variation techniques in *Midare* by Yatsuhashi by means of hierarchical
analytical method derived from Schenker.

A671 1976   Morgan, Robert. "Dissonant Prolongation: Theoretical and Com-
                 positional Precedents." *Journal of Music Theory* 20/1: 49–91.
Taking Schenker's analysis of Stravinsky's piano sonata from *Das Meisterwerk*
II, Morgan examines the possibility of dissonant prolongations, citing Babbitt's
work on Bartók.

A672 1976   Salzer, Felix. "Haydn's Fantasia from the String Quartet Op. 76,
                 No. 6." In *The Music Forum* IV. New York: Columbia University Press:
                 161–94.

Citing Schenker's essay "Die Kunst der Inprovisation," shows how "the bass can . . . be understood as a coherent compositional plan that allows the improvising composer to prolong, to elaborate, and to exploit all of its possibilities." (162)

A673 1976 Schachter, Carl. "Rhythm and Linear Analysis: A Preliminary Study." In *The Music Forum* IV. New York: Columbia University Press: 281–334. Reprinted in *Unfoldings: Essays in Schenkerian Theory and Analysis,* ed. by Joseph N. Straus. Oxford: Oxford University Press, 1984: 17–53.

Answering the criticism that Schenker's theory "fails to do justice to rhythm," Schachter outlines Schenker's own ideas on rhythm, surveys recent scholarship, and begins to formulate a theory of rhythm based on Schenker's theories. (281)

A674 1976 Smith, Charles. "Analysis symposium: Brahms, *Der Tod, das ist die kühle Nacht*, Op.96, No. 1." *In Theory Only* 2/6: 35–43. (35)

Shows how the "song can be heard as an interlocking of a Schenkerian model with a diminished-seventh-chord-progression model." (35)

A675 1976 Smoliar, Stephen W. "SCHENKER: A Computer Aid for Analyzing Tonal Music." *Music Project Report No. 6, Department of Computer and Information Science, University of Pennsylvania.* Reprinted in *SIGLASH Newsletter* 10/1–2 (1977): 30–61.

"SCHENKER is an interactive programming language in which a music theorist can formulate and verify analyses of tonal compositions." It utilizes a "command set" derived from Schenker's terminology and allows "often-used sequences of rules [to be] grouped together under the same name." (30)

A676 1976 Travis, Roy. "J. S. Bach, *Invention No. 1 in C Major*: Reduction and Graph." *In Theory Only* 2/7: 3–7.

A voice-leading graph without commentary.

A677 1976 Travis, Roy. "J. S. Bach, *Invention No. 13 in A Minor*: Reduction and Graph." *In Theory Only* 2/8: 29–33.
Response: *In Theory Only* 8/7 (1985): 15–27 (J. Adrian).

A voice-leading graph without commentary.

A678 1975 Barford, Philip. "Music in the Philosophy of Schopenhauer." *Soundings* 5: 29–43.

Discusses Schopenhauer's views on music as outlined in *The World as Will and Representation*; mentions his importance for Kurth and Schenker.

A679 1975 Berry, Wallace, Sylvan Kalib, William Poland, and Charles J. Smith. "Analysis Symposium: Mozart Symphony No. 40." *In Theory Only* 1/7: 8–36.

Transcription of a panel discussion held at the University of Michigan (4 October 1975) expounding upon various analytical views of Mozart's G Minor Symphony.

A680 1975   Browne, Richmond. "Initial Readings in Schenker." *In Theory Only* 1/1: 4–5.

Proposes a list of introductory Schenkerian materials including works of Salzer, Katz, Kalib, Krueger, and Mitchell.

A681 1975   Dahlhaus, Carl, trans. by Carroll Prather. "Some Models of Unity in Musical Form." *Journal of Music Theory* 19/1: 2–30.

Discusses the ideas of musical form from the schematic representations of Marx to the organicist theories of Halm and Schenker.

A682 1975   Frankel, Robert, with Stanley Rosenschein and Stephen Smoliar. "The Modeling of Musical Perception on a Digital Computer via Schenkerian Theory." *Moore School of Electrical Engineering Music Report* [University of Pennsylvania] 4.

A preliminary report, which was expanded into their 1976 *Computers and the Humanities* article (see **A665** above).

A683 1975   Gould, Murray. "Schenker's Theory in the World of Teacher and Student." *College Music Symposium* 15: 133–49.

Transcription of a panel, chaired by David Beach and involving Richmond Browne, Charles Burkhard, Murray Gould, and Oswald Jonas, regarding the applicability of the Schenkerian approach to classroom teaching in music theory.

A684 1975   Greenberg, Beth. "Brahms Rhapsody in G Minor Op. 79/2: A Study of Analyses by Schenker, Schoenberg, and Jonas." *In Theory Only* 1/9–10: 21–9.

A comparative analysis based on Schenker's reading of the piece in *Harmonielehre*, Jonas's appendix (to the Borgese translation *Harmony*), and Schoenberg's analysis in *Structural Function of Harmony*.

A685 1975   Kassler, Michael. "Explication of Theories of Tonality." *Computational Musicology Newsletter* 2/1: 17.

A report of Kassler's work on computers and Schenkerian analysis.

A686 1975   Kassler, Michael. "Proving Musical Theorems I: The Middleground of Heinrich Schenker's Theory of Tonality." Technical Report 103, University of Sydney, Basser Department of Computer Science. ISBN 0-909-20312-1.

Because he perceives Schenker's theory to be "informal . . . unclear, ambiguous, [and] inconsistent," Kassler has "[replaced] Schenker's descriptions and examples [with a structure of] sufficient formalization that its constituent processes can be manipulated by computer." (4)

A687 1975   Levy, Morten. "The Naïve Structuralism of Heinrich Schenker." *Musik and Forskning* 1: 20–32.

The approach to musical thought and to musical analysis developed by Heinrich Schenker is compared to certain holistic trends in structural linguistics. Schenker's work, though seriously limited in some respects, deserves the greatest attention from musicologists who aim at introducing structuralistic or semiological thought into musicology. (RILM; used by permission)

A688 1975 Rothgeb, John. "Strict Counterpoint and Tonal Theory." *Journal of Music Theory* 19/2: 260–84.

Describes the advantages of studying counterpoint: (1) gradually increasing complexity and aural training; and (2) "reflects certain norms of perceptual interpretation of tonal relations." (261)

A689 1975 Smith, Charles. "J. S. Bach: Six suites pour violoncello seul: interpretation musicale et instrumentale." *In Theory Only* 1/8: 20–7.

A review of an edition of the suites by Diran Alexandian that seems to use Schenkerian analytical notation, but does not.

A690 1974 Beach, David. "The Origins of Harmonic Analysis." *Journal of Music Theory* 18/2: 274–306.

Discusses the origins of the Roman-numeral approach to harmonic analysis, surveying writings of Rameau, Kirnberger, Schutz, Weber, and others. Examines the theories of Schenker as a departure from that tradition.

A691 1974 Levy, Edward. "Structural Analysis in Interdisciplinary Arts Courses." *College Music Symposium* 14: 102–21.

Describes methods of analysis for interdisciplinary to study: make "connections among the disciplines, historical allusions, [or provide] social commentary or information about style." Suggests showing music as "an organic totality of interacting levels and nested layers." (105)

A692 1973 Block, A. F. "And Now We Begin: A Survey of Recent Theory Texts." *College Music Symposium* 13: 97–105.

Discusses factors in the "crisis in the teaching of music theory," such as "(1) changes in the discipline of music itself; (2) a reexamination of the role of the music theorist; (3) new theories about how people learn; and (4) the changing student population." (98)

A693 1973 Dahlhaus, Carl. "Schoenberg and Schenker." *Proceedings of the Royal Musical Association* 100: 209–15. Reprinted in *Schoenberg and the New Music: Essays by Carl Dahlhaus,* trans. by Derrick Puffett and Alfred Clayton. Cambridge: Cambridge University Press, 1987: 134–40. ISBN 0–521–33251–6.

Discusses the differences between the two theories as regards the nature of dissonance: "Schenker denies the concept of the 'essential' dissonance and Schoenberg that of the 'incidental.'" (209)

A694 1973 Hauschild, Peter. "Bemerkungen zu Beethovens Klaviernota-
          tion." *Beethoven Jahrbuch* 9: 147–65.
Examines editions by Schenker, Schmid, and Unverricht, concluding that "autograph oddities should not be held sacrosanct." (147)

A695 1973 Hilse, Walter, tr. "The Treatises of Christoph Bernhard." In *The
          Music Forum* III. New York: Columbia University Press: 1–196.
Examines Bernhard's three treatises, *Von der Singe-Kunst oder Manier, Tracta-
tus compositionis augmentatus*, and *Ausgefühlicher Bericht vom Gebrauche der
Con- und Dissonantien.* Bernhard's discussion of diminution technique and his
reduction of recitative passages into simpler models seems, in a small way, to
foreshadow Schenker's thinking.

A696 1973 Imbrie, Andrew W. " 'Extra' Measures and Metrical Ambiguity in
          Beethoven." In *Beethoven Studies* I, ed. by Alan Tyson. New
          York: Norton, 45–66. Reprinted in *Approaches to Tonal Analysis*,
          Garland Library of the History of Western Music, Vol. 14: 41–63.
          ISBN 0-82-40746-7.
Examines metric ambiguity in the sonata op. 10/3 and the first movement of the
Fifth Symphony, using Schenker's analysis from *Der Tonwille* I as a point of
departure.

A697 1973 Mann, Alfred. "Haydn's *Elementarbuch:* A Document of Classic
          Counterpoint Instruction." In *The Music Forum* III. New York:
          Columbia University Press: 197–238.
Documents Mozart's study of Fux's *Gradus* under Haydn.

A698 1973 Mitchell, William J. "Beethoven's *La Malinconia* from the String
          Quartet Op. 18, No. 6: Techniques and Structure." In *The Music
          Forum* III. New York: Columbia University Press: 269–80.
Examines the work from the linear-stuctural vantage point; discusses "relationships between the *Adagio* and the following *Allegretto quasi Allegro*" in order to
"[gain insight into] the unified career of the work." (269)

A699 1973 Orenstein, Arbe. "Some Unpublished Music and Letters of Mau-
          rice Ravel" In *The Music Forum* III. New York: Columbia Uni-
          versity Press: 291–334.
Discusses some unpublished material of Ravel, located in private collections.

A700 1973 Salzer, Felix. "Chopin's Etude in F Major, Op. 25 No. 3: The
          Scope of Tonality." The *The Music Forum* III New York: Colum-
          bia University Press: 281–90. Analyzes the work from the
          Schenkerian vantage point; discusses the meaning of the middle
          B major section in the context of F major.

A701 1973 Schachter, Carl. "Bach's Fugue in B Flat Major (WTC Book I, No. 21)." In *The Music Forum* III. New York: Columbia University Press: 239–268. Reprinted in *Unfoldings: Essays in Schenkerian Theory and Analysis,* ed. by Joseph N. Straus. Oxford: Oxford University Press, 1984: 239–259.

Discusses the difficulties in fugal analysis, such as "important thematic elements constantly [shifting] from voice to voice [making] it difficult to determine the controlling outer-voice structure." (239)

A702 1972 Drabkin, William. "Some Relationships between the Autographs of Beethoven's Sonata in C Minor, Opus 111." *Current Musicology* 13: 38–47.

Presents a discussion of the manuscript, citing previous versions by Schenker and Unverricht.

A703 1972 Walker, Alan. "Schenker: A Musician's Musician." *Composer* 43: 9–10.

Discusses the *Funf Ürlinie-Tafeln*; describes three "reservations" about Schenker: (1) his "neglect" of rhythm, (3) the idea that "all works do not share a common background"; and (3) that Schenker "wasn't interested in criticism." (10)

A704 1971 Beeson, Roger. "Background and Model—A Concept in Musical Analysis." *Music Review* 32/4: 349–59.

Examines the various meanings of the term *background* in its specific "spatio-visual" meaning and as used by music analysts of the "functional school" and the "Schenkerian school." (349)

A705 1971 Clarkson, Austin. "Analysis Symposium: Brahms Op. 105/1." *Journal of Music Theory* 15/1–2: 6–32. Reprinted in *Readings in Schenker Analysis and Other Approaches*, ed. by Maury Yeston. New Haven: Yale University Press: 230–74.

Surveys analytical literature; presents a literary-historical analysis of the piece, focusing on the text and the compositional history.

A706 1971 Laufer, Edward. "Analysis Symposium: Brahms Op. 105/1." *Journal of Music Theory* 15/1–2. Reprinted in *Readings in Schenker Analysis and Other Approaches*, ed. by Maury Yeston. New Haven: Yale University Press: 254–74.

Presents a Schenkerian analysis of the song, paying special attention to Brahms's use of motives.

A707 1971 Rothgeb, John. "Design as a Key to Structure in Tonal Music." *Journal of Music Theory*15/1–2: 230–53. Reprinted in *Readings in Schenker Analysis and Other Approaches*, ed. by Maury Yeston. New Haven: Yale University Press:72–93.

Discusses "the design of the surface—and its implications for the study of voice leading," showing how "changes in surface design usually coincide with crucial structural points, and accordingly such changes must be given the most thoughtful attention in deriving or verifying an analysis." (72–3)

A708 1970 Boretz, Benjamin. "Meta-Variations." *Perspectives of New Music* 8/1: 1–74, 8/2: 49–110, 9/1: 23–42.
A series of three articles drawn from his dissertation: "An Epistemic Approach to the Resolution of Both Traditional and Related Current Musical Puzzles," "Sketch of a Musical System," and "Analytic Fallout." The middle section outlines "a possible model for a tonal syntax based on that of Schenker."

A709 1970 Clifton, Thomas. "An Application of Goethe's Concept of *Steigerung* to the Morphology of Diminution." *Journal of Music Theory* 14/2: 165–89.
Deals with "the critical problems of relating Mozart's compositional procedures to certain eighteenth-century notions of organic form, particularly as revealed in Goethe's concept of *Steigerung*; . . . the technical problem of demonstrating that the capacity of a few simple and typical musical shapes to contribute to the control of varying time-spans of a composition is a significant, though of course not unique feature in the creation of organic form." (167)

A710 1970 Loeb, David. "Mathematical Aspects of Music." In *The Music Forum* II. New York: Columbia University Press: 110–29.
After discussing music as a semantic system, Loeb discusses mathematics in the study of music, including musicology and the compositional process. Also discusses the role of the computer in music.

A711 1970 Lockwood, Lewis. "The Autograph of the First Movement of Beethoven's Sonata for Violoncello and Pianoforte, Opus 69." In *The Music Forum* II New York: Columbia University Press): 1–109.
Discusses the lack of autograph facsimiles of Beethoven's music, including sketches. Focuses his analysis on the publication of the autograph of op. 69.

A712 1970 Mitchell, William. "The Prologue to Orlando di Lasso's *Prophetiae Sybillarum*." In *The Music Forum* II. New York: Columbia University Press: 264–73.
After describing the inefficacy of the "Roman legions"—i.e., traditional Roman-numeral analysis—to describe tonal relationships, Mitchell analyzes Lasso's work according to the linear ideas of Heinrich Schenker.

A713 1970 Novack, Saul. "Fusion of Design and Tonal Order in the Mass and Motet: Josquin Desprez and Heinrich Isaac." In *The Music Forum* II. New York: Columbia University Press: 187–263.

Discusses the history of tonality, suggesting that "it is the fusion of design and tonal structure that provides us with the diversity and richness of compositional order in the history of tonal music." (107)

A714 1970 Parks, Richard. "Voice Leading and Chromatic Harmony in the Music of Chopin." *Journal of Music Theory* 20/2: 189–214.
Discusses analyses of Chopin's music by Gerald Abraham and Henry Hadow regarding Chopin's use of "use of altered chords in passages where they do not appear to function in their conventional harmonic roles." Employs Schenker's method to investigate these "harmonic parentheses." (189)

A715 1970 Salzer, Felix. "Chopin's Nocturne in C-sharp Minor, Op. 27, No. 1." In *The Music Forum* II. New York: Columbia University Press: 283–92.
Discusses form and tonal structure in the work, singling out key motives.

A716 1970 Schachter, Carl. "Landini's Treatment of Consonance and Dissonance: A Study in 14th Century Counterpoint." In *The Music Forum* II. New York: Columbia University Press: 130–86.
Discusses the treatment of intervals by Landini, questioning whether thirds and sixths belong to the sphere of consonance, dissonance, or "whether they might properly form an intermediary category of their own." (131)

A717 1970 Travis, Roy. "Tonal Coherence in the First Movement of Bartók's Fourth String Quartet." In *The Music Forum* II. New York: Columbia University: 298–371.
Proposes "not merely to demonstrate that this movement is tonal [but also examine] the exact means by which the overwhelming impression of tonality is achieved." Stresses that we "must hear the structure in terms of the details, and the details in terms of the structure." (298–9)

A718 1969 Beach, David. "A Schenker Bibliography." *Journal of Music Theory* 13/1: 2–37. Reprinted in *Readings in Schenker Analysis and Other Approaches*, ed. by Maury Yeston New Haven: Yale University Press: 275–311.
Divided into two sections: primary and secondary sources. Contains an initial essay providing much information about the sources listed in the appendix.

A719 1968 Eibner, Franz. "Die musikalischen Grundlagen des Volkstumlichen Österreichischen Musiziergutes." *Jahrbuch des Österreichischen Volksliedwerkes* 17: 1–21.
An application of Schenker's method to Austrian folk music, studying vocal polyphony and the overtones of the Alphorn. Contains a discussion of Schenker's basic ideas.

A720 1968 Harris, Simon. "The Schenkerian Principle." *Composer* 29/3: 30–2.

Criticizes the Schenkerian approach, since "one cannot point to evidence of the existence of [prolongation]." Suggests that "the entire reasoning underlying the analytical system is circular." (31)

A721   1967   Beach, David. "The Functions of the Six-Four Chord in Tonal Music." *Journal of Music Theory* 11/1: 2–31.
Contains three parts: "a critical examination of the different viewpoints [on the six-four chord]; the properties of the six-four chord [as viewed by Schenker]"; and analytical application demonstrating "the necessity for interpreting correctly a structure as seemingly insignificant as the six-four chord." (2–3)

A722   1967   Bergquist, Peter. "Mode and Polyphony around 1500: Theory and Practice." In *The Music Forum* I. New York: Columbia University Press: 99–161.
Questions the assumption that the writings of contemporaneous theorists should determine the analytical course taken. Focuses on the writings of Pietro Aaron, especially in regard to mode and counterpoint.

A723   1967   Kaufmann, Harald. "Aushöhlung der Tonalität bei Reger." *Neue Zeitschrift für Musik* 128: 28–33.
Cites Schenker's analysis of Reger's Bach Variations from *Das Meisterwerk* II as well as Riemann's writings, showing Reger's "undermining" of tonality through his use of nonfunctional progressions.

A724   1967   Mitchell, William, and Felix Salzer. "A Glossary of the Elements of Graphic Analysis." In *The Music Forum* I. New York: Columbia University Press: 260–68.
Presents some of the symbols used in the graphs of *The Music Forum*. Notes that "Variants of the symbols and abbreviations here presented are easily conceivable, as are additional symbols not included herein." (260)

A725   1967   Mitchell, William. "The *Tristan* Prelude: Techniques and Structure." In *The Music Forum I* (New York: Columbia University Press): 162–203. Reprinted in *Approaches to Tonal Analysis*, Garland Library of the History of Western Music, Vol. 14. New York: Garland, 1985: 160–202. ISBN 0-824-7463-7.
"[Approaches] the work in terms of its linear-harmonic elements . . . to arrive at a view of the entire work as a unified, articulated structure." Suggests that "there are discoverable morphological meanings in the lines and harmonies [that] can pave the way to the comprehension of an embracing structure reaching from the beginning to the end." (162–3)

A726   1967   Neumann, Hans, and Carl Schachter. "The Two Versions of Mozart's Rondo." In *The Music Forum* I. New York: Columbia University Press: 1–34.

Examines Mozart's Rondo K. 494; presents comments on sources and surveys the literature on the rondo in general. Concludes with a graphic analysis of and commentary on the piece.

A727 1967 Perle, George. "The Musical Language of *Wozzeck.*" In *The Music Forum* I New York: Columbia University Press: 204–59.

Examines the elements of pitch organization that "generate the context within which themes and motives operate." Describes "certain means of integration and differentiation that are characteristic features of *Wozzeck*'s language." (204)

A728 1967 Regner, Eric. "Layered Music-Theoretic Systems." *Perspectives of New Music* 6/1: 52–62.

Defines a *layered system* as "a set of rules which, when applied to a specific musical work, assign *values* to certain parameters, called *system parameters*. The nature of these parameters depends on the nature of the system being used." Uses Kassler's mathematical model of Schenker's system. (52)

A729 1967 Salzer, Felix. "Tonality in Early Medieval Polyphony: Towards a History of Tonality." In *The Music Forum* I. New York: Columbia University Press: 35–98.

Describes medieval polyphony as "modal-contrapuntal" tonality (as opposed to major-minor tonality); shows directed motion in organum of Leoninus and Perotinus.

A730 1966 Federhofer, Hellmut. "Zur neuesten Literatur über Heinrich Schenker." In *Saarbrücker Studien zur Musikwissenschaft* 1, ed. by W. Wiora. Festschrift J. Müller-Blattau : 69–78.

Cites two articles of Dahlhaus (from *Musikforschung* 12 1959: 523–5 and *Bach-Jahrbuch* 49 1962: 58ff) that criticize Schenker's theory of the *Ursatz.*

A731 1966 Travis, Roy. "Directed Motion in Schoenberg and Webern." *Perspectives of New Music* 4/2: 84–9.

Examines Schoenberg's op. 19/2 and Webern's op. 27 from a linear perspective, following the example of Felix Salzer, showing "origins and goals of motion" through graphic analysis. (85)

A732 1965 Kaufmann, Harald. "Fortschritt und Reaktion in der Analysen-lehre Heinrich Schenkers." *Neue Zeitschrift für Musik* 126: 8–9. Reprinted in *Das Orchester* 13 (1965): 44–9 and *Spurlinien: Analytische Aufsätze über Sprache und Musik.* Vienna: Elisabeth Lafite, 1969: 37–46. Reviewed by C. Dahlhaus in *Musik und Bindung* 2/9 (1970): 395.

Describes Schenker's view on twentieth-century music based on quotations of his from *Meisterwerk* II and III; discusses his "arrogant" and "aristocratic" views. Examines the influence of Goethe on his ideas; takes issue with the "static" nature of the background.

A733 1965   Treitler, Leo. "Musical Syntax in the Middle Ages: Background to an Aesthetic Problem." *Perspectives of New Music* 4/12: 75–85.

Insofar as it is "only against the background of a musical syntax that we can speak of unity and variety," Treitler examines the issue of musical "order" and "syntax" from a historical basis. (76)

A734 1964   Jonas, Oswald. "Heinrich Schenker und grosse Interpreten." *Österreichische Musikzeitung* 19/12: 584–9.

Describes Schenker's assessment of musicians, such as Johannes Messchaert, Karl Straube, Joseph Joachim, and Pablo Casals, as found in his diaries.

A735 1964   Silberman, Israel. "Teaching Composition via Schenker's Theories." *Journal of Research in Music Education* 12/4: 295–303.

Demonstrates that Schenker's theory can be useful "to develop a method of composition based primarily on the Classical style." Employs notation that is "not entirely Schenkerian [but is] close enough to give the reader a genuine notion of Schenker's analysis." Provides an (admittedly curious) analysis of Beethoven's op. 2/1 and a new composition derived from that "model." (295–7)

A736 1963   Jonas, Oswald. "Zur realen Antwort in der Fuge bei Bach." In *Bericht über den internationalen musikwissenschaftlichen Kongreß, Kassel 1962*. Bärenreiter: Kassel: 365ff.

A study of the fugues from the WTC, documenting Bach's use of real answers.

A737 1963   Jonas, Oswald. "Ein textkritisches Problem in der Ballade Op. 38 von Frederic Chopin." 1963 *Acta Musicologica* 35/2–3: 155–8.

Transcribes correspondence among Brahms, Ernst Rudorff, and Schenker regarding op. 38 in Breitkopf's *Chopin-Gesamtausgabe*.

A738 1962   Kerman, Joseph. "A Romantic Detail in Schubert's *Schwanengesang*." *Musical Quarterly* 48/1: 36–49.

Contains a discussion of Schenker's essay on *Ihr Bild* from *Der Tonwille* I.

A739 1962   Westergaard, Peter. "Some Problems in Rhythmic Theory and Analysis." *Perspectives of New Music* 1/1: 180–90. Reprinted in *Perspectives on Contemporary Music Theory*, ed. by Bejnamin Boretz and Edward T. Cone. New York: Norton, 1972: 226–237.

Discusses the "relationship of rhythm and meter, [and] phrase and cadence to the location of the structural downbeat." Examines the rhythmic theories of Cooper and Meyer, showing the concept of "architectonic levels" to be derivative of Schenker's concept of structural levels with regard to pitch. (181)

A740 1961   Jonas, Oswald. "Die Kunst des Vortrags nach Heinrich Schenker." *Musikerziehung* 15/3: 127–29.

An examination of Schenker's writings on performance from the *Nachlass*.

A741 1961 Oster, Ernst. "Register and the Large Scale Connection." *Journal of Music Theory* 5/1: 54–71. Reprinted in *Readings in Schenkerian Analysis and Other Approaches*, ed. by Maury Yeston. New Haven: Yale University Press: 54–71.

Describes the importance of register as an agent of musical unity, citing Schenker's concept of the "obligatory register." Shows how "tones which, viewed superficially, have nothing to do with each other enter into a relationship merely through the register in which they appear." (56)

A742 1961 Zuckerkandl, Viktor. "Die Tongestalt." *Eranos-Jahrbuch* 29: 293ff.

Contains a linear analysis of the melody of Schubert's *Schnitter-Tod*, showing basic melodic diminutions.

A743 1960 Eibner, Franz. "Die Stimmführung Chopins in der Darstellung Heinrich Schenkers." *Congress Copenhagen*: 155–8.

Discusses Schenker's analyses of Chopin's music.

A744 1959 Forte, Allen. "Schenker's Conception of Musical Structure." *Journal of Music Theory* 3/1: 1–30. Reprinted in *Readings in Schenkerian Analysis and Other Approaches*, ed. by Maury Yeston. New Haven: Yale University Press: 3–37.

Provides an overview of Schenker's work, including an explication of his graph of Schumann's op. 39/2 from *Der freie Satz*. Identifies five areas in music theory where Schenker's ideas could contribute: constructing a theory of rhythm, studying the development of triadic tonality, studying compositional technique, improving theory instruction, and understanding modern music.

A745 1959 Travis, Roy. "Towards a New Concept of Tonality?" *Journal of Music Theory* 3/2: 257–84.

      Responses: 1960 *Journal of Music Theory* 4/1: 85–98 (E. Oster).

                      1960 *Journal of Music Theory* 4/2: 274–5 (H. Neumann).

                      1961 *Journal of Music Theory* 5/1: 152–6 (A. Komar).

Asks "to what extent can the techniques of tonal coherence . . . be applied to certain sonorities and melodic procedures characteristic of the newest music?" Presents Schenker-based analyses of *Le Sacre du Printemps* and two pieces from Bartók's *Mikrokosmos*, showing how they "[illustrate] in a striking way the fascinating transformations which triadic principles and techniques may undergo in their non-triadic applications." (257)

A746 1958 Eibner, Franz. "Chopins kontrapuntisches Denken." *Chopin Jahrbuch*: 103–30.

Examines Chopin's counterpoint from the Schenkerian vantage point.

A747 1958 Federhofer, Hellmut. "Die Funktionstheorie Hugo Riemanns und die Schichtenlehre Heinrich Schenkers." *Bericht über des International Musikwissenschaftlichen Kongreß Wien, 1956*: 183–90.

Translation: 1991   "La theoria funzionale di Hugo Riemann a la theoria degi strati di Heinrich Schenker." *Azzaroni*: 233–43.

A comparative study of the analytical systems of Schenker and Riemann that was expanded in his 1981 book.

A748 1958 Hirschkorn, Kurt. "Die Stimmführung als Leitstern des Geigers: Die Bedeutung Heinrich Schenkers." *Musikerziehung* 12: 233–4.

Discusses the importance of Schenker's ideas for performers.

A749 1958 Kessler, Hubert. "On the Value of Schenker's Ideas for Analysis of Contemporary Music." *Periodical of Theory-Composition, Illinois State Teacher's Association* 1: 1–11.

Suggests that some of Schenker's ideas (such as the general concept of prolongation) may be brought to bear on contemporary music. Anticipates in some ways the "neo-Schenkerian" movement.

A750 1958 Kolneder, Walter. "Sind Schenkers Analysen Beiträge zur Bacherkenntnis?" *Deutsche Journal für Musikwissenschaft* 3: 59–73.

Discusses Schenker's analysis of Bach's BWV 940 from *Das Meisterwerk* I, questioning whether it actually leads to a better understanding of Bach's music. Suggests that Schenker's work as a whole is valuable, but in studying it one must be wary of his critical nature and his "detours" (i.e., his discussions of nonmusical matters). (72)

A751 1958 Reynolds, William. "Unity in Music." *Journal of Music Theory* 2/1: 97–104.

Describes methods of analysis that involve "consideration of harmonic relationships . . . together with other unified elements such as melodic line, rhythmic balance, and structural and formal details." Suggests that traditional Roman-numeral "harmonic dissection" is "well-nigh meaningless." (97)

A752 1958 Schmid, Edmund. "Autographie und Originalausgaben Beethovens: Auswertung eines vergleichs." *Neue Zeitschrift für Musik* 119/12: 746–7.

Discusses Schenker's *Erläuterungsausgeben* and his writings on the importance of the autograph and first printings of music from *Der Tonwille*.

A753 1956 Jonas, Oswald. "On the Study of Chopin's Manuscripts." *Chopin Jahrbuch* 142–55.

Discusses how studying the autographs "give us insight into the workshop of the composer." Describes the correspondence between Brahms and Rudorff in preparation for the publication of the Chopin *Gasamtausgabe* by Breitkopf. (142)

A754 1954 Furtwängler, Wilhelm. "Heinrich Schenker: Ein zeitgemasses Problem." In *Ton und Wort.* Wiesbaden: F. A. Brockhaus: 198–204.
Translations: 1977 *Suono e parola* (Fógola: Torino).
1985 *Sonus* 6/1: 1–5 (J. Emerson).
Describes his acquaintance with Schenker's ideas from his reading of the *Neunte*. Emphasizes the importance of *Fernhören* (long-range hearing) and a conception of the organic whole.

A755 1952 Hartmann, Heinrich. "Heinrich Schenker und Karl Marx." *Österreichische Zeitung für Musikwissenschaft* 7/2: 46–52.
Criticizes Schenker's idea that "the new music, which has no longer anything to do with the *Urlinie*, is unable to bring forth any new masterpieces." Suggests that "one can never conclude . . . that the classical masterworks are formed according to the laws of the *Urlinie*." (48–9)

A756 1950 Salzer, Felix. "Directed Motion—The Basic Factor of Musical Coherence." *Journal of the American Musicological Society* 3: 157.
Abstract of a paper read 18 December 1949 at the Society meeting examining directed motion in the music of Scarlatti, Schubert, and Hindemith. Shows that "listening to and grasping the music's direction gives an understanding of the functions of tones and chords in relation to the meaning of the musical motion as a whole." (157)

A757 1950 Wingert, Hans. "Über die Urlinie und Ihrer Schöpfer. Eine Würdigung." *Zeitschrift für Musik* 111: 244–6.
An introduction to Schenker's ideas, suggesting that they may not be fruitful for the analysis of modern music.

A758 1949 Mann, Michael. "Schenker's Contribution to Music Theory." *Music Review* 10: 3–26.
Response: *Musical Review* 10: 248 (O. Deutsch).
Compares Schenker with Rameau, Kurth, and Halm; presents an overview of Schenker's works and speculations on his place in history. Ultimately rejects Schenker's method as "inseparably bound up with the conservatism which characterizes his view of music history, and as therefore essentially sterile in tendency." (26)

A759 1949 Oster, Ernst. "The Dramatic Character of the *Egmont* Overture." *Musicology* 2/3: 269–85. Reprinted in *Aspects of Schenkerian Theory*, ed. by David Beach. New Haven: Yale University Press: 209–22.

Describes the inherent drama in Beethoven's overtures, demonstrating that the dramatic nature is subsidiary to the voice leading. Suggests that "the determining factor in the greatness of Beethoven's overtures lies in how, from a purely musical standpoint, he wrote compositions of a dramatic nature." (269)

A760 1947 Federhofer, Hellmut. "Die Musiktheorie Heinrich Schenkers." *Schweizerliche Musikzeitung* 87/2: 265–8.
A general introduction to Schenker's ideas, comparing them to Kurth's; describes Schenker's reductive techniques and the relationship between harmony and counterpoint.

A761 1947 Oster, Ernst. "Chopin's Fantasie-Impromptu: A Tribute to Beethoven." *Musicology* 1/4: 407–29. Reprinted in *Aspects of Schenkerian Theory*, ed. by David Beach. New Haven: Yale University Press:189–208.
Discusses Chopin's reluctance to have the work published; examines the work's relationship to Beethoven's Sonata in C-sharp Minor, op. 27/2.

A762 1946 Mitchell, William. "Heinrich Schenker's Approach to Detail." *Musicology* 1/2: 117–28. Reprinted in *Theory and Practice* 10/1–2 (1985): 49–62.
Discusses the concept of the 5–6 intervallic exchange and the difference between *Stufe* and a "chord of detail." Examines bars 113–121 of Brahms's Fourth Symphony.

A763 1943 Dale, Frank Knight. "Heinrich Schenker and Musical Form." *Journal of the American Musicological Society* 17/3: 12–3. Reprinted in *Theory and Practice* 10 (1985): 23.
Describes the concept of linear progressions; suggests that by using Schenker's method, we may "achieve a far more comprehensive grasp of musical form than that permitted by the usual approach." (13)

A764 1938 Jonas, Oswald. "Nachtrag zu Schenkers Aufsatz über Schindler." *Der Dreiklang* 9/10: 200–7. Reprinted in *Musikerziehung* 18 (1965): 205–9.
Discusses Schindler's biography of Beethoven, especially noting his comments about Beethoven's piano technique and various comments about performance in general.

A765 1938 Vrieslander, Otto. "Eine Stelle aus Chopins Scherzo op. 54." *Der Dreiklang* 9/10: 208–14.
Publishes a letter from Schenker that clarifies the meaning of m. 266 of Chopin's op. 54, where the last eighth-note of the printed edition is A-sharp, but the manuscript shows B. Schenker demonstrates, by examining the motivic structure, that the B is correct.

A766 1938 Sessions, Robert. "The Function of Theory." *Modern Music* 15/4: 257–62. Reprinted in *Roger Sessions on Music: Collected Essays*, ed. by Edward T. Cone Princeton: Princeton University Press, 1979: 263–68.

Discusses works of Hindemith (*Unterweisung im Tonsatz*), Krenek (*Über neue Musik*), and Schenker (*Der freie Satz*), describing Schenker's as "the most pretentions and . . . provocative." Ultimately judges the works of Hindemith and Krenek as "pertinent and vital," while Schenker "vitiates the fundamental soundness of his approach" by not considering "actual problems." (267)

A767 1937 Aurelius Augustinus, trans. by Oswald Jonas and Felix Salzer. "Musik." *Der Dreiklang* 3 (June): 65–7.

A translation of book 7, chapter 2, a discussion between master and pupil about "the various forms of the number of tones and their interrelationship." (65)

A768 1937 Bamberger, Carl. "Zur Frage der Dirigentenziehung." *Der Dreiklang* 4/5 (July/August): 105–9.

Describes a plan of musical education for conductors, consisting of piano accompanying, conducting works with soloists, and studying to develop discriminating hearing.

A769 1937 Berl, Paul. "'Das 'Freudethemen' aus Beethovens IX. Sinfonie." *DerDreiklang* 2 (May): 33–40.

A thorough explanation of the sixteen-measure theme, showing graphic analyses and providing commentary.

A770 1937 Elias, Angie. "Zwei Stücke aus Schumanns *Album für die Jugend*." *Der Dreiklang* 7 (October): 161–3.

Examines the first two pieces, *Melodie* and *Soldatenmarsch*, providing voice-leading graphs and analytical commentary for each piece.

A771 1937 Heimler, Hans. "Ein Vorkämpfer für die Erhaltung der Handschriften Mozarts." *Der Dreiklang* 3 (June): 82–4.

Discusses Franz Lorenz's book, *In Sachen Mozarts*, which states that "each note has its predestined place, its secret mission," hinting at the idea of organic coherence.

A772 1937 Jonas, Oswald. "Ein Bach-Präludium. Ein Weg zum organische Hören." *Der Dreiklang* 1 (April): 12–7. Reprinted in *Musikerziehung* 20 (1967): 205–9.

Explains Schenker's approach to musical analysis from the *Klang* through the foreground using Bach's Prelude in F Major.

A773 1937 Jonas, Oswald, and Felix Salzer. "Der Nachlaß Heinrich Schenkers." *Der Dreiklang* 1 (April): 17–21.

Describes the contents of Schenker's *Nachlass*, including unfinished projects on thoroughbass and performance and many *Urlinie* graphs.

A774 1937 Jonas, Oswald. "Musikalische meisterhandschriften." *Der Dreik-lang* 1 (April): 22–6 and 2 (May): 55–60.
Discusses the importance of studying composer's manuscripts, as they may clarify motivic relationships and connections. Frequently, editors change slurs, but the composer's notation also contains keys to understanding and should be preserved.

A775 1937 Jonas, Oswald. "Bewußtes oder unbewußtes Schaffen?" *Der Dreiklang* 2 (May): 53.
Discusses the question of whether the master composers had knowledge of the *Urlinie* through an analysis of the F Major Prelude of Bach.

A776 1937 Jonas, Oswald. "Die Krise der Musiktheorie." *Der Dreiklang* 3 (June): 67–74. Describes the deleterious effect of Rameau's emphasis on the vertical aspect of music. Quotes Georg Sorge's sarcastic comment in *Compendicum Harmonicum* (1760), "C-E-G-B-D-F should be a chord! Why not, rather, name the entire piano or the entire organ a chord?" Goes on to discuss the advantages of the Schenker system. (71–2).

A777 1937 Jonas, Oswald. "Mozarts Ewige Melodie." *Der Dreiklang* 3 (June): 84–92. Reprinted in *Musikerziehung* 30/3 and 30/4: 118–21 and 158–60.
Discusses the nature of melody as the *Auskomponierung* of the chord of nature (*Klang*), i.e., the first five partials of the overtone series; shows the underlying coherence of many Mozart examples, focusing on hidden motivic repetitions.

A778 1937 Jonas, Oswald. "Die Analyse im praktischen Unterricht." *Der Dreiklang* 4/5 (July/August): 98–104.
Discusses the benefits to be gained for performers by the study of Schenker's ideas, especially concerning the projection of motivic relationships.

A779 1937 Jonas, Oswald. "Miscellen." *Der Dreiklang* 4/5 (July/August): 113–20.
Jonas's article contains criticisms of editors, a general study of diminution, a sketch study of Beethoven's op. 23, a review of two recent *Beethoven Jahrbücher*, and an essay on "the decline of music."

A780 1937 Jonas, Oswald. "Über neue Musik." *Der Dreiklang* 6 (September): 133–7.
Describes tonality as the condition sine qua non for music, as expressed in the overtone series; rejects the term *atonal*.

A781 1937 Jonas, Oswald. "Beethoveniana." *Der Dreiklang* 6 (September): 148–56.

Provides a review of *Beethoven Jahrbuch* 7, discusses the significance of Beethoven's sketches (especially for showing motivic relationships), and discusses interpretation issues in improvisatory works.

A782 1937   Oster, Ernst. "Neue Urtext ausgeben von Mozart." *Der Dreiklang* 2 (May): 62–3.

Discusses errors in the Peters edition of Mozart's works when compared to the autograph, especially concerning slurring.

A783 1937   Oster, Ernst. "Vom Sinn des langen Vorschlags." *Der Dreiklang* 6 (September): 140–7.

   Translation: 1982   *Theory and Practice* (Robert Kosovsky)

Discusses the meaning and proper performance of the long appoggiatura, citing examples of Mozart, Haydn, Schubert, and Bach. Shows how the appoggiaturae may be significant in terms of the motivic parallelism.

A784 1937   Salzer, Felix. "Die Historische Sendung Heinrich Schenkers." *Der Dreiklang* 1 (April): 2–12.

Describes the state of music theory before Schenker, citing the decline in "the instinct for the tonal language of the masterworks" of the late nineteenth and early twentieth centuries and the effect this had on "artistic understanding." Describes Schenker as "saving" this musical instinct through the originality of his theories. (5)

A785 1937   Simon, Erich. "Der Wert des Photogramm-Archivs für den ausübenden Musiker." *Der Dreiklang* 4/5 (July/August): 110–2.

Describes the value of manuscript study by providing a list of mistakes in the Breitkopf edition of the Wind Quintet of Mozart (K. 452), showing wrong notes, missing or incorrect slurs, performance indications, and errors in orthography.

A786 1937   Wolf, Hans. "Schenkers Persönlichkeit in Unterricht." *Der Dreiklang* 7 (October): 176–84.

Reminiscences of Schenker's lessons from a former student. Wolf describes Schenker's teaching through quotations drawn from the lessons. Includes a discussion of Schenker's analysis of Haydn's *Kaiserhymne*.

A787 1937   Zauner, Victor. "Wort und Ton bei Mozart: Bemerkungen anläßlich der Neuen *Don Giovanni* Übertragungen." *Der Dreiklang* 2 (May): 41–53.

Examines the German translation of *Don Giovanni* prepared by Siegfried Anheisser and Hermann Roth. Discusses the relationship between words and music, and cites examples from the original Italian, examining the effectiveness of the translation.

A788 1937   Zuckerkandl, Victor. "Zur jüngsten Aufführung des *Don Carlos*." *Der Dreiklang* 4/5 (July/August): 128.

Discusses the Act III trio from *Don Carlos*, as performed by the Wiener Staatsoper under Bruno Walter, who perform the middle section and the repeat, despite a "stage tradition" to the contrary.

A789 1936 Jonas, Oswald. "Das Wiener Photogramm-Archiv." *Anbruch* 18/1: 6–7.
A discussion of the significance of the archive.

A790 1936 Plettner, Arthur. "Heinrich Schenker's Contribution to Theory: Viennese Scholar Sought Broader Base for Analysis of Composition." *Musical America* 56/3: 14, 136. Reprinted in *Theory and Practice* 10/1–2: 11–4.
Discusses the difference between "genius" and "talent" and Schenker's conception of the organic whole; expresses concern that "many pages . . . are marred by lapses into bitter political tirades . . . [which are] out of place in works of this nature." Speculates on the influence of Schenker on music theory. (14)

A791 1935 Katz, Adele. "Heinrich Schenker's Method of Analysis." *Musical Quarterly* 21/3: 311–29. Reprinted in *Theory and Practice* 10/1–2 (1985): 77–95.
A technical introduction to Schenker's method, showing that "the fundamental principles which govern the music of all great composers are the same." Demonstrates the approach on Bach's prelude BWV 846. (312)

A792 1935 Reich, Willi. "Ein Meister der Musikforschung." *Anbruch* 19[?]: 14–16.
Discusses two methods of musical analysis, "synthetic" and "analytical," as examined in the works of Kurth and Schenker, respectively. Describes Schenker's concept of organic coherence and his idea of *Auskomponierung*. Discusses Schenker's publications and his founding of the Photogramm-Archiv.

A793 1935 Sessions, Robert. "Heinrich Schenker's Contribution." *Modern Music* 12: 170–8. Reprinted in *Sonus* 6/1 (1985): 6–14. Reprinted in *Critical Inquiry* 2/1 (1975).
Discusses Schenker's concepts of *Stufe, Tonikalisierung, and Auskomponierung*. Criticizes the concept of the *Ursatz* as "far too primitive as a description of the actual events which constitute a musical work." (176)

A794 1935 Waldeck, A., and N. Broder. "Musical Synthesis as Expounded by Heinrich Schenker." *The Musical Mercury* 11/4: 56–64. Reprinted in *Theory and Practice* 10 (1985): 9–14.
Discusses the literature on Schenker as being either "reverently laudatory or impatiently hostile." Examines the vital and revitalizing role Schenker's theory can play in the study of music. (9)

A795 1935 Weisse, Hans. "The Music Teacher's Dilemma." *Proceedings of the Music Teachers National Association*: 122–31. Reprinted in *Theory and Practice* 10/1–2 (1985): 29–48.

Discusses the "crisis in the theory of music" and the "chasm between theory and practice." Presents a hypothetical dialogue between Mozart and a music theorist examining K. 533. (123)

A796 1935 Zuckerkandl, Victor. "Bekenntnis zu einem Lehrer." *Anbruch* 17/5: 121–3.

Describes Schenker's teaching as being grounded in the work itself ("tones and tones only"), not hermeneutic descriptions or formal schemes. (121)

A797 1935 Zuckerkandl, Victor. "The Importance of Heinrich Schenker's Teaching." *The Musical Times* 76: 705.

A translation of an excerpt from his *Anbruch* article (see **A796** above). The editor mentions an English translation of *Kontrapunkt* (see **T1** above). I have not been able to verify its existence.

A798 1934 Jonas, Oswald. "The Photogram-Archives in Vienna." *Music and Letters* 15/4: 344–7.

An announcement about the Photogramm-Archive, stressing its importance for musical study. Discusses the reactions of composers to the printed editions, suggesting they are often unreliable. Names some of the more important holdings.

A799 1934 Reich, Willi. "Kant, Schenker, und der Nachläufer." *Dreiundzwanzig* 15/16: 29–32.

      Response: 1934 Eine Wiener Musikzeitschrift 15/16 (JC XXXVIII: 54) (O. Jonas).

Essentially a review (critique) of Jonas's *Das Wesen des Musikalischen Kunstwerkes*, Reich describes Schenker's system as "impotent" and Jonas as a "silly follower." (30–2)

A800 1933 Citkowitz, Israel. "The Role of Heinrich Schenker." *Modern Music* 11: 18–23. Reprinted in *Theory and Practice* 10/1–2 (1985): 15–22.

Discusses the state of music theory and the role of the theorist. Describes Schenker as the man born to meet the "Herculean" task of removing the "cancerlike growth of theoretical speculation" and reuniting theory with performance. Stresses the originality of Schenker's ideas. (18–9)

A801 1933 Jonas, Oswald. "Heinrich Schenker." *Allgemeine Musik Zeitung* 60/36–37: 425–7, 437–88.

Discusses Schenker's uniting of harmony and counterpoint as well as the concept of the *Stufe* and his explanation of the overtone series. Touches upon sutuctural levels, and mentions Schenker's musical and editorial activities.

A802 1930 Albersheim, Gerhard. "Heinrich Schenker: Grundlegen und Bedeutung Seines Werkes." *Rheinische Theater-und Musik-Zeitung*: 15/16: 259–61.
After an introduction to Schenker's ideas stressing the relationship of strict counterpoint to free composition, Albersheim applies the ideas to a folksong, *Alle Vögel sind schon da*.

A803 1930 Riezler-Stettin, Walter. "Die Urlinie." *Die Musik* 22/7: 502–10. Response: 1930 *Die Musik* [?] (R. Brünauer) (JC: XXI: 24).
Discusses the *Urlinie* throughout Schenker's works (through *Meisterwerk* II); suggests that "sometimes Schenker gets into a dangerous conflict with artistic reality of the foreground." Discusses Schenker's ideas on organicism. (505)

A804 1930 Vrieslander, Otto. "Heinrich Schenker." *Kunstwart* 43/9: 181–9.
A general introduction to Schenker's life and works.

A805 1926 Bamberger, Carl. "Das Schenker-Institut am neuen Wiener Konservatorium." *Anbruch* 18/1: 7–8.
A discussion of the newly founded Schenker-Institut, a forum where Schenker's ideas could be propagated.

A806 1926 Vrieslander, Otto. "Heinrich Schenker." *Die Musik* 19: 33–8.
Speculates on reasons for Schenker's publishing the *Harmonielehre* anonymously, and the significance of the designation "von einem Künstler." Stresses the organic conception of the works of the great masters. Contains a photograph of Schenker on the facing page.

A807 1925 Carrière, Paul. "Schenker's *Urlinie*." *Allgemeine musikalische Zeitung* 52/7–8: 139–40, 163–5.
A criticism of Schenker's work.

A808 1925 Vrieslander, Otto. "Carl Philipp Emanuel Bach als Theoretiker." *Von Neuer Musik*: 222–79.
Discusses the significance of the theoretical writings of Bach, especially his *Versuch über das wahre Art, das Klavier zu spielen*.

A809 1923 Dahms, Walter. "Heinrich Schenkers Persönlichkeit." *Allgemeine Musik Zeitung* 32/32: 511–2.
Describes the "theoretical and practical chaos" that preceded Schenker; describes his teaching as "truly 'modern' teaching, a new teaching . . . [that] straightens up those paralyzed in tradition." Nontechnical description of his works. (511)

A810 1923 Vrieslander, Otto. "Heinrich Schenker und sein Werk." *Anbruch* 15/2–3: 41–4.

An overview of Schenker's works and aesthetic, stating the importance of the works of the "great masters" for him, and their being the "quintessential center" of his teaching. (43).

A811 1922 Moorman, Ludwig. "Das Werk Heinrich Schenker: Eine Über-sicht." *Die Musikantgilde* 1/7: 80–4.
An overview of Schenker's works.

A812 1920 Halm, August. "Heinrich Schenker, *Neue musikalische Theorien und Phantasien*." *Der Merker* 11: 414–17, 505–7.
An essay-review dicussing the *Harmonielehre* and *Kontrapunkt*.

A813 1918 Dahms, Walter. "Heinrich Schenker zu seinem 50. Geburtstag am 19. Juni 1918." *Konservative Monatschrift* 9: 647–9.
Written as a tribute to Schenker; discusses his works, stressing Schenker's originality and "restless creativity." Defends Schenker's polemics.

A814 1917 Halm, August. "Heinrich Schenker." *Die Freie Schulgemeinde* 7: 11–5.
A nontechnical discussion of Schenker's works through the *Erläuterungsausgabe* of op. 109.

ADDITIONAL SOURCES

A815 2002 Karnes, Kevin. "Another Look at Critical Partisanship in the Viennese *Fin-de- Siècle*: Schenker's Reviews of Brahms's Vocal Music, 1891–92." *Nineteenth-Century Music* 26/1: 73–93.
Based on the author's dissertation (see **D7** below); discusses Schenker's reviews of Brahms's opp. 104 and 107 (see **S1** and **S3** above).

A816 2002 Rothstein, William. "Conservatory Schenker versus University Schenker." *Tijdschrift voor musiektheorie* 3/2: 239–41.
Discusses the differences in the pedagogy of Schenker's approach in the conservatory and the university, suggesting that Schenker's approach "combines elements of both educational traditions, [yet is] too 'artistic' to be fully integrated into a traditional musicology department, [and] too 'intellectual' to fit within a traditional conservatory." (239)

A817 2001 Darcy, Warren. "Rotational Form, Teleological Genesis, and Fantasy-Projection in the Slow Movement of Mahler's Sixth Symphony." *Nineteenth-Century Music* 25/1: 49–74.
The slow movement of Mahler's Sixth Symphony exemplifies the fundamental principle of rotational form: two thematic complexes, A and B, are stated four times, the final statement or rotation producing a synthesis of the two ideas (AB AB AB A/B). This quadruple rotational structure is punctuated by two "fantasy

projections" that suggest an unattainable utopian vision. The telos or goal of the movement (the synthesis of A and B) coincides with, in Schenkerian terms, the arrival of the Kopfton or structural tone. (RILM; used by permission)

A818 2000   Schachter, Carl. "Playing What the Composer Didn't Write: Analysis and Rhythmic Aspects of Performance." In *Pianist, Scholar, Connoisseur: Essays in Honor of Jacob Lateiner.* Stuyvesant: Pendragon: 47–68.

Examines Mozart's K. 330 sonata, Mendelssohn's op. 19/1, and the third movement from Beethoven's First Symphony from Schenker's viewpoint, stated in *Kontrapunkt*, that "notational symbols hide more than they make explicit." (RILM; used by permission)

A819 1999   Burgnaro, Michele. "Analisi e meta-analisi: Schenker e l'arte del comprendere." *Diastema* 13/2.

Discusses the relationships between analysis and performance; examines connections between Schenker's and Heiddeger's ideas.

A820 1991   Modena, Elena. "Analisi Schenkeriana e libertá compositiva: alcuneticolaritá strutturali dell' *Intermezzo* op. 118/1 di J. Brahms." *Analisi* 5: 23–31.

An analysis, according to Schenkerian ideas, of Brahms's op. 118/1.

A821 1992   Snarrenberg, Robert. "Zen and the Way of the Soundscroll." *Perspectives of New Music* 30/1: 222–37.

A study of Schenker's essay on the E-flat Minor Prelude from WTC 1 (from *Der Tonwille* 1) in light of Zen theories and James Kirtland Randall's *A Soundscroll.*

A822 1990   Willner, Channan. "Händel's Borrowings from Telemann: An Analytical View." In *Trends in Schenkerian Research*, ed. by Allen Cadwallader. New York: Schirmer: 145–68.

Discusses Händel's use of borrowed compositional material from Telemann's *musique de table*, and "[addresses] the compositional implications of the rhythmic, motivic, stylistic, and tonal similarities and differences."(145)

A823 1989   Rahn, John. "New Research Paradigms." *Music Theory Spectrum.* 11/1: 84–94.

Discusses the two leading movements in music theory, the Schenkerian approach and the mathematical approach of Babbitt. Also discusses the combination of music theory with other disciplines.

A824 1986   Smith, Charles. "The Functional Extravagance of Chromatic Chords." *Music Theory Spectrum* 8: 94–139.
   Responses: 1987   *Music Theory Spectrum* 9: 173–85. (D. Beach).
                    1987   *Music Theory Spectrum* 9: 186–94. (C. Smith).

Examines both the chordal and the linear approaches "in order to determine the reasons for their individual failures." Suggests, since "neither one can say much about chromatic music without the cooperation and collusion of the other," a hybrid approach, encompassing both Roman-numeral and linear analysis. (94)

A825 1983 Eibner, Franz. "Schenker—quo vadis?" *Tritonus* "Reproduzent 1984–Besinnung zur Kunst," December: 36–9.
[Not examined]

A826 1981 Federhofer, Hellmut. "Was ist ein Generalbaß-Satz?" *Muzikološki Zbornik* 17: 57–64.
Examines Schenker's analysis of *Ich bin's, ich sollte Büßen* from the *Fünf Urlinie-Tafeln.*

A827 1980 Schachter, Carl. "Rhythm and Linear Analysis: Durational Reduction." In *The Music Forum* V. New York: Columbia University Press: 197–232. Reprinted in *Unfoldings: Essays in Schenkerian Theory and Analysis,* ed. by Joseph N. Straus. Oxford: Oxford University Press, 1984: 54–78.
Shows that "by indicating tonal events in durational proportion and by specifying the larger metrical divisions, [durational reduction] can sometimes clarify aspects of rhythmic organization not directly revealed by graphic analyses that deal mainly with voice leading and harmony." (197)

A828 1979 Lester, Joel. "Articulation of Tonal Structures as a Criterion for Analytic Choices." *Music Theory Spectrum* 1: 67–79.
Describes Schenker's view of form as an organic tonal structure in which the separate themes function to articulate that structure and are not autonomous in themselves.

A829 1965 Eibner, Franz. "Die aktuella Arbeit im Heinrich Schenker—Seminar an der Akademie für Musik und darstekllender Kunst im Wien." In *Österreichischer Musikrat, Mitgleid des Conseil International de la Musique der Unesco* 1: 10–3.
[Not examined]

A30 1962 Federhofer, Hellmut. "Heinrich Schenker." In *Anthony van Hoboken: Festschrift zum 75. Geburtstag,* ed. by Joseph-Schmidt-Görg. Mainz: Schott.
Describes the founding of the *Meisterarchive* at the Austrian National Library; discusses Schenker's works, and contains an overview of recent Schenkerian literature.

A831 1957–8 Eibner, Franz. "Die Obertonreihe als Erscheinung und als Idee." *Musikerziehung* 11: 83–5.
[Not examined]

A832 1957–8   Eibner, Franz. "Tonleiter, Tonart, Tongeschlecht und Dia-
tonie." *Muzikerziehung* 11: 96–113.
[Not examined]

A833 1992   Gołąb, Maciej. "*Pentezilea* na sopran i orkiestre op. 18 Karola
Szymanowskiego: Zagadnienia semantyki, skladni, formy i tech-
niki dzwiekowej." *Muzyka* 37/1: 21–38.
Discusses Szymanowskiego's *Pentezilea* in light of Schenker's *Ursatz* concept.
Employs "semantic analysis" as well.

A834 1994   Beach, David. "Harmony and Linear Progression in Schubert's
Music." *Journal of Music Theory* 38: 1–20.
Examines the interaction of harmony and voice leading in three instrumental
works by Schubert: The first movement of the string quartet in C (D. 956), the
string quartet in G (D. 887), and the Quartettsartz (D. 703). (RILM; used by
permission)

A835 1996   Schachter, Carl, trans. by David Aijon. "La reconciliacion de op-
uestos: Elementos cromaticos en los dos primeros movimientos
de las sonatas para piano op. 31 num. 1 y op. 53 de Beethoven."
Quodlibet 6: 47–59.
[Not examined]

A836 1990   Beach, David. "More on the Six-Four." *Journal of Music Theory*
34/2: 281–90.
Continues his 1990 article (see **A321** above), including examples of the unresolved cadential six-four and the "apparent" cadential six-four that is, in reality,
passing.

Chapter 4

Books on Schenker and His Approach

SYMPOSIA, COLLECTIONS OF ESSAYS, MONOGRAPHS, AND TEXTBOOKS

B1   TBA   Burstein, Poundie, and David Gagné, eds. *A Celebration of Carl Schachter*. Stuyvesant: Pendragon Press. [?]
Scheduled to include "Reminiscences of Carl Schachter as a Teacher" (T. Jackson), "Rhythmic Displacement in the Music of Bill Evans" (S. Larson), "Tonal and Thematic Structure in Brahms: The String Quintet, Op. 88" (W. Petty), "Circular Motion in Chopin's Late B-Major Nocturne" (W. Rothstein), "The Spirit and Technique of Schenker Pedagogy" (A. Cadwallader/D. Gagné), and others.

B2   TBA   Korsyn, Kevin. *Schenker: A Philosophical Interpretation* [forthcoming].
Based in part on his 1996 *Intégral* article and his 1988 *Theoria* article, Korsyn discusses the philosophical basis of Schenker's thought.

B3   2002   Korsyn, Kevin. *Decentering Music: A Critique of Contemporary Musical Research*. Oxford: Oxford University Press. ISBN 0-195-10454-4.
"Examines the struggle for the authority to speak about music at a time when the humanities are in crisis; links the institutions that support musical research, including professional associations and universities, to complex historical changes such as globalization and the commodification of knowledge. Suggests unexpected relationships between works of musical scholarship and the cultural networks in which they participate." (from the publisher)

B4   2002   Lipp, Gerhard. *Das musikanthropologische Denken von Viktor Zuckerkandl*. Musikethnologische Sammelbände 18. Tutzing: Schnein ISBN 3-795-2107-39.

Publication of the author's dissertation examining the life and works of Zuckerkandl. Chapters I.3 and II.2–3 deal specifically with his studies with Schenker, the influence of Schenker's philosophy upon Zuckerkandl, and Zuckerkandl's "continuation" of Schenker's theories in his own works.

B5   2002   Плотников, Борис. *Очеки и Зтюды по Методологии Музыкального Анализа*. Краноярск: Краноярская ак, адемия музыки и театра.

> [2002   Plotnikov, Boris. *Essays and Studies on the Methodology of Musical Analysis*. Krasnoyarsk: Krasnoyarsk Academy of Music and Theatre.]

Contains three parts: essays, analytical studies, and appendices. The first part serves to introduce Schenker's theories (pp. 12–89) as well as some other modes of analysis, including Larry Solomon's parametric analysis, set theory, and semiotics (pp. 90–168). In part 2 (pp. 169–249), Schenker's approach is combined with musical dramaturgy and applied to works of Rimsky-Korsakov, Medtner, Shostakovich, and Debussy. The work includes, as an appendix, a translation of Renwick's online Schenkerian glossary (see **E41** below).

B6   2000   Spurný, Lubomír: *Heinrich Schenker—dávný neznámý*. Olomouc: Univerzita Palackého—vydavatelství. ISBN 8-0244-0055-3.

A Czech introduction to Schenker's analytic method; contains excerpts from *Harmonielehre* and *Der freie Satz* in additions to translations of an analyrical essay from *Der Tonwille* and four of Schenker's critical essays (see chapter 2). The author discusses Schenker's theories in the context of Sechter and Riemann, and discusses the polemic of Federhofer and Dahlhaus regarding their reactions to voice-leading analysis. He then proceeds to explain Schenker's organic model from *Der freie Satz*, followed by a discussion of Schenker's thought vis-à-vis Goethe and Hegel. The work concludes with a Polish-Czech glossary of Schenkerian terms.

B7   1999   Schachter, Carl, and Heidi Siegel. *Schenker Studies II*. Cambridge: Cambridge University Press. ISBN 0-521-47011-0.
          Review: 2000   *Notes* 57: 99–101 (J. Boss).

Each of the book's chapters is an elaboration of a paper originally presented at the Second Schenker Symposium (1992) at the Mannes College of Music (see Appendix A). Each chapter is indexed and annotated separately in chapter 3.

B8 1998 Cadwallader, Allen, and David Gagné. *Analysis of Tonal Music: A Schenkerian Approach*. New York: Oxford University Press. ISBN 0-19-510232-0.

Reviews: 2001 *Music Theory Spectrum* 23/2: 264–77 (F. Samarotto).

2001 *Tijdschrift voor muziektheorie* 6/1 (P. Scheepers).

2000 *Music Analysis* 19: 130–34. (V. Vaughan).

1997 *Intégral* 11 (D. Neumeyer and J. Hook).

A textbook intended for advanced undergraduates or graduate students; assumes familiarity with traditional tonal theory and form, and species counterpoint; contains sample analyses and a bibliography for further reading.

B9 1998 Плотников, Борис. *К Вопросу О Расширении Аналит, ического Кругозора Педагогов-Музыкантов: Пр, актический аспект идей и метода Генриха Шенкера*. Краноярск: Краноярская академия музыки и театра.

[1998 Plotnikov, Boris. *On Expanding the Analytical Outlook of Teachers of Music: Practical Aspects of the Theory of Heinrich Schenker*. Krasnoyarsk: Krasnoyarsk Academy of Music and Theatre.]

Published as a brochure; contains a biographical sketch and an introduction to Schenker's method based on Forte/Gilbert and Schachter/Salzer. Emphasizes the role of species counterpoint in explaining more complicated tonal procedures. Examines Beethoven's op. 2/1, Cherny's op. 299/1, Prokofiev's Second Piano Sonata, Mozart's C Minor Fantasia (bass-line sketch), and Medtner's op. 26 march.

B10 1998 Schachter, Carl. *Unfoldings: Essays in Schenkerian Theory and Analysis,* ed. by Joseph N. Straus. Oxford: Oxford University Press, 1999. ISBN 0-19-512590-8.

Reviews: 2001 *Music Theory Spectrum* 23/2: 242–7.

2000 *Music and Letters* 81: 656–9 (N. Helsby).

2000 *Intégral* 13: 217–28 (D. Gagné).

1999 *Indiana Theory Review* 20/2 217–28 (A. Davis).

1999 *Music Theory Online* 5/4 (D. Damschroder).

A reprinting/re-editing of eleven of Schachter's articles drawn from various sources (indexed separately in chapter 2); contains a "dialogue between author and editor" discussing Schachter's educational philosophy vis-à-vis Schenkerian theory.

B11 1997 Będkowski, Stanisław, Agnieszka Chwiłek, and Iwona Lindstedt. *Analiza schenkerowska*. Kraków: Musica Iagellonica. ISBN
8-370-99071-1.
An introduction to Schenkerian analysis based on the 1982 Forte/Gilbert text,
with many examples from *Der freie Satz*. After an introduction on Schenker's
theory and graphic notation, the ordering of chapters reverses *freie Satz*, and proceeds from foreground to background, including a section on musical form.

B12 1997 Gauldin, Robert. *Harmonic Practice in Tonal Music*. New York:
Norton. ISBN 0-393-97074-4.
      Review: 1999 *Notes* 56/2: 382–4 (J. Check).
A textbook, aimed at undergraduates, that introduces linear-reductive analysis
as well as the implication-realization theories of Meyer. Includes appendices on
acoustics, scales and modes, orchestration, and conducting patterns.

B13 1997 Snarrenberg, Robert. *Schenker's Interpretive Practice*. Cambridge:
Cambridge University Press. ISBN 0-521-49726-4.
      Reviews: 2001 *Theory and Practice* 26: 141–51 (J. Rothgeb).
                    1999 *Notes* 55: 651–3 (J. W. Sobaskie).
                    1999 *Journal of Aesthetics and Art Criticism* 57: 78–80
                          (A. Alterman).
                    1998 *Dissonanz* 56: 42–3.
"Schenker's desire to portray musical experience had four aims: to present a
theoretical account of musical effects encountered in European music of the
eighteenth and nineteenth centuries; to represent the mind set shared among
composers of that music; to convey the expressive interaction of musical effects
in individual artworks; and to promote continued creative and re-creative participation in the musical tradition. The center of Schenker's interpretive practice,
grounded in humanism, lies in the interweaving of technical analysis with metaphor and imagery." (from the publisher)

B14 1997 Suurpää, Lauri. *Music and Drama in Six Beethoven Overtures:
Interaction between Programmatic Tensions and Tonal Structure*.
Sibelius Academy, Studia Musica No. 8. Helsinki: Hakapaino Oy.
ISBN 952-9658-567.
Employs "Schenkerian analysis, and plot as described in literary theory, specifically in structuralism"; suggests "that the programmatic quality of the works can
best be understood as the outcome of an interaction between the relatively distinct extramusical allusions created by the foreground and the basic tonal tensions of more remote levels"

B15 1996 Blasius, Leslie David. *Schenker's Argument and the Claims of
Music Theory*, Cambridge Studies in Music Theory and Analysis,

Vol. 9. New York: Cambridge University Press. ISBN 0-521-55085-8.

Reviews: 1999 Journal of Aesthetics and Art Criticism 57: 78–80 (A. Alterman).

1998 *Österreichische Musikzeitschrift* 53: 74–4 (M. Ebyl).

1998 *Contemporary Music Review* 17/2: 115–8 (R. Monelle).

1997 *Musicology Australia* 20: 110–1 (M. Kassler).

1997 *Musical Times* 39–41 (W. Drabkin).

"As the thesis of this study . . . I proceed from the assumption that Schenker's late analysis entails a powerful if unacknowledged epistemological argument, directed first . . . at the psychologies of music perception available at the opening of the new century, and second . . . at the sciences of history which flourished simultaneously, and that the strength of his argument is to be found in the combination of these two strands." (xvi)

B16 1996 Dreyfus, Laurence. *Bach and the Patterns of Invention.* Cambridge, Mass.: Harvard University Press. ISBN: 0-674-06005-X.

Reviews: 2001 *Theory and Practice* 26: 112–40 (K. Braunschweig).

1998 *Fanfare* 21: 343–5. (L. Dreyfus).

1999 *Journal of the American Musicological Society* 52/3: 627–33 (S. Crist).

Discusses the genesis of many of Bach's works, examining his relationship to his contemporaries; adopts a position critical of Schenkerian and "organicist" analysis, preferring to take a thematic approach. Cites Schenker's analysis of the C Minor Fugue from WTC I.

B17 1996 Kinderman, William, and Harald Krebs, eds. *The Second Practice of Nineteenth-Century Tonality.* Lincoln and London: University of Nebraska Press. ISBN 0-803-22724-8.

Review: 1998 *Musikforschung* 51/1: 114–5 (D. de la Motte).

A collection of eleven essays, most of which were presented at a conference titled "Alternatives to Monotonality" at the University of Victoria, British Columbia (1989); entries are cited separately in chapter 3.

B18 1996 McColl, Sandra. *Music Criticism in Vienna, 1896–1897: Critically Moving Forms.* New York: Oxford University Press. ISBN 0-19-816564-1.

Examines the writings of a host of Viennese music critics, from Hanslick to Schenker, to provide a "slice history" of a one-year period in terms of its critical and aesthetic outlook and various political tensions.

B19 1996 Tuchowski, Andrzej. *Integracja strukturalna w świetle przemian stylu Chopina.* Kraków: Musica Iagellonica. ISBN 83-7099-048-7.

Discusses several of Chopin's late compositions, including the Ballades, the Barcarolle, and the F Minor Fantasia, in addition to several other pieces, utilizing a curious graphing technique that examines contour, motivic relationships, and intervallic structures.

B20   1995   Burns, Lori. *Bach's Modal Chorales*, Harmonologica Series, No. 9. Stuyvesant: Pendragon Press. ISBN 0-945-19374-2.

Studies Bach's chorales based on modal cantus firmi; extends Schenkerian techniques to account for a modal background.

B21   1995   Drabkin, William, with Susanna Pasticci and Egidio Pozzi. *Analisi Schenkeriana: Per un' interpretazione organica della struttura musicale*, Quaderni de Musica/Realta, Vol. 32. Lucca: Libreria musicale italiana. ISBN 8-870-96138-9.

Discusses (1) Schenker's life, works, and musical thought, (2) fundamental principles of Schenker's theory, and (3) the fundamental structure as a model of compositional elaboration. The next six chapters are devoted to analyses of complete pieces by Bach, Beethoven, Haydn, and Mozart, for which *Urlinie* graphs are provided. The book includes a bibliography of Schenker's works, secondary sources, and a German-English-Italian Schenker lexicon.

B22   1995   Eybl, Martin. *Ideologie und Methode: Zum Ideengeschichlichen Kontext von Schenkers Musiktheorie*. Tutzing: Schneider. ISBN 3-795-20816-5.

      Review: 1999   *Die Musikforschung* 52: 260–1.

Examines the evolution of Schenker's thought and the historical context from which it came. Includes, as an appendix, a catalog of Schenker's estate sale after his death.

B23   1995   Forte, Allen. *The American Popular Ballad of the Golden Era, 1924–1950*. Princeton: Princeton University Press. ISBN 0-691-04399-X.

      Reviews: 1999   *Sonneck Society Bulletin* 25/2: 63–4 (M. Pisani).
                     1998   *Music Analysis* 17/2: 256–9 (A. Moore).

Examines the musical design of popular songs of Gershwin, Carmichael, Porter, and others, according to Schenker's principles.

B24   1995   Gilbert, Steven. *The Music of George Gershwin*. New Haven: Yale University Press. ISBN 0-300-06233-8.

      Reviews: 1997   *Journal of Music Theory* 41/2: 319–29 (C. Folio).
                     1997   *Notes* 53/4: 1165–6 (G. Block).
                     1997   *Music and Letters* 78: 118–22 (C. Hailey).
                     1997   *Journal of Musicological Research* 16/4 (R. Wiecki).
                     1997   *American Studies* 38: 139–49 (B. Williams).

1996 *BBC Music Magazine* 4/10: 23 (J. Gibbons).
Discusses the music, from a Schenkerian point of view, in order to determine structural underpinnings.

B25 1995 Marston, Nicholas. *Beethoven's Piano Sonata in E, Op. 109.* Oxford: Oxford University Press. ISBN 0-193-15332-7.

Review: 1997 *Music Theory Online* 3/1 (M. Friedmann).

Examines and transcribes all manuscript sources for the work in addition to early printed additions, and studies Beethoven's sketchbooks and letters in order to understand the genesis of the work and its place in Beethoven's oeuvre. Considers the form of the work as a whole, suggesting that the individual movements are structurally incomplete and that closure occurs only at the end of the final movement.

B26 1995 Poulin, Pamela, ed. *J. S. Bach's Precepts and Principles for Playing the Thorough Bass or Accompanying in Four Parts.* Oxford: Oxford University Press. ISBN 0-198-16225-1.

A study of the work, presumably dictated by Bach to one of his students; consists of the facsimile, translation, commentary, and transcription (into modern clef) of the musical examples. Examines the work for clues into Bach's compositional and pedagogical practice; notes the its importance for Schenker.

B27 1995 Renwick, William. *Analyzing Fugue: A Schenkerian Approach.* Stuyvesant: Pendragon Press.

Reviews: 2000 Online Review: http://www.music.qub.ac.uk/ tomita/bachbib/review/bb-review Renwick-AnaFugue.html

1998 *Music Theory Spectrum* 20: 137–40 (C. Sabourin).

1997 *Intégral* 11: 101–33 (D. Smyth).

1996 *Music and Letters* 77/1: 116–9 (L. Pike).

1996 *Notes* 53/1: 93–4 (H. Platt).

1995 *Intégral* 9 (R. Gauldin).

Discusses the difficulties of fugal analysis from a Schenkerian perspective, noting that all voices carry essentially the same motivic/melodic content; considers the effect of this upon the voice-leading and tonal structure.

B28 1994 Thiemel, Matthias. *Tonale Dynamik: Theorie, musikalische Praxis und Vortragslehre seit 1800,* Berliner Musik Studien, Vol. 12 Köln: Tank. ISBN 3-89564-027-1.

A publication of the author's dissertation on the history of dynamics in tonal music (see **D82** below).

B29 1993 Luccio, Ricardo. *La musica come processo cognitivo.* Milano: Guerini.

Discusses cognitive models of music, citing Schenker and Chomsky. Notes the emphasis of current methods on stressing "the phenomenological and behavioral elements of profound structures or of general cognitive principles." (RILM; used by permission)

B30   1993   Cook, Nicholas John. *Beethoven: Symphony No. 9*, Cambridge Music Handbooks. Cambridge: Cambridge University Press. ISBN 0-521-3903-9.
   Translation: 1996   Cook, Nicholas. *Beethoven: 9. Sinfonia*. Athínai: Ekdoseis Stachy.
A study of the symphony, discussing it as a cultural symbol; cites analytical literature, including Schenker's 1911 monograph.

B31   1993   Dale, Catherine. *Tonality and Structure in Schoenberg's Second String Quartet, Op. 10*. New York: Garland Press. ISBN 0-815-30951-1.
Publication of the author's dissertation (see **D159** below).

B32   1993   Meeùs, Nicholas. *Heinrich Schenker: Une Introduction*. Liège: Mardaga. ISBN 2-870-09506-6.
   Reviews: 1996   *Music Analysis* 15/2–3: 367–72 (J. Rink).
              1996   *Revue de musicology* 82/2: 377–8 (S. Gut).
A introduction to Schenker and his works; discusses (1) the man and his works; (2) the theory of *Free Composition*; and (3) evaluations and criticisms of the theory. Includes an excellent (albeit unannotated) bibliography of primary and secondary materials, arranged chronologically, as well as a French-German glossary of terms.

B33   1993   Murtomäki, Veijo. *Symphonic Unity: The Development of Formal Thinking in the Symphonies of Sibelius*, Studia Musicologica Universitatis Helsingiensis 5. Helsinki: University of Helsinki.
   Review: 1995   *Music Theory Spectrum* 17/1: 124–8 (D. Loeb)
A publication of the author's dissertation on the later symphonies of Sibelius.

B34   1993   于蘇賢. 申克音樂分析理論概要. 北京: 人民音樂出版社。

   [1993 Yu, Su-xian. *Introduction to Schenkerian Analytical Concepts*. Beijing: People's Music Publications.]
An introduction to Schenker's method. Chapters include harmonic analysis, contrapuntal analysis, melodic analysis, structure and prolongation, double function (i.e., chords functioning as both contrapuntal and harmonic), mixture, application of contrapuntal prolongation and structure, form, and tonality. Contains numerous musical analyses, many drawn from Felix Salzer's *Structural Hearing* (see **B92** below).

B35 1992 Neumeyer, David, and Susan Tepping. *A Guide to Schenkerian Analysis.* Englewood Cliffs: Prentice Hall. ISBN 0-0287-1325-7.
      Reviews: 1993 *Music Theory Spectrum* 15/1: 89–93 (F. Samarotto).
              1993 *Intégral* 7: 179–94 (N. Hubbs).
A general introduction to Schenker's ideas; focuses on the bass and the upper voice in turn rather than together. Suggests that the text may, in conjunction with other sources, make up the material for a course.

B36 1992 Komar, Arthur J. "Linear-Derived Harmony." Dedham, Mass: Ovenbird Press.
      Review: 1992 *College Music Symposium* (M. Rodgers.)
Organized in terms of chord groupings: (1) basic tonal harmonic unit, the three-chord grouping; (2) diatonic and chromatic four-chord groupings; (3) techniques for harmonizing melodies; and (4) pedagogical tools geared to the preceding three parts. Suggests that the books may serve to introduce Schenker's ideas. (v)

B37 1991 Goląb, Maciej. *Chromatyka I tonalnosc w muzyce Chopina.* Kraków: PWM. Translated into German as *Chopins Harmonik: Chromatik in ihrer Beziehung zur Tonalität.* Köln: Bela Verlag, 1995.
Examines the relationship between chromaticism and tonality in Chopin's late music; applies Schenkerian analytical methodology.

B38 1990 Cadwallader, Alan, ed. *Trends in Schenkerian Research.* New York: Schirmer. ISBN 0-02-870551-3.
      Reviews: 1994 *Theory and Practice* 19: 121–52 (W. Everett).
              1993 *Notes* 49/3: 1048–53 (A. Keiler).
              1993 *Music Analysis* 12/2: 266–85 (M. Russ).
              1992 *Musical Quarterly* 76/2: 242–63 (T. Jackson).
              1991 *Music Theory Spectrum* 13/2: 265–73 (M. Brown).
A collection of nine essays on topics in Schenkerian analysis; indexed separately in chapter 3.

B39 1990 Federhofer, Hellmut. *Heinrich Schenker als Essayist und Kritiker: gesammelte Aufsätze, Rezensionen und kleinere Berichte aus dem Jahren 1891–1901*, Studien und Materialien zur Musikwissenschaft 5. Hildesheim: Georg Olms Verlag. ISBN 3-487-07960-7.
      Reviews: 1997 *Musicology Australia* 20: 110–11 (M. Kassler).
              1996 *Die Musikforschung* 49/2: 224–5 (I. Fellinger).
              1992 *Music and Letters* 73/3: 436–7 (N. Marston).
              1992 *Notes* 48/4: 1306–7 (T. Christensen).
              1992 *Dix-huitieme siécle* 24: 590 (M. Baridon).
              1992 *Die Musikforschung* 45/4: 451–2. (M. Heinemann).
              1991 *Music Research Forum* 6: 73–4 (R. Bowen).

A collection of more than a hundred essays and reviews of Schenker's, cataloged separately in chapter 2, with page references to this text.

B40   1990   Siegel, Heidi, ed. *Schenker Studies.* Cambridge: Cambridge University Press. ISBN 0-521-36038-2.
          Reviews: 1996   *Revue de musicologie* 82/2: 374–5. (S. Gut).
                         1994   *Theory and Practice* 19: 121–52 (W. Everett).
                         1993   *Music Analysis* 12/2: 266–85) (M. Russ).
                         1993   *Notes* 49/3: 1048–53 (A. Keiler).
                         1992   *Die Musikforschung* 45/2: 177–8.
                         1992   *Musical Quarterly* 76/2: 242–63 (T .Jackson).
                         1991   *Music Theory Spectrum* 13/2: 265–73 (M. Brown).
                         1991   *Music and Letters* 72/1: 141–4 (N. Marston).
A collection of fourteen essays (one including an extensive bibliography) based on papers read at the 1985 Schenker Symposium at the Mannes College of Music; cataloged separately in chapter 3.

B41   1989   Cavett-Dunsby, Esther C. *Mozart's Variations Reconsidered: Four Case Studies* New York: Garland Press. ISBN 0-824-02340-4.
          Reviews: 1994   *Mozart-Jahrbuch*: 195–7 (U. Knorad).
                         1991   *Music Analysis* 10: 1–2: 207–14 (T. Jones).
Publication of the author's dissertation (see **D158** below).

B42   1989   Rothstein, William. "Phrase Rhythm in Tonal Music." New York: Macmillan. ISBN 0-02-872191-8.
Composed in two parts: theoretical underpinnings (definition of the concepts with examples from the literature) and analytical applications (to music of Haydn, Mendelssohn, Chopin, and Wagner). Applies Schenkerian precepts to the analysis of rhythm.

B43   1988   Cube, Felix-Eberhard von. *The Book of the Musical Artwork: An Interpretation of the Musical Theories of Heinrich Schenker,* Studies in the History and Interpretation of Music, Vol. 10, trans. and provided with an afterword by David Neumeyer, George Boyd, and Scott Harris. Lewiston, N. Y.: The Edward Mellon Press. ISBN 0-889-46436-7.
          Reviews: 1991   *Theory and Practice* 16: 215–9 (P. Burstein).
                         1990   *Die Musikforschung* 43/4: 390–1 (H. Federhofer).
                         1988   *Indiana Theory Review* 9/2: 135–44 (W. Drabkin).
Consists of three parts: (1) the tonal system; (2) the entelechy and biogenesis of the musical artwork; and (3) analyses. After a thorough exegesis of the workings of the tonal system, von Cube outlines the "nine stages of biogenesis" (of which the *Ursatz* is the seventh). The third part contains "scientifically unbiased, irreproachable, irrefutable" analyses of works ranging from Greek melodies through Jarnach's *Hymnus* of 1957 (see Composer Index). (203)

B44 1988 Dunsby, Jonathan, and Arnold Whitall. *Music Analysis in Theory and Practice.* New Haven: Yale University Press. ISBN 1-878-82279-9.

Reviews: 1989 *Journal of Music Theory* 33/1: 165–89 (P. van den Toorn).

1989 *Journal of Musicological Research* 9/2–3: 174–8 (M. D. Green).

1989 *Music Analysis* 8/1–2: 177–86. (M. Musgrave).

1988 *Theory and Practice* 13: 133–50. (T. Greer).

1988 *Journal of Music Theory Pedagogy* 2/2: 297–311 (M. Rodgers).

In the first part, "Aspects of Tonal Analysis," the authors include three chapters on Schenker: "Schenker the Theorist" (pp. 23–28), "Schenkerian Analysis" (pp. 29–52), and "Developments in Schenker: Katz and Salzer" (pp. 53–61). Cites and explains Schenker's analysis of "Ich bin's, ich solte Büßen" from the *Fünf Urlinie-Tafeln.*

B45 1987 Bent, Ian, and William Drabkin. *Analysis.* New York: Norton. ISBN 0-393-02447-4.

Translation: 1990 *Analisi musicale.* (Torino: Edizion di Torino).

An expansion of the *New Grove* article on analysis (1980); contains discussions of the major approaches to musical analysis as well as an extensive glossary and bibliography.

B46 1987 Cook, Nicholas. *A Guide to Musical Analysis.* London: Dent.

Translation: 1991 *Guida all'analisi musicale* (Milano: Guerini).

A general discussion of methods of musical analysis. See pp. 27–66 for a discussion of Schenkerian analysis.

B47 1987 Dembski, Stephen, and Joseph N. Straus, eds. "Milton Babbitt: Words about Music." Madison: University of Wisconsin Press.

Review: 1994 *Notes* 50/4: 1411–2 (R. Swift)

Discusses Schenker in chapter 5 (pp. 121–62) *passim,* especially the sections "The Schenker Synthesis and a Bach Chorale [no. 217]" and "Schenker's Analysis of a Bach Chorale [no. 117] and Some Additional Parallelisms."

B48 1987 Grave, Floyd K., and Margaret Grave. *In Praise of Harmony: The Teachings of Abbé Georg Joseph Vogler.* Lincoln: University of Nebraska Press. ISBN: 0-803-22128-2.

Discusses the writings of Vogler, who represented chord functions with Roman numerals and employed a reductive analysis that foreshadowed Schenker's.

B49 1986 Kucukalic, Zija. *Die Struktur des Kunstwerks: mit besondere Berücksichtigung der Musik.* Lier & Boog Studies 3. Amsterdam: Rodopj. ISBN 90-6203-608-2.

The identity of a musical artwork is determined from a phenomenological perspective; the different levels of a musical work are analyzed to create a basis for evaluating a music work. (RILM; used by permission)

B50   1986   Lester, Joel. *The Rhythms of Tonal Music.* Carbondale: Southern Illinois University Press. ISBN 0-8093-1282-4.
A discussion of various methods of rhythmic analysis, including the approaches derived from Schenker.

B51   1986   Neumeyer, David. *The Music of Paul Hindemith.* New Haven: Yale University Press. ISBN 0-00-03287-0.
Employs methodology similar to Schenker's in his analysis of Hindemith's music, which, though hierarchic, "has no limited set of *a priori* constructs like Schenker's *Ursätze*."

B52   1985   Federhofer, Hellmut. *Heinrich Schenker: Nach Tagebücher und Briefen in der Oswald Jonas Memorial Collection, University of California, Riverside,* Studien zur Musikwissenschaft, Vol. 3. Hildesheim: Georg Olms Verlag. ISBN 3-487-07462-X.
　　　Reviews:　　1988   *Music Analysis* 7/2: 233–8 (W. Rothstein).
　　　　　　　　　1987   *Music and Letters* 68/3: 279–81 (W. Drabkin).
　　　　　　　　　1986   *Journal of the American Musicological Society* 39/3: 667–77 (W. Pastille).
　　　　　　　　　1986   *Neue Zeitschrift für Musik* 147/12: 78–9 (P. Cahn).
　　　　　　　　　1986   *Österreichische Musikzeitung* 41/6: 337–38 (R. Stephan).
A biographical study of Schenker based on his correspondence and diaries. Consists of (1) biography; (2) connections to artists, scholars, and writers on music; (3) music critics; (4) opinions about authors, philosophers, writers and literary works; (5) Schenker's worldview; and (6) Schenker in the intellectual context of his time and posterity. Contains a listing of literature and index of names.

B53   1985   Sloboda, John A. *The Musical Mind: The Cognitive Psychology of Music,* Oxford Psychology Series, Vol. 5. Oxford: Clarendon Press, 1985. ISBN 0-19-852114-6.
　　　Reviews:　　1986   *Music Perception* 3/4: 427–9. (D. Butler).
　　　　　　　　　1987   *Music Analysis* 6/1–2: 179–91. (E. Graebner).
　　　　　　　　　1986   *British Journal of Music Education* 3/2: 240–2 (G. Pratt).
　　　　　　　　　1987   *Council for Research in Music Education Bulletin* 94: 77–82 (J. Sherbon and K. Miklaszewski).
　　　　　　　　　1988   *Journal of Music Theory Pedagogy* 2/1:163–72 (E. Marvin).
　　　　　　　　　1988   *Musikforschung* 41/2: 191–2 (H. de la Motte-Haber).

1986 *Music and Letters* 67/3: 320–1 (C. Longuet-Higgins).
1986 *Musik-Psychology* 3: 210–2
1987 *Musical Times* 128/1729: 142–3 (F. Sparshott).
1985 *Nature* 315/6021: 696 (E. Clarke).

Surveys literature on the application of cognitive psychology to the study of music; includes a list of introductory reading. Attempts to "highlight and elucidate some basic characteristics of musical skills and the cognitive mechanisms which serve them." (vi)

B54 1985 Stein, Deborah. *Hugo Wolf's Lieder and Extensions of Tonality.* Ann Arbor: UMI Research Press. ISBN 0-053-71469-1.

Publication of the author's dissertation (see **D189** below).

B55 1985 Wason, Robert. *Viennese Harmonic Theory from Albrechtsberger to Schenker and Schoenberg.* Ann Arbor: UMI Research Press. ISBN 0-835-71586-8.

Reviews: 1989 *Journal of Music Theory* 33/1: 214–21 (S. Hefling).
1986 *Music Theory Spectrum* 8: 140–2 (W. Caplin).

Publication of the author's dissertation (see **D197** below).

B56 1984 Deliege, Célestin. *Les fondaments de la musique tonale: Une perspective analytique post-schenkerienne.* Paris: J. C. Lattès. ISSN 0242-7834.

Reviews: 1986 *Journal of Music Theory* 30/1: 122–30. (J. Swain).
1986 *Muzyka* 31/4: 106–10 (Z. Helman).
1987 *Revue de musicology* 73/1: 139–43 (G. Le Coat).
1987 *Revue musicale de Suisse romande* 38/1: 41–2 (G. Le Coat).

Contains a critical description of Schenker's method and suggests amendments; discusses theories of modulation, generative theories, prosaic structure, thematic perspectives, and an appendix on stylistic/semantic analysis.

B57 1984 Thaler, Lotte. *Organische Form in der Musiktheorie des 19. und beginnenden 20. Jahrhunderts*, Berliner musikwissenschaftliche Arbeiten, Vol. 25. München and Salzburg: Katzbichler.

Publication of the author's dissertation (see **D183** below).

B58 1983 Beach, David, ed. *Aspects of Schenkerian Theory.* New Haven: Yale University Press. ISBN 0-300-02803-2.

Review: 1988 *Musikforschung* 41/1: 88–9 (H. Federhofer).
1985 *Journal of Music Theory* 29/1: 169–77 (P. McCreless).
1984 *In Theory Only* 7/7–8: 51–7 (D. Damschroder).

1984   *Music Analysis* 3/3: 277–84 (A. Keiler).
1984   *Theory and Practice* 9/1–2: 119–24 (C. Hatch and D. Bernstein).
1984   *Music and Letters* 65/1: 83–7 (C. Ayrey).
1984   *Music Teacher* 63/7: 20 (J. Fenton).
1984   *Österreichische Musikzeitung* 38/7–8: 452.
1984   *Nineteenth-Century Music* 8/2: 164–76. (R. Swift).
1983   *Choice* 20: 1147.
1983   *Times Literary Supplement* (1 July): 697 (C. Whittle).

A collection of ten essays on various topics in Schenkerian theory; cataloged separately in chapter 3.

B59   1983   Lerdahl, Fred, and Ray Jackendoff. *A Generative Theory of Tonal Music*. Cambridge: MIT Press. ISBN 0-262-62107-X.
    Reviews: 1987   *Journal of Aesthetics and Art Criticism* 46/1: 94–8 (R. Cantrick).
        1987   *Musiktheorie* 2/2: 192–4 (C. Dahlhaus).
        1986   *Musicology* 9: 72–3.
        1986   *Muzyka* 31/4: 100–6 (Z. Helman).
        1985   *Music Theory Spectrum* 7: 190–202 (E. Hantz).
        1985   *Music Analysis* 4/3: 292–303 (D. Harvey).
        1984   *In Theory Only* 8/6: 27–52 (R. Cohn).
        1984   *The Musical Times* 125: 273 (W. Drabkin).
        1984   *Nineteenth-Century Music* 8/2: 168–9 (R. Swift).
        1984   *Journal of Music Theory* 28: 271–94 (J. Peel and W. Slawson).
        1984   *Notes* 41: 502–5 (F. Retzel).
        1984   *Journal of the American Musicological Society* 37: 196–205 (J. Swain).
        1984   *Computer Music Journal* 8/4: 56–64 (P. Child).
        1984   *Music Perception* 2/2: 275–90 (B. Rosner).
        1983   *Psychomusicology* 3/1–2: 60–7 (H. Cady).
        1983   *Canadian University Music Review* 4: 141–83 (C. Deliège).

Presents a theory, derivative of Schenker in its use of reduction and hierarchical organization. Designed to model the experiences of the listener, which are expressed as rules and preferences regarding metric and grouping structure and governing the time-span and prolongational reductions.

B60   1983   Rushton, Julian. *The Musical Language of Berlioz*. Cambridge: Cambridge University Press: chapters 11–4. ISBN 0-521-24279-7.

Employs Schenkerian analysis in an analysis of Berlioz's music, despite acknowledging that "Schenkerian analysis may . . . bring out what Schenker would have interpreted as negative signals, indicating ineptitude, lack of richness, a deplorably Rameau-based education"—which are "characteristic, and potentially expressive, features of Berlioz's music." (173)

B61 1982 Federhofer, Hellmut. *Heinrich Schenkers Verhältnis zu Arnold Schönberg*, Mitteilungen der Kommission für Musikforschung, Vol. 33. Wien: Verlag der Österreichischen Akademie der Wissenschaften.

Discusses the correspondence between Schenker and Schoenberg, noting similarities and differences in their aesthetic outlooks, and providing transcriptions of said correspondence.

B62 1982 Forte, Allen, and Stephen Gilbert. *Introduction to Schenkerian Analysis*. New York: Norton. ISBN 0-393-95192-8.

Reviews:	1984	*Music Theory Spectrum* 6: 110–21 (L. Laskowski).
	1983	*Music Analysis* 2/3: 281–90 (J. Marra).
	1983	*In Theory Only* 7/4: 45–51 (P. Bergquist).
	1984	*Journal of Music Theory* 28/1: 113–23 (R. Kamien).
	1984	*Nineteenth-Century Music* 8/2: 164–76. (R. Swift).
	1984	*Musical Quarterly* 70: 269–78 (J. Dubiel).
	1984	*Notes* 41: 268–70 (C. Wilner).
	1986	*Muzyka* 31/4: 91–4 (A. Tuchowski).
	1987	*Svensk tidskrift för musikfoskining* 69: 160–2.
Translation:	1992	Forte, Allen, and Steven Gilbert. *Introduccion al analisis Schenkeriano*. Barcelona: Labor.

Introduces the graphing process in a pedagogical sequence, moving from simpler to more complex issues; contains exercises with pointed commentary to aid the student. Unfortunately, many examples are poorly copied; instructor's manual available separately.

B63 1982 Lester, Joel. *Harmony in Tonal Music*, 2 vols. New York: Alfred A. Knopf.

Reviews:	1983	*Music Theory Spectrum* 5: 132–6 (D. Neumeyer).
	1984	*Journal of Music Theory* 28/1: 142–54 (P. Breslauer).

Although the text assumes no knowledge of Schenker's theories, they are used to teach basic harmonic principles. Lester shows the student, after basic chords are identified, "how [the connections between chords] fill in larger progressions." (vi)

B64 1981 Federhofer, Hellmut. *Akkord und Stimmführung in den musiktheoretisch Systemen von Hugo Riemann, Ernst Kurth und Heinrich Schenker 1981*, Veröffentlichung der Staatlichen Instituts für Musikforschung, Vol. 21. Wien: Verlag der Österreichischen Akademie der Wissenschaften. ISBN 3-700-10385-9.

> Translation: 1991 "Per una critica della theoria funzionale." *Azzaroni*: 245–64 [orig. pp. 11–31].
> Reviews: 1983 *Music Analysis* 2/1: 102–4 (W. Drabkin).
>   1983 *Journal of Music Theory* 27/1: 99–110 (D. Neumeyer).
>   1982 *Music Theory Spectrum 4*: 131–7 (J. Rothgeb).
>   1982 *Notes* 38: 843–844 (C. Willner).
>   1982 *Svensk Tijdschrift för Musikforskining* 64: 84–6 (I. Bengtsson).
>   1984 *Neue Musikzeitung* 33/1 (K. Plum).

Chapters include "On Criticism of *Funktionstheorie*," "Linear Counterpoint and Harmony in the Music Theory of Ernst Kurth," "On Criticism of the Concepts of *Stufe* and Counterpoint in Heinrich Schenker's Music Theory," "Convergence and Divergence in the Voice-Leading Analyses," "Voice-Leading Analyses, *Substanzgemeinschaft*, and Procedural Characteristics of Music," and "The Problem of Tonality."

B65 1980 Albersheim, Gerhard. *Die Tonsprache*, Mainzer Studien zur Musikwissenschaft, Vol. 15. Tutzing: Schneider, 1980.

> Review: 1982 *Musikforschung* 35/3: 323–4 (C. Mollers).

Part 1 discusses music as a grammar; part 2 discusses musical theory and practice of the twentieth century, devoting chapters to Riemann, Schenker, Schoenberg, Hindemith, and serial music.

B66 1979 Epstein, David. *Beyond Orpheus: Studies in Musical Structure.* New York: Cambridge University Press. ISBN 0-262-05016-1.

> Reviews: 1981 *Music Theory Spectrum* 3: 150–7 (G. Wittlich).
>   1987 *Brio* 24/2: 71–2 (J. Wagstaff).
>   1979 *Jounal of the Arnold Schoenberg Institute* 3/2: 194–202 (J. Dunsby).
>   1981 *Theory and Practice* 6/2: 47–53 (W. Rothstein).
>   1983 *Journal of Music Theory* 25/2: 319–26 (A. Whitall).
>   1983 *Music Analysis* 2: 225–7 (J. Harvey).
>   1982 *In Theory Only* 6/2: 31–9 (S. Larson).
>   1979 *Notes* 36: 357–8 (L. Stempl).
>   1979 *Music and Letters* 69/3: 407–9 (K. Agawu).
>   1979 *Music and Musicians* 28/5: 38–40 (M. Barry).

1980   *Journal of Aesthetics and Art Criticism* 38: 480–2 (W. Webster).
1982   *Journal of Music Theory* 26/1: 208–10 (D. Epstein).
1982   *Journal of Music Theory* 26/1: 211–2 (A. Whitall).

Describes Schenker and Schoenberg as "complementary historical figures," and employs both of their analytical ideas in the discussions contained in the book, which are concerned to a large degreed with composers' use of time. (x)

B67   1979   Forte, Allen. *Tonal Harmony in Concept and Practice*, 3rd ed. New York: Holt, Rinehart and Winston.

Designed to "prepare the student for advanced study of tonal music." Employs figured bass to indicate voice-leading and vertical structures. Includes chapters on large-scale structures and linear intervallic patterns. (v)

B68   1979   Plum, Karl-Otto. *Untersuchungen zu Heinrich Schenkers Stimmführungsanalyse*. Kölner Beiträge zur Musikforschung. Regensburg: Gustav Boße Verlag.

Reviews: 1983   *Music Analysis* 2/1: 102–4 (W. Drabkin).
            1981   *Music and Letters* 62: 212–5 (J. Dunsby).
            1981   *Musikforschung* 34: 509–11 (E. Seidel).

Provides an introduction to Schenker's theories and terminology; examines Bach's works for solo string instruments from a harmonic, formal, motivic-thematic, rhythmic, and voice-leading perspective.

B69   1978   Aldwell, Edward, and Carl Schachter. *Harmony and Voice Leading*. New York: Harcourt Brace Jovanovich (2nd ed. 1989).

Focuses on a few harmonic relationships at a time, "[making] it possible to show examples from the literature at a much earlier stage than in other approaches." Focuses on linear expansion of harmonies, e.g., prolongations. (vi)

B70   1978   Brooks, Richard, and Gerald Warfield. *Layer Dictation: A New Approach to the Bach Chorales*. New York: Longman. ISBN 0-582-28046-X.

Proposes a layered approach to dictation based on Schenker's ideas of prolongation. Proceeds from the premise that, "with the chordal structure in front of him, the student can more easily perceive which of the four voices contains the contrapuntal motion." (iii)

B71   1978   Laskowski, Larry. *Heinrich Schenker: An Annotated Index to His Analyses of Musical Works*. Stuyvesant: Pendragon. ISBN 0-918-72807-X.

Reviews: 1979   *Journal of Music Theory* 23/2: 304–7 (H. Krebs).
            1979   *Notes* 36/1: 98–9 (J. Rothgeb).

Scours the works of Schenker, cataloging his musical examples. Cites example number and commentary as well as the general type of analysis (e.g., a foreground graph) in Schenker's original works and then-available translations.

B72 1977 Narmour, Eugene. *Beyond Schenkerism: The Need for Alternatives in Musical Analysis*. Chicago: University of Chicago Press. ISBN 0-226-56847-4.

Reviews: 1981 *The American Organist* 15/1: 12 (C. Heaton).
1980 *Music Review* 41/2: 154–5 (D. Chittum).
1980 *Musikforschung* 33/3: 372–74 (H. Federhofer).
1979 *Music and Letters* 60/1: 86–90 (A. Whittall).
1979 *Nineteenth-Century Music* 2/3: 267–9 (J. McCalla).
1979 *Indiana Theory Review* 3/1: 7–15 (R. Hatten).
1979 *Journal of Music Theory* 23/7: 287–304 (S. Haflich).
1979 *Humanities Association Review* 30/1–2: 114–8 (A. Cohen).
1979 *Journal of the American Musicological Society* 32/3: 586–91 (J. LaRue).
1978 *Journal of Research in Music Education* 26/4: 481–6 (J. Rothgeb).
1978 *Musical Times* 119/1622: 331 (W. Drabkin).
1978 *Interface* 7/2–3: 169–71 (F. Weiland).
1978 *Perspectives of New Music* 17/1: 196–210 (H. Martin).
1978 *Perspectives of New Music* 17/1: 161–95 (A. Keiler).
1978 *Perspectives of New Music* 17/1: 196–210 (H. Martin).
1978 *Theory and Practice* 3/2: 28–42 (J. Rothgeb).
1978 *Zeitschrift für Musiktheorie* 9/2: 52–4 (W. E. Caplin).
1978 *Choice* 15/3: 410.
1977 *Journal of Aesthetics and Art Criticism* 36/4: 505–7 (K. Dreyfus).
1977 *Notes* 34/4: 857–59 (R. Solie).

Attempts to "refute the principal beliefs of Schenkerian theory and to dispute many of the analytical practices of its followers . . . [demonstrating] that Schenkerian voice-leading principles produce analytical results that are patently indefensible." (ix)

B73 1977 Yeston, Maury, ed. *Readings in Schenker Analysis and Other Approaches*. New Haven: Yale University Press. ISBN 0-300-02114-3.

Reviews: 1977 *Choice* 14/11: 1510.
            1980 *Musikforschung* 33/3: 371–2 (H. Federhofer).
            1978 *Musical Times* 119/1622: 331 (W. Drabkin).
            1978 *Music and Musicians* 27/6: 40–1 (M. Barry).
            1978 *Nineteenth-Century Music* 2/3: 267–9 (J. McCalla).
            1978 *Österreichische Musikzeitung* 33/9: 468.
A collection of essays, some reprinted from diverse sources, others original. Contains three analysis symposia on Mozart K. 344, Schubert op. 94/1, and Beethoven op. 53. The essays have been cataloged separately in chapter 3.

B74 1976 Berry, Wallace. *Structural Functions of Music*. Englewood Cliffs: Prentice Hall. ISBN 0-13-853903-0.
Reviews: 1977 *Tempo* 122: 20–4 (J. Samson).
"An inquiry into *tonal, textural, and rhythmic structures in music,* and into conceptual and analytical systems for the study of these fundamental elements." (xi)

B75 1976 Flechsig, Hartmut. *Studien zu Theorie und Methode musikalischer Analyse*, Beiträge zur Musikforschung, Vol. 1. München: Katzbichler.
Presents an overview of analytical methodologies, including Schenker's.

B76 1976 Warfield, Gerald. *Layer Analysis: A Primer of Elementary Tonal Structures*. New York: David McKay Company. ISBN 0-679-30297-2.
A workbook designed to introduce undergraduate students to the concept of structural levels. Contains exercises of four to six measures in length drawn from the literature; also, appendices on layer notation, divergences with Schenker, and supplementary readings.

B77 1976 Yeston, Maury. *The Stratification of Musical Rhythm*. New Haven: Yale University Press. ISBN 0-300-01884-3.
An early application of Schenker's ideas applied to rhythm, where "the weight of analysis will be thrown towards an elucidation of rhythmic structure that is characterized by levels of meaning." Distinguishes between pitch to rhythm and rhythm to pitch approaches.

B78 1975 Westergaard, Peter. *An Introduction to Tonal Theory*. New York: Norton. ISBN 0-393-09342-5.
Takes species counterpoint as its "central pedagogical means . . . to understand the complex and varied voice-leading patterns of actual eighteenth- and nineteenth-century music in terms of simpler patterns." Also formulates a theory of tonal rhythm. (vii)

B79 1974 Henneberg, Gudrun. *Theorieen zur Rhythmik und Metrik Mögtlichkeiten und Grenzen rhythmischer und metrischer Analyse,* *dargestellt am Beispiele der Wiener Klassik*, Mainzer Studien zur Musikwissenschaft, Vol. 6. Tutzing: Schneider.

Responses: 1976   *Musikforschung* 29/2: 183–6 (C. Dahlhaus).
               1977   *Musikforschung* 30/2: 191–3 (G. Henneberg).

A survey of theories of rhythm and meter from the eighteenth century to the present, examining their strengths and weaknesses. Considers the relationship of rhythm and meter and tonal structure.

B80   1973   Zuckerkandl, Victor. *Sound and Symbol II: Man the Musician.* Princeton: Princeton University Press. ISBN 0-691-01812-X.

Review: 1975   *Journal of Aesthetics and Art Criticism*: 356 (B. Morton).

The influence of Schenker is clear throughout, but especially in chapter 9, "Hearing Organic Structure." Zuckerkandl discusses the general concept of "musicality" before addressing the subjects of the "musical ear" (cognition) and "musical thought" (the creative process).

B81   1971   Komar, Arthur. *Theory of Suspensions.* Princeton: Princeton University Press.

Reviews: 1971   *Australian Journal of Music Education* 9: 55 (A. McCredie).
               1971   *Choice* 8/9: 1186.
               1972   *Journal of Music Theory* 16/1–2: 210–9 (J. Rothgeb).
               1973   *Musical Quarterly* 59/2: 320–2 (C. Hatch).
               1972   *Notes* 29/1: 52–4 (G. George).

Publication of the author's dissertation; see **D233** below.

B82   1969   Salzer, Feliz, and Carl Schachter. *Counterpoint in Composition: The Study of Voice-Leading.* New York: McGraw-Hill. ISBN 07-054497-2.

Reviews: 1969   *Perspectives of New Music* 8/1: 151–4 (S. Persky).
               1969   *Journal of Music Theory* 13/2: 307–16. (J. Rothgeb).
               1971   *Beiträge zur Musikwissenschaft* 13/3: 226–7 (J. Wilbrandt).
               1970   *Dansk Musiktidsskrift* 45/4: 112–3 (M. Levy).
               1970   *Music in Education* 34/341: 36 (L. Orrey).
               1971   *Music and Musicians* 20/11: 46–7 (W. Shaw).

Translation: 1992   Baroni, Mario, et al. *Contrappunto e composizione.* Torino: Edizioni di Torino.

A textbook, influenced by the Schenker approach, that "treats counterpoint not only as a self-contained discipline but also in relation to other aspects of musical design." The first part introduces the five species, and the second deals with pro-

longed counterpoint, including a chapter on voice-leading techniques in historical perspective. (viii)

B83 1969 Zuckerkandl, Victor. *Sound and Symbol: Music and the External World.* Princeton: Princeton University Press. ISBN 0-691-
01759-X.

Considers four main topics: tone, motion, time, and space. Seeks to understand
music's place in society by examining the question (paraphrasing Kant), "[W]hat
must the world be like, what must I be like, if between me and the world the phenomenon of music can occur." Schenker's influence is evident throughout, but
especially in part 2. (7)

B84 1968 Cone, Edward. *Musical Form and Musical Performance.* New
York: Norton. ISBN 0-390-97676.
Reviews: 1971 *Perspectives of New Music* 9/2 and 10/1: 271–90.
(W. Berry).

Consists of three essays: "The Nature of Musical Form," "Problems of Performance," and "Form and Style." Describes long-term rhythmic features such as "extended upbeats" and "structural downbeats," establishing hierarchic relationships.

B85 1967–87 *The Music Forum,* 6 volumes (1967, 1970, 1973, 1976, 1980,
and 1987), ed. by Felix Salzer and William J. Mitchell (later,
Carl Schachter).
Reviews: 1982 *Music Analysis* 1/2: 203–9 (W. Drabkin).
1982 *Journal of Musicological Research* 4/1–2: 193–
205 (S. Fuller).
1982 *Music and Letters* 63/1–2: 107–11 (J. Dunsby).
1978 *Music and Letters* 59/1: 79–82 (W. Drabkin).
1974 *Notes* 30/4: 778–9 ((J. Webster).
1972 *Music Educator's Journal* 59/1 (H. Clarke).
1972 *Journal of Research in Music Education* 20/1 (W.
Newmann).
1971 *Perspectives of New Music* 9/2 and 10/1: 314–22
(A. Komar).
1971 *Notes* 27/2: 220–22 (L. Rowell).
1969 *Music Review* 30/4 (A. F. Thomas).
1969 *Die Musikforschung* 22/3 (H. Federhofer).

A periodical devoted to the propagation of Schenker's ideas, including contributions by "those who have applied his approach rigorously to a literature of limited historic scope [as well as those] who recognize the more universal values
that lie dormant in his ideas and are capable of providing valuable insights into
earlier and later music." (ix)

B86 1965 Green, Douglass M. *Form in Tonal Music.* (2nd ed., 1979) New
York: Holt, Rinehart, and Winston. ISBN 0-030-20286-8.

A textbook on the standard formal categories, seeking to equip the student with the "ability to approach a piece of music unencumbered by *a priori* notions as to what characteristics it should or should not have, and to discover, it might be said in *innocence*, the structure of the music." Acknowledges a debt to Felix Salzer for the view of form as the "interaction of tonal structure and design." (vii)

B87   1960   Cooper, Grosvernor, and Leonard B. Meyer. *The Rhythmic Structure of Music*. Chicago: University of Chicago Press. ISBN 0-226-11522-4.

Reviews: 1963   *Journal of the American Musicological Society* 16/2: 370–2 (H. Tischler).

1962   *Music and Letters* 43/1: 72–4 (A. Hutchings).

1962   *Notes* 20/1: 60–1 (W. Berry).

1961   *Journal of Music Theory* 5: 129–34. (E. B. Kohs.)

1961   *Instrumentalist* 15/7: 14.

1961   *Journal of Research in Music Education* 9/1: 77–8 (C. L. Gary).

1961   *Musical Courier* 163/8: 46 (F. Werlé).

1961   *Tempo* 59: 32 (P. Evans).

Suggests that "rhythmic structure is perceived . . . as an organic process in which smaller rhythmic motives, while possessing a shape and structure of their own, also function as integral parts of a larger rhythmic organization." The idea of "architectonic levels" suggests parallels with Schenker. (2)

B88   1959   Zuckerkandl, Victor. *The Sense of Music*. Princeton: Princeton University Press. LCCN 57–8670.

A relatively nontechnical study of musical cognition based on Schenker's ideas. Discusses melody, texture and structure, meter and rhythm, polyphony, harmony, and the interaction of melody and harmony.

B89   1956   Meyer, Leonard B. *Emotion and Meaning in Music*. Chicago: University of Chicago Press. (2nd ed., 1961).

Reviews: 1956   *Canadian Music Journal* 1/4: 71–6 (G. B. Payzant).

1957   *Chicago Review* 11/2: 97–100 (M. G. Raskin).

1957   *High Fidelity [Musical America]* 7/4: 29–30 (R. D. Darrell).

1957   *Journal of Aesthetics and Art Criticism* 16/2: 285–6 (J. Portnoy).

1957   *Journal of Music Theory* 1/1: 110–2 (D. Kraechenbuehl).

1957   *Music and Letters* 38/3: 278–9 (F. Howes).

1958   *Monthly Musical Report* 88/988: 149–50 (P. T. B.).

1957   *Musical Quarterly* 43/4: 553–7 (E. A. Lippman).

1958   *Music Review* 19/1: 64–7 (G. A. Marco).

1958 *Musical Times* 99/1380: 82 (H. Raynor).
1956 *Notes* 14/1: 253–4 (R. S. Hill).
1957 *New Yorker* 32/46: 63–5 (W. Sargeant).
1957 *Pan Pipes* 50/1: 41 (E. G. Gilliand).
1956 *Yale Review* 46/4: 627–29 (K. Konnelly).

Meyer is "concerned with an examination and analysis of those aspects of meaning which result from the understanding of and response to relationships inherent in the musical process" rather than extramusical relationships. Considers how musical meaning is conveyed. (3)

B90 1955 Forte, Allen. *Contemporary Tone Structures*. New York: Bureau of Publications, Teacher's College, Columbia University.

Reviews: 1957 *Journal of Music Theory* 1: 112–8 (H. Boatwright).
1956 *Etude* 74/6: 8 (W. Mitchell).
1956 *Journal of Research in Music Education* 4/1: 85–92 (J. Verrall).
1956 *Music and Letters* 37/2: 187–9 (H. Keller).
1955 *Notes* 13/3: 431–2 (H. Livingston).

Rebuttal: 1958 *Journal of Music Theory* 1/2: 201–5. (A. Forte).

Response: 1959 *Journal of Music Theory* 2/1: 85–92 (H. Boatwright).

After an introductory section outlining the methodology, Forte applies Schenker's method to Stravinsky's *Petrouchka*, Bartók's Fourth String Quartet, and Schoenberg's *Phantasy for Violin*.

B91 1953 Langer, Susanne K. *Feeling and Form*. New York: Charles Scribner's Sons.

Discusses Schenker's theories; rejects the idea that composers begin to with a "blueprint" of the *Urlinie* and "deliberately [compose] the piece within its frame." (124)

B92 1952 Salzer, Felix. *Structural Hearing: Tonal Coherence in Music*. 2 vols. New York: Charles Boni. Reprint ed., New York: Dover Publications, 1969. ISBN 0-486-22275-6.

Reviews: 1952 *Journal of the American Musicological Society* 5: 260–95 (M. Babbitt).
1953 *Musical Quarterly* 39: 126–8 (N. Broder).
1953 *Music and Letters* 34: 329–32 (W. H. Mellers).
1963 *Dansk musiktidsskrift* 38/7: 284–5 (M. Levy).
1952 *International Musician* 51/5: 28 (J. R.).
1952 *Musical Courier* 145/10: 30.
1980 *Musikforschung* 33/4: 513–4 (H. Rösling).
1953 *Monthly Musical Record* 83/946: 85–7.

1953   *Musical Times* 94/1324: 236 (M. Carner).

1952   *Notes* 10/3: 439 (O. Jonas).

Translations: 1977   *Strukturelles Hören: der tonale Zusammenhang in der Musik*, Taschenbücher zur Musikwissenschaft, Vol. 10–11 Wilhelmshaven Heinrichshofen. (2nd ed., 1983) ISBN: 3-795-90220-7.

Reviews: 1978   *Musica* 32/6: 581–2 (C. Kühn).

1978   *Tibia* 3/3: 189–91 (A. Riethmüller).

Discusses elements of Schenker's theory, the pedagogy of structural hearing, and "the implications and consequences of structural hearing as they concern problems of musical understanding, interpretation and musicology." Contains musical examples ranging from chant to contemporary music. (xvii–xviii)

B93   1950   Routley, Erik. *The Church and Music*. London: Gerald Duckworth & Co.

Contains a brief analogy comparing Schenker's way of thinking to the analysis of a sermon in order to expose the essential meaning, or being able to distinguish "what is peripheral from what is central." (243)

B94   1950   Federhofer, Hellmut. *Beiträge zur musikalischen Gestaltanalyse*. Graz: Akademische Druck- und Verlagsanstalt.

Review: 1951   *Music and Letters* 32: 177–80 (M. Cooper).

Discusses the theories of Schenker, Kurth, Riemann, and Bernhard. Includes foreground graphs of Mozart's A Minor Sonata, K. 310, Bach's Prelude and Fugue in D major (WTC II), and Brahms's Intermezzo op. 118/1.

B95   1948   Daniskas, John. *Grondslagen voor de Analytische Vormleer der musiek*. Rotterdam: W. L. and J. Brusse.

Review: 1951   *Journal of the American Musicological Society* 4/1: 51–5 (A. Ringer).

Criticizes Schenker's concept of the *Ursatz* and *Urlinie* as being static and insufficient to describe the complexities of the music.

B96   1945   Katz, Adele. *Challenge to Musical Tradition: A New Concept of Tonality*. New York: Da Capo Press.

"The purpose of this book is: (1) to show how [the law of tonality] has functioned for over two hundred years; (2) to clarify the difference between its practical application and the theoretical explanation of its function; (3) to point out the various factors . . . that have led to its decline; (4) to demonstrate various instances of mistaken identity, which contemporary composers cite as containing the germ plasms of the atonal and polytonal systems; and (5) to investigate these systems, to find the new concept of unity they express." (xxviii)

B97   1939   Mitchell, William J. *Elementary Harmony*. New York: Prentice Hall. ISBN 11-11-91934-8.

Suggests that "more than the ability to label chords, the student needs to have awakened in him a sense of musical direction, an awareness of the difference between goals of motion and details of motion." Presents basic Schenkerian ideas of harmonic reduction and simple prolongations. (viii)

B98 1937 Jonas, Oswald, and Felix Salzer, eds. *Der Dreiklang: Monatschrift für Musik*. Vienna: Krystall Verlag (April 1937–February 1938). Reprint ed. Hildesheim: Georg Olms Verlag, 1989. ISBN 3-487-09074-0.

A short-lived collaboration between Jonas and Salzer containing articles describing facets of music illuminated by Schenker's approach; contains several hitherto unpublished essays of Schenker. Articles are separately indexed in chapters 2 and 3.

B99 1935 Salzer, Felix. *Sinn und Wesen der abendlandischen Mehrstimmigkeit*. Vienna: Saturn-Verlag.
    Reviews: 1935 *Music and Letters* 16/3: 249–50 (E. Lockspeiser).
               1935 *The Musical Times* 76: 614–5 (M. Calvecoressi).

An early application of Schenker's ideas to Renaissance music. The main part of the book is a discussion of the motet from the thirteenth through the sixteenth centuries, considering the problems of form and musical unity, tenor repetition and its relation to structure, and the "obstacles" to *Auskomponierung*. Contains a separate booklet of scores and graphic analyses.

B100 1932 Jonas, Oswald. *Einführung in die Lehre Heinrich Schenkers: Das Wesen des musikalischen Kunstwerks*. Vienna: Universal Edition. U-E 26.202.
    Review: 1935 *Music and Letters* 16/4: 341 (E. Lockspeiser)
    Translation: 1972 Rothgeb, John. *Introduction to the Theory of Heinrich Schenker*. New York: Longman. ISBN 0-582-28227-6.
    Reviews: 1984 *Nineteenth-Century Music* 8/2: 164–76. (R. Swift).
               1983 *Music Theory Spectrum* 5: 127–31 (B. Campbell).
               1983 *Times Literary Supplement* (1 July): 697 (C. Wintle)
               1983 *Journal of Music Theory* 27/2: 273–81 (W. Rothstein).
               1982 *Choice* 19/11–2: 1568.
               1982 *Cum notis variorum* 65: 19 (J. Swackhammer).
               1974 *Musikforschung* 27/2: 251 (H. Federhofer).
               1972 *Musikerziehung* 26/2: 93.
               1972 *Neue Zeitschrift für Musik* 134/2: 123–4 (C. Dahlhaus).

The first introduction to Schenker's method, predating *Der freie Satz*; discusses the various agents of prolongation and the concepts of the *Urlinie* and *Ursatz*.

Contains two appendices on the relationship of words and tones, and Schenker's editorial work with the Photogramm-Archiv.

B101   1926   Roth, Hermann. *Elemente der Stimmführung (Der Strenge Satz).*
                  1. Heft: Ein- und Zweistimmigkeit. Stuttgart: Carl Grüninger
                  Nachf. Ernst Klett.

A treatise on strict composition according to the Fux-Schenker approach. In his foreword, Roth says, "after Fux, the [study of counterpoint] thanks Heinrich Schenker's highly significant interpretation and formation of the Fuxian teaching most of all . . . especially the theory of prolongation undertaken there." (7)

Chapter 5

Dissertations and Theses
on Schenker and His Approach

D1 2002 Traut, Donald G. "Displacement and Its Role in Schenkerian Theory." Ph.D. diss., University of Rochester, Eastman School of Music. UMI Number 3045252.

Using the work of Rothstein as a starting point, the author discusses the roles played by rhythmic displacement and normalization, commenting on Schenker's use of diagonal lines to show conceptual normalization of foreground displacement. Examines Schenker's analysis of Stravinsky's Piano Concerto from *Das Meisterwerk* II.

D2 2001 Bribitzer-Stull, Matthew P. "Thematic Development and Dramatic Association in Wagner's *Der Ring des Nibelungen*." Ph.D. diss., University of Rochester, Eastman School of Music. UMI Number 3023448.

Describes four categories of thematic development: thematic mutation, thematic transformation, contextual reinterpretation, and thematic metamorphosis. Investigates the views of tonality of Schenker and Bailey. Discusses the interaction of tonality, drama, and motive as they influence form in the work.

D3 2001 Burchard, John E. "*Prometheus* and *Der Musensohn*: The Impact of Beethoven on Schubert Reception." Ph.D. diss., Rutgers University. UMI Number 3034247.

Examines critical and analytical reactions to Schubert's music, citing the writings of Schenker and Tovey.

D4 2001 Gamble, Charles. "The framing interval and its role in the integration of melody and form in four early works by Aaron Copland." Ph.D. diss., City University of New York. UMI Number 9997089.

Shows how melodic events can be understood as the embellishment of a particular interval and that these intervals operate on various lavels of structure and determine the musical form.

D5 2001 Goldenberg, Yosef. "Prolongation of Seventh Chords in Tonal Music." Ph.D. diss., Hebrew University of Jerusalem.

Discusses the problems of seventh-chord prolongations; states that it (1) violates the control of strict counterpoint over free composition; and (2) violates the normative distinction between horizontalization of chordal tones in skips and stepwise motion via non-chordal tones (since the seventh and octave are adjacent tones within the same harmony).

D6 2001 Hoskisson, Darin. "The Finale of Brahms's Piano Quintet, Op. 34." M.M. thesis, Louisiana State University.

Notes Brahms's utilization of rhythmic and metric irregularities, as well as the more typical thematic/motivic transformation, to establish the themes and relate them to one another. Explores his use of developing variations, connecting surface events to the large-scale voice leading. Shows Brahms's use of the linkage technique to connect this movement to the other three.

D7 2001 Karnes, Kevin. "Heinrich Schenker and Musical Thought in Late Nineteenth-Century Vienna." Ph.D. diss., Brandeis University. UMI Number 3004964.

Discusses the context for Schenker's early work; describes the influence of Eduard Hanslick and Friedrich von Hausegger and others on his writings. Includes two chapters on music criticism and speculative aesthetics, which focus on the Schenker-Bruckner connection. Discusses the relationship of music criticism and the birth of musicology.

D8 2001 Landis, Raymond. "Developing Variation in the Chorale Preludes for Organ, Opus 122 by Johannes Brahms." DMA doc., University of Cincinnati. UMI Number 3014169.

Discusses Schoenberg's concept of the developing variation; applies both Schenkerian and Schoenbergian analytical techniques.

D9 2001 Marvin, William. "Tonality in Selected Set Pieces from Wagner's *Die Meistersinger von Nürnberg*: A Schenkerian Approach." Ph.D. diss., University of Rochester, Eastman School of Music. UMI Number 3034650.

Surveys Schenker's writings to "better understand his ambivalent attitude towards Wagner," and examines Schenker's conception of motive and *Aufhaltung* (delay). Analyzes the chorales of Acts I and III, and three excerpts sung by Hans Sachs. Contains information on the non-tonic opening and auxiliary cadence. Discusses the "rules," rhetorical and tonal, of the master songs, focusing on

Walther's arias, including the various versions of the prize song. (RILM; used by permission)

D10 2001 Russakovsky, Luba. "The Altered Recapitulation in the First Movement of Haydn's String Quartets." Ph.D. diss., Hebrew University of Jerusalem.

Combines traditional analytic procedures with Schenker's voice-leading approach; suggests that the retransitional dominant is of crucial importance, and that its delay causes a redistribution of areas of tension and relaxation.

D11 2001 Trolier, Kimberly A. "Analytical Topics in Bach's Flute Sonatas." DMA doc., Temple University. UMI Number 3031564.

Reviews the secondary literature on the flute sonatas, and describes Bach's concertante procedures. Analyzes the chamber works BWV 1013 and 1032 according to Schenkerian techniques.

D12 2001 Walker, David. "Computer-Aided Collaboration in a Graduate-Level Music Analysis Course: An Exploration of Legitimate Peripheral Participation." Ph.D. diss., University of Toronto. UMI Number NQ58954.

Describes an experiment in which students in a Schenkerian analysis course posted their work on the Internet and employed computer conferencing to discuss issues raised in the class.

D13 2000 Bates, Vicky. "A Comparative Analysis Based on the Theories of Schenker and Schoenberg Using Brahms's F Minor Sonata, Op. 120, No. 1." M.M. thesis, Bowling Green State University.

Explores the work using both theorists' ideas; suggests a third analytical approach to fill in the leftover "gaps."

D14 2000 Cutler, Timothy. "Orchestration and the Analysis of Tonal Music: Interaction between Orchestration and Other Musical Parameters in Selected Symphonic Compositions, c. 1785–1835." Ph.D. diss., Yale University. UMI Number 9973669.

Examines the possibilities of codifying orchestration and discusses Schenker's approach to orchestration, gleaned from his writings. Discusses the interaction between scoring and form, tonal structure, motivic development, register, and voice leading.

D15 2000 Henry, Margaret. "Motivic Cross References in Schumann's *Liederkreis*, Op. 39." Ph.D. diss., University of Rochester, Eastman School of Music. UMI Number 9968745.

Explores motivic connections at various levels of structure, especially as related to programmatic interest; notes the large-scale binary division of the cycle into two groups of six songs.

D16   2000   Hsieh, Wenchi. "Robert Schumann's Piano Sonata Op. 22 in G
               Minor: An Analytical Study and the Performer's Perspective."
               M.M. thesis, California State University. UMI Number 1400815.
Contains graphic analyses with commentary geared toward aiding the performer's interpretation.

D17   2000   Hwang, Seung-Yee. "The Higher-Level Neighboring Motive in
               the First Movement of Beethoven's Last Piano Sonata in C Minor,
               Op. 111." M.M. thesis, University of Texas at Austin.
Discusses Schenker's concept of motive and discusses the permeation of the
voice-leading levels by the neighbor-note motive.

D18   2000   Larson, Brook. "The Application of Schenkerian Analysis to
               Choral Performance." DMA doc., Arizona State University. UMI
               Number 9976321.
Discusses basic Schenkerian ideas to be employed by choral directors with little
analytical experience.

D19   2000   Latham, Edward. "Linear-Dramatic Analysis of Twentieth-Cen-
               tury Opera." Ph.D. diss., Yale University. UMI Number 9973717.
Discusses Stanislavski's method of dramatic analysis, coupled with Schenker's
musical analysis. Constructs a linear-dramatic analytical methodology to be applied to operatic roles. Considers characters from *Porgy and Bess, Peter Grimes,
Pélleas et Mélisande,* and *Moses und Aron.*

D20   2000   McDonell, Twila Schemmer. "Using Schenkerian Analysis: Mov-
               ing from Analysis to Performance in the First Movement of W. A.
               Mozart's Concerto in G for Flute and Orchestra, K. 313." DMA
               doc., Northwestern University. UMI Number 3030537.
Surveys Schenker's theories and defines terms; applies the analytical techniques
to K. 313.

D21   2000   Pomeroy, David. "Towards a New Practice: Chromaticism
               and Form in Debussy's Orchestral Music." Ph.D. diss., Cornell
               University.
Examines "structural discontinuity" in Debussy; discusses interaction between
triadic tonality and symmetrical collections. Discusses the non-goal-directed
tendencies of his music.

D22   2000   Sayers, Richard. "Tonal Organization in Selected Early Works of
               Aaron Copland." Ph.D. diss., Catholic University of America.
               UMI Number 9969553.
Examines works from Copland's two early periods (pre-1928 and 1928–35)
according to modified Schenkerian techniques; discusses added-note chords,
bitonality, octatonic and whole-tone influences, and jazz style.

D23   2000   Schüler, Nico. "Methods of Computer-Aided Musical Analysis: History, Classification, and Evolution." Ph.D. diss., Michigan State University. UMI Number 9985460.

The dissertation "lays out a historical framework for computer-assisted music analysis, showing how it has been related to the development of computer technique and information theory, and how it has been applied to aesthetics." Contains a 150-page bibliography of sources dealing with computer-aided analysis. (ii)

D24   1999   Cunningham, Robert. "Harmonic Prolongation in Selected Works of Rachmaninoff 1910–1931." Ph.D. diss., Florida State University. UMI Number 9922657.

Examines several of the preludes using Schenkerian techniques.

D25   1999   Braskey, Jill. "Rehearsing the Tritone: Examining Schenker's sharp $\hat{4}$/flat $\hat{5}$ Hypothesis." M.A. thesis, University of Buffalo.

Taking as her starting point the Brown/Dempster/Headlam *Spectrum* article of 1997 (see **A100** above) Braskey (1) explores a historical approach to tritone modulations; (2) critiques the three classifications of tritone modulations and analyzes that result; and (3) explores ways by which one might analyze music containing tritone modulations.

D26   1999   Daigle, Paulin. "Les fonctions harmoniques et formelles de la technique 5-6 a plusieurs niveaux de structure dans la musique tonale." Ph.D. diss., McGill University.

Discusses the 5-6 exchange technique in the theoretical writings and in music literature. Examines a series of excerpts from the eighteenth through the twentieth centuries demonstrating this technique at various structural levels.

D27   1999   Kyung, Sandra. "Chaconne from Johann Sebastian Bach's Partita No. 2: Linear Analysis." M.M. thesis, California State University, Long Beach.

A voice-leading graph with commentary, using both Schenkerian techniques and traditional analysis.

D28   1999   Metz, Andreas. "Large-Scale Tonal Issues in Maurice Ravel's *Histoires Naturelles*." M.A. thesis, University of British Columbia.

Employs "Robert Mueller's concept of the 'tonal pillar,' which is slightly extended and modified . . . combined with quasi-Schenkerian graphing and traditional harmonic analysis." Suggests that the resultant analytical process will be effective for the study of "Ravel's early music if not Impressionistic music in general."

D29   1999   Nitzberg, Roy. "Voice-Leading and Chromatic Techniques in Expositions of Selected Symphonies by Joseph Haydn, Introducing a New Theory of Chromatic Analysis." Ph.D. diss., City University of New York. UMI Number 9946207.

Combines the theoretical ideas of Schenker and Henry Burnett (presenting "the chromatic aggregate . . . as linear arrays and eleven-note areas"); applies these ideas to the music of Haydn and Mozart.

D30   1999   Samarotto, Frank. "A Theory of Temporal Plasticity in Tonal Music: An Extension of the Schenkerian Approach to Rhythm with Special Reference to Beethoven's Late Music." Ph.D. diss., City University of New York. UMI Number 9946218.

Describes a "temporal plasticity framework" comprised of six elements (three pitch elements and three rhythmic elements): Uninterpreted Pitches, Tonal Structure, Tonal Hierarchy, Uninterpreted Durations, Rhythmic Structure, and Metric Hierarchy. Demonstrates his theories through analyses of the music of Haydn and Beethoven.

D31   1999   Schneider, Mathieu. "Les *Métamorphoses* de Richard Strauss. In Memoriam." M.M. thesis, Université Marc-Bloch, Strasbourg.

Discusses the significance of the title; suggests that it is tied as much to the process of variation as to tonal structure. Suggests parallels with Kafka's *Die Verwandlung*. Provides voice-leading graphs and commentary.

D32   1999   Schulze, Sean. "An Ignored Fantasy: An Examination of Beethoven's Fantasy for Piano Op. 77." DMA doc., University of Arizona.

Surveys the fantasy as a genre; uses both Schenkerian and traditional means of analysis to examine the work.

D33   1999   Song, Moo-Kyoung. "An Unresolved Conflict between Form and Structure: A Schenkerian Analysis of the First Movement of Brahms's Second Violin Sonata in A Major, Op. 100." M.M. thesis, University of Texas at Austin.

Examines the work from the Schenkerian perspective, focusing on Brahms's use of the tonic *Stufe* to begin the development section; discusses interpretation of the sonata as thematic design or tonal structure. Provides several analytic interpretations.

D34   1999   Turner, Mitchell. "Toward a General Theory of Pitch Structure: Unity Between Horizontal and Vertical Pitch-Class Sets." Ph.D. diss., University of Georgia.

Establishes criteria for assessing the structural importance of pc sets for non-tonal works that are then used to produce a graphic analysis. "Provides the foundation for a general theory of pitch structure analysis of post-tonal music by establishing a primary assumption regarding atonal stability conditions and showing a consistent methodology for the determination of pitch structure."

D35 1999 Weng, Li-Shuang. "An Analytic Investigation of Schumann's *Scenes from Childhood* Opus 15." M.A. thesis, University of Southern California.

Explores the thirteen pieces of the *Kinderszenen*; focuses on "(1) determination of the primary tone in the reductive graphs, (2) ambiguities of various typologies of the song form and (3) the use of traditional and non-traditional key relationships."

D36 1998 Anson-Cartwright, Mark. "The Development Section in Haydn's Late Instrumental Works." Ph.D. diss., City University of New York. UMI Number 9908291.

Surveys theoretical literature on development sections; examines (1) foreground characteristics; (2) use of augmented sixth chords, especially enharmonic reinterpretation of either the chord of resolution or the augmented sixth itself; (3) historical significance of Haydn's developments. Focuses analysis on Symphonies 93, 100, 102, and 103.

D37 1998 Brooks, Noel. "A Schillingerian and Schenkerian Approach to George Gershwin's '*I Got Rhythm* Variations.'" M.M. thesis, University of Western Ontario. UMI Number MQ32470.

Reviews relevant literature; explains the Schillingerian variation techniques. Demonstrates how Gershwin used these techniques to produce "effective and coherent" variation.

D38 1998 Clemens, John. "Combining *Ursatz* and *Grundgestalt*: A Schenkerian-Schoenbergian Analysis of Coherence in Hugo Wolf's *Italienisches Liederbuch*." Ph.D. diss., University of Cincinnati. VMI number 9833720.

Suggests that "the analytic tools developed from Schoenberg's concepts provide a means for expanding the Schenkerian perspective" to account for features of music outside his area of interest.

D39 1998 Cockell, James. "Schenkerism and the Hungarian Oral Tradition." M.A. Thesis, University of Alberta. UMI Number MQ34305.

Suggests that Schenkerian analysis can be used "as a tool for comparative musicology . . . as well as a tool for interpreting improvisational aspects of performance."

D40 1998 Davis, Andrew. "Incorporating Schenkerian Concepts into the First Year of the Undergraduate Music Theory Curriculum." M.M. Thesis, University of Amherst.

Surveys the main concepts of Schenkerian theory; examines ways in which they might be implemented in the first year of study (in both aural and written theory). Includes a bibliography of literature on the influence of Schenkerian analysis in pedagogy.

D41   1998   Lehmann, Kennett. "Tonal Unity and Quality Of Motion: A Schenkerian Study." Ph.D. diss., University of Washington. UMI Number 9836203.

Discusses Schenker's *Auskomponierung* concept from a cognitive point of view; examines the various techniques of prolongation in the upper and lower voice.

D42   1998   Nelson, Thomas. "The Fantasy of Absolute Music (Pastoral)." Ph.D. diss., University of Minnesota. UMI Number 9834924.

In the context of a study of nineteenth-century aesthetics, Nelson develops a theory of romantic tonality based on examination of Schubert song, focusing on his use of the flat submediant. Art by Klinger, Poussin, and Watteau; essays by Nietzsche, Schiller, Schenker, and Wackenroder; and music by Beethoven, Brahms, Mahler, Marenzio, Mozart, Schubert, and Wagner are examined.

D43   1998   Pavlov, Sara. "The Neapolitan Chord in the Works of Chopin." M.A. Thesis, Hebrew University of Jerusalem.

Examines the different ways in which Chopin used the Neapolitan chord, as a harmonic, melodic, and contrapuntal entity; shows how the position of the chord (five-three versus six-three) affects the structural voice leading.

D44   1998   Swift, Angela. "The Dark Side of William Albright's *Organbook III*: Multiple Perspectives of the Six Etudes of Volume II." DMA doc., University of Cincinnati.

Examines compositional technique using pitch-class set theory, gestural analysis, and Schenkerian techniques; includes a biographical sketch and a survey of organ works.

D45   1998   Wampler, Stephen. "A Brass Player's Guide to the Transcription and Performance of J. S. Bach's 'Six Suites For Violoncello Solo.' " DMA doc., University of Washington.

Discusses the difficulties of performing the suites on a brass instrument; surveys manuscript and transcription sources; provides analytical justification for performance dicisions.

D46   1998   Watts, Donald. "Toward an Understanding of the Pedagogical Value of Hierarchical Structure in Tonal Pitch Dictation." Ph.D. diss., University of Maryland, College Park.

Discusses the dissemination of Schenkerian theory; reviews several undergraduate textbooks. Formulates a method that "encourages student perception of the integration of melody and harmony in tonality and proposes a step-by-step routine for utilizing that insight in the dictation process."

D47   1998   Underwood, Michael. "A Schenkerian Analysis of the First Movement of Gustav Mahler's Third Symphony." M.M. thesis, Bowling Green State University.

Examines the work through a Schenkerian perspective; suggests that the directional tonality should be represented by an incomplete background line in D minor that ends in F major.

D48 1997 Asada, Chizuko. "Schenkerian Analysis of Sonata No. 9, Op. 68 by Alexander Scriabin." M.M. thesis, California State University at Long Beach. UMI Number 1387554.
Examines the work from Schenker's point of view; supplies graphic analysis and commentary.

D49 1997 Dent, Cedric. "The Harmonic Development of the Black Religious Quartet Singing Tradition." Ph.D. diss., University of Maryland.
Employs traditional tonal theory, jazz theory, and Schenkerian analysis; "identifies and traces threads of harmonic development through the genre, which define stylistic epochs." Supplies transcriptions for the works analyzed. (RILM; used by permission)

D50 1997 Edwards, Stephen. "Extremes of Contrast in Mozart's Sonata-Form Movements." Ph.D. diss., University of Texas.
Explores issues of unity and contrast, revealed through Schenkerian analysis, in Mozart's K. 284, 309, and 280.

D51 1997 Inwood, Mary. "The Long Christmas Dinner." Ph.D. diss., New York University. UMI Number AAI9810479.
Examines Hindemith's opera based on his own analytical techniques plus those of Salzer and Schenker. Examines correspondence between Hindemith and Wilder.

D52 1997 Mirchandani, Sharon. "Ruth Crawford Seeger's Five Songs, Suite no. 2, and Three Chants: Representations of America and Explorations of Spirituality." Ph.D. diss., Rutgers University.
Proposes to examine Seeger's music with eclectic methods, such as those found in the writings of Straus, Perle, Forte, LaRue, and Schenker. Also explores issues of spirituality and gender.

D53 1997 Penfold, Nigel. "Schubert: Piano Sonata in C Major, No. 15, D. 840, *Relique*: An Analysis of the First Movement Following the Theories of Heinrich Schenker." M.A. thesis, Reading University.
A Schenkerian analysis of the movement, providing voice-leading graphs and commentary.

D54 1997 Sayrs, Elizabeth. "Approaches to Wolf: Schenker, Transformation, Function." Ph.D. diss., Ohio State University. UMI Number 9801781.

Uses Schenkerian theory, function theory, and transformational voice leading to examine songs of Wolf. Provides an overview of the theoretical methodologies, the analyses themselves, and conclusions drawn therefrom.

D55   1997   Setar, Katherine. "An Evolution in Listening: An Analytical and Critical Study of Structural, Acoustic, and Phenomenal Aspects of Selected Works by Pauline Oliveros." Ph.D, diss., University of Southern California. UMI Number 9902864.

Uses Schenker's method with others (traditional morphologies, vowel/formant theory) to examine *Sound Patterns*, *O Ha Ah*, and *I of IV*. Discusses Oliveros's stylistic evolution.

D56   1997   Shim, Elizabeth. "Schenkerian Analyses of Frederic Chopin's Mazurkas, Opuses 6, 7, and 17." M.A. thesis, University of Southern California. UMI Number 1384920.

Discusses the significance of the mazurka to Chopin; applies Schenkerian techniques and discusses how the analyses may inform performance.

D57   1997   Skeirik, Kaleel. "Tonal Syntax in the First Movement of Sibelius's Sixth Symphony." Ph.D. diss., University of Cincinnati. UMI Number 9735055.

Replaces the *Ursatz* with a "modal background" to explain large-scale progression in Sibelius's Sixth Symphony (Dorian I-VII-I). Discusses the interaction of modal and functional harmony.

D58   1996   Blatz, Catherine. "A Comparison of Schenkerian and Conventional Theories of Form." M.M. Thesis, University of Alberta. UMI Number MQ22055.

Studies Schenker's approach to form, especially the relationship between improvisation and the fundamental structure. Employs Derrida's concept of "supplement."

D59   1996   Cahn, Steven. "Variations in Manifold Time: Historical Consciousness in the Music and Writings of Arnold Schoenberg." Ph.D. diss., State University of New York, Stony Brook. UMI Number 9713848.

Examines several pieces in regards to "continuity, discontinuity, social history, and the phenomenology of creativity." Interprets Schoenberg's writings with regard to a host of others; studies his polemics against Schenker, Riemann, and Spengler.

D60   1996   Duke, Daniel. "The Piano Improvisations of Chick Corea: An Analytical Study." Ph.D. diss., Louisiana State University. UMI Number 9720348.

Applies Schenkerian methodology to transcriptions of five improvisations; studies the relationship of improvisation to composition and classical music to jazz.

D61   1996   Foulkes-Levy, Laurdella. "A Synthesis of Recent Theories of Tonal Melody, Contour, and The Diatonic Scale: Implications for Aural Perception and Cognition." Ph.D. diss., State University of New York, Buffalo. UMI Number 9704876.

Examines the theories of Schenker, Lerdahl/Jackendoff, Morris, Clough, and Hegyi in regard to basic musicianship training.

D62   1996   Kessler, Deborah. "Schubert's Late Three-Key Expositions: Influence, Design, and Structure." Ph.D. diss., City University of New York. UMI Number 9618079.

Examines four sonata-form movements that feature three-key expositions, noting motivic features, including large-scale neighboring motion flat $\hat{6}$-$\hat{5}$ in the bass, manifested in the foreground as the flat VI key area.

D63   1996   McGire, David. "Revisiting the Return: The Structural Dilemma of the Recapitulation in the Schenkerian Account of Classical Sonata Form." Ph.D. diss., State University of New York at Buffalo. UMI Number 9617888.

Suggests that Schenker's interpretation of sonata form is flawed; examines the "contradiction . . . between the structural voice leading of the returning second key material and the background voice leading of the reprise as a whole."

D64   1996   Moreno-Rojas, Jairo. "Theoretical Reception of the Sequence and Its Conceptual Implications." Ph.D. diss., Yale University. UMI Number 9632449.

Examines treatment of the sequence in the writings of Heinichen, Rameau, Fétis, Riemann, Koch, Galeazzi, Rejcha, and Marx. Explores the fusions of the ideas (the mediation of harmony and counterpoint) expressed by these writers in the works of Schenker (the *Außensatz*) and Forte (the linear intervallic pattern).

D65   1996   Rytting, Bryce. "Structure versus Organicism in Schenkerian Analysis." Ph.D. diss., Princeton University. UMI Number 9707285.

Discusses the gap between Schenker's original terminology and American usage, which relies on metaphors drawn from architecture rather than biology. Discusses facets of Schenker's thought (and graphs) that are best understood in light of his biological metaphors.

D66   1996   Taggart, Bruce. "Rhythmic Perception and Conception: A Study of Bottom-Up and Top-Down Interaction in Rhythm and Meter." Ph.D. diss., University of Pennsylvania.

Views rhythm and meter as operative on the lowest level of hierarchy only; admonishes both cognitive psychology and Schenkerian theory for failing to distinguish between "direct perception" and "indirect conception"; formulates an analytical approach based on Narmour's implication-realization model.

D67 1996 Walter, Ross. "Paul Hindemith's Sonata for Trombone: A Performance Analysis." D.M.A. doc., Louisiana State University. UMI Number 9706370.

Part of a lecture-recital; employs pitch-class set theory and Schenkerian analysis; presents solutions to performance difficulties encountered in the work.

D68 1995 Bain, Jennifer. "Selected Antiphons of Hildegard von Bingen: Notation and Structural Design." D.M.A. doc., McGill University.

Examines *O quam mirabilis est, Hodie aperuit, Nunc gaudeant, O virtus sapientie*, and *O virgo ecclesia*. Discusses historical context, and compares three analyses of *O quam mirabilis est* by Bronarski, Cogan, and Pfau. Applies Schenkerian analytical techniques to the three other antiphons.

D69 1995 Carter, Lee. "Progress in the Rake's Return." Ph.D. diss., City University of New York. UMI Number 9521257.

Incorporates Schenkerian techniques, motivic analysis, and pitch-class set theory, which allows for "[making] connections and [measuring] distinctions between diverse elements." (RILM; used by permission)

D70 1995 Dabrusin, Ross. "Deriving Structural Motives: Implications for Music Performance." Ph.D. diss., New York University. UMI No. 9528283.

Discusses the benefit to the performer of motivic analysis across structural levels.

D71 1995 Fung, Eric. "The Performance of Chopin's First Movement of Piano Sonata in B Minor, Op. 58: A Schenkerian Approach." B. A. thesis, Chinese University of Hong Kong.

Examines Schenker's analysis of Chopin's G-flat Major etude, his writings on performance, and the writings of others on the relationship of analysis to performance; applies these ideas to the B Minor Etude.

D72 1995 Leite, Zilei. "Applications of Reductive Analytical Techniques in the Phrygian Settings of the *Orgelbüchlein* by Johann Sebastian Bach." M.M. thesis, University of North Texas.

Examines the modal and tonal traits of four chorale preludes (BWV 602, 611, 620, and 621). Applies Schenker's ideas to the works as well as using Burns's ideas (1991, 1993, 1994) of reworking Schenker's ideas to make them more amenable to modal works.

D73 1995 Lubben, Robert. "Analytic Practice and Ideology in Heinrich Schenker's *Der Tonwille* (with) *Cantata Harmonia Mundi* (Original Composition)." Ph.D. diss., Brandeis University.

Examines the analyses included in *Der Tonwille,* providing translations of twelve essays (see above). The essays in *Der Tonwille,* says Lubben, "[describe] Schenker's reliance on organicist and idealist metaphors [and] reveal the interdependence of Schenker's musical thought and his political, religious, and social views."

D74 1995 Petty, Wayne. "Compositional Techniques in the Keyboard Sonatas of Carl Philipp Emanuel Bach: Reimagining the Foundations of a Musical Style." Ph.D. diss., Yale University. UMI Number 9615215.

Examines various approaches to Bach's music, maintaining that analytical approaches should be consistent with the practices known to Bach (figured bass and improvisation). Studies sonata-form works of Bach, Haydn, and Beethoven, noting that "features of C. P. E. Bach's style, often regarded as merely eccentric, develop musical ideas that can be uncovered through analysis."

D75 1995 Roller, Jonathan. "An Analysis of Selected Movements from the Symphonies of Charles Ives Using Linear and Set Theoretical Analysis Models." Ph.D. diss., University of Kentucky. UMI Number 9614461.

Analyzes three excerpts from three analytic standpoints: Symphony I/ii (Schenkerian theory); Symphony III/iii ("linear" analysis, using tools borrowed from Schenker plus some original symbols); Symphony IV/i (set theory). Displays the interconnectedness of sets in the third section by means of an original graphing technique.

D76 1995 Sly, Gordon. "An Emerging Symbiosis of Structure and Design in the Sonata Practice of Franz Schubert." Ph.D. diss., University of Rochester, Eastman School of Music. UMI Number 9514927.

Notes Schubert's proclivity for "[replicating] the exposition's broad modulation scheme in the recapitulation such that the tonic serves as the goal of, rather than the point of departure for, the tonal motion of that section." Suggests that these tonal plans undermine the usual conception of the interrupted sonata form.

D77 1995 Teboul, Jean-Claude. "Le concept de la tonalite selon Heinrich Schenker (1868–1935) application aux 27 etudes de Chopin." Ph.D. diss., University of Paris IV-Sorbonne.

Views Schenekrian analysis as "deconstruction" and applies it to the twenty-seven etudes of Chopin.

D78 1995 Wilde, Howard. "Towards a New Theory of Voice-Leading Structure in Sixteenth-Century Polyphony." Ph.D. diss., Royal Holloway, University of London.

After a survey of theoretical approaches to Renaissance music, Wilde proposes a set of "hypothetical voice-leading archetypes" based on sixteenth-century cadence theory; applies theoretical model to excerpts from Josquin to Gesualdo.

D79   1994   Blasius, Leslie. "Schenker's Argument (with) *Still* (Original Composition)." Ph.D. diss., Princeton University. UMI Number 9519125.
Suggests that "the structure of Schenker's mature analysis is philological. The analysis embodies a history of music in the same way in which a text or a language can be determined to embody a history. The synthesis of an introspective methodology and a historiological structure is made possible by Schenker's subscription to a closed canon, by his shift of the musical presence from the empirically available human who listens or performs or even composes to the specific and transcendental musical object." (RILM; used by permission)

D80   1994   Boyd, James. "Tonality, Genre, and Form: Mahler's *Lieder eines Fahrender Gesellen.*" Ph.D. diss., University of Michigan. UMI Number 9513305.
Discusses analytical precedents for monotonal and non-monotonal works; examines the *Gesellenlieder* to determine the function and significance of its directional tonality. Includes discussions of the Mahler's texts.

D81   1994   Klonoski, Edward. "A Critical Examination of Schenker's Theory of Linear Progressions." Ph.D. diss., Ohio State University. UMI Number 9427735.
Distinguishes "linear progression" from "line" by defining the former as "a connection between two voices of different structural rank." Provides guidelines for determining "when one of the boundary tones of a progression has been transferred to a new register, which in turn provides a mechanism for distinguishing between inverted progressions and those in their original form." (RILM; used by permission)

D82   1994   Thiemel, Matthias. "Tonale Dynamik: Theorie, musikalische Praxis und Vortragslehre seit 1800." Ph.D. diss., Albert-Ludwigs-Universität Freiburg, Breisgau.
Examines the history and meaning of dynamics in tonal music; consults texts of Riemann, Kurth, Marx, and Asafiev. Explores the Schenkerien idea of *Fernhören*. Also considers the "relation between tension and intensity, the dialectic of meter and phrase, understanding of notation, the notion of balance in sound." Published by Tank (Köln) in 1994.

D83   1994   Weiner, Brien. "Notes from the Middleground: The Convergence of *Ur-Idee* and *Urlinie* in Schenker's *Erläuterungsausgabe* of Beethoven's Op. 101." Ph.D. diss., Yale University. UMI Number 9523249.

Contains a translation of the "analytic sections" (as opposed to the editorial and performance commentary) of Schenker's critical edition as well as a reproduction of his edition of the score of op. 101. Includes his own graphs and commentary on Schenker's edition.

D84 1994 Whittle, Barbara B. "The Cultural Context of the Theories of Heinrich Schenker." Ph.D. diss., Open University. DLX44–3056.

Discusses how divorcing Schenker's method from his philosophical ideas "profoundly impoverishes" it; examines the influence of Goethe, Nietzsche, Kant, and Schopenhauer on Schenker's thought. A thorough introduction to Schenker's milieu.

D85 1994 Yribarren, Martin. "Melodic and Tonal Coherence in the Organ Works of César Franck: An Approach Employing Basic Shape and Structural Levels." Ph.D. diss., University of Southern California. UMI Number 9625281.

Explores thirteen works using Schenkerian and Schoenbergian concepts, showing the relationship between them. Pays particular attention to motivic processes.

D86 1993 Barket, James. "The Speaker of the Orchestra: An Analytical Study of the Bass Line in the Fourth Movement of Beethoven's Ninth Symphony." DMA doc., University of North Carolina. UMI Number 9419155.

Studies the bass line in relation to the tonal structure of the overall movement; provides exercises to aid performers' aural comprehension. Employs Schenker's and LaRue's analytical systems.

D87 1993 Hampson, Barbara. "Schenker and Schoenberg: A Critical Comparison of Two Analytical Methods, with Reference to the *Appasionata* Sonata (1st Mvt.)." M.A. thesis, McMaster University.

Compares the two analytical systems, showing their similarities.

D88 1993 Krause, Drew. "Musical Ambiguity in Analysis and Composition: Problems of Pattern, Value, Form, and Structure." D.M.A. doc., University of Illinois. UMI Number 9329088.

Employs eclectic analytical systems such as gestalt theory, linguistics, serialism, etc. Critiques the systems of Schenker and Meyer for downplaying musical ambiguity.

D89 1993 Mayfield, Connie. "The Structural Function of Motives in the Piano Sonatas of Arnold Bax." Ph.D. diss., University of Kansas.

Describes Bax's process of developiong variation; describes and employs Schenkerian and Schoenbergian techniques for motivic analysis. Provides tables of motives for purposes of showing transformations and relationships across movements.

D90   1993   Mori, Paul. "Vivaldi's Bassoon Concerto Variants: A Schenkerian Approach." D.M.A. diss., Peabody Institute of the Johns Hopkins University. UMI Number 9327536.

Applies a Schenkerian perspective, examining "register, structure, and functionality." Suggests that, "Ultimately, Vivaldi's solo bassoon lines are derivations of functional bass structures." Provides an introduction to Schenkerian analysis and a history of the instrument through the time of Vivaldi. (RILM; used by permission)

D91   1993   Rawlins, Robert. "The Implication-Realization Model: An Approach to Melodic Analysis." Ph.D. diss., Rutgers University. UMI Number 9333444.

Examines Meyer/Narmour's implication-realization theory; suggests that it is "complementary" to Schenkerian analysis because it "operates most strongly in the domain where the latter's explanatory powers begin to dissipate—that involving the temporal succession of melodic events at the surface level." (RILM; used by permission)

D92   1992   Arnold, Janice. "The Role of Chromaticism in Chopin's Sonata Forms: A Schenkerian View." Ph.D. diss., Northwestern University. UMI Number 9309337.

Examines the function of chromatic elements at various structural levels. Suggests three categories of chromaticism: embellishing, procedural, and generative.

D93   1992   Anderson, Norman. "Aspects of Early Major-Minor Tonality: Structural Characteristics of the Music of the Sixteenth and Seventeenth Centuries." Ph.D. diss., Ohio State University. UMI Number 9227220. Avaliable online at http://web.presby.edu/~danderso/diss/.

Provides a description of musical features during the transitory period from the modal system to the diatonic system, the fifteenth and sixteenth centuries. Employs the Schenker system to examine the underlying tonality in the examples.

D94   1992   Barrington, Barrie. "The Four 'Mephisto' Waltzes of Franz Liszt." Ph.D. diss., University of British Columbia. UMI Number N80816.

Examines the four waltzes, commenting especially on tonality in the third waltz, where a dual tonic complex is revealed. Examines the programmatic influences of Lenau's *Faust*.

D95   1992   Berardinelli, Paula. "Bill Evans: His Contributions as a Jazz Pianist and an Analysis of His Musical Style." Ph.D. diss., New York University.

Employs LaRue and Schenker analysis; discusses Evans's contributions to jazz pianistic style.

D96 1992 Bonds, Nancy. "An Analysis of Joan Tower's *Wings* for Solo Clarinet." D.M.A. doc., Arizona State University.
Employs Hindemith's and Schenker's methods of analysis as well as traditional formal analysis.

D97 1992 Gibeau, Peter. "Chromaticism as a Middleground Phenomenon in selected Mazurkas of Chopin." Ph.D. diss., University of Wisconsin, Madison. UMI Number 9224153.
Examines the mazurkas of Chopin, showing a highly refined structure with chromatic tonal relationships functioning in the middleground (usually in conjunction with motivic parallelisms).

D98 1992 Johnson, Lisa. "Mozart's Quintet for Clarinet and Strings: An Analytic Study." D.M.A. doc., City University of New York. UMI Number 9218240.
Examines the historical development of the instrument and historical context of the work; offers an analysis with insights to inform performances of the work; provides suggestions for ornamentation.

D99 1992 Marcozzi, Rudy. "The Interaction of Large-Scale Harmonic and Dramatic Structure in the Verdi Operas Adapted from Shakespeare." Ph.D. diss., Indiana University.
Examines *Macbeth*, *Othello,* and *Falstaff* in terms of tonal structure and dramatic design.

D100 1992 Nivans, David. "Brahms and the Binary Sonata: A Structuralist Interpretation." Ph.D. diss., University of California, Los Angeles. UMI Number 9213700.
Binary sonata refers to "those that have principal and secondary themes that are repeated with no intermediate, autonomous development section." Examines the sonatas in light of the approaches of Schoenberg and Schenker/Salzer.

D101 1992 Powell, Hiram. "The Extant Sonatas of Six Sonates pour le Violon by Joseph Boulogne 'Le Chavalier' Saint-Georges: A Hybrid Analysis." Ph.D. diss., Florida State University. UMI Number 9222413.
Utilizes the analytical systems of Schenker and Ratner plus an idea of Agawu's.

D102 1992 Smith, Peter. "Formal Ambiguity and Large-Scale Tonal Structure in Brahms's Sonata-Form Recapitulations." Ph.D. diss., Yale University.
Examines the means by which Brahms "substantiated the traditional practice of recapitulation in the late nineteenth-century historical context" and "reconcile[d] its inherent repetitious structure with his proclivity for continuous formal development"; examines the baroque and classical influences on Brahms. (RILM; used by permission)

D103 1992 Wenger, Barbara. "A Schenkerian Analysis of the Allegro Movement of Piano Sonata, Op. 31, No. 3 by Ludwig van Beethoven." M.A. Thesis, Eastern Michigan University. UMI Number 1347619.

Discusses the differences between Schenkerian and traditional methods of analysis; includes graphic analysis and commentary.

D104 1991 Burns, Lori. "J. S. Bach's Chorale Harmonizations of Modal Cantus Firmi." Ph.D. diss., Harvard University. UMI Number 9211661.

Applies Schenkerian methodology to chorales based on modal cantus firmi; highlights mode-defining characteristics in the analyses.

D105 1991 Cummings, Craig. "Large Scale Coherence in Selected Nineteenth-Century Piano Variations." Ph.D. diss., University of Indiana.

Examines four sets of variations (one each by Beethoven and Schumann, and two by Brahms) according to Schenkerian techniques; includes a history of variation form.

D106 1991 Don, Gary W. "Music and Goethe's Theories of Growth." Ph.D. diss., University of Washington. UMI Number 9131638.

Explains Goethe's theory of the archetype as well as the concepts of polarity and intensification in light of the theories of Marx, Hauptmann, and Schenker. Explores Schoenberg's *Grundgestalt* concept as well as Stravinsky's views on polarity in music.

D107 1991 Goldwurm, Giuliano. "Le theorie musicali di H. Schenker: L. B. Meyer e E. Narmour: Un percorso di analisi comparata." M.M. Thesis, University of Bologna.

A comparison of the theories of Schenker, Meyer, and Narmour.

D108 1991 Layton, Richard Douglas. "Large-Scale Tonal Connections in Robert Schumann's *Dichterliebe*." Ph.D. diss., University of Maryland at College Park. UMI Number 9222716.

Analyzes each song separately and as part of the cycle; includes discussion of the text, which supports the musical analysis.

D109 1991 Moore, Hillarie Clark. "The Structural Role of Orchestration in Brahms's Music: A Study of the Third Symphony." Ph.D. diss., Yale University. UMI Number 9136171.

Explores the connection between orchestration and voice leading, considering such aspects as register and doubling; integrates orchestration graphs with voice-leading graphs.

D110 1991 Reynolds, M. Fletcher. "Music Analysis for Expert Testimony in Copyright Infringement Litigation." Ph.D. diss., University of Kansas.

Discusses the roles in analysis of infringement cases, such as formal, functional, semiotic, and Schenkerian approaches; noting that "many cases reveal the presentation of haphazard and theoretically basesless analyses," Reynolds suggests that revision is needed. (RILM; used by permission)

D111 1991 Snarrenberg, Robert. "Writing (Figures) Music." Ph.D. diss., University of Michigan. UMI Number 9135696.

Examines the metaphors of concealed repetition and musical procreation in the writings of Schenker; discusses Schenker's highly figurative writing style and discusses the problems of translation.

D112 1990 Potgieter, Zelda. "The Structural and Style-Critical Analyses of Heinrich Schenker and Jan La Rue with Reference to J. Brahms, Piano Sonata Opus 1." M.M. thesis, University of Port Elizabeth [South Africa].

Applies the two analytical methodologies to Brahms's op. 1.

D113 1990 Galand, Joel. "Heinrich Schenker's Theory of Form and Its Application to Historical Criticism, with Special Reference to Rondo-Form Problems in Eighteenth and Nineteenth-Century Instrumental Music." Ph.D. diss., Yale University. UMI Number 9316059.

Surveys concepts of form in Schenker's writings and places them in the contexts of historical theory and current analytical approaches; examines rondo and ritornello techniques of Mozart, Haydn, and others.

D114 1990 Davis, Glen. "Levels Analysis in Jazz Tunes." D.M.A. doc., Ohio State University.

This thesis presents new concepts, terminology, and notation considered by the author to be logical extensions of Schenkerian analysis that are necessary for a meaningful levels analysis of jazz tunes. It is the author's belief that this thesis reveals, at least in part, how equivalent structural levels in jazz are similar to, and dissimilar from, equivalent structural levels as seen in earlier tonal art music. Eighteen complete levels analyses of jazz tunes composed from the 1930s through the 1960s are presented in part 1. Part 2 presents the new concepts, terminology, and notation, and explains their applications for graphing structural levels in jazz tunes. (RILM; used by permission)

D115 1990 Hubbs, Nadine. "Musical Organicism and Its Alternatives." Ph.D. diss., University of Michigan. UMI Number 9034443.

Works to define organicism, and surveys the historical influences on musical organicism. Discusses the use of the organic metaphor by Schenker. Concludes with an analysis of a work of Marilyn Shrude.

D116 1990 Murtomäki, Veijo. "Sinfoninen ykseys: Muotoajattelun kehitys Sibeliusken sinfonioissa." Ph.D. diss., University of Helsinki.
Studies the later symphonies of Sibelius (nos. 4–7) using Schenkerian and paradigmatic analysis. Translated into English and published in 1993 by the University of Helsinki (see **B33** above)

D117 1990 Nash, Laura. "Aspects of an Evolving Tonal Language: A Study of Chorale-Based Compositions by the Leipzig *Thomaskirche* Cantors, 1618–1722." Ph.D. diss., Yale University. UMI Number 9121110
Describes prolongational techniques of five consecutive cantors: Johann Schein, Tobias Michael, Sebastian Knupfer, Johann Schelle, and Johann Kuhnau.

D118 1989 Brown, Matthew. "A Rational Reconstruction of Schenkerian Theory." Ph.D. diss., Cornell University. UMI Number 8924538.
Reconstructs Schenkerian theory according to the Covering-Law Model—a scientific model first postulated by positivist philosophers in the 1930s and explored more fully in the 1940s through the 1960s by Carl Hempel. Tries to "correct some of the problems [he sees] in Schenker's own presentation of the theory." (3)

D119 1989 Chenevert, James. "Simon Sechter's *The Principles of Musical Composition*: A Translation of and Commentary on Selected Chapters." Ph.D. diss., University of Wisconsin, Madison. UMI Number 8917091.
Translates the following chapters: "On the Laws of Meter in Music," "On Single-Voice Composition," "On Two- and Three-Voice Composition, insofar as it Arises from Four-Voice Composition," "Rhythmic Sketches," and "On Strict Composition." Commentary focuses on Sechter's harmonic reduction process as an antecedent of Schenker's.

D120 1989 Cumming, Naomi. "Analytical and Aesthetic Concepts in the Work of Leonard B. Meyer." Ph.D. diss., University of Melbourne. UMI Number 8910123.
Explores Meyer's theories of rhythmic grouping and linear structure as outlined in his writings; contrasts his approach with Schenker's.

D121 1989 Horn, Geoffrey. "Dual *Urlinien* in the Concerto Practice of Wolfgang Amadeus Mozart, as Demonstrated in the Three Concerti in E Flat for Horn and Orchestra: K. 417, K. 447, and K. 495." Ph.D. diss., University of Michigan. UMI Number 9001642.

Suggests coexisting *Urlinien* in the solo and tutti sections of the three concerti, each with its own obligatory register.

D122 1989 Krantz, Steven. "Rhetorical and Structural Functions of Mode in Selected Motets of Josquin Des Prez." Ph.D. diss., University of Minnesota. UMI Number 9005239.

Transcribes twenty-six motets previously unavailable; studies cadences as then confirm or undermine the mode, and notes the melodic presentation of modally significant intervals on the middleground.

D123 1989 Petito, Sue. "The Piano Works of Luigi Dallapiccola (1904–1975): An Analysis for Performance." Ph.D. diss., New York University. UMI Number 9016420.

Employs style and structural analysis (LaRue and Schenker) and synthesizes then, using them to inform performances of the works.

D124 1989 Porter, Charles. "Interval Cycles and Symmetrical Formations as Generators of Melody, Harmony, and Form in Alban Berg's String Quartet Op. 3." Ph.D. diss., City University of New York. UMI Number 9000059.

Examines Berg's embedded interval cycles as they relate to the symmetrical form in his op. 3. Uses graphic analysis to depict the interval cycles at various levels of structure.

D125 1989 Sabourin, Carmen. "A Schenkerian Study of J. S. Bach's *Two-Part Inventions* Presented in Their Original Ordering." Ph.D. diss., Yale University. UMI Number 9019021.

Examines the pedagogical intent of the pieces, by retaining the ordering from Friedmann Bach's *Clavierbüchlein*; shows how the middleground voice leading substantiates this ordering. Discusses the problems of using Schenkerian analysis to explicate the eighteenth-century compositional style.

D126 1989 Viljoen, Nicol. "Motivic Design and Tonal Structure in the Mazurkas of Frederic Chopin, as Illustrated in Graphic Analyses Based on the Theoretical Concepts of Heinrich Schenker." Ph.D. diss., University of the Orange Free State [Bloemfontein, South Africa].

Studies selected mazurkas, showing the interaction of counterpoint, harmony, and motive.

D127 1988 Albright, Larry. "Computer Realization of Human Music Cognition." Ph.D. diss., University of North Texas. UMI Number 8900326.

Models the process of music cognition (based on Krumhansl/Kessler, Jones, and Schenker) on the computer by analyzing MIDI "performances."

D128 1988   Barrow, Paul. "Franz Schubert's Unfinished Symphony: A Comparative Analysis." M.M. thesis, Bowling Green State University.
Examines the symphony using Schenkerian graphic techniques; compares this to other analytical writings that focus on non-structural issues.

D129 1988   Burstein, L. Poundie. "The Non-tonic Opening in Classical and Romantic music." Ph.D. diss., City University of New York. UMI Number 8915577.
Studies works that either (1) do not begin on the tonic, or (2) suppress the tonic until the end of the work, and (3) works that start and end in different keys; invokes Schenker's notion of the auxiliary cadence to explain these works.

D130 1988   DeBellis, Mark. "Music and the Representational Content of Experience." Ph.D. diss., Princeton University.
Studies the issue of Schenkerian analysis reflecting the representational content of a listener's experience, where given sounds are heard in relation to simpler background structures.

D131 1988   Everett, Walter. "A Schenkerian View of Text Painting in Schubert's Song Cycle *Winterreise*." Ph.D. diss., University of Michigan. UMI Number 8907027.
Examines musical-textual relationships and intersong motivic unity; explores Schubert's treatment of three central themes: delusions and illusions, memories and dreams, and the traveler's grief. Suggests that *Gute Nacht* encapsulates many of the poetic and musical themes, serving as an overture.

D132 1988   Eybl, Matrin. "Heinrich Schenkers frühe Veröffentlichungen, 1891–1898." DMP Diplomarbeit. Universität Wien.
A study of Schenker's early publications in light of what they reveal of his early musical philosophy. Notes the "numerous references between Schenker's articles and the writings of Wagner, Hauptmann, Hanslick, Ambros, and Riemann." Suggests that "Schenker's texts offer us the opportunity to explore at least three questions of the view of art between the Romantic era and modern times: the question of the role of reflection in artistic creativity and its influence on the creativity of the works; the question of the historicity of the musical effect and systems of musical rules; and finally the problem of endangered formal unity." (5)

D133 1988   Gagné, David. "Performance Medium as a Compositional Determinant: A Study of Selected Works in Three Genres by Mozart." Ph.D. diss., City University of New York. UMI Number 9111460.
Discusses the influence of performance medium on form and design; discusses a piano sonata, string quartet, and symphony of Mozart from the Schenkerian per-

spective. Examines "texture, articulation, melodic design, register, dynamics, phrase structure, and rhythm. The nature of form, harmonic structure and prolongations, voice leading, motivic structure, and chromaticism are also considered." (RILM; used by permission)

D134 1988 Gleason, James. "A Schenkerian Analysis of the Petronian Motets of the Montpellier Codex." M.S. thesis, Wright State University.
Builds on Hart's 1977 dissertation; suggests three types of prolongation in the motets: a single sonority, movement between two structural sonorities, or the prolongation of a single sonority but beginning or ending outside the "tonic." Discusses treatment of consonance and dissonance, and internal compositional logic.

D135 1988 Mosley, David. "Gesture, Sign, and Song: An Interdisciplinary Approach to Robert Schumann's *Liederkreis* Op. 39." Ph.D. diss., Emory University. UMI Number 8816955.
Applies the gestural-semiotic analysis of Mead/Pierce and the reductive method of Schenker; considers musical-text relationships. Also examines relevant writings of Schumann and Eichendorff.

D136 1988 Perone, James. "Pluralistic Strategies in Musical Analysis: A Study of Selected Works of William Albright." Ph.D. diss., State University of New York.
Applies eclectic analytical methodologies to Albright's music, including Schenkerian graphing, pitch-class set theory, group theory, and gestural analysis.

D137 1988 Smith, Timothy Allen. "A Taxonomy of Pitch Formations, and an Implication-Realization Analysis of Folk-Hymn Melodies from the *Repository of Sacred Music, Part Second*, 'Kentucky Harmony,' 'Southern Harmony,' and 'Sacred harp.' " D.M.A. doc., University of Oregon. UMI Number 8825874.
Applies Schenkerian methodology coupled with Narmour/Meyer's implication-realization theory to folk melodies.

D138 1987 Adrian, John. "The Development Section That Begins with the Tonic." Ph.D. diss., University of Rochester, Eastman School of Music.
Examines some fifty compositions, noting the presence of the tonic chord at the beginning of the development section. Provides two explanations: first, a return to the tonic chord (as distinct from the tonic *Stufe*) is termed an "apparent tonic"; the second explanation is the tonic as initiator of structural motion toward the dominant (a "real" tonic). This gives rise to the "ternary sonata form" with a thrice-articulated tonic.

D139 1987 Elliot, Scott. "A Study of Tonal Coherence in Jazz Music as Derived from Linear Compositional Techniques of the Baroque Era." M.M. thesis, Dusquesne University. UMI Number 1330262.
Uses Schenkerian ideas to trace linear patterns in jazz; suggests that "jazz and Baroque music are similar in structure."

D140 1987 Goldenzweig, Hugo. "Selected Piano Etudes of Frederic Chopin: A Performance Guide." Ph.D. diss., New York University. UMI Number 8803584.
Includes Schenkerian graphs and phenomenological narratives based on Clifton/ Ferrara. Also considers form, texture, dynamics, and style. Includes a videotape performance of the twenty-seven etudes by the author.

D141 1987 Jordan, Alan. "Harmonic Style in Selected Sibelius Symphonies." Ph.D. diss., Indiana University. UMI Number 8506112.
Discusses the First, Fourth, and Seventh Symphonies using Schenkerian reductive techniques; notes Sibelius's proclivities for third-related harmonies and weakly defined tonal centers.

D142 1987 Kaufman, Rebecca. "Expanded Tonality in the Late Chamber Works of Sergei Prokofiev." Ph.D. diss., University of Kansas. UMI Number 8727617.
Examines four works (see index) using the methodology of Heinrich Schenker.

D143 1987 Kraus, Joseph. "Contexts for Chromatic Third Relations in the Late String Quartets and Quintets of Wolfgang Amadeus Mozart. (Volume I: Text. Volume II: Musical Examples and Figures.)" Ph.D. diss., University of Rochester, Eastman School of Music. UMI Number 8705756.
Analyzes the development sections of the late string quartets and quintets of Mozart, exploring his use of the altered mediant and submediant triads; establishes how these harmonies function in the large-scale tonal unfolding of the work.

D144 1987 Larson, Steven. "Schenkerian Analysis of Modern Jazz." Ph.D. diss., University of Michigan. UMI Number 8813034.
Examines questions concerning the application of Schenkerian theory to jazz improvisations; explores "five performances of a single composition by three different pianists. Analyses of these performances lead to a consideration of relationships between improvisation and composition, and between technique and art."

D145 1987 Morrison, Charles. "Interactions of Conventional and Nonconventional Tonal Determinants in the String Quartets of Béla Bartók." Ph.D. diss., University of British Columbia.

Surveys approaches to tonality in Bartók; describes four types of progression—conventionally functional progressions, nonconventional tonicizing progressions, fifth progressions, and linear progressions—and discusses each. Explores the applicability of Schenker's method and employs it in a discussion of the Sixth Quartet.

D146 1987 Stewart, Celia. "An Introduction to the Analytical Techniques of Heinrich Schenker, with an Analysis of the *Andante Cantabile* from W. A. Mozart's Piano Sonata in B Flat, K.333." Honors thesis, Georgia State University.

General introduction to Schenker's ideas with graphic analyses of the piece and commentary.

D147 1987 Tepping, Susan. "Fugue Process and Tonal Structure in the String Quartets of Haydn, Mozart, and Beethoven." Ph.D. diss., Indiana University.

Examines the music from a Schenkerian perspective, showing that the entrance of the fugal subject generally correlates with an important point in the tonal structure; explores the relationship between thematic organization and tonal design.

D148 1986 Ballan, Harry. "Schoenberg's Expansion of Tonality, 1899–1908." Ph.D. diss., Yale University. UMI Number 8627258.

Explicates Schoenberg's early works by using Schenkerian theory; examines in particular Schoenberg's use of mediants as a dominant substitute at all levels of structure.

D149 1986 Crotty, John. "Design and Harmonic Organization in Beethoven's String Quartet Op. 131." Ph.D. diss., University of Rochester, Eastman School of Music.

The analysis is from a Schenkerian perspective. Divergences between formal design and harmonic organization are of special interest.

D150 1986 Ebcioglu, Kemal. "An Expert System for Harmonization of Chorales in the Style of J. S. Bach." Ph.D. diss., State University of New York at Buffalo. UMI Number 8609106.

Translates Bach's chorale style into ca. 270 "rules" for purposes of computer-generated harmonization. The program "acquaints" the computer with properties of voice leading drawn from Schenker.

D151 1986 Harrison, Daniel. "A Theory of Harmonic and Motivic Structure for the Music of Max Reger." Ph.D. diss., Yale University. UMI Number 9619469.

Examines pitch structures in Reger's music, focusing on the *Intermezzo*, op. 45/5, the "Larghetto" from *Träume am Kamin*, op. 143/1, and the first eighteen measures of the *Introduktion, Variationen, und Fuge uber ein Orig-*

inalthema, op. 73. Employs Schenkerian and Riemannian analytical techniques; cites Schenker's own analysis of Reger from *Das Meisterwerk in der Musik* II.

D152 1986 Smaldone, Edward. "Linear Analysis of Selected Post-Tonal Works of Arnold Schoenberg: Toward an Application of Schenkerian Concepts to Music of the Post-tonal era (and) String Quartet, No. 2 (Original Composition)." Ph.D. diss., City University of New York. UMI Number 8629741.

Examines works of Schoenberg (op. 15/1, op. 19) and Debussy (*Jimbo's Lullaby*) with Schenker-based techniques.

D153 1986 Swinburne, Caroline. "Schenker in Perspective: A Critique of Schenkerian Theory as Applied to Chopin's Fourth Ballade." M.M. Thesis, Goldsmith College.

A critique of Schenker's theories.

D154 1986 Wagner, Naphtali. "The Apparent Tonic in Western Music of the 18th–19th Century." Ph.D. diss., Hebrew University of Jerusalem.

Examines how apparent tonics are used in tonal music of the eighteenth and nineteenth centuries, and provides a theoretical framework for determining whether a given chord is a true or an apparent tonic.

D155 1986 Wick, Norman. "A Theory of Rhythmic Levels in Tonal Music." Ph.D. diss., University of Wisconsin. UMI Number 8614404.

Builds on the work of Rothstein and Schachter; formulates a theory wherein "the metrical framework is formed by the initiating points of linear progressions, arpeggiations, unfoldings, neighboring motions, and so forth." Meter at middleground levels is subject to five types of metrical transformation: extension, elision, layering, expansion, and discontinuity. Employs traditional Schenkerian pitch notation with added indications of rhythmic functions. (RILM; used by permission)

D156 1986 Williamson, Richard. "Linear and Motivic Connections in Two Brahms Motets." M.A. thesis, Eastman School of Music.

Examines op. 74, *Warum ist das Licht gegeben*, and op. 29, *Es ist das Heil uns kommen Her*, from the Schenkerian viewpoint, focusing on motivic unity.

D157 1985 Antonelli, Amy. "A Critical, Analytical Study of Selected Works by Robert Evett." Ph.D. diss., Catholic University of America. UMI Number 8515028.

Employs both *Grundgestalt*, traditional formal analysis, and Schenkerian techniques to examine the music; contains biographical information on Evett.

D158 1985 Cavett-Dunsby, Esther. "Mozart's Variations Reconsidered: Four Case Studies (K. 613, K. 501, and the Finales of K. 421 [417b] and K. 491)." Ph.D. diss., King's College.

An evaluation of form and structure in the composer's variations in light of Schenkerian theory. The sophistication of Mozart's compositional technique is demonstrated by his transformation of the middleground and foreground voice-leading structure of the theme in consecutive variations. (RILM 89–09480; used by permission)

D159 1985 Dale, Catherine. "Schoenberg's Second String Quartet Op. 10: A Schenkerian-Schoenbergian Study." M.M. thesis, King's College.

Consists of three parts: (1) analytical methodology describing the analytical techniques of Schenker and Schoenberg, (2) analysis in prose describing form, tonality, motivic relationships, etc., and (3) voice-leading graphs comprising more than a hundred pages.

D160 1985 Gerling, Cristina. "Performance Analysis for Pianists: A Critical Discussion of Selected Procedures." D.M.A. doc., Boston University. UMI Number 8602344.

Questions whether one theory is sufficient to provide complete understanding of a piece of music; analyzes pieces according to Riemann/Kurth (BWV 916). Schenker (Chopin op. 10/1), Rufer/Réti (Haydn Hob. XVI: 36), and Cooper/Meyer (Beethoven op. 81a). Also analyzes two works (Brahms's op. 117/2 and Debussy's *Ce qu'a vu le vent d'Ouest*) using an "eclectic approach . . . in which all component parts of the work are taken into account and the score itself suggests the method for the interpretation."

D161 1985 Locke, Benjamin Ross. "Performance and Structural Levels: A Conductor's Analysis of Brahms's Op. 74, No. 2, *O Heiland, Reiss Die Himmel Auf* and Op. 29, No. 2, *Schaffe In Mir, Gott, Ein Rein Herz*." D.M.A. doc., University of Wisconsin. UMI Number 8528431.

Applies analytical findings from Schenkerian analysis to performance; provides suggestions for warm-ups, rehearsal technique, tempos, and conducting gestures.

D162 1985 Pancharoen, Natchar. "Part I: 'Sextet for Strings and Woodwinds' (Original Composition). Part II: Distinguishing Musical Styles within the Romantic Era through Schenkerian Analysis." Ph.D. diss., Kent State University. UMI Number 8514178.

Investigates the question of whether Schenkerian graphs are useful for distinguishing stylistic features. Analyzes works of Berlioz, Franck, Schubert, and Mahler; includes an introduction to Schenker's ideas.

D163 1985 Pastille, William. "Ursatz: The Musical Philosophy of Heinrich Schenker." Ph.D. diss., Cornell University. UMI Number 8525718.

Traces the importance of idealism, organicism, and morphology in Schenker's thought; outlines the development of the concepts of organicism and the *Ursatz* in Schenker's published works.

D164 1985 Russom, Philip. "A Theory of Pitch Organization for the Early Works of Maurice Ravel." Ph.D. diss., Yale University. UMI Number 8601009.

Examines "referential scale collections" that are composed out as melodies and harmonies; uses the parlance of set theory with the graphing techniques of Schenkerian theory. (RILM; used by permission)

D165 1985 Simon, Mark. "Part I: Concerto for Alto Saxophone and Orchestra (Original Composition). Part II: The Modular Technique of Michael Tippett." DMA doc., Cornell University. UMI Number 8504501.

In the "modular technique," the material is "divided into a number of discrete units defined by certain parameters such as tempo or instrumentation . . . then shuffled upon each other" with the interest being in their interaction rather than their thematic development. Examines tonal and atonal relationships using "Schenker-inspired" graphs and pitch-class set theory. (RILM; used by permission)

D166 1985 Sobaskie, James. "A Theory of Associative Harmony for Tonal Music." Ph.D. diss., University Of Wisconsin. UMI Number 8601123.

Derived from the writings of Schenker, Schoenberg, Boatwright, Boretz, and Babbitt, Sobaskie's theory "offers explanations for certain little-understood aspects of tonal structure and provides a basis for speculation regarding the dissolution of the tonal system and the emergence of the centric and other post-tonal repertoires." (RILM; used by permission)

D167 1985 Walts, Anthony. "The Significance of the Opening in Sonata Form: An Analytical Study of the First Movements from Three String Quartets by Joseph Haydn." Ph.D. diss., Yale University. UMI Number 8613636.

Includes a survey of relevant literature; discusses the opening of the sonata form as generating the motivic material to be developed and ushering in the initial tonic, from which tonal motion originates. Describes the similarities and differences of the three movements.

D168 1985 Whitlock, Prentice. "The Analysis, Development of Form, and Interpretation of the Epistle Sonatas of Wolfgang Amadeus Mozart (1756–1791)." Ph.D. diss., New York University. UMI Number 8510781.

Applies Schenkerian methodology to the sonatas, written between 1772 and 1780, and compares the form to the sonata-allegro "stereotype." Includes a section on how analysis may aid performers.

D169 1984 Cinnamon, Howard. "Third-Relations as Structural Elements in Book II of Liszt's *Annees de Pelerinage* and Three Later Works." Ph.D. diss., University of Michigan. UMI Number 8502781.
Describes Liszt's compositional evolution to suggest a continuity of practice from the eighteenth through the early twentieth centuries. Shows how Liszt "develops new structural procedures based upon harmonic relationships made available within the chromatic tonal system of the nineteenth century [and employs them in his later pieces] that are often cited for their relationship to twentieth-century practice." (v)

D170 1984 Fowler, Andrew. "Multilevel Motivic Projection as a Compositional Process in Tonal Music." Ph.D. diss., University of Texas at Austin. UMI Number 8421706.
Surveys the historical development of the concept of motivic repetition (makes mention of *Grundgestalt* as well as Schenker's hidden repetitions); posits criteria for evaluating the significance of a motivic projection.

D171 1984 Holcomb, Margaret. "Rhythmic Theories in Schenkerian Literature: An Alternative View." Ph.D. diss., University of Texas at Austin. UMI Number 8508280.
Proposes a three-level metric scheme of foreground meter and "a complementary scheme of time span organization with the middleground and background." (RILM; used by permission)

D172 1984 Konecne, Julie. "Harmonic Reduction Techniques in Music Analysis, 1770–1917." Ph.D. diss., University of Iowa. UMI Number 8423575.
Examines the writings of Kirnberger, Vogler, Johann Bernhard Logier, August Frederic Kollmann, Simon Sechter, and Ernst von Stockhausen as possible precursors of Schenker's reductive analysis.

D173 1984 Stolet, Jeffrey. "The Temporal Placement of Pitch and Pitch-Class Structures in Tonal Music." Ph.D. diss., University of Texas at Austin. UMI Number 8513304.
"Proposes an alternative to the orthodox Schenkerian approach of representing tonal structure at deep levels, [changing] the mode in which the tonal contents of a piece are represented from pitch-specific representations, containing strong registral associations, to a pitch-class format with fewer registral ties, at some middleground level." (RILM; used by permission)

D174 1983 Anderson, Norman. "The Development of the Concept of 'Line' in the Writings of Heinrich Schenker." M.M. thesis, University of

Texas at Austin. Available online at http://web.presby.edu/~ danderso/thesis/.

Traces the development of the *Urlinie* concept through Schenker's published writings; cites criticisms of the concept.

D175 1983   Bante-Knight, Mary. "Tonal and Thematic Coherence in Schubert's Piano Sonata in B Flat." Ph.D. diss., Washington University. UMI Number 8402191.

Employs the analytical approaches of Schenker, Schoenberg, and LaRue to demonstrate that "(1) Schubert did indeed have a great concern for proportion and balance; (2) tonal and thematic cohesiveness does exist among all movements of the sonata; and (3) each movement functions as a necessary and vital part of a total entity." (RILM; used by permission)

D176 1983   Cadwallader, Allen. "Multileveled Motivic Repetition in Selected Intermezzi for Piano of Johannes Brahms." Ph.D. diss., University of Rochester, Eastman School of Music. UMI Number 8308592.

An examination of seven Brahms intermezzi, exploring how "the basic motive elaborates and decorates the headtone of the structural melodic line. Subsequent repetitions of the motive at various levels prolong the headtone, retarding the descent of the Urlinie until the latter parts of a piece."

D177 1983   Debaise, Joseph. "George Crumb's *Music for a Summer Evening*: A Comprehensive Analysis." Ph.D. diss., University of Rochester, Eastman School of Music.

Employs eclectic analytical approaches, including Schenker (foreground and middleground reductions), pitch-class set theory, and numerology, to explain compositional structure and design in the work.

D178 1983   De Zeeuw, Anne. "Tonality and the Concertos of William Walton." Ph.D. diss., University of Texas at Austin. UMI Number 8414357.

Because no "single theoretical model accounts fully for the tonal organization of these compositions," De Zeeuw produces an integrated theoretical system using "Rameau, Schenker, and five other 20th-century theories." (RILM; used by permission)

D179 1983   Gebuhr, Ann. "Structuralism in Music: A Review of Recent Ideas." Ph.D. diss., Indiana University. UMI Number 8321374.

Surveys the development of the structuralist movement; examines writings of Salzer, Forte, Yeston, Narmour, Berry, and Epstein for their structuralist content.

D180 1983   Korsyn, Kevin. "Integration in Works of Beethoven's Final Period." Ph.D. diss., Yale University. UMI Number 8411528.

Discusses the problems and nature of analysis, "with the aim of establishing a dialectic between our analytical assumptions and our analyses of individual compositions, so that the general and the specific are intertwined." Examines compositional integration between movements.

D181 1983 Stewart, James. "Heinrich Schenker's *Kontrapunkt* I and II: A Translation and Commentary." Ph.D. diss., Ohio State University. UMI Number 8403579.

The first complete English-language translation of *Kontrapunkt*; includes complete bibliographical references and passages of text from which Schenker cited, as well as musical examples omitted by Schenker (from secondary sources); moves Schenker's "asides, commentaries and source citations" to footnotes.

D182 1983 Swain, Joseph. "Limits of Musical Structure." Ph.D. diss., Harvard University. UMI Number 8322452.

Compares the style theories of LaRue, Meyer, and Rosen; presents a limited hierarchical view of musical structure (comparing Schenker and Meyer); suggests that "human capacity to perceive abstract stimuli and language is limited, and that hierarchical mechanisms that organize these types of information are the principal means by which listeners can extend such capacity." (RILM; used by permission)

D183 1983 Thaler, Lotte. "Organische Form in der Musiktheorie des 19. und beginnenden 20. Jahrhunderts." Ph.D. diss., Technische Universität Berlin.

A discussion of organicism in music-theoretical writings and in nonmusical writings; surveys the writings of Goethe, Halm, Schenker, and Mersmann. Published by Katzbilcher (Munich) in 1984.

D184 1982 Campbell, Bruce. "Beethoven's Quartets Opus 59: An Investigation into Compositional Process." Ph.D. diss., Yale University. UMI Number 8619443.

Examines the Razumovsky quartets using Schenkerian and Schoenbergian processes; includes summaries of the approaches and reviews analytical language used to explicate the compositional process.

D185 1982 Hantz, Edward. "Towards a Psychology of Tonal Music." Ph.D. diss., University of Michigan. UMI Number 8215005.

Deals with the musical perception and melodic memory; examines how listeners process and use musical information; examines what listening strategies have in common with Schenker's ideas of *Stufe* and *Ursatz*.

D186 1982 Hatten, Robert. "Toward a Semiotic Model of Style in Music: Epistemological and Methodological Bases." Ph.D. diss., Indiana University. UMI Number 8300851.

Views style as a theoretical and historical construct based on readings in linguistics, structuralism, and semiotics; examines the writings of Eco, Schenker, Meyer, Narmour, Rosen, Jackendoff/Lerdahl, and Keiler.

D187 1982 Navien, Charles Francis. "The Harmonic Language of *L'horizon chimérique* by Gabriel Fauré." Ph.D. diss., University of Connecticut. UMI Number 8309251.

Examines Fauré's synthesis of tonality and modality in *L'horizon chimérique*; shows the modal influences as subservient to the tonal.

D188 1982 Peel, John Milton. "From Parsifal to The Pythia: Reveria on the Prelude: Herzeleide: Introduction to The Pythia." Ph.D. diss., Princeton University. UMI Number 8223307.

Combines "Schenkerian-type" graphs and pitch-class set theory to analyze Act II, scene 2, in *Parsifal*.

D189 1982 Stein, Deborah. "Extended Tonal Procedures in the Lieder of Hugo Wolf." Ph.D. diss., Yale University. UMI Number 8425337.

Based on the theory and methodology of Heinrich Schenker, extended and supplemented with new analytical concepts and methods where necessary (e.g., replacing the diatonic *Ursatz* with a progressive tonal scheme where appropriate); presents Schenker's theory as a "norm" against which Wolf's extended tonal procedures can be gauged.

D190 1982 Taylor, Paul. "Thematic Process and Tonal Organization in the First Movement Sonata Forms of Max Reger's Nine Sonatas for Violin and Piano." Ph.D. diss., Catholic University of America. UMI Number 8221465.

Examines nine works of Reger from two perspectives, thematic process and tonal organization; divides Reger's oeuvre into three periods: (1) opp. 1, 3, and 41; (2) opp. 72–122; and (3) op. 139.

D191 1982 Yokota, Erisa. "Heinrich Schenker no ongakukan kôsatsu— Harmonielehre (1906) o chûshin to shite." M.A. diss., Ochanomizu Women's University, Tokyo.

Compares Schenker's ideas from the *Harmonielehre* to Riemann's theories.

D192 1981 Bollinger, John. "An Integrative and Schenkerian Analysis of the B-flat Minor Sonata of Frederic Chopin." Ph.D. diss., Washington University. UMI Number 8201728.

Seeks to "provide extensive integrative and Schenkerian analytical procedures specifically designed to permit modern pianists to conceive the four-movement Sonata as a totally integrated composition." (RILM; used by permission)

D193 1981 Damschroder, David. "The Structural Foundations of 'The Music of the Future': A Schenkerian Study of Liszt's Weimar Repertoire." Ph.D. diss., Yale University. UMI Number 8124336.

Examines music of Liszt, Wagner, and Berlioz; notes that background and middleground structures are consistent with Schenker's theories, and that their novelty lies in the foreground.

D194 1981 Levenson, Irene. "Motivic-Harmonic Transfer in the Late Works of Schubert: Chromaticism in Large and Small Spans." Ph.D. diss., Yale University. UMI Number 8124373.

Examines Schubert's chamber music 1824–8; asserts that "not only can [chromaticism in the] motive be said to *affect* the harmonic plan in Schubert's late works, but in a great number of cases, chromatic motivic material *determines* large-scale harmonic structure." (vi)

D195 1981 Riggins, Herbert. "Heinrich Schenker's Graphic Notation and Contemporary Variants." Ph.D. diss., University of Texas at Austin. UMI Number 8208242.

Examines Schenker's notation used in *Der freie Satz* and the *Fünf Urlinie-Tafeln*, comparing it to Mitchell's glossary from *The Music Forum*, Salzer's *Structural Hearing*, and Warfield's *Layer Analysis*. Concludes that "Schenker's mature analytic symbols are entirely adequate for his theory and that departures from his model in the name of improvement are either not improvements or reflect a different theory." (RILM; used by permission)

D196 1981 Rothstein, William. "Rhythm and the Theory of Structural Levels." Ph.D. diss., Yale University. UMI Number 8125672.

Formulates a theory of rhythmic levels based on Schenker's analyses and his "often half-articulated" comments throughout his writings.

D197 1981 Wason, Robert. "Fundamental Bass Theory in Nineteenth-Century Vienna." Ph.D. diss., Yale University 1981.

Discusses figured bass and harmonic theory in early-nineteenth-century Vienna; traces the influence of Sechter, through Bruckner, to Schenker and Schoenberg.

D198 1980 Krebs, Harald. "Third Relation and Dominant in Late 18th- and Early 19th-Century Music." Ph.D. diss., Yale University. UMI Number 8025208.

Examines use of the mediant and submediant at various structural levels, especially in the works of Schubert and Chopin, where they were used with increasing frequency and independence.

D199 1980   Yadeau, William. "Tonal and Formal Structure in Selected Larger Works of Chopin." D.M.A. doc., University of Illinois. UMI Number 8026622.
Examines three works (opp. 38, 49, and 61) by means of voice-leading graphs and commentary; makes suggestions for interpretation based on the analysis.

D200 1979   Ferencz, George. "Application of the Analytical Techniques of Heinrich Schenker and Grosvernor W. Cooper/Leonard B. Meyer." M.A. thesis, Kent State University.
Contains one chapter on each theory, with separate application to Brahms's Rhapsody op. 119/4.

D201 1979   Hoyt, Reed. "The Bassline in Tonal Music: Its Relationship to Melodic and Harmonic Structure." Ph.D. diss., University of Pennsylvania. UMI Number 7928144.
Examines the Schenkerian model, implication-realization theory, and traditional harmonic theory, with a preference for the implication-realization model; "suggests a new method of treating harmony unfettered by rules for chord progression, and of looking at tonal structure without assumptive analytical prototypes." (RILM; used by permission)

D202 1979   Lamb, James. "A Graphic Analysis of Brahms, Opus 118, with an Introduction to Schenkerian Theory and the Reduction Process." Ph.D. diss., Texas Tech University. UMI Number 8013258.
Analyzes the six intermezzi that comprise op. 118; contains an introduction to Schenker's theory.

D203 1979   Pittman, Daniel. "Percy Grainger, Gustav Holst, and Ralph Vaughan Williams: A Comparative Analysis of Selected Wind Band Compositions." D.M.A. doc., Memphis State University. UMI Number 8001188.
Provides biographical sketches of the composers; uses Schenkerian analysis to discuss tonality, harmony, melody, rhythm, form, instrumentation, and performance practice.

D204 1979   Porter, Steven. "Rhythm and Harmony in the Music of the Beatles." Ph.D. diss., City University of New York. UMI Number 7913156.
Surveys popular music in the United States and Britain; discusses the complete output of the group, and focuses his analyses on developing terminology for studying rhythm and harmony in popular music.

D205 1978   Blum, Harold. "A Structural Analysis of Beethoven's Op. 31, No. 2." M.M. thesis, Kent State University.
An analysis according to Schenkerian techniques; includes a brief summary of Schenker's ideas.

D206 1978 Miller, Mina Florence. "The Solo Piano Music of Carl Nielsen: An Analysis for Performance." Ph.D. diss., New York University. UMI Number 7824097.

Employs structural analysis, style analysis, and Schenkerian analysis to explain Nielsen's piano music; bases her explanation of effects on archival studies and interviews with Nielsen's family.

D207 1978 Phillips, Edward. "A Theory of Pitch Structures in a Selected Repertoire of Early German Chorale Melodies." Ph.D. diss., Yale University. UMI Number 7916475.

Examines a selection of melodies ca. 1500–45, noting the pitch structures over short and long spans; emphasizes the importance of the third as a scale degree and as a linear pattern.

D208 1978 Proctor, Gregory. "Technical Bases of Nineteenth-Century Chromaticism." Ph.D. diss., Princeton University. UMI Number 7807490.

Rejects the notion of a single "common practice" spanning the music ca. 1600–1900. Rather, divides the three-hundred-year period into overlapping systems of "classical diatonic tonality" and "nineteenth-century chromatic tonality." (v)

D209 1978 Simon, Tom. "An Analytical Inquiry into Thelonius Monk's *Ruby, My Dear*." M.M. thesis, University of Michigan.

Discusses problems of analyzing jazz improvisation; includes a transcription of the 1959 improvisation and a graphic analysis based on that transcription.

D210 1977 Adrian, John Stanley. "Heinrich Schenker's Early Theory of the Scale-Step." Ph.D. diss., University of Alberta.

Examines the theory of tonicization and the *Stufe*, which allows chromaticism into the diatonic system.

D211 1977 Dagnes, Edward. "A Musical and Textural Analysis of J. S. Bach's *Christ Lag in Todesbanden* (BWV 4)." M.M. thesis, University of Michigan.

Considers the implications of Luther's text governing the musical design; approaches the music with Schenkerian techniques, noting that the cantata is a "fascinating amalgam of musicality and spirituality in Bach's genius." (1)

D212 1977 Hart, Josephine. "Musical Structure in the Thirteenth-Century Motet: An Analytical Study of the Motets in the Old Corpus of the Montpellier Manuscript." D.M.A. diss., University of Oregon. UMI Number 7719342.

Examines the thirty motets using Schenkerian methodology; discusses the texts in an appendix.

D213 1976   Greenberg, Beth. "A Study of Chromaticism in the Mozart String
Quartet in G Major, K. 387." M.M. thesis, University of Michigan.
Studies the effect of chromaticism at various structural levels in the quartet; in-
cludes a copy of the autograph.

D214 1976   Neumeyer, David. "Counterpoint and Pitch Structure in the Early
Music of Hindemith." Ph.D. diss., Yale University. UMI Number
7630240.
Examines the music of Hindemith, noting his style shift around 1930; explores
the similarities between Hindemith's and Schenker's analytical systems.

D215 1976   Szkodzinski, Louise. "A Study of Editorial Markings in Three
Beethoven Sonatas." D.M.A. diss., Indiana University.
A comparative study of Beethoven editions by Bülow, Tovey, Schenker, Schna-
bel, and others compared to the "urtext" edition of Breitkopf; focuses on opp.
2/1, 53, and 101.

D216 1975   Bashour, Frederick. "A Model for the Analysis of Structural
Levels and Tonal Movement in Compositions of the Fifteenth
Century." Ph.D. diss., Yale University. UMI Number 7524499.
Examines the eighty-four chansons of Dufay as well as compositions from his
contemporaries, combining "the melodic principles of Gregorian chant theory
and the contrapuntal principles of discant theory . . . with the concepts of prolongation, structural levels, and essential voice-leading."

D217 1975   Smith, Charles. "Beethoven's Eighth Symphony: An Analysis
from No Particular Point of View." M.M. thesis, University of
Michigan.
Although the analysis is from "no particular point of view," it is very much influenced by Schenkerian thinking, with its sketches in "quasi-musical notation."

D218 974   Austin, John. "A Survey of the Influence of Heinrich Schenker on
American Music Theory and Its Pedagogy Since 1940." M.M.
thesis, North Texas State University. UMI Number 1306953.
Surveys the Schenkerian literature since 1940 in periodicals, research papers,
and textbooks; provides a biographical sketch and introduction to Schenker's
basic concepts.

D219 1974   Flechsig, Hartmut. "Studien zu Theorie und Methode musikalischer Analyse." Ph.D. diss., Universität Heidelberg.
Examines various methods of musical analysis, grouping them into two broad
categories: (1) analyses based on information theory; and (2) theories of representation, expression, and symbolism, with Schenker falling into the former category. Published in 1976 by Katzbichler in the Beiträge zur Musikforschung
series (see **B75** above).

D220 1974 Narmour, Eugene. "The Melodic Structure of Tonal Music: A Theoretical Study." Ph.D. diss., University of Chicago.

An extension of Cooper/Meyer's rhythmic approach exploring the implications and realizations melodies. Proposes five melodic types: gap-filling, triadic, axial, linear, and compound.

D221 1973 Gould, Murray. "Species Counterpoint and Tonal Structure." Ph.D. diss., New York University. UMI Number 7401984.

Makes an inquiry "into the rationales and predispositions of the species system in order to determine its limits as a vehicle for tonal composition." Considers whether passages in species counterpoint should be "interpreted *as* tonal compositions or as structural-level models of tonal compositions." (5–6)

D222 1973 Kalib, Sylvan. "Thirteen Essays from the Three Yearbooks *Das Meisterwerk in Der Musik* by Heinrich Schenker: An Annotated Translation." Ph.D. diss., Northwestern University. UMI Number 7330626.

Contains (1) a digest introducing the concepts of Schenker and his aesthetic philosophy; (2) the text of the thirteen essays (see **T6** above); and (3) commentary on the essays.

D223 1973 Stewart, Milton. "Structural Development in the Jazz Improvisational Technique of Clifford Brown." Ph.D. diss., University of Michigan. Reprinted in *Jazzforschung* 6–7 (1974–5): 141–273.

Considers whether hierarchical analysis may be profitably applied to jazz improvisation; uses concepts of Schenker, Saltzer, Boretz, and Chomsky.

D224 1971 Mast, Paul B. *"Oktaven u. Quinten, u. a.*: A Critical Edition of Brahms' Notebook with Schenker's Commentary Translated and Compared by Paul B. Mast." Ph.D. diss., University of Rochester, Eastman School of Music.

A translation of Brahms's study, later published in *The Music Forum.*

D225 1970 Boretz, Benjamin. "Meta-Variations: Studies in the Foundation of Musical Thought (with) Group Variations I (Original Composition)." Ph.D. diss., Princeton University.

"[Attempts] to discover principles to account for the conceptual richness of music and to provide a radically simplified map of what is understood about music." The section "Sketch of a Musical System" outlines "a path toward a possible foundation model for all music" based on Schenker.

D226 1970 Kaderavek, Milan. "I: Stylistic Aspects of the Late Chamber Music of Leos Janácek: An Analytic Study. II: Composition: Music for Orchestra." D.M.A. doc., University of Illinois.

Considers the music from the Schenkerian perspective and also in light of Janácek's idea of *napevký mluvý* (speech melody); traces the influence of folk melodies in the instrumental works.

D227 1970   Kudlawiec, Dennis. "The Application of Schenkerian Concepts of Musical Structure to the Analysis Segment of Basic Theory Courses at the College Level." Ed.D. diss., University of Illinois at Urbana-Champaign. UMI Number 7114836.

Considers (1) the basic tenets of Schenker's theories; (2) their implications for the study of the structure of music and for the technique of musical analysis; (3) the extent to which textbooks in current use reflect the theories; and (4) the implications of Schenker's theories for change in theory textbooks and in the theory curriculum. (5)

D228 1970   Lester, Joel. "A Theory of Atonal Prolongations, as Used in an Analysis of the Serenade, Op. 24, by Arnold Schoenberg." Ph.D. diss., Princeton University.

Discusses the inadequacies of previous atonal analyses; suggests that prolongational analysis may be fruitful for the explanation of atonal works. Examines the transitory period from Schoenberg's atonal to his twelve-tone works.

D229 1969   Arnn, John. "The Harmonic Language of Selected Piano Works by Fauré." M.M. thesis, Indiana University.

Uses Salzer-based Schenkerian ideas to examine sonority, chord progressions, and cadence structure in Fauré's works.

D230 1969   Morgan, Robert. "The Delayed Structural Downbeat and Its Effect on the Tonal and Rhythmic Structure of Sonata Form Recapitulation." Ph.D. diss., Princeton University.

Examines the view that "form emerges as a result of the interaction of rhythm and tonality"; examines Chopin's B Minor Sonata, Tchaikovsky's Sixth Symphony, Strauss's *Tod und Verklärung*, and Mahler's Sixth Symphony.

D231 1968   Chesnut, John. "Mozart as a Novice: Compositional Problem Solving in Mozart's Earliest Known Works." M.M. thesis, New England Conservatory of Music.

Examines Mozart's first nineteen known works using Schenkerian techniques.

D232 1968   Komar, Arthur. "Theory of Suspensions: A Study of Metrical and Pitch Relationships in Tonal Music." Ph.D. diss., Princeton University.

Formulates a theory of tonal meter based on Schenker's ideas; a probing inquiry into the nature of the suspension at various structural levels. Published by Princeton in 1971 (see **B81** above).

D233 1968 Pierce, Anne. "The Analysis of Rhythm in Tonal Music." Ph.D. diss., Brandeis University.
An early application of Schenker's hierarchical concepts to rhythm and meter. Suggests the term *integrative levels* with the hierarchy of note, > motif, > phrase, > phrase group, etc.

D234 1967 Brewer, Robert. "Variations in Current Terminology Relating to Modulation." M.M. thesis, Indiana University.
Examines theories of modulation as expressed in the writings of Schenker, Schoenberg, Goetschius, Hindemith, Piston, Forte, and others; summarizes them and suggests a codification of terms.

D235 1967 Dubbiosi, Stelio. "The Piano Music of Maurice Ravel: An Analysis of the Technical and Interpretive Problems in the Pianistic Style of Maurice Ravel." Ph.D. diss., New York University.
Contains analyses of each piano work of Ravel according to Schenker's principles.

D236 1967 Howard, Joseph. "Application of Schenker Principles for the Interpretation of Mozart Sonata K. 333." M.M. thesis, Kent State University.
Includes an introduction to Schenker's ideas, the analysis itself, a discussion of the value of Schenker's ideas for interpretation, and possibilities for the extending of Schenker's system to the music of Debussy, Bartók, and Stravinsky.

D237 1967 Kassler, Michael. "A Trinity of Essays: Toward a Theory That Is the Twelve-Note Class System, Toward Development of a Constructive Tonality Theory Based on Writings by Heinrich Schenker, Toward a Simple Programming Language for Musical Information Retrieval." Ph.D. diss, Princeton University. UMI Number 6802490
The essay concerning Schenker "develops a logistic system whose theorems are di-linear major-minor compositions, whose axioms are Schenker's three major-mode Ursätze, and whose rules of inference correspond to a selection of Schenker's techniques of prolongation." (RILM; used by permission)

D238 1967 Riley, John. "A Critical Examination of George Russell's Lydian Chromatic Concept of Tonal Organization for Improvisation." M.M. thesis, Indiana University.
Examines Russell's approach to tonality in light of Hindemith's and Schenker's theories.

D239 1967 Slatin, Sonia. "The Theories of Heinrich Schenker in Perspective." Ph.D. diss., Columbia University. UMI Number 6715521.
An introduction to Schenker's ideas; contains a valuable chapter of biographical data, correcting several errors. Includes a section on the state of music theory at

Schenker's time and a section on "criticisms and contributions." Appendices include a glossary of analytical symbols and many musical examples from *Der freie Satz*.

D240 1962 Kalib, Sylvan S. "The Hindemith System: A Critique." M.M. thesis, DePaul University.

Refutes Hindemith's conception of the overtone series using Schenker's ideas; also uses Schenkerian analytical techniques to show that Hindemith's readings of degree progressions are, in many cases, incorrect.

D241 1960 Krueger, Theodore. "*Der freie Satz* by Heinrich Schenker: A Complete Translation and Re-editing. Volume I: The Complete Text. Volume II: Supplement of Musical Examples." Ph.D. diss, University of Iowa. UMI Number 6001558.

The first English translation of *Der freie Satz*; includes a glossary of graphic symbols and an introduction to Schenker's ideas.

D242 1956 Miron, Nathan. "The Analytical System of Hindemith and Schenker as Applied to Two Works of Arnold Schoenberg." M.M. thesis, North Texas State College (i.e., University of North Texas).

A response to Knod's thesis, "[attempting] to fill in one of the gaps resulting from [her] insufficient sampling." Analyzes *Gurrelieder* and the Fourth String Quartet according to Hindemith's and Schenker's ideas.

D243 1955 Knod, Grace. "A Comparison of the Hindemith and Schenker Concepts of Tonality." M.M. thesis, North Texas State College (i.e., University of North Texas).

Compares Hindemith's and Schenker's concept of tonality vis-à-vis the "conventional" concept; illustrates these with examples representing "a fifty-year period from the late thirteenth century to the present day." (v)

D244 1952 Thompson, William. "A Clarification of the Tonality Concept." Ph.D. diss., Indiana University. UMI Number 0004380.

Attacks the traditional understanding of tonality; examines the concepts of tonality set forth by Hindemith and Schenker. Additional Sources of Interest.

ADDITIONAL SOURCES OF INTEREST

D245 2002 Chong, Eddy. "Extending Schenker's *Neue musikalische Theorien und Phantasien*: Towards a Schenkerian Model for the Analysis of Ravel's Music." Ph.D. diss., University of Rochester, Eastman School of Music. UMI Number 3045246.

D246 2001 Smith, Elizabeth Lena. "Motivic Unity in Beethoven's Piano Sonata Op. 10/1: A Schenkerian Analysis." M.M. thesis, Florida State University.

D247 1997 Bird, Melvin. "Franz Schubert, Piano Sonata D. 840: An Analytical Study." M.M. thesis, Reading University.

D248 1997 Penfold, Nigel. "Schubert: Piano Sonata in C Major, No. 15, D. 840, Relique: An Analysis of the First Movement Following the Theories of Heinrich Schenker." M.A. thesis, Reading University.

D249 1995 Foster, Peter. "Brahms, Schenker and the Rules of Composition." Ph.D. diss., Reading University. DDM Code 61cmFosP.

D250 1994 Marvin, William. "Tonal Design and Structural Levels in the Finale from Act Two of Mozart's *Die Zauberflöte*." M.A. thesis, University of Rochester, Eastman School of Music.

D251 1994 McKee, Eric J. "The Interaction of Tonal Structure and Phrase Structure as an Aspect of Form in Tonal Music." Ph.D. diss., University of Michigan. UMI Number 9500995.

D252 1991 Coeurdevey, Annie. "La formation du langage tonal en France dans la première Moitié du XVIe siècle: Etienne Moulinié." Ph.D. diss., University of Tours.

D253 1990 Miller, Malcolm. "Richard Wagner's *Wesendonck Lieder:* An Analytical Study with Consideration of the Orchestrations by Felix Motti and Hans Werner Henze." Ph.D. diss., King's College. DDM Code: 01anMilm.

D254 1988 Pitre, Richard. "Preliminary Considerations for a Theological Anthropology of Music." M.M. thesis, Jesuit School of Theology.

D255 1987 Smith, Richard. "Foreground Rhythmic Structuring: A Preliminary Study." M.M. thesis, King's College.

D256 1986 McBright, Lesley. "Latent Background versus Manifest Foreground: An Investigation into the Organic Evolution of the First Movement of Chopin's B-flat Minor Piano Sonata, op. 35." M.M. thesis, Goldsmith's College.

D257 1978 Plum, Karl-Otto. "Die Schenkersche Theorie und ihre Anwendung auf die Analyse der Bachschen Solokompositionen für

Streichinstrumente." Ph.D. diss., Universität Köln. DDM Code
79anPluK.

D258 1974 Hallnäs, Lars. "Heinrich Schenker, Arnold Schering och frågan
'Vad är musik?' " Ph.D. diss., University of Uppsala.

D259 1975 Debruyn, Randall. "Contrapuntal structure in contemporary tonal
music: a preliminary study of tonality in the twentieth century."
D.M.A. diss., University of Illinois.
Examines works of Bartók, Ives, Hindemith, Stravinsky, and Hovhaness according to Schenkerian-based linear analysis.

Chapter 6

Electronic Schenker Resources

This chapter has been divided into two sections: (1) articles and essays from online journals involving Schenker, and (2) miscellaneous Web pages. The quality of the Web sites varies greatly, as does their accessibility. Various types of Web sites have been omitted from this list: entries in online encyclopedias, abstracts of conference presentations, syllabi for university courses, postings from online message boards, and online versions of print journals. Likewise, subscription services such as RILM, RISM, IIMP, and the like have been excluded.

PART 1: ARTICLES AND ESSAYS INVOLVING SCHENKER

E1   2002   Kelly, Robert T. "The Effect of Being Passing: A Philosophical Basis for the Importance of Analysis."
http://www-student.furman.edu/users/r/rkelley/schenker.htm

E2   2001   Burstein, L. Poundie. "Mozart *in medias res*." *Electronic Journal of Music Theory and Analysis* 2/1.
http://musictheoryresources.com/members/MTA_2_1b.htm

E3   2000   Gallardo, Cristóbal. "Schenkerian Analysis and Popular Music." *Transcultural Music Review* 5.
http://www.sibetrans.com/trans/trans5/garcia.htm

E4   2000   Karpinski, Gary S. "Lessons from the Past: Music Theory Pedagogy and the Future." *Music Theory Online* 6/3.
http://smt.ucsb.edu/mto/issues/mto.00.6.3/mto.00.6.3.karpinski.html

E5   2000   Pozzi, Egidio. "Concetto teorico e significato analitico delle successioni lineari: il Largo della Ciacona op. II n. 12, di Arcangelo Corelli." *Analytica* 1/1.
Italian: http://www3.muspe.unibo.it:8080/gatm/Ita/Vol/1/fr_egidio_pozzi_ita. html
English: http://www3.muspe.unibo.it:8080/gatm/Eng/Vol/1/1indx%20eng. htm

E6   2000   Sanguinette, Giorgio. "Analisi e variazioni di tempo: la Polacca op. 53 di Chopin." *Analytica* 1/2.
Italian: http://www3.muspe.unibo.it:8080/gatm/Ita/Vol/2/fr_sanguinetti_ita.htm
English: http://www3.muspe.unibo.it:8080/gatm/Eng/Vol/2/fr_sanguinetti_en.htm

E7   1999   Alpern, Wayne. "Music Theory as a Mode of Law: The Case of Heinrich Schenker, Esq." *Cardozo Law Review Online.*
http://www.cardozo.yu.edu/cardlrev/v20n5–6/alpern.pdf

E8   1999   Boss, Jack F. "Schenkerian-Schoenbergian Analysis and Hidden Repetition in the Opening Movement of Beethoven's Piano Sonata Op. 10, No. 1." *Music Theory Online* 5/1.
http://smt.ucsb.edu/mto/issues/mto.99.5.1/mto.99.5.1.boss.html

E9   1999   Damschroder, David A. "Review of Carl Schachter, *Unfoldings: Essays in Schenkerian Theory and Analysis.*" *Music Theory Online* 5/4.
http://smt.ucsb.edu/mto/issues/mto.99.5.4/mto.99.5.4.damschro.html

E10   1999   Koozin, Timothy. "On Metaphor, Technology, and Schenkerian Analysis." *Music Theory Online* 5/3.
http://smt.ucsb.edu/mto/issues/mto.99.5.3/mto.99.5.3.koozin.html

E11   1999   Suurpää, Lauri. "Tonaalisen musiikin analyysi: historiaa ja lähtökohtia." *Tieteessä Tapahtuu* 1.
http://www.tsv.fi/ttapaht/991/suurpaa.htm

E12   1999   Tuchowski, Andrzej. "Chopin's Integrative Technique and Its Repercussions in 20th-Century Polish Music." *Polish Music Journal* 2/1
http://www.usc.edu/dept/polish_music/PMJ/issues.html

E13   1998   Barbose, Joel Luis. "Estudo para clarineta de Gaetano Donizetti." *Urucungo* 1/1.
http://www.svn.com.br/urucungo/barbosa/barbosa1.htm

E14   1998   Broman, Per F. "Report from the 'Skagerack Network' Analysis Workshop at Lyseby Conference Center in Oslo, Norway, November 20–23, 1997." *Music Theory Online* 4/1.
http://smt.ucsb.edu/mto/issues/mto.98.4.1/mto.98.4.1.broman.html

E15 1998 Drabkin, William. "L'analisi come strumento pratico: un argomento da prendere in considerazione." *Analitica* 0.
http://www3.muspe.unibo.it:8080/gatm/Ita/Vol/0/fr_drabkin-it.htm

E16 1998 Zbikowski, Lawrence M. "Metaphor and Music Theory: Reflections from Cognitive Science." *Music Theory Online* 4/1.
http://smt.ucsb.edu/mto/issues/mto.98.4.1/mto.98.4.1.zbikowski.html

E17 1998 Lester, Joel. "How Theorists Relate to Musicians." *Music Theory Online* 4/2.
http://smt.ucsb.edu/mto/issues/mto.98.4.2/mto.98.4.2.lester.html

E18 1998 Schmalfeldt, Janet. "On Keeping the Score." *Music Theory Online* 4/2.
http://smt.ucsb.edu/mto/issues/mto.98.4.2/mto.98.4.2.schmalfeldt.html

E19 1998 Ulhoa, Mario. "Gavotte I BWV 995: Reducao e performance musical." *Urucungo* 1/1.
http://www.svn.com.br/urucungo/ulloa/ulloa1.htm

E20 1997 Agmon, Eytan. "The Bridges That Never Were: Schenker on the Contrapuntal Origin of the Triad and Seventh Chord." *Music Theory Online* 3/1.
http://smt.ucsb.edu/mto/issues/mto.97.3.1/mto.97.3.1.agmon.html

E21 1997 Broman, Per F. "Report from the Third Triennial ESCOM Conference in Uppsala, Sweden, 7–12 June, 1997." *Music Theory Online* 3/4.
http://smt.ucsb.edu/mto/issues/mto.97.3.4/mto.97.3.4.broman.html

E22 1997 Cheong, Wai-ling. "Theory Reception in China: Report on Journals of Central Conservatory and Shanghai Conservatory of Music." *Music Theory Online* 3/4.
http://smt.ucsb.edu/mto/issues/mto.97.3.4/mto.97.3.4.cheong.html

E23 1997 Lacerda, Marcos Branda. "Breve resenha das contribuiçoes de Schenker e Schoenberg para a análise musical." [A Summary of the Contributions of Schenker and Schoenberg to Musical Analysis]. *Revista eletrônica de musicologia 2.*
http://www.cce.ufpr.br/~rem/REMv2.1/vol2.1/BreveResenha/BreveResenha.html

E24 1997 Meeùs, Nicholas. "Music Theory and Analysis in France and Belgium." *Music Theory Online* 3/4.
http://smt.ucsb.edu/mto/issues/mto.97.3.4/mto.97.3.4.meeus.html

E25 1996 Agmon, Eytan. "Beethoven's Op. 81a and the Psychology of Loss. Dedicated to the Memory of Yizhak Rabin, 1922–1995." *Music Theory Online* 2/4.
http://smt.ucsb.edu/mto/issues/mto.96.2.4/mto.96.2.4.agmon.html

E26   1996   Agmon, Eytan. "Conventional Harmonic Wisdom and the Scope of Schenkerian Theory: A Reply to John Rothgeb." *Music Theory Online* 2/3.
http://mto.societymusictheory.org/issues/mto.96.2.3/mto.96.2.3.agmon.html

E27   1996   Chew, Geoffrey. "Musical Aesthetics."
http://www.tcd.ie/music/aesthetics/aesthetics.html

E28   1996   Grauer, Victor A. "Toward a Unified Theory of the Arts." *Music Theory Online* 2/6.
http://smt.ucsb.edu/mto/issues/mto.96.2.6/mto.96.2.6.grauer.html

E29   1996   Rothgeb, John. "Re: Eytan Agmon on Functional Theory." *Music Theory Online* 2/1.
http://smt.ucsb.edu/mto/issues/mto.96.2.1/mto.96.2.1.rothgeb.html

E30   1996   Willner, Channan. "Handel, the Sarabande, and Levels of Genre: A Reply to David Schulenberg." *Music Theory Online* 2/7.
http://smt.ucsb.edu/mto/issues/mto.96.2.7/mto.96.2.7.willner.html

E31   1995   Pastille, William. "Schenker's Value-Judgments." *Music Theory Online* 4/6.
http://smt.ucsb.edu/mto/issues/mto.95.1.6/mto.95.1.6.pastille.html

E32   N. D.   Moore, Ken C. "Modern Psychoacoustics and Its Impact on Schenkerian Analysis."
http://www.hpsl.demon.co.uk/schenk/index.html

PART 2: MISCELLANEOUS WEB PAGES INVOLVING SCHENKER

E33   Campbell, Bruce. "Quotations from the Works of Heinrich Schenker."
http://www.msu.edu/~bruce/schenkerquotes.htm

E34   Chernov, Eric B. "Mannes College of Music Schenker Symposia."
http://www.ursatz.com/SCHENKER/

E35   Humal, Mart. "Schenkeri Analüüs Ja Poolkadents."
http://www.usesoft.ee/tmk/Muusika/01juuni_m2.htm

E36   Jackson, Timothy. "Center for Schenkerian Studies."
http://www.music.unt.edu/the/Center%20for%20Schenkerian%20Studies.htm

E37   New York Public Library: The Oster Collection.
http://www.nypl.org/research/lpa/mus/mus.majcoll.html

E38 Oliver, William D. "Schenker Analysis" from "The Singing Tree: A Novel Interactive Musical Interface." M.S. thesis, University of Rochester, 1997. http://feynman.stanford.edu/people/Oliver_www/singhtml/node18.html

E39 Pankhurst, Tom (tompankhurst@lineone.net). http://www.schenkerguide.com

E40 Ramunno, Sandra. "Schenkerian Analysis: Valuable Asset for Music Critics." http://desktop12.cis.mcmaster.ca/~mus701/sandra/valuable.htm

E41 Renwick, William, and Dave Walker. "Schenker-Analysis Glossary." http://www.humanities.mcmaster.ca/~renwick/glosstart.htm

E42 Solomon, Larry. "Schenkerian Primer." http://solo1.home.mindspring.com/schenker.htm

E43 Walker, David. "Schenkerian Analysis." http://www.media.mcmaster.ca/walker/Schenker_Intro/schenkeri1.htm

E44 Wang, PoWei."Schenker." http://powei.hypermart.net/Articles/Schenker.htm

E45 Oswald Jonas Memorial Collection at University of California, Riverside: http://library.ucr.edu/spcol/schenker.shtml

E46 Checklist for the Oswald Jonas Memorial Collection. http://www.oac.cdlib.org/dynaweb/ead/ucr/schejona/

E47 Wiener Singakademe. "Konzerte mit Werken von Heinrich Schenker." http://wienersingakademie.at/archive/k_schenk.html

E48 Universität für Musik und Darstellende Kunst "Lehrgang für Tonsatz nach Heinrich Schenker" http://www.mdw.ac.at/schenkerlehrgang

Appendix A

Schenker Symposia

1984   March 19–20 University of Notre Dame: *Critical Perspectives*
on Schenker: Toward a New Research Paradigm

Patrick McCreless	Rhetoric, Schenker, and Early Beethoven
Scott Burnham	Beethoven's Schenker: *Urlinie* and the Heroic Style
Allan Keiler	The Problem of Derivation in Schenker's Formal Language
Joseph Lubben	God, Country, *Ursatz*: Internal Challenges to Schenkerian Hierarchy
Peter Smith	Structural Tonic or Apparent Tonic?: Parametric Conflict, Phenomenological Perspective, and a Continuum of Articulative Possibilities
David Neumeyer	Thirty-two Ways to Filter Schubert Through Your Ears: The Confrontation of Ideology and Schenkerian Analytic Practice
Joseph Dubiel	What Did Schenker Mean by Prolongation?

1985   March 15–17 Mannes College of Music: *First International*
Schenker Symposium

John Rothgeb	Schenkerian Theory and Manuscript Studies: Modes of Interaction
Heidi Siegel	A Source for Schenker's Study of Thorough Bass: His Annotated Copy of J. S. Bach's "Generalbass-büchlein"
William Pastille	Music and Morphology: Goethe's Influence on Schenker's Musical Ontology
Irene Schreier	Schenker's *Kunst des Vortrags*
Saul Novack	An Historical Overview of the Significance of Foreground, Middleground, and Background
David Stern	Schenkerian Theory and the Analysis of Renaissance Music

James Baker	Schenkerian Analysis: Key to Late-Romantic Extended Forms
Roy Travis	Some Applications of Linear-Structural Analysis to Britten's *Death in Venice*
David Loeb	Dual-Key Movements
Harald Krebs	The Background Level in Tonally Deviating Works of the Early 19th Century
Eric Wen	Enharmonic Transformation in the First Movement of Mozart's Piano Concerto in C Minor, K. 491
David Beach	Beethoven's Piano Sonata in A-flat Major, Op. 110: The Concealed Motivic Structure of the Adagio and Arioso
Charles Burkhart	Departures from the Norm in Schumann's *Liederkreis*
Larry Laskowski	J. S. Bach's "Binary" Dance Movements: Form and Voice Leading
Edward Laufer	Interpolations and Parenthetical Passages
Jonathan Dunsby	The Development of Schenkerian Theory in Great Britain
William Rothstein	The Americanization of Heinrich Schenker
John Rothgeb	Archival Material
Allan Cadwallader	Foreground Motivic Ambiguity: Its Clarification at Middleground Levels in Selected Late Piano Works by Johannes Brahms
Patrick McCreless	Schenker and Chromatic Tonicization: A Reappraisal
Roger Kamien	Aspects of the Neopolitan Sixth Chord in Mozart's Music
Carl Schachter	Either/Or

1986 April 26 University of Hartford, Symposium on the Life and Music of Heinrich Schenker

Hellmut Federhofer	Heinrich Schenker's Life and Work as Reflected in His Correspondence and Diaries
Patrick Miller	A Stylistic Overview of Schenker's Published Music
Concert	Published music of Heinrich Schenker, preserved on disc MHS 522205H (Musical Heritage Society)

1992 March 27–29 Mannes College of Music: Second International Schenker Symposium

| David Beach | The Interaction of Design and Structure in Tonal Music |

John Rink	"Structural Momentum" and Closure in Chopin's Nocturne, Op. 9, No. 2
John Rothgeb	Misleading Associations
William Pastille and Allen Cadwallader	Schenker's Unpublished Work with the Music of Johannes Brahms
Timothy Jackson	Diachronic Transformation and Accentual Reinterpretation in Brahms's *Haydn Variations*
William Renwick	Schenker's Theory and Invertible Counterpoint
Eric Wen	Bass Line Articulations of the *Urlinie*
Arthur Maisel	*Un bacio-ancora? Un altro bacio!*
Roy Travis	Convergence on a Chord Form in the Rite of Spring, or The Case of the Indigestible F Sharp
Edward Laufer	On Sibelius, and the Seventh Symphony in Particular
Richard Cohn	Schenker's Theory, Shenkerian Theory: Pure Unity or Constructive Conflict?
Kevin Korsyn	Schenker's Organicism Reexamined
Joel Lester	Notions of Prolongation and Hierarchical Structure in Eighteenth-Century Theory
Ronald Rodman	Retrospection and Reduction: Telemann's Middleground Reductions of his *Zwanzig kleine Fugen*
William Rothstein	The True Principles for the Use of Harmony: Schulz, Schenker, and the *Stufe*
David Loeb	Instrumental Technique and Compositional Design
David Gagné	"Symphonic Breadth": Structural Style in Mozart's Symphonies
Wayne Petty	C. P. E. Bach and the Fine Art of Transposition
L. Poundie Burstein	Comedy, Structure, and Haydn's Symphonies
Carl Schachter	The Adventures of an F Sharp: Tonal Narration and Exhortation in Donna Anna's First-Act Recitative and Aria
David Goldman	Adumbrations of a Theory of Rhythm in Schenker's Erläuterungsausgabe of Beethoven's Sonata Op. 101
Frank Samarotto	Strange Dimensions: Regularity and Irregularity in Deep Levels of Rhythmic Reduction
Roger Kamien	Conflicting Metrical Patterns in Accompaniment and Melody in Works by Mozart and Beethoven
Charles Burkhart	Mid-bar Downbeat Revisited
Robert Kosovsky	Levels of Understanding: A Guide to Schenker's Nachlass Heidi Siegel When "Freier Satz" Was Part of Kontrapunkt

Saul Novack   Analysis and Historical Musicology
Joseph Straus   Schenker Studies in the Late Twentieth-Century
Naphtali Wagner   Schenker and Cognitive Studies
Christine Berl   The Composer's Point of View
Edward Aldwell   The Performer's Point of View
Steve Larson   Jazz Performance Practice and Analytic Method

**1999   March 12–14, Mannes College of Music: Third International
Schenker Symposium**

L. Poundie Burstein   Schenker's Concept of the Auxiliary Cadence
Roger Kamien   "Auxiliary Cadences" Beginning on a Root-Position
                                Local Tonic Chord: Some Preliminary Observations
Lauri Suurpää   Non-tonic Openings in Two Beethoven Introductions
Edward Laufer   Notes on the Auxiliary Cadence
Panayotis Mavromatis   The Early Keyboard Prelude as an Agent in the
                                Formation of Schenkerian Background Prototypes
Channan Willner   Baroque Styles and the Analysis of Baroque Music
Robert Cuckson   Settings of *Mit Fried und Freud ich fahr dahin* in
                                Bach's Cantata No. 83 and Brahms's Op. 74, No. 1
Frank Samarotto   Hearing Angels: Schenker's Two Organicisms
Nicholas Marston   Schenker and Interruption: Don't Hear Everything
                                You Believe
David Gagné   Unity in Diversity: The Retained Tone
Peter H. Smith   Outer-Voice Conflicts: Their Analytical Challenges
                                and Artistic Consequences
Deborah Kessler   Motive and Motivation in Schubert's Three-Key
                                Expositions
Giorgio Sanguinetti   "Tonal Field" and Drama: The Duet between
                                Elisabetta and Carlo in Act II of Verdi's *Don Carlo*s
Wayne Petty   Chopin's "Funeral March" Sonata and the Influence
                                of Beethoven
Eric Wen   "Wie Frühlingsblumen blüht es": The First
                                Movement of Brahms's Violin Sonata, Op. 100
Eric McKee   The Role of the Extended Anacrusis in Mozart's
                                Instrumental Music
Joel Galand   The Large-Scale Formal Role of the Solo Entry
                                Theme in the Eighteenth-Century Concerto
Mark Anson-Cartwright   Tonal Conflicts in Haydn's Development Sections:
                                The Role of C Major in Symphonies Nos. 93 and 102
Wayne Alpern   Schenkerian Jurisprudence: Echoes of Schenker's
                                Legal Education in His Musical Thought

Heidi Siegel	Looking at the *Urlinie*: Schenker and the Visual Arts
Timothy Jackson	Schenker as Composition Teacher: The Correspondence with Reinhard Oppel
Olli Väisälä	Projections of Post-triadic Harmonies in Debussy
James Baker	The Structural Bass in Nineteenth- and Twentieth-Century Music
Eytan Agmon	Structural Levels and Harmonic Theory: Toward a Reconciliation
William Rothstein	Corelli's Cadences
Carl Schachter	*Che Inganno!* The Analysis of Deceptive Cadences
David Loeb	The Analysis of East Asian Music
Arthur Maisel	Gershwin's Surface Motivic Repetitions with Hidden Sources
Steve Larson	Displacement in the Music of Bill Evans
Robert Snarrenberg	Forms and Uses of Musical Memory
William Benjamin	Schenker's Theory and Virgil's Construction of the World
Nicholas Cook	Detail and Difference in the Writings of Schenker
Kevin Korsyn	Communicating with Schenker's Adversaries
William Pastille	Music and Life: Some Lessons

2001   May 12–13, University of Utrecht: Symposium Heinrich Schenker

Hans Maas	Schenker Analysis and the Unaccompanied Melody
Paul Scheepers	Schenker Analysis: The Need for a Dogmatic Approach
Nicholas Meeù	Teaching Schenker at the Sorbonne
Carl Schachter	Taking Care of the Sense
Håkon Austbro	A Pianist's Reflection on Schenker
Oliver Schwab-Felisch	Functions of the Obscure: Chromaticism in Selected Slow Introductions by Beethoven
Martijn Hooning	Linearity in Early Twentieth-Century Music
Discuss	Schenker Reception in Europe and the United States

2002   June 27–30, Mannes College of Music: The Mannes Institute on Schenkerian Theory and Analysis

Heidi Siegel	The State of the Discipline: Past, Present, and Future
Nicholas Cook	Panelist
Frank Samarotto	Panelist
Carl Schaqchter	Panelist
David Gagné	Schenkerian Pedagogy at the Crossroads
Matthew Brown	Panelist

Charles Burkhart	Panelist
William Rothstein	Panelist
Robert Snarrenberg	Panelist
Carl Schachter	Three Analyses: Schubert's *Die Neigierige*, Mozart's K. 481 Violin Sonata, Beethoven's "Waldstein" Sonata
Charles Burkhart	Schenkerian Paradigms and Their Extension
William Rothstein	Schenkerian Syntax: Variations on Three Themes
Frank Samarotto	Analyses after Schenker: Reconsidering the Legacy
Matthew Brown	Schenkerian Theory as a Theory of Tonality
Nicholas Cook	Understanding the Schenker Project
Robert Snarrenberg	Lines of Interpretation

Appendix B

Chronology of Schenker's Life and Works

1868
19 June: Born to Johann and Julia Schenker at Wisniowzyk (Podhayze), Galacia

1874
Moriz Schenker (younger brother) born

1880
Marcus Schenker (eldest brother) dies in Lemburg

1884
Enters the University of Vienna to study law

1887
Johann Schenker (father) dies
Enters the Wiener Conservatorium für Musik und Darstellende Kunst

1889
Rebekah Schenker (eldest sister) dies in Gradiska

1890
Awarded Juris Dr. from University of Vienna

1891
Writes first essay for *Musikalisches Wochenblatt*, Leipzig

1892
Writes one article for *Musikalisches Wochenblatt*
Writes two articles for *Die Zukunft*, Berlin

1893
Serenade für Waldhorn performed by Louis Salwart and Martha Horning,
    5 August

One article for *Musikalische Wochenblatt* (9 March)
Seven articles for *Die Zukunft*

1894

Serenade für Waldhorn performed by Salwart and Marie Baymeyer, 5 March
Seven articles for *Neue Revue*
One article for *Musikalisches Wochenblatt*
Six articles for *Die Zukunft*

1895

One article for *Die Zukunft* (27 April)
Publishes *Der Geist des musikalischen Technik* for *Musikalisches Wochenblatt*
Seventeen articles for *Die Zeit* (beginning 21 March)
Meeresstille and *Blumengrüß* performed by Edouard Gärtner, 19 January
Eight articles for *Neue Revue*

1896

Twenty-six articles for *Die Zeit*
Two articles for *Die Zukunft*
One article for *Neue Revue*

1897

Eight articles for *Neue Revue*
One article for *Die Zukunft*
Die Nachtigallen (text Eichendorff) 19 June (unpublished)
Das Sträußchen (text Goethe) 23 June (unpublished)
Harfenspieler (text Goethe) 10 August (unpublished)
Zwei Klavierstücke Op. 1 for Doblinger (D. 1740)

1898

Sechs Lieder Op. 3 for Breitkopf (DLV 4760)
Fantasie Op. 2 for Breitkopf (KlB 22290)
5 Klavierstücke Op. 4 (KlB 22055)
Zweistimmige Inventionen Op. 5 (KlB 22366)
Die Braut (text Müller) 14 August (unpublished)
One article for *Neue Revue*

1899

Concert tour with Johannes Messchaert (7 Jan. – 3 Feb.)
Performed *Legende aus* Op. 2 and *Klavierstück* Op. 4/2 on 8 and 13 January
Publishes *Ländler* Op. 10
Auf die Nacht in Spinnstub'e (Text Heyse) July (unpublished)

1900

Syrische Tänze performed by Schenker and Moriz Violin, 26 January (published by Weinberger, J. W. 1092a/b)

Wiegenlied Op. 3/2 sung by Gärtner, accompanied by Alexander von Zemlinsky, 16 November

1901

One article for *Wiener Abendpost*

1902

Ausklang, Op. 3/4 sung by Gärtner, 19 March

C. P. E. Bach Klavierwerke in 2 vols. through Universal Edition, Vienna

1903

Vorüber performed (choir directed by Schenker), 18 November

Syrische Tänze performed by Ferruccio Busoni and Berlin Philharmonic (in Arnold Schoenberg's orchestration), 5 November

1904

Schenker performs his arrangement of Phillip Emmanuel Bach's A Minor Concerto (Orchestra conducted by Moriz Violin), 3 November

Ein Beitrag zur Ornamentik published through Universal Edition, Vienna

Four-handed arrangement of six Händel organ concerti

1905

Heimat and *Nachtghüß Op. 6/1–2* sung by Gärtner, 26 January

1906

Schenker's arrangement performed in England by Richard Epstein, 15 April

Publishes revised version of *Ornamentik*

Harmonielehre published anonymously as "einem Künstler" through Cotta, later Universal

Edition

1908

Instrumenations-Tabelle published pseudonymically as "Arthur Niloff" through Universal Edition

1910

Kontrapunkt I published through Universal Edition

Critical edition of J. S. Bach's Chromatic Fantasy and Fugue

1911

Selig ist der Mann and *Ich will der Kreuzstab gerne tragen* performed
Schenker's arrangement of C. P. E. Bach's F Major Concerto for Two Pianos
   performed by Paul de Conne and Moritz Violin, 13 January
Schenker's arr. of C. P. E. Bach's A Minor Concerto performed by Anna
   Voileanu; his arrangement of G. F. Händel's B Major Concerto for two
   harps performed by Steranie Goldner and Angela Novak; his arrangement
   of C. P. E. Bach's F Major Concerto performed by Aurelre Cerné and Stella
   Wang, 17 May

1912

Beethoven: Neunte Sinfonie

1913

Erläuterungsausgaben der letzten fünf Sonaten Beethoven: Op. 109

1914

Erläuterungsausgaben der letzten fünf Sonaten Beethoven: Op. 110

1915

Erläuterungsausgaben der letzten fünf Sonaten Beethoven: Op. 111

1916

One article for *Der Merker*

1919

Marries Jeannette Korngold (née Schiff) 11 November

1920

Erläuterungsausgaben der letzten fünf Sonaten Beethoven: Op. 101

1921

Begins *Der Tonwille Booklets* (1921–4)
Beethoven's Sonata op. 27, no. 2, Facsimile with Commentary

1922

Publishes *Kontrapunkt* II through Universal Edition

1923

One article for *Die Music*, subsequently published in *Meisterwerk II*
One article for *Die Musikanten Gilde*, reprinted from *Tonwille* I

1925

Publishes *Beethovens fünfle Sinfonie* (reprinted from *Der Tonwille*) through
A. Gutmann Verlag and Universal Edition
Publishes *Das Meisterwerk in der Musik I* through Drei Masken Verlag, Munich
One article for *Moderne Welt*

1926

Publishes *Das Meisterwerk in der Musik II* through Drei Masken Verlag,
Munich

1927

Founds (with Anthony von Hoboken) the Photogramm-Archiv in the National
Library
One article for *General-Anzeiger für Bonn und Umgemend*

1929

One article for *Der Kunstwart*

1930

Published *Das Meisterwerk in der Musik* III through Drei Masken Verlag,
Munich

1931

Two articles for *Der Kunstwart*

1932

Publishes *Fünf Urlinie-Tafeln* through Universal Edition and The David
Mannes School
One article for *Der Kunstwart*

1933

Publishes *Johannes Brahms: Oktaven u. Quinten* through Universal Edition
One article for *Deutsche allgemeine Zeitung*
One article for *Der Kunstwart*
One article for *Basler National-Zeitung*

1935

Dies in Vienna, 14 January
Der freie Satz published posthumously

Glossary of Schenkerian Terms

Anstieg (initial ascent): an ascending span leading to the first one of the *Urlinie*.
Fr: montée initiale; It: ascesa iniziale; Po: wznoszączy ciąg inicjalny;
Cz: vzestupdr; Ru: Первоначальный подъем; Cn: 上升
Ausfaltung (unfolding): the horizontal unfolding of an interval of a chord;
typically appears as a single melodic line.
Fr: deployment; It: dispiegamento; Po: rozposarcie interwału;
Cz: rozvinutí či melodizace intervalu; Ru: Развертывание; Cn: 横向展延
Ausführung (realization): the composition itself; the final stage of *Auskomponierung*.
Fr: realization; It: realizzazione; Po: urzeczywistnienie; Cz: uskutečnění;
Ru: Проведение; Cn: 察觉认知
Auskomponierung (composing out): the process through which the chord of
nature is prolonged in time and transformed from a vertical into a horizontal
occurrence.
Fr: déploiement compositionnel; It: elaborazione compostiva;
Po: rozkomponowanie; Cz: horizontální rozkomponování;
Ru: Развертывани/высочинение; Cn: 延长；装饰
Baßbrechung (bass arpeggiation): the structural arpeggiation of the bass in the
Ursatz, moving from I to V and back to I.
Fr: arpégiation de la basse; It: arpeggio del basso; Po: rozłożony akord basowy;
Cz: bassový rozklad; Ru: Басовое арпеджирование; Cn: 低音分解式
Brechung (arpeggiation): refers to the arpeggiation of a chord at various levels
of structure.
Fr: arpégiation; It: arpeggio; Po: rozłożony; Cz: rozklad; Ru: Арпеджирование;
Cn: 分解式
Deckton (covering tone): a tone of a middle voice that hovers above the *Urlinie*.
Fr: note de couverture; It: nota di copertura; Po: dźwięk przykrywający;
Cz: prodleva ve vrchním hlase; Ru: Покрывающий тон; Cn: 覆层音
Dehnung (expansion): the expansion of a linear progression in time.
Fr: expansion; It: espansione; Po: rozwinięcie; Cz: rozšiřování;
Ru: Расширение; Cn: 扩充

Diminution: the filling out of large intervals with smaller ones, prolonging their content in time; does not necessarily denote the reverse process of augmentation.
Fr: diminution; It: diminuzione; Po: diminuce; Cz: diminuce;
Ru: Диминуция; Cn: 减值

Durchgang (passing tone): the term is applied to all notes and/or chords that are passing in function, including neighboring notes, suspensions, and appoggiaturae as well as the foreground passing tone.
Fr: ton écoulement; It: nota di passaggio; Po: průchodná; Cz: průchod;
Ru: Проходящий тон; Cn: 经过乐

Hintergrund (background): the first stage of the *Auskomponierung* process, consisting of the *Ursatz* plus some basic diminutions.
Fr: arrière-plan; It: livello profondo; Po: warstwa głęboka; Cz: základní vrstva;
Ru: консонантный; Cn: 背景

Höherlegung (higher placement): procedure through which a tone due in a particular octave is transferred to a higher octave.
Fr: transfert de register ascendant; It: trasposizione al registro superiore;
Po: górne przeniesienie oktawowe; Cz: přenesaní oktávy vzhurů;
Ru: Восходящий егистровый сдвиг; Cn: 上行音区转移

Kopfton: (head tone): the first note of the *Urlinie*, either $\hat{3}$, $\hat{5}$, or $\hat{8}$. May also refer to the first note of a span.
Fr: note de tête; It: nota principale; Po: dźwięk czołowy; Cz: primární tón;
Ru: Заглавный тон; Cn: 始发音

Koppelung (octave coupling): the process by which a structural connection is achieved between a tone and its counterpart in the higher or lower octave.
Fr: couplage; It: abbinamento; Po: sprzężenie; Cz: spojení vazba;
Ru: копуляция; Cn: 八度连接

Mischung (mixture): the incorporation of elements of the minor system in the major and vice versa.
Fr: mixture; It: alternanza Magg./min.; Po: przenikanie trybów;
Cz: mísení, prolínání tónorodu; Ru: Микстура, смешение; Cn: 混合

Mittelgrund (middleground): the intermediate stage of *Auskomponierung*, in which the individuality of the composition becomes more apparent.
Fr: plan moyen; It: livllo medio; Po: warstwa środkowa; Cz: střední vrstva;
Ru: Средний план; Cn: 中景

Nebennote (neighboring note): a note adjacent stepwise above or below a given note. May be complete or incomplete (an appoggiatura).
Fr: note voisine; It: nota di volta; Po: střídavý tón; Cz: vedlejší tón;
Ru: Вспомогательный тон; Cn: 邻近音

Nebennote-Harmonie (neighboring-note chord): a chord consisting of concurring neighboring notes.
Fr: l'harmonie de la note du voisin; It: accordo construito su una nota di volta;
Po: střídavý tón zgoda; Cz: vedlejší tón harmonie;
Ru: Гармония вспомогательного тона; Cn: 邻近和声

Oberdezime (upper tenths): a common diminution pattern in which the parallel tenths serve to prolong the opening chord.

Fr: supérieur dixième; It: decimal sopra il basso; Po: górny dziesiąty; Cz: hořejší desátý; Ru: Верхняя децима; Cn: 上部十度

Obbligate Lage (obligatory register): the register in which the *Urlinie* begins, and in which it is understood to terminate.

Fr: register oblige; It: registro obbligato; Po: obowiązujący rejestr; Cz: obligátní poloha; Ru: Обязательный регистр; Cn: 责任音区

Schicht (stratum, structural level): refers to the various stages or levels of the *Auskomponierung* process, consisting of the background, middleground, and foreground.

Fr: niveau structurel; It: livello strutturale; Po: warstwy; Cz: vrstvy; Ru: Слой, Структурный уровень; Cn: 结构性层次

Stimmentausch (exchange of voices): occurs when one tone of a chord moves to another member of the same chord during a simultaneous exchange of those tones with another voice, e.g., the succession I – V@^{6} – I^6 with $\hat{3}$ – $\hat{2}$ – $\hat{1}$ in the soprano.

Fr: echange des voix; It: scambio delle voci; Po: wymina głosów; Cz: výměna hlasů; Ru: Взаимообмен голосов; Cn: 声音交换

Stufe (scale degree): triads built on the scale-degrees I, II, III, IV, V, VI, or VII that are understood to control a longer passage of music; not simply triads as such.

Fr: degree; It: grado armonico fondamentale; Po: stopień; Cz: stupeň; Ru: Ступень, гармоническая ункция; Cn: 音级

Theiler (divider): the division of the arpeggiating I by its upper fifth (V) or, less commonly, lower fifth (IV).

Fr: diviseur; It: divisore; Po: dzienik; Cz: rozdělovník; Ru: Делитель; Cn: 划分点

Tieferlegung (lower placement): procedure through which a tone that is due in a particular octave is transferred to a lower octave.

Fr: transfert de register descendant; It: trasposizione al registro inferiore; Po: dolne przeniesienie oktawowe; Cz: podní oktávové přenesení; Ru: Нисходящий регистровый сдвиг; Cn: 下行音区转移

Übergreifen (upper shift; overlapping): the procedure through which a tone is due in a middle voice appears directly in a higher octave in the upper voice.

Fr: surmarche; It: scavalcamento delle voci; Po: eksterioryzacja; Cz: přesah; Ru: Перекрывание; Наложение; Cn: 超越

Unterbrechung (interruption): occurs when the *Urlinie* halts at $\hat{\underset{V}{2}}$, necessitating its repetition and conclusion with $\hat{\underset{I}{1}}$. In Schenker's view, the interruption is the basis of musical form.

Fr: interruption; It: interruzione; Po: przerwanie; Cz: přerušení; Ru: Перерыв; Cn: 阻断

Untergreifen (lower shift): occurs when a span is interrupted and a lower, middle-voice note is taken, which is then led back up to the point at which the span had been abandoned, and from which point the original span now proceeds.

Fr: sous-marche; It: movimento da una voce interna; Po: interioryzacja; Cz: ukrytí, podsah; Ru: Движение; Cn: 出自内声部的运动

Urlinie (fundamental line): the descending line in the upper voice that fills out one of the intervals of the chord of nature, $\hat{3} - \hat{1}$, $\hat{5} - \hat{1}$, or $\hat{8} - \hat{1}$. In his earlier works, Schenker names the reduction of the upper voice the *Urlinie*.

Fr: ligne fondamentale; It: linea fondamentale; Po: pralinia, linia pierwotna; Cz: základní linie; Ru: Первичная линия; Cn. 基本线条

Ursatz (fundamental structure): the basic two-voice contrapuntal setting from which the composition is ultimately understood to evolve, consisting of the *Urlinie* and the *Baßbrechung*.

Fr: structure fondamentale; It: struttura fondamentale; Po: budowa pierwotna; Cz: základní složení; Ru: Первичная структура; Cn: 基本结构

Vordergrund (foreground): The lowest level of structure; essentially the composition itself with ornamental pitches removed.

Fr: l'avant-plan; it: livello esterno; Po: warstwa powiezchniowa; Cz: svrchní vrstva; Cn: 前景.

Bibliography

Beach, David. "A Schenker Bibliography." *Journal of Music Theory* 13/1 (1969): 2–37.
———. "A Schenker Bibliography." In *Readings in Schenkerian Analysis and Other Approaches,* ed. by Maury Yeston. New Haven: Yale University Press (1977): 274–309.
———. "A Schenker Bibliography: 1969–1979." *Journal of Music Theory* 23/2 (1979): 275–86.
———. "The Current State of Schenkerian Research." *Acta Musicologica* 57 (1985): 145–75.
———. "Schenkerian Theory." *Music Theory Spectrum* 11/1 (1989): 3–14.
Damschroder, David, and David Russell Williams, eds. *Music Theory from Zarlino to Schenker: A Bibliography and a Guide,* Harmonologica, Vol. 4. Stuyvesant: Pendragon Press, 1990.
Federhofer, Hellmut. *Heinrich Schenker: Nach Tagebücher und Briefen in der Oswald Jonas Memorial Collection, University of California, Riverside.* Studien zur Musikwissenschaft, Vol. 3. Hildesheim: Georg Olms Verlag, 1985.
———. *Heinrich Schenker als Essayist und Kritiker: Gasammelte Aufsätze und Kleinere Berichte aus dem Jahren 1891–1901,* Studien und Materialen zur Musikwissenschaft, Vol. 5. Hildesheim: Georg Olms Verlag, 1990.
Fink, Michael. *Varieties and Trends in Music Analysis: A Commentary on the Literature.* Los Alamitos, Calif: Southwest Regional Laboratory for Educational Research and Development, 1972.
Gołąb, Maciej. "Głowne nurty badań Schenkerowskich. Bibliografia z lat 1904–1984." *Muzyka* 31/4 (1986): 67–84.
Kosovsky, Robert: *The Oster Collection: Papers of Heinrich Schenker: A Finding List.* Unpublished typescript. New York Public Library, 1990.
Lang, Robert and JoAn Kunselman. *Heinrich Schenker, Oswald Jonas, Moriz Violin: A Checklist of Manuscripts and Other Papers in the Oswald Jonas Memorial Collection,* University of California Catalogues and Bibliographies, Vol. 10. Berkeley: University of California Press, 1994.
Laskowski, Larry. *Heinrich Schenker: Index to Analyses,* Annotated Reference Tools in Music, Vol. 1. Stuyvesant: Pendragon Press, 1978.
Lewis, Christopher Orlo. "Into the Foothills: New Directions in Nineteenth-Century Analysis." *Music Theory Spectrum* 11/1 (1989): 15–23.
Meeùs, Nicholas. *Heinrich Schenker: Une Introduction.* "Chaptire IV: Bibliographie schenkerienne (pp. 91–124)." Liège: Mardaga, 1993.

Neumeyer, David, and Rudy T. Marcozzi. "An Index to Schenkerian Analyses of Beethoven Piano Sonatas and Symphonies." *Indiana Theory Review* 6/1–2: 101–17.

Rast, Nicholas. "A Checklist of Essays and Reviews by Heinrich Schenker." *Music Analysis* 7/2 (1988): 121–32.

Rink, John. "A Select Bibliography of Literature Related to Schenker by British Authors or in British Publications since 1980." in *Schenker Studies*, ed. by Heidi Siegel. Cambridge: Cambridge University Press, 1990: 190–2.

Ziffer, Agnes, ed. *Katalog des Archivs für Photogramme Musikalischer meisterhandschriften / Widmung Anthony van Hoboken*. Veröffentlichungen der österreichischen nationalbibliothek, Vol. 3. Wien: Georg Prachner Verlag, 1967.

Author Index

A

Adams, F. John **T10**
Adorno, Theodore W. **A379, A565**
Adrian, John Stanley **A282, A318, A502, A267**R**, D138, D210**
Agawu, Victor Kofi, **A67, A95, A253, A362, A363, A428, A503, B66**R
Agmon, Etyan **E20, E25, E26**
Aigner, Thomas **A72**
Akopian, Levon, **A96**
Albersheim, Gerhard **A802, B65**
Albright, Larry Eugene **D127**
Aldwell, Edward **B69**
Alpern, Wayne **A29, E7**
Anderson, Norman Douglas **D93, D174**
Annibaldi, Claudio **T30, A286, A375**
Anson-Cartwright, Mark **D36, A131**
Arias, Enrique Alberto **A564**
Arnn, John **D229**
Arnold, Janice Margaret **D92**
Asada, Chizuko **D48**
Austin, John Charles **D218**
Ayrey, Craig **A565, B58**R**, T12**R

B

Babbitt, Milton **A283, 284, B47, B92**R
Badura-Skoda, Paul **A566**
Bain, Jennifer **D68**

Baker, James M. **A319, A524, A607**
Ballan, Harry Reuben **D148**
Bamberger, Carl **Bio22, A768, A805**
Bamberger, Jeanne **A663**
Bante-Knight, Mary Martha **D175**
Barbose, Joel **E13**
Barcaba, Peter **A285, A320, A364**
Barce, Ramón **T31**
Barford, Philip **A678**
Barket, James Charles **D86**
Baroni, Mario **A68, B82**T
Barrington, Barrie M. **D94**
Barrow, Paul **D128**
Barskii, Viktor **A504**
Bashour, Frederick **A627, D216**
Bass, Richard **A388, A389**
Bates, Vicky Marie **D13**
Beach, David W. **A69, A97, A170, A197, A198, A225, A321, A365, A429, A430, A445**R**, A446**R**, A482**R**, A505, A525, A526, A643, A690, A718, A721, A824**R**, A834, B58**
Beeson, Roger **A171, A704**
Benjamin, William E. **A30, A132, A567**
Bent, Ian **T21, T36, T50, T51, T62, A254, A286, A458, B45**
Bergquist, Peter **A608, A722, B62**R
Berl, Paul **A769**
Bernard, Jonathan **A199**

Bernhard, Christoph **A695**
Berry, Wallace **A609, A679, B74, B84ᴿ, B87ᴿ**
Bird, Melvin **D247**
Blasius, Leslie David **B15, D79**
Blatz, Catherine Ann **D58**
Block, A. F. **A692**
Blum, Harold Tremeer **D205**
Blume, Jürgen **A366**
Boatwright, Howard **A644, B90ᴿ⁽²⁾**
Bollinger, John Simon **D192**
Bonds, Nancy **D96**
Boretz, Benjamin **A708, D225**
Borio, Gianmarino **A2**
Boss, Jack **A200, B7ᴿ, E8**
Botstein, Leon **A98**
Boyd, James William **D80**
Bozikova, Milena **A31, A133**
Brandenburg, Seighard **A638ᴿ**
Braskey, Jill **D25**
Brenneis, Clemens **A667**
Breslauer, Peter **A390, B63r**
Brewer, Robert Edwin **D234**
Bribitzer-Stull, Matthew **D2**
Broder, Nathan **A794, B89ᴿ**
Broman, Per F. **A32, E14, E21**
Brooks, Noel K. C. **D37**
Brooks, Richard **B70**
Brower, Candace **A408ᴿ**
Brown, Matthew Gordon **A70, A99, A100, A226, A367, A459, A545, B38ᴿ, B40ᴿ, D118**
Browne, Richmond **A680**
Bullard, John **A559**
Burchard, John E. **D3**
Burdick, Michael F. **A665**
Burgnaro, Michele **A819**
Burkhart, Charles **A287, A322, A527, A610, A628**
Burkholder, J. Peter **A227**
Burnham, Scott G. **A228, A255**

Burns, Lori Anne **A101, A201, A229, B20, D104**
Burstein, L. Poundie **T56ᴿ, A33, A71, A528, B1C**

C
Cadwallader, Allen Clayton **A34, A35, A102, A256, A257, A323, A391, A392, A393, A506, A529, B8, B38, D176**
Cahn, Steven Joel **D59**
Campbell, Bruce **D184, E33, B100ᴿ**
Caplin, William **A507, B55ᴿ, B72ᴿ**
Carpenter, Patricia **A395**
Carrière, Paul **A807**
Carter, Lee Chandler **D69**
Cavanaugh, Lynn **A134**
Cavett-Dunsby, Esther **A395, A396, A460, B41, D158**
Chenevert, James Henry **D119**
Cheong, Wai-ling **E22**
Cherlin, Michael **A397**
Chesnut, John **D231**
Chew, Geoffrey **A290, A369, A531, E27**
Chiang, Yu-ring **A135**
Chong, Eddy **D245**
Christensen, Thomas **A324, A568, B39ᴿ**
Cinnamon, Howard **A202, A230, A258, A259, A461, A508, A531, A541ᴿ, A569, D169**
Citkowitz, Israel **A800**
Clark, Suzannah **A36, A72**
Clark, William **A369, A570**
Clarke, David Ian **A370**
Clarke, Eric F. **A371, A372**
Clarkson, Austin **A705**
Clemens, John **D38**
Clifton, Thomas **A709**
Cockell, James Edward **D39**

Coeurdevey, Anne **A232, A260, D252**

Cohn, Richard L. **A233, A261, A262, A263, A264, B59**[R]

Cone, Eward T. **A645, B84**

Cook, Nicholas John **A37, A38, A172, A173, A231, A288, A289, A373, A374, A398, A431, A432, B30, B30**[T]**, B46, B46**[T]

Cooper, Grosvernor **B87**

Covach, John **A103**

Crotty, John Edward **D149**

Cube, Felix-Eberhard von **B43**

Cumming, Naomi Helen **D120**

Cummings, Craig C. **D105**

Cunningham, Robert E. **D24**

Cutler, Timothy S. **D14D**

D

Dabrusin, Ross **D70**

Dagnes, Edward **D211**

Dahlhaus, Carl **A532, A571, A681, A693, A732**[R]**, B59**[R]**, B79**[R]**, B100**[R]

Dahms, Walter **S148**[R(2)]**, A809, A813**

Daigle, Paulin **D26**

Dale, Catherine **A234, A291, B31, D159**

Dale, Frank Knight **A763**

Dalmonte, Rossana **A68**

Damiani, Giovanni **A235**

Damschroder, David Allen **A326, A433, A487, B10**[R]**, B58**[R]**, D193, E9**

Daniskas, John **B95**

Darcy, Warren **A327, A817**

Davis, Andrew **B10**[R]**, D40**

Davis, Glen Roger **D114**

Debaise, Joseph **D177**

DeBellis, Mark **A1, D130**

Debruyn, Randall **D259**

Deliège, Célestin **A462, A509, B56, B59**[R]

Dempster, Douglas J. **A100, A262, A367**

Dent, Cedric Carl **D49**

Deutsch, Walter **A292**

DeZeeuw, Anne Marie **D178**

Don, Gary W. **A136, A328, A399, D106**

Drabkin, William **Bio4, S125**[R]**, S128**[R]**, S134**[T]**, T23**[R]**, T36, T50, T51, A14, A137, A375, A416, A488, A510, A572, A638**[R]**, A702, B15**[R]**, B21, B43**[R]**, B45, B52**[R]**, B59**[R]**, B64**[R]**, B67**[R]**, B68**[R]**, B72**[R]**, B85**[R(2)]**, E15**

Dreyfus, Lawrence **B16**

Dubiel, Joseph **A329, A330, B62**[R]

Duke, Dainel Alan **D60**

Dunsby, Jonathan Mark **T12**[R]**, T26, A331, A376, A434, A473**[R]**, A511, A533, A591, A611, A646, B44, B66**[R]**, B68**[R]**, B85**[R]**E**

E

Ebcioglu, Kemal **D150**

Edwards, G. **A293**

Edwards, Stephen Perry **D50**

Eibner, Franz **S125**[R]**, S128**[R]**, S151**[R]**, A719, A743, A746, A825, A829, A831, A832**

Elias, Angie **A770**

Elliker, Calvin **A205**

Elliot, Scott Nelson **D139**

Ellison, Paul M. **A3**

Emmerson, Simon **A371**

Epstein, David **T12r, B66, B66**[R]

Erwin, Charlotte E. **A592**

Everett, Walter Tripp **A104, A294 A332, A435, A463, B38**[R]**, B40**[R]**, D131**

Eybl, Martin **A39, A138, B22, D132**

F
Federhofer, Hellmut **Bio7, S134^R,
A105, A139, A203, A236, A237,
A377, A400, A436, A464, A532^R,
A573, A574, A730, A747, A760,
A826, A830, B39, B43^R, B52,
B58^R, B61, B64, B72^R, B73^R,
B85^R, B94, B100^R**
Ferencz, George Joseph **D200**
Fessel, Pablo **A15**
Flechsig, Hartmut **B75, D219**
Folio, Cynthia **A295, B24^R**
Forbes, Elliott **T10**
Forte, Allen **Bio6, A73, A74, A401,
A437, A489, A512, A534, A535,
A536, A575, A612, A636, A744,
B23, B62, B62^T, B67, B90, B90^R**
Foster, Peter **D249**
Foulkes-Levy, Laurdella **A106, D61**
Fowler, Andrew Judson **D170**
Frankel, Robert E. **A637, A665, A682**
Fung, Eric W. M. **D71**
Furtwängler, Wilhelm **A754G**

G
Gagné, David **A40, A204, A333,
A438, B1, B8, B10^R, D133**
Galand, Joel **A174, D113**
Gamble, Charles **D4**
Garcia, Christóbal **E3**
Gauldin, Robert **A629, B12, B27^R**
Gebuhr, Ann **D179**
Geiringer, Karl **Bio14**
Gerling, Cristina Capparelli **A175,
A379, D160**
Gibeau, Peter **A238, D97**
Gilbert, Stephen **A107, A513, B24,
B62, B62^T**
Gjeringen, Robert O. **A465**

Gleason, James Anthony **D134**
Gligo, Niksa **A379**
Gluck, Marion A. **A666**
Gołąb, Maciej **A265, A266, A267,
A402, A466, A467, A468, A883,
B37**
Goldenberg, Yosef **D5**
Goldenzweig, Hugo **D140**
Goldschmidt, Harry **A667**
Goldwurm, Giuliano **A176, D107**
Gould, Murray J. **T13, A683, D221**
Grave, Floyd K. **A613 B48**
Grave, Margaret **B48**
Graybill, Roger **A380, A380^R, A403**
Green, Douglas M. **B86**
Greenberg, Beth **A684, D213**
Greer, Taylor **A296**
Grossman, Orin **T4**
Grunsqeig, Werner **A239**
Gut, Serge **T35^R, A140, A469, B32^R,
B40^RH**

H
Hallnäs, Lars **D258**
Halm, August **A812, A814**
Hampson, Barbara Louise **D87**
Hanson, John **A267**
Hantz, Edward Charlton **D185, B65^R**
Hantz, Edwin **A576**
Harris, Simon **A720**
Harrison, Daniel G. **D151**
Hart, Josephine Spencer **D212**
Hartmann, Heinrich **A755**
Hatten, Robert S. **A172^R, A647,
B72^R, D186**
Hauschild, Peter **A694**
Headlam, David **A100, A491**
Hearts, Daniel **A614**
Hefling, Stephen E. **A108, A439,
B55^R**
Heimler, Hans **A771**

Helman, Zofia **A404, A470, B56ᴿ, B59ᴿ**
Hendersonellers, Brian **A240**
Henneberg, Gudrun **B79, B79ᴿ**
Henry, Margaret Elaine **D15**
Hill, David S. **A141**
Hilse, Walter **A695**
Hinton, Stephen **A76, A334, A405**
Hirschkorn, Kurt **A748**
Holcomb, Margaret Ann **D171**
Holland, Mark **A577**
Horn, Geoffrey **D121**
Horton, Charles **D631**
Hoskisson, Darin **D6**
Howard, Joseph **D236**
Hoyt, Reed Jerabek **A491, A492, A493, D201**
Hsieh, Wenchi **D16**
Hubbs, Nadine **A297, B35ᴿ, D115**
Hughes, Matt **A648**
Hush, David **A578**
Hwang, Seung-Yee **D17I**

I
Imbrie, Andrew W. **A696**
Inwood, Mary B. **D51**
Irving, Howard **A406J**

J
Jackendoff, Ray **A514, A651, B59**
Jackson, Timothy L. **A4, A41, A42, A109, A110, A177, A268, B38ᴿ, B40ᴿ, E36**
Jan, Steven B. **A269**
Jarzebska, Alicja **A16**
Johns, Donald **A299**
Johnson, Douglas **A638**
Johnson, Lisa **D98**
Jonas, Oswald **Bio1, Bio8, A668, A734, A736, A737, A740, A753, A764, A772, A773, A774, A775,** A776, A777, A778, A779, A780, A781, A789, A798, A799, A801, B92ᴿ, B98, B100
Jordan, Alan **D141**
Jost, Peter **A298**
Judd, Christle Collins **A494K**

K
Kaderavek, Milan R. **D226**
Kalib, Sylvan Sol **T6, A679, D222, D240**
Kalisch, Volker **A142**
Kamien, Roger **T12ᴿ, A77, A335, A471, A537, A538, A579, A669, B62ᴿ**
Karnes, Kevin Charles **A815, D7**
Karpinski, Gary S. **E4**
Kassler, Jamie Croy **A539**
Kassler, Michael **A649, A685, A686, D238, B15ᴿ, B39ᴿ**
Katz, Adele **A791, B96**
Kaufman, Rebecca Sue **D142**
Kaufmann, Harald **A723, A732**
Keiler, Allan R. **A143, A381, A540, A650, B38ᴿ, B40ᴿ, B58ᴿ, B72ᴿ**
Keller, Wilhelm **A144**
Kelly, Robert T. **E1**
Kerman, Joseph **A738**
Kessler, Deborah **D62**
Kessler, Hubert **A749**
Kholopov, Yurii Nikolaevich **A631**
Kielian-Gilbert, Marianne **A472**
Kinderman, William **A407, B17**
Klonoski, Edward W. **D81**
Knod, Grace **D243**
Köhler, Rafael **A146**
Kolneder, Walter **A750**
Komar, Arthur J. **A206, A408, A745ᴿ, B36, B81, B85ᴿ, D232**
Koozin, Timothy **E10**
Korde, Shirish **A580**

Korsyn, Kevin Ernest **T34ᴿ, A147, A241, A409, B2, B3, D180**
Kosovsky, Robert **A43, A783ᵀ**
Kramer, Lawrence **A270**
Krantz, Steven **D122**
Kraus, Joseph Charles **D143**
Krause, Drew Stafford **D88**
Krebs, Harald Manfred **A148, A300, A410, A495, A593, B17, B71ᴿ, A198**
Krims, Adam **A17, A17ᴿ**
Krueger, Theodore Howard **T3, D241**
Kucukalic, Zija **B49**
Kudlawiec, Dennis Paul **D227**
Kurth, Ulrich **A440**
Kyung, Sandra Eun Joo **D27L**

L
Lacerda, Marcos Branda **A178, E23**
Lai, Eric **A242**
Laitz, Steven **A149**
Lamb, James Boyd **D202**
Lamblin, André **A473**
Landis, Raymond **D8**
Langer, Susanne K. **B91**
Larson, Brook Carter **D18**
Larson, Steven Leroy **T23ᴿ T25, A44, A89, A111, A112, A113, A150, A151, A207, A243, A441, A447ᴿ, A541, A581, B66ᴿ, D144**
Laskowski, Larry **A337, A338, B62ᴿ, B71ᴿ**
Latham, Edward **D19**
Laufer, Edward **T12ᴿ, A45, A114, A301, A412, A706**
Layton, Richard Douglas **D108**
Legrand, Raphäelle **A115**
Lehmann, Kennett **D41**
Leite, Zilei de Oliveira **D72**
Lerdahl, Fred **A78, A79, A90, A113ᴿ, A411, A514, A651, B59**

Lester, Joel **A179, A594, A828, B50, B63, D229**
Levenson, Irene Montefiore **A208, D194**
Levy, Edward **A632, A691**
Levy, Morten **A687, B82ᴿ**
Lewin, David **A46, A582**
Lewin, Harold **A596**
Lewis, Christopher **A413, A595**
Lindstedt, Iwona **B11**
Lipp, Gerhard **B4**
Littlefield, Richard **A80, A271**
Locke, Benjamin Ross **D161**
Lockwood, Lewis **A711**
Loeb, David **A338, A670, A710, B33ᴿ**
Loeschmann, Horsch B. **T27, T28**
London, Justin M. **A81, A339**
Lubben, Robert Joseph **T39, T51ᴿ, T62, A244, D73**
Lubet, Alex **A583**
Luccio, Ricardo **B29M**

M
Maas, Hans **A5**
Maisel, Arthur **A47, A340, A425, A528ᴿ, A598**
Mann, Alfred **A697**
Mann, Michael **A758**
Marcozzi, Rudy **A542, D99**
Marion, Gregory **A180**
Mark, Christopher **A496**
Marsden, Alan **A443**
Marston, Nicholas John **A116, A272, A382, A474, B25, B40ᴿ**
Martin, Henry **A442, A652, B72ᴿ**
Marvin, William **D9, D250**
Mast, Paul **T14, D224**
Mathis, Michael **A152**
Maxwell, John **A597**
Mayfield, Connie E. **D89**
Mazur, Krzysztof **T54**

McBright, Lesley **D256**
McColl, Sandra **B18**
McCreless, Patrick Phillip **T23ᴿ,**
 A153, A302, A303, A341, A383,
 A414, A543, B58ᴿ
McIrvine, Edward **A584**
McKee, Eric **A48, A49, A154, D251**
McNamee, Ann K. **A497**
Medina, Cedilia **A18**
Medina, Juan Pablo **A18**
Meehan, J. R. **A615**
Meeùs, Nicolas **T35, A6, A82, A245,**
 A342, B32, E24
Mesnage, Marcel **A83**
Metz, Andreas **D28**
Meyer, Leonard B. **B89**
Miller, Malcolm B. **A475, D253**
Miller, Mina Florence **D206**
Miller, Patrick **A304, A476**
Mirchandani, Sharon **D52**
Miron, Nathan **D242**
Mitchell, William J. **T2ᴿ, A698, A712,**
 A724, A725, A762, B90ᴿ, B97
Modena, Elena **A273, A820**
Montgomery, Kip **A209**
Moore, Allen F. **A181, B23ᴿ**
Moore, Hillarie Clark **D109**
Moorman, Ludwig **A811**
Moreno-Rojas, Jairo **A7, D64**
Morgan, Robert **A117, A639, A640,**
 A671, D230
Mori, Paul Alan **D90**
Morrison, Charles Douglas **A305,**
 D145
Mosley, David Lee **D135**
Moss, Lawrence **A653**
Murtomäki, Veijo **A155, B33, D116**
Musgrave, Michael **T12ᴿ, B44ᴿN**

N
Narmour, Eugene **A515, B72, D220**
Nash, Laura **D117**

Nattiez, Jean-Jacques **A275**
Navien, Charles Francis **D187**
Nekljudov, Yurii **A274**
Nelson, Thomas Keith **D42**
Neumann, Frederick **A444**
Neumann, Hans **A726**
Neumeyer, David Paul **A70ᴿ, A80,**
 A118, A271, A445, A445ᴿ⁽²⁾,
 A446, A447, A585, A599, A633,
 B8ᴿ, B35, B43ᵀ, B51
Nitzberg, Roy J. **D29**
Nivans, David B. **D100**
Noden-Skinner, Cheryl **A516**
Nogueira, Ilza Maria Costa **A343**
Noro, Aiko **T11**
Novack, Saul **A344, A544, A713O**

O
Oppel, Rheinhard **Bio3**
Orenstein, Arbe **A699**
Oster, Ernst **Bio2, T12, A654, A741,**
 A745ᴿ, A759, A761, A782, A783,
 E37P

P
Palmer, Robert **A655**
Palmer, Virginia **A546**
Pancharoen, Natchar **D162**
Pankhurst, Thomas A. **E39**
Parish, George **A616**
Parker, Roger **A545**
Parks, Richard S. **A714**
Pastille, William Alfred **T18, T23ᴿ,**
 T29, T32, A34, A50, A182, A256,
 A345, A346, A415, A448, A517,
 B52ᴿ, D163, E31
Pavlov, Sara **D43**
Peel, John Milton **D188**
Peles, Stephen **A119**
Penfold, Nigel **D53, D248**
Perle, George **A727**
Perone, James Edward **D136**

Perry, Jeffrey **A120**
Petito, Sue **D123**
Petty, Wayne Christopher **T24, A51, A52, A53, A210, D74**
Phillips, Edward Rooker **A600, D207**
Phipps, Graham H. **A477, A518**
Pierce, Alexandra **A211**
Pierce, Anne Alexandra **D233**
Pitre, Richard **D254**
Pittman, Daniel Sayle, Jr. **D203**
Platt, Heather Anne **A212, B27ᴿ**
Plenckers, Leo J. **A19**
Plettner, Arthur **A790**
Plotnikov, Boris **T63, A20, A91, A189ᵀ, B5, B9**
Plum, Karl-Otto **A416, A532ᴿ, B64r, B68, D257**
Poland, William **A679**
Pomeroy, David B. **D21**
Pople, Anthony **A157, A547**
Popovic, Linda **A158**
Porter, Charles **D124**
Porter, Steven Clark **D204**
Poulin, Pamela **B26**
Powell, Hiram Clayton **D101**
Pozzi, Egidio **A68, B21, E5**
Proctor, Gregory **T12ᴿ, A384, A417, D208**
Puffett, Derrick **S125ᴿ, S128ᴿ, T50ᴿ, T51, A347, A693ᵀ**
Purroy Chicot, Pedro **A478R**

R
Rahn, John **A367ᴿ, A617, A634, A823**
Rast, Nicholas **A418**
Rawlins, Robert C. **D91**
Redmann, Bernd **A159**
Regner, Eric **A728**
Reich, Willi **A792, A799**
Renoldi, Marco **A183**

Renwick, William J. **T50ᴿ, A17ᴿ, A54, A55, A184, A276, A277, A307, A419, B27, E41**
Reynolds, M. Fletcher **D110**
Reynolds, William H. **A555ᴿ, A751**
Riedel, Johannes **A618**
Riezler-Stettin, Walter **A803**
Rigaudière, Marc **A420**
Riggins, Herbert Lee **A384, A406, A417, A601, A602, D195**
Riley, John Howard **D238**
Rink, John S. **T16ᴿ, A56, A185, A246, A348, A421, A449, B32ᴿ**
Rodgers, Michael **B36ᴿ, B44ᴿ**
Rodman, Ronald **A81, A213**
Roller, Jonathan Brian **D75**
Rosen, Charles **S149ᴿ, A84**
Rosenschein, Stanley J. **A637, A665, A682**
Roth, Hermann **B101**
Rothfarb, Lee Allen **A479**
Rothgeb, John **T7, T23, T34, T36, T50, A121, A349, A380ᴿ, A519, A548, A603, A619, A630ᴿ, A656, A688, A707, B13ᴿ, B64ᴿ, B71ᴿ, B72ᴿ⁽²⁾, B81ᴿ, B82ᴿ, B100ᵀ, E29**
Rothstein, William Nathan **T8, T16ᴿ, A21, A122, A186, A214, A308, A350, A384ᴿ, A422, A480, A520, A620, A816, B42, B52ᴿ, B66ᴿ, B100ᴿ, D196**
Routley, Erik **B93**
Russ, Michael **A160, A247, A351**
Russakovsky, Luba **D10**
Russom, Philip Wade **D164**
Rytting, Bryce Wallis **D65S**

S
Sabourin, Carmen **A187, A215, B27ᴿ, D125**
Salzer, Felix **A481, A549, A621, A672, A700, A715, A724, A729,**

A756, A767, A773, A784, B82, B85, B92, B98, B99

Samarotto, Frank Paul A57, B8ᴿ, B35ᴿ, D30

Samson, Jim A216, A423, A550, B74ᴿ

Sanguinetti, Giorgio T40, T41, T42, T43, T44, T45, T46, T47, T48, T49, A188, E6

Saslaw, Janna A123

Sayers, Richard D22

Sayrs, Elizabeth Paige D54

Scarpellini Pancrazi, Franco A278

Schachter, Carl E. T12ᴿ, T23ᴿ, A8, A9, A22, A58, A161, A189, A217, A218, A219, A220, A309, A310, A311, A352, A385, A424, A451, A452, A453, A551, A552, A586, A657, A658, A659, A673, A701, A716, A726, A818, A827, B7, B10, B69, B82, B85

Scheepers, Paul A19ᴿ, A23

Schmalfeldt, Janet A124, A279, A312, A498, E18

Schmid, Edmund A752

Schneider, Mathieu A85, D31

Schoffman, Nachum A554

Schubert, Giselher A313

Schulenberg, David A353, A499

Schüler, Nico D23

Schulze, Sean D32

Schwab-Felisch, Oliver A10

Sessions, Robert S151ᴿ, A766, A793

Setar, Katherine Marie D55

Shaftel, Matthew A59

Sharpe, Robert A. A248, A555

Shim, Elizabeth D56

Siegel, Heidi T5, T9, T16, T36, T50, A60, A354, A425, B7, B40

Silberman, Israel A735

Simms, Bryan R. A592, A660

Simon, Erich A785

Simon, Mark D165

Simon, Tom D209

Skeirik, Kaleel Charles D57

Slatin, Sonia D239

Sloboda, John A B53

Sly, Gordon C. A24, A190, D76

Smaldone, Edward Michael D152

Smith, Charles Justice S123ᴿ, A163, A661, A674, A679, A689, A824, A824ᴿ, D217

Smith, Elizabeth Lena S246

Smith, Peter Howard A25, A86, A191, A221 A222, D102

Smith, Richard D255

Smith, Timothy Allen D137

Smoliar, Stephen A623, A637, A665, A675, A682

Smyth, David A61, A249, B27ᴿ

Snarrenberg, Robert Bio5, T50ᴿ, T62, A223, A280, A821, B13, D111

Snyder, John L. A314

Sobaskie, James William A455, B13ᴿ, D166

Solie, Ruth A622, B72ᴿ

Solomon, Larry A355, E42

Somfai, László A558

Song, Moo-Kyoung D33

Spicer, Mark A164

Spurný, Lubomír T57, T58, T59, T60, T61, B6

Stein, Deborah Jane A556, B54, D189

Stephan, Rudolf S134ᴿ, A641, B52ᴿ

Stern, David A356, A357, A587, A604

Stewart, Cecelia D146

Stewart, James T15, D181

Stewart, Milton Lee D223

Stilles, Ramón A533ᵀ

Stock, Jonathan A251

Stolet, Jeffrey Marshall D173

Stopford, John **A591**
Straus, Joseph N. **A125, A454, A557**
Street, A. **A386**
Strunk, Steven **A166**
Suppan, Wolfgang **A126**
Suurpää, Lauria **A62, A63, A88, A167, A250, B14, E11**
Swain, Joseph Peter **A482, B59ᴿ, D182**
Swift, Angela **D44**
Swift, Robert **B47ᴿ, B58ᴿ, B59ᴿ, B62ᴿ, B100ᴿ**
Swinburne, Caroline **D153**
Szkodzinski, Louise **D215T**

T
Taggart, Bruce **D66**
Tamamoto, Akiko **T11**
Tanenbaum, Faun S. **A500, A624**
Taylor, Paul **D190**
Teboul, Jean-Claude **T53, A26, A35ᵀ, A192, D77**
Tepping, Susan **A426, A483, A559, A605, B35, D147**
Thaler, Lotte **B57, D183**
Thiemel, Matthias **B28, D82**
Thym, Jürgen **T23, A625**
Todd, R. Larry **A168**
Traut, Donald **A11, A27, D1**
Travis, Roy **A456, A676, A677, A717, A731, A745**
Treibitz, C. Howard **A560**
Treitler, Leo **A588, A626, A733**
Tschierpe, Rudolph **Bio13**
Tuchowski, Andrzej **A12, B19**
Turner, Mitchenn M. **D34**
Turnstall, Patricia **A635U**

U
Underwood, Michael Paul **D47V**

V
Van Beek, Johan **A127**
Van den Toorn, Pieter **A169, A193, B44ᴿ**
Viljoen, Martina **A252**
Viljoen, Nicol **A252, A315, A561, D126**
Violin, Moritz **Bio24**
Vrieslander, Otto **S148ᴿ⁽²⁾, A765, A804, A806, A808, A810W**

W
Wagner, Aleksandra **A522, A606**
Wagner, Naphtali **A64, A194, A457, D154**
Waldeck, A. **A794**
Walker, Alan **A703**
Walker, David **D12, E43**
Walsh, Stephen **A521**
Walter, Ross Alex **D67**
Walts, Anthony Albert **D167**
Wampler, Stephen George **D45**
Warfield, Gerald **B70, B76**
Wason, Robert Wesley **T23ᴿ, A562, B55, D197**
Watts, Donald Earl **D46**
Webster, James **A281, A358, B85ᴿ**
Weiner, Brien **T37, D83**
Weisse, Hans **A795**
Wen, Eric **A13, A65, A359, A360, A484, A589**
Weng, Li-Shuang **D35**
Wenger, Barbara F. **D103**
Westergaard, Peter **A739, B78**
Whitall, Arnold **B44, B66ᴿ⁽²⁾**
White, John D. **A92**
Whitlock, Prentice Earle **D168**
Whittle, Barbara B. **D84**
Wick, Norman Lee **A224, A316, A361, D155**
Wilde, Howard **D78**

Williams, Alastair **A93**
Williams, David Russell **A326**
Williamson, John Gordon **A128,
A145, A486**
Williamson, Richard Anthony **A94,
D156**
Willner, Channan **A66, A317, A427,
A822, B64ᴿ, E30**
Wilson, Paul **A523**
Wingert, Hans **A757**
Winkler, Peter K. **A642**
Wintle, Christopher **S143ᴿ, T12ᴿ,
T55, A28, A485, A501, A590,
B100ᴿ**
Witten, David **A129**

Wolf, Hans **A786Y**

Y
Yadeau, William **D199**
Yan-Di, Yang **A195, A196**
Yeston, Maury **A662, B73, B77**
Yokota, Erisa **D191**
Yribarren, Martin John **D85**
Yu, Su-xian **B34Z**

Z
Zauner, Victor **A787**
Zbikowski, Lawrence **E16**
Zuckerkandl, Victor **A126, A742,
A788, A796, A797, B80, B83, B88**

Topical Index

I. Introductions, Surveys, and Explanations

A3, A54, A82, A183, A195, A238, A250, A278, A292, A369, A378, A420, A473, A504, A601, A602, A606, A631, A680, A719, A724, A742, A744, A757, A760, A762, A763, A772, A790, A791, A794, A800, A801, A802, A804, A806, A810, A811, A812, A813, A814, A829, A830, A831, A832, B6, B11, B21, B32, B34, B35, B43, B44, B45, B68, B100, D146, D162, D163, D195, D202, D223, D240

II. Analytical Studies

A5, A21, A22, A33, A39, A40, A49, A56, A69, A72, A77, A83, A97, A121, A127, A137, A154, A161, A165, A170, A189, A205, A208, A212, A213, A214, A216, A253, A257, A260, A265, A273, A276, A279, A293, A294, A298, A307, A308, A309, A310, A321, A332, A333, A335, A338, A352, A360, A382, A391, A395, A396, A398, A406, A412, A421, A427, A428, A449, A452, A453, A457, A462, A465, A481, A483, A484, A485, A492, A493, A500, A501, A511, A530, A542, A546, A548, A555, A558, A561, A566, A567, A572, A579, A585, A590, A597, A599, A609, A614, A617, A621, A624, A625, A638, A641, A653, A655, A658, A659, A661, A663, A666, A667, A672, A674, A676, A677, A679, A698, A700, A701, A702, A705, A706, A707, A711, A715, A726, A736, A737, A738, A741, A743, A746, A752, A753, A756, A759, A761, A765, A769, A770, A771, A775, A781, A782, A783, A819, A820, A822, A826, A834, B7, B10, B14, B16, B19, B25, B27, B28, B30, B37, B38, B41, B45, B54, B58, B73, B75, B85, B98, D3, D6, D8, D11, D14, D27, D29, D32, D35, D36, D43, D50, D53, D56, D74, D86, D90, D92, D97, D99, D103, D104, D105, D108, D109, D117, D125, D126, D128, D129, D133, D143, D147, D149, D154, D158, A167, D168, D175, D180, D184, D192, D199, D202, D203, D205, D207, D211, D213, D215, D217, D231, D236, D244, D246, D247, D248, D250, D256, D257, D258

III. Repertoire Outside Schenker's Sphere of Inquiry
a. Pre-tonal Music

A344, A357, A368, A438, A440, A494, A499, A544, A549, A557, A578, A587, A600, A604, A627, A671, A712, A713, A716, A722, A729, A733, B99, D68, D78, D93, D122, D134, D212, D216, D252

b. Late-Nineteenth-Century/Chromatic Music

A73, A79, A85, A95, A108, A110, A117, A128, A131, A132, A145, A152,
A153, A155, A158, A160, A168, A226, A232, A259, A296, A327, A351, A383,
A388, A407, A424, A433, A437, A461, A469, A486, A495, A512, A516, A528,
A531, A556, A567, A576, A593, A608, A629, A633, A723, A725, A817, A824,
B17, B33, B54, B60, D2, D9, D21, D24, D47, D48, D54, D57, D80, D85, D94,
D116, D141, D142, D151, D162, D164, D169, D187, D188, D189, D190,
D193, D198, D208, D226, D229, D235, D245, D253

c. Post-tonal Music

A27, A47, A90, A125, A134, A157, A199, A230, A234, A242, A291, A305,
A306, A319, A343, A363, A387, A401, A441, A454, A456, A489, A496, A503,
A508, A518, A523, A524, A547, A565, A583, A595, A596, A598, A607, A610,
A620, A636, A652, A717, A727, A731, A745, A749, A780, B31, B90, B96, D4,
D19, D22, D28, D31, D34, D44, D51, D52, D55, D69, D75, D89, D96, D123,
D124, D145, D148, D152, D157, D159, D165, D177, D178, D206, D214,
D228, D238, D259

d. Popular and World Music

A59, A89, A99, A101, A103, A104, A107, A111, A151, A166, A181, A243,
A251, A340, A435, A463, A513, A580, A581, A642, A670, B23, B24, D39,
D49, D60, D95, D114, D137, D139, D144, D204, D209, D223

IV. Criticism and/or Revision

A16, A32, A37, A61, A70, A80, A81, A96, A100, A114, A118, A140, A144,
A148, A164, A187, A193, A196, A201, A206, A229, A233, A247, A262, A263,
A266, A466, A271, A300, A402, A403, A445, A446, A447, A466, A509, A514,
A532, A626, A647, A689, A694, A703, A732, A750, A758, A766, A793, A799,
A803, A807, B20, B51, B56, B59, B72, B74, B92, B95, D5, D25, D63, D66,
D72, D78, D81, D115, D118, D120, D121, D153, D220, A720

V. Rhythm and Meter

A11, A18, A48, A57, A66, A75, A186, A224, A258, A264, A287, A316, A317,
A336, A337, A350, A380, A422, A444, A451, A490, A505, A506, A535, A640,
A662, A673, A696, A739, A818, A827, B10, B38, B50, B74, B77, B78, B79,
B81, B84, B85, B87, B89, D1, D30, D66, D88, D91, D120, D155, D171, D173,
D196, D232, D233, D255

VI. Historical, Philosophical, and Epistemological Studies

A1, A15, A34, A35, A36, A38, A43, A60, A76, A98, A105, A109, A116, A126,
A130, A135, A139, A162, A173, A175, A182, A188, A223, A228, A231, A235,
A239, A241, A244, A246, A252, A268, A272, A280, A286, A288, A289, A297,
A304, A320, A326, A345, A346, A349, A367, A373, A374, A379, A381, A397,
A399, A400, A405, A409, A410, A418, A425, A448, A458, A459, A460, A474,

A476, A510, A517, A519, A539, A540, A553, A554, A559, A559, A462, A570,
A588, A618, A622, A638, A650, A664, A668, A678, A690, A754, A755, A767,
A773, A774, A779, A784, A785, A787, A788, A789, A798, A805, A809, A815,
A821, A825, B2, B3, B4, B10, B13, B15, B18, B22, B26, B38, B39, B52, B55,
B57, B71, B85, B91, B98, D7, D65, D73, D79, D83, D84, D111, D113, D115,
D119, D132, D163, D172, D174, D181, D197, D210, D222, D224, D239, D241

VII. Motivic Relationships and Form
A7, A13, A14, A24, A28, A44, A45, A46, A52, A55, A58, A62, A63, A65, A71,
A86, A102, A120, A122, A143, A149, A163, A169, A174, A176, A184, A190,
A198, A202, A210, A218, A219, A220, A225, A249, A256, A261, A269, A281,
A282, A301, A311, A314, A315, A318, A322, A323, A334, A341, A342, A356,
A358, A359, A385, A389, A390, A392, A393, A429, A431, A434, A471, A472,
A497, A525, A529, A533, A534, A536, A538, A545, A551, A552, A582, A584,
A586, A589, A605, A612, A619, A628, A630, A643, A644, A654, A656, A669,
A777, B10, B40, B42, B58, B85, B100, D10, D15, D17, D26, D33, D62, D63,
D70, D76, D83, D89, D100, D102, D131, D138, D151, D156, D167, D170,
D176, D194, D230, D251

VIII. Analysis and Performance
A68, A91, A172, A179, A217, A295, A364, A376, A430, A439, A498, A520,
A527, A537, A541, A632, A740, A748, A764, A778, B98, D16, D18, D20, D45,
D67, D70, D71, D86, D98, D140, D160, D161, D192

IX. Pedagogy
A4, A6, A8, A9, A23, A25, A50, A106, A112, A119, A124, A129, A150, A197,
A204, A211, A215, A267, A277, A330, A354, A362, A365, A375, A384, A408,
A413, A415, A416, A417, A419, A426, A475, A478, A480, A487, A488, A502,
A526, A594, A603, A657, A683, A688, A692, A697, A735, A751, A768, A776,
A786, A795, A796, A797, A816, A828, B8, B9, B11, B12, B21, B34, B35, B36,
B43, B46, B50, B58, B62, B63, B67, B69, B70, B74, B76, B78, B82, B86,
B97, B101, D18, D40, D46, D61, D218, D221, D227

X. Computer Applications
A355, A615, A617, A623, A637, A648, A649, A665, A675, A682, A685, A686,
A728, D12, D23, D127, D150, D237

XI. Relationships between Schenker and Others/Comparative Analyses
A2, A7, A53, A64, A74, A87, A93, A94, A123, A142, A146, A159, A178, A180,
A185, A191, A192, A194, A200, A203, A209, A221, A222, A236, A237, A245,
A248, A274, A283, A284, A290, A299, A312, A313, A324, A325, A329, A339,
A353, A361, A366, A377, A386, A394, A423, A436, A450, A464, A477, A479,

A491, A543, A550, A563, A568, A571, A573, A574, A592, A611, A613, A646, A660, A681, A684, A693, A695, A699, A714, A720, A730, A734, A747, A792, A808, B47, B48, B57, B61, B64, B66, B75, B85, B94, D13, D37, D38, D51, D52, D58, D59, D64, D82, D85, D87, D96, D101, D107, D112, D119, D148, D157, D159, D160, D183, D191, D200, D201, D219, D234, D240, D242, D243, D249

XII. Interdisciplinary Approaches
A10, A12, A17, A19, A20, A26, A29, A30, A41, A42, A51, A67, A78, A84, A88, A113, A115, A133, A135, A138, A141, A147, A156, A171, A177, A207, A227, A240, A254, A255, A270, A275, A285, A302, A303, A328, A370, A371, A372, A404, A411, A414, A432, A442, A443, A455, A470, A482, A507, A514, A521, A564, A577, A591, A634, A635, A645, A651, A687, A691, A704, A708, A709, A710, A823, A833, B5, B29, B49, B53, B59, B65, B80, B83, B88, B93, D41, D42, D55, D58, D77, D88, D110, D106, D130, D135, D136, D137, D166, D177, D179, D182, D185, D186, D225, D254

Composer Index

Note: Unless otherwise specified, *quartet* or *quintet* refers to a string quartet or quintet, and *sonata* refers to a piano sonata

Anonymous
Alleluia, LU 779 **A554**
En ma dame, HAM 19d **A554**
Vos n'aler, HAM 19e **A554**
Estampie, HAM 40c **A554**
Cunctiponens genitor, HAM 27b **A554**
Benedicamus domino, HAM 28c **A554**
Melody to the First Pythian Ode **B43**
Trop lonc temps **B43**
Hymn to Apollo **B43**
Hymn to the Muse **B43**
Hymn to the Sun-God **B43**

Babbitt, Milton (b. 1916)
Compositions for Twelve Instruments **A578**

Johann Sebastian Bach (1685–1750)
Clavierübung III: Manualtier Kyries **A276**

BWV Anh. 114	*Menuet* in G Major **B21**	
BWV Anh. 115	*Menuet* in G Minor **B21**	
BWV 18	*Durch Adams Fall ist ganz verderbt* **A201**	
BWV 38	Cantata, "Aus thefer Noth" **A356**	
BWV 60	Cantata, "O Ewigkeit" **A673**	
BWV 78	Cantata, "Jesu der du meine Seele" **A584**	
BWV 90	Cantata, "Es reißet euch" **A356**	
BWV 111	Cantata, "Was mein Gott will" **B96**	
BWV 140	Cantata, "Wachet Auf," **A356**	
BWV 147	Cantata, "Herz und Mund" **A356**	

BWV 176	*Christ, unser Herr, zum Jordan kam* **A201**
BWV 232	Mass in B Minor **A30**
BWV 244	St. Matthew Passion **S149, S141, S143, A141, A178,** **A338, A356, A567, A651, A826**
BWV 298	*Dies sind die zehn heil'gen Gebote* **A229**
BWV 314	*Gelobt seiest du, Herr Jesu Christ* **A229**
BWV 377	*Mach's mit mir, Gott, nach deiner Güt* **A446**ᴿ
BWV 436	*Wie Schön Leuchtet der Morgenstern* **A446**ᴿ
BWV 589	*Allabreve* **A570**
BWV 602	*Lob sei dem allmachtigen Gott* **D72**
BWV 611	*Christum wir sollen loben schon* **D72**
BWV 620	*Christus, Der uns selig macht* **D72**
BWV 621	*Da Jesus an dem Kreuze stund* **D72**
BWV 654	*Schmücke dich, o liebe Seele* **A641**
BWV 772	Two-Part Invention in C Major **A541, A676, B43**
BWV 774	Two-Part Invention in D Minor: **D125**
BWV 777	Two-Part Invention in E Major **A426**
BWV 778–86	Two-Part Inventions **D125**
BWV 779	Two-Part Invention in F Major **A5, A19, B43**
BWV 784	Two-Part Invention in A Minor **A599, A677, A677**ᴿ**, B27**
BWV 794	Three-Part Sinfonia in F Major **A548**
BWV 797	Three-Part Sinfonia in G Minor **A548**
BWV 812	French Suite no. 1 in D Minor **A48**
BWV 813	French Suite no. 2 in C Minor **A321**
BWV 814	French Suite no. 3 in B Minor **A48**
BWV 815	French Suite no. 4 in E-flat Major **A48, A302, A453**
BWV 817	French Suite no. 6 in E Major **A48, A337 A446**ᴿ
BWV 825	Partita no. 1 in B Flat Major **A65, A527, A567**
BWV 828	Partita no. 4 in D Major **A65**
BWV 830	Partita no. 6 in E Minor **A352**
BWV 846	WTC I, Prelude and Fugue in C Major **S159, A79, A206,** **A355, A453, A488, A671, B8, B21, B43**
BWV 847	WTC I, Prelude and Fugue in C Minor **S147, A45, A485,** **B43**
BWV 850	WTC I, Prelude and Fugue in D Major **B43**
BWV 851	WTC I, Prelude and Fugue in D Minor **A707**
BWV 852	WTC I, Prelude and Fugue in E-flat Major **S135**
BWV 853	WTC I, Prelude and Fugue in E-flat Minor **A65, A641,** **A821, B27**
BWV 855	WTC I, Prelude and Fugue in E Minor **A453, A567, B27**
BWV 856	WTC I, Prelude and Fugue in F Major **A772, A775**
BWV 858	WTC I, Prelude and Fugue in F-sharp Major **A345, B27**

BWV 861   WTC I, Prelude and Fugue in G Minor **A609**
BWV 865   WTC I, Prelude and Fugue in A Minor **A446ᴿ**
BWV 866   WTC I, Prelude and Fugue in B-flat Major **A701**
BWV 867   WTC I, Prelude and Fugue in B-flat Minor **A570**
BWV 868   WTC I, Prelude and Fugue in B Major **A257**
BWV 869   WTC I, Prelude and Fugue in B Minor **A690, B43**
BWV 870   WTC II, Prelude and Fugue in C Major **B27**
BWV 871   WTC II, Prelude and Fugue in C Minor **A741**
BWV 872   WTC II, Prelude and Fugue in D Major **B94**
BWV 891   WTC II, Prelude and Fugue in B-flat Minor **B27**
BWV 903   Chromatic Fantasy and Fugue **S127, A353, A741**
BWV 924   Little Prelude in C Major **S138, A375**
BWV 925   Little Prelude in D Major **S138**
BWV 926   Little Prelude in D Minor **S139**
BWV 939   Little Prelude in C Major **S139**
BWV 940   Little Prelude in D Minor **S146, A750, B43**
BWV 941   Little Prelude in E Minor **S146**
BWV 942   Little Prelude in A Minor **S146**
BWV 971   Italian Concerto **A741**
BWV 989   *Aria variata* **A257**
BWV 996   Suite for Lute **A673**
BWV 999   Little Prelude in C Minor **S139, A707**
BWV 1003   Sonata no. 3 in A Minor for Unaccompanied Violin **S146, A65**
BWV 1006   Partita no. 3 in E Major for Solo Violin **S146, A352, A452, B43**
BWV 1008   Suite no. 2 in D Minor for Unaccompanied Violoncello **A624**
BWV 1009   Suite no. 3 in C Major for Unaccompanied Violonello **S147**
BWV 1010   Suite no. 4 in E-flat Major for unaccompanied Violonello **A220**
BWV 1011   Suite no. 5 in C Minor for Unaccompanied Violoncello **A65**
BWV 1018   Sonata in F Minor for Violin **A338**
BWV 1020   Violin Sonata in G Minor **A707**
BWV 1032   A Major Flute Sonata **A295**
BWV 1050   Brandenburg Concerto no. 5 **A662**
BWV 1051   Brandenburg Concerto no. 6 **A338, A585**
BWV 1068   Orchestral Suite no. 3 in D **A13**
BWV 1079   Musical Offering **A641, A673**
D Minor Chaccone **A542**

Carl Philipp Emanuel Bach (1714–88)

W. 55	Sonata in C Major **S138**
W. 113	*Sonata für Kenner und Liebhaber* I, 1 **S138**
H. 261 (W. 57/2)	*Sonatas für Kenner und Liebhaber* II, 2-II **A548**
H. 38 (W. 62/4)	Sonata no. 4 **A548**
H. 253 (W. 55/3)	Sonata no. 3 **A707**
H. 71 (W. 63/2)	G Minor *Probestück* **A52, A53**
H. 173 (W. 57/6)	Sonata in F Minor **A52, A55**
H. 72 (W. 63/3)	A Major *Probestück* **A52, A53**

Johann Christian Bach (1735–82)

G. 10	*La Clemenza di Scipione* **A546**

Béla Bartók (1881–1945)

Op. 20	Eight Improvisations **A503, A523**
Op. 30	**A523**
Op. 88	Piano Sonata **A535**
Op. 14	Piano Suite **A535**
Op. 52	Quartet no. 1 **A535**
Op. 95	Quartet no. 4, **A305, B90**
Op. 105	*Mikrokosmos* V: 132 **A596**
Op. 119	Quartet no. 6 **D145**

Ludwig van Beethoven (1770–1827)

Op. 2/1	Sonata no. 1 in F Minor, **S136, A2, A45, A65, A735, A628, A735, A628, A691, A827, B8, D173**
Op. 2/2	Sonata no. 2 in A Major
Op. 2/3	Sonata no. 3 in C Major **A673**
Op. 7	Sonata no. 4 in E-flat Major **A453, A527, A836**
Op. 10/1	Sonata no. 5 in C Minor **A2, A302, A836, B21**
Op. 10/2	Sonata no. 6 in A-flat Major **A186**
Op. 10/3	Sonata no. 7 in D Major **A77, A501, A696**
Op. 13	Sonata no. 8 in C Minor "Pathétique" **A206, A761**
Op. 14/1	Sonata no. 9 in E Major **A586, A827**
Op. 14/2	Sonata no. 10 in G Major **A673**
Op. 18/2	Quartet no. 2 in G Major **A62**
Op. 18/3	Quartet no. 3 in D Major **A71**
Op. 18/6	Quartet no. 6 in B-flat Major **A698, A762**
Op. 21	Symphony no. 1 in C Major **A310, A818, D14**
Op. 23	Vionlin Sonata no. 4 in A Minor **A779**
Op. 24	Violin Sonata no. 5 in F Major "Spring" **A218, A453**
Op. 26	Sonata no. 12 in A-flat Major **A120, A137, A365, A836**

Op. 27/1	Sonata no. 13 in E-flat Major, **A451, B43**
Op. 27/2	Sonata no. 14 in C-sharp Minor **A57, A761**
Op. 31/1	Sonata no. 15 in D Major **A835**
Op. 31/2	Sonata no. 16 in D Minor **A45, A77, D173, D205**
Op. 31/3	Sonata no. 17 E-flat Major **A77, A493, D103, D173**
Op. 35	Piano Variations **A116**
Op. 49/1	Sonata no. 19 in G Minor **B43**
Op. 49/2	Sonata no. 20 in G Major **S138, B8**
Op. 50/1	Quartet **A329**
Op. 53	Sonata no. 21 in C Major "Waldstein" **A72, A180, A321, A464, A526, A643, A655, A824, A835, A837**
Op. 55	Symphony no. 3 in E-flat Major "Eroica" **S148, A460, A548, A721, A836, D14**
Op. 57	Sonata no. 23 in F Minor "Appassionata" **S141, A2, A527, D87**
Op. 59/1	Quartet no. 7 in F Major "Razumovsky" **A490, A673**
Op. 59/2	Quartet no. 8 in E Minor **B96**
Op. 59/3	Quartet in C Major **A110**
Op. 62	*Corolan* Overture **A110**
Op. 67	Symphony no. 5 in C Minor **S135, S139, S140, S145, A334, A696, D14**
Op. 68	Symphony no. 6 in F Major "Pastorale" **A189, D14**
Op. 69	Sonata for ViolonVioloncello **A711**
Op. 72b	*Leonore* Overture no. 3 **A341**
Op. 74	Quartet in E-flat **A10, A382**
Op. 77	Fantasy in G Minor **D32**
Op. 78	Sonata no. 24 in F-sharp Major ("Für Therese") **A673**
Op. 81a	Sonata in E-flat Major "Lebewohl" **A321**
Op. 84	*Egmont* Overture **A759**
Op. 90	Sonata no. 27 in E Minor **A374, D70**
Op. 96	Violin Sonata no. 10 in G **A365**
Op. 97	Piano Trio no. 6 in B Flat "Archduke" **A548**
Op. 101	Sonata no. 28 in A Major **S134, A65, A138, A334, A570**
Op. 109	Sonata no. 30 in E Major **S131, A45, A334, A400, A474, A759, D30, D105**
Op. 110	Sonata no. 31 in A-flat Major **S132, S1446, A57, A127, A334. A429, A669, A673, D30, D180**
Op. 111	Sonata no. 32 in C Minor **S133, A702, D17**
Op. 119/3	Bagatelle in D Major **D30**
Op. 119/7	Bagatelle in C Major **D30**
Op. 119/8	Bagatelle in C Major **D30**
Op. 119/1	Bagatelle in G Minor **B8**

Op. 125	Symphony no. 9 in D Minor **S130, A172, A173, A272, A281, A302, A358, A626, B30, D106**, **D14**, **D180**
Op. 126/2	Bagatelle in G Minor **A498**
Op. 126/5	Bagatelle in G Major **A498**
Op. 127	Quartet no. 12 in E-flat Major **A49**
Op. 131	Quartet no. 14 in C-sharp Minor **D30**
Op. 132	Quartet no. 15 in A Minor **A427, D180**
WoO 60	Bagatelle **A511**

Alban Berg (1885–1935)

Op. 2/2	*Scheideweg* **A565, D34**
Op. 5/3	Four Pieces for Clarinet **A595**
Op. 7	*Wozzeck* **A47, A489, A727, D34**
1907, -25	*Schliesse mir die augen beide*, both versions **B43**
1935	*Lulu* **A547, D34**

Hector Berlioz (1803–69)

Op. 14	*Symphonie fantastique* **A110, D162**

Georges Bizet (1838–75)

Op. 27/7	*Jeux d'enfants* **A673**

Johannes Brahms (1833–97)

Op. 9	Variations on a Theme by Schumann **D105**
Op. 19/5	*An eine Äolsharfe* **A58**
Op. 24	Variations and Fugue on a Theme by Händel **S142, D105**
Op. 29/2	*Schaffe In Mir, Gott, Ein Rein Herz* **D161**
Op. 34	Piano Qunitet in F Minor **D6**
Op. 38	Violoncello Sonata no. 1 in E Minor **A110**
Op. 39/11	Waltz **A707**
Op. 39/14	Waltz **A45**
Op.43/1	*Von ewiger Liebe* **A212**
Op. 45	Deutsches Requiem **A330**
Op. 51/1	Quartet no. 1 in C Minor **A221, A534**
Op. 53	Alto Rhapsody **A536**
Op. 54	*Schicksalslied* **A110**
Op. 56	Variations on a Theme of Haydn **A41, A42**
Op. 63/5	*Meine Liebe ist Grün* **B43**
Op. 67/2	String Quartet no. 4 **A715**
Op. 73/1	Symphony no. 2 in D **A65, A367, A551**
Op. 74/2	*O Heiland, Reiss Die Himmel Auf* **D161**
Op. 76/6	Intermezzo in A Major **A391**
Op. 76/7	Intermezzo in A Minor **A65, A257, A446ᴿ, D176**

Op. 79/2   Rhapsody in G Minor **A684**
Op. 81   *Tragic* Overture **A110**
Op. 83   Piano Concerto no. 2 in B-flat Major **A824**
Op. 88   Quintet no. 1 in F Major **A147**
Op. 95/5   *Vorschneller Schwur* **A212**
Op. 96/1   *Der Tod, das ist die kühle Nacht* **A88, A666, A674**
Op. 98   Symphony no. 4 in E Minor **A110, A221, A762**
Op. 99   Violoncello Sonata no. 2 in F Major **A221, A403**
Op. 101   Piano Trio no. 3 in C Minor **A110**
Op. 104   Songs **A815**
Op. 104/2   *Nachtwache* **A330**
Op. 105/1   *Wie Melodien zieht es mir* **A705, A706**
Op. 105/2   *Immer leise wird mein schlummer* **B43**
Op. 105/4   *Auf dem Kirchhofe* **A425**
Op. 107   Songs **A875**
Op. 108   Violin Sonata no. 3 in D Minor **A110**
Op. 114   Trio for Viola, Violoncello, and Piano in A Minor **A632**
Op. 116   Seven Fantasias **A533**
Op. 116/4   Intermezzo in E Major **D176**
Op. 116/7   Capriccio in D Minor **A761**
Op. 117   Fantasias **A392**
Op. 117/2   Intermezzo in B-flat Minor **A102, A506, D176**
Op. 117/3   Intermezzo in C-sharp Minor **D176**
Op. 118   Six Piano Pieces **D202**
Op. 118/1   Intermezzo in A Minor **B94**
Op. 118/2   Intermezzo in A Major **A65, A391, A392, A820, D176**
Op. 119/1   Intermezzo in B Minor **A34, A35, A529, A645, D176**
Op. 119/2   Intermezzo in E Minor **A34, A35, A392, D176**
Op. 119/4   Rhapsody in E-flat Major **A150, D200**
Op. 120/1   Clarinet/Viola Sonata no. 1 in F Minor **A86, D13**
Op. 120/2   Clarinet/Viola Sonata no. 2 in E-flat Major **A65, A318**

Benjamin Britten (1913–76)
Op. 88   *Death in Venice* **A456**
Op. 25   Quartet **A496**

Anton Bruckner (1824–96)
Op. 107   Symphony no. 7 **A110**
Op. 108   Symphony no. 8 **A132**
Op. 109   Symphony no. 9 **A114**

William Byrd (1543–1623)
Mass for five voices, *Credo* **A357**

Luigi Cherubini (1760–1842)
Medée Overture **A110**

Frederic Chopin (1810–49)
Ballades nos. 1, 2, 4 **A214**

Op. 1	Rondo **A459**
Opp. 6, 7, 17	Mazurkas **D56, D126**
Op. 6/1	Mazurka in F-sharp Minor **A714**
Op. 6/2	Mazurka in C-sharp Minor **A561**
Op. 9/2	Nocturne in E-flat Major **A56, A714**
Op. 9/3	Nocturne in B Major **A21**
Opp. 10, 25	Etudes **D77**
Op. 10/1	Etude in C Major **A91, A202**
Op. 10/3	Etude in E Major **A164, A836**
Op. 10/5	Etude in G-flat Major **S146**
Op. 10/6	Etude in E-flat Major **S146**
Op. 10/8	Etude in F Major **A149, A606**
Op. 10/12	Etude in C Minor **A420, A477**
Op. 15/2	Nocturne in F-sharp Major **S147, S149, A14, A628**
Op. 24/1	Mazurka in G Minor **A548**
Op. 24/2	Mazurka in C Major **A14, A21**
Op. 25/3	Etude in G-flat Major "Butterfly" **A661**
Op. 25/3	Etude in F Major **A700**
Op. 25/12	Etude in C Minor **A673**
Op. 27/1	Nocturne in C-sharp Minor **A715**
Op. 28/2	Prelude in A Minor **A14, A21, A164, A366, A472, A493, A509, B43**
Op. 28/3	Prelude in G Major **A827**
Op. 28/4	Prelude in E Minor **A45, A81, A189, A219, A366, A714**
Op. 28/5	Prelude in D Major **A217**
Op. 28/6	Prelude in B Minor **A258**
Op. 28/8	Prelude in F-sharp Minor **A265**
Op. 28/9	Prelude in E Major **B43**
Op. 28/10	Prelude in C-sharp Minor **B43**
Op. 28/18	Prelude in F Minor, **A453**
Op. 28/20	Prelude in C Minor **B43**
Op. 30/3	Mazurka **A315**
Op. 31	Scherzo no. 2 in B-flat Minor **A300, A407**
Op. 32/1	Nocturne in B Major **A21**
Op. 33/1	Mazurka in G-sharp Minor **A352**
Op. 34/1	Waltz in A-flat Major **S147, A14, A21**
Op. 34/2	Waltz in A Minor **D70**

Op. 35	Sonata no. 2 in B Flat **A51, D192**
Op. 36	Impromptu no. 2 in F-sharp Minor **A527**
Op. 38	Ballade no. 2 in F Major **A147, A214, A407, A593, A737, D199**
Op. 40/1	Polonaise in A Major "Militare" **A350**
Op. 40/2	Polonaise in C Minor **A65**
Op 41/3	Mazurka in B Major **A21, A58**
Op. 48/1	Nocturne in C Minor **A619**
Op. 49	Fantasy in F Minor **A407, A424, A714, D199**
Op. 50/3	Mazurka in C-sharp Minor **A22**
Op. 54	Scherzo no. 4 in E Major **A765**
Op. 56/2	Mazurka in C Major **A561**
Op. 58	Sonata no. 3 in B Minor **A21, D71, D231**
Op. 59/2	Mazurka in A-flat Major **A688**
Op. 60	Barcarolle **A421**
Op. 61	Polonaise-Fantasie in A-flat Major **A21, A122, A164, A423, A449, D199**
Op. 62/1	Nocturne in B Major **A21**
Op. 66	Fantasie-Impromptu in C-sharp Minor **A761**
Op. 68	Four Mazurkas **A265**
Op. IIb/3	Trois nouvelles etudes **A26**

Loyset Compére (1445–1518)
Missa alles regretz **A713**

Aaron Copland (1900–90)

1923	*As It Fell upon a Day* **D22**
1923–8	Two Pieces for String Quartet **D22**
1925	Music for the Theatre **D22**
1942	Statements for Orchestra **D22**
1947	Piano Blues **D22**

Armando "Chick" Corea (b. 1941)
Ballad for Anna **D60**
Noon Song **D60**
Sometime Ago **D60**
Song for Sally **D60**
Song of the Wind **D60**

Arcangelo Corelli (1653–1713)

| Op. 3/1 | Trio Sonata **A590** |
| Op. 5 | Violin Sonatas **A37** |

Luigi Dallapiccola (1904–1975)

1935	Musica per tre Pianoforte **D123**
1939–41	Piccolo Concerto per Muriel Couvreux **D123**
1949	Tre Episodi dal Balletto *Marsia* **D123**
1942–3	Sonatina Canonica in E-flat Major **D123**
1952	Quaderno Musicale di Annalibera **D123**

Claude Debussy (1862–1918)

1902	*Pelleas et Mélisande* **B96**
1910	*La fille aux cheveux de lin* **B96**
1895	*Prelude á l'apres-midi d'un faune* **A226**
1908	*Jimbo's Lullaby* **D152**
1913	*Les tierces alternées* **B96**
1904	*L'isle Joyeuse* **A530**
1910	*Voiles* **A575, B96**
1901	Pour le Piano **B96**
1910	*Minstrels* **B96**
1891	*Beau Soir* **A824**

Guillaume Dufay (1400–74)
Trop lonc temps **A627**

Gabriel Fauré (1845–1924)

Op. 46/1	*Les Présents* **A296**
Op. 51/4	*La Rose* **A296**
Op. 61	Una Sainte from *Le Bonne Chanson* **A296**

John Field (1782–1837)
Nocturne no. 1 in E Flat **A56**
Nocturne no. 9 in E Flat **A56**

César Franck (1822–90)

Op. 8	Sonata for Violin and Piano in A Major **D162**
Op. 25	Andantino in G Minor **D85**
Opp. 28–33	Six Pieces, 1860–62 **D85**
Opp. 35–7	Trois Pieces, 1878 **D85**
Opp. 38–40	Trois Chorals, 1892 **D85**
Op. 46	Symphonic variations **D85**

George Gershwin (1898–1937)
I Got Rhythm variations **D37**
Rhapsody in Blue **A340, A513**

Concerto in F **A513**
Oh, Lady Be Good **A51**

Edvard Grieg (1843–1907)
Op. 12/4   *Elfentanz* **B43**
Op. 23   Peer Gynt Suite no. 1 **A446**

Georg Friedrich Händel (1685–1759)
HWV 67   "Arrival of the Queen of Sheba" from *Solomon* **A822**
HWV 102   Canata: *Dalla guerra amorosa* **A4**
HWV 108   Cantate: *Dolce mio ben, s'io taccio* **A4**
HWV 115   Cantata: *Fra pensieri quel pensiero* **A4**
HWV 309   Organ Concerto Op. 7/4 **A822**
HWV 315   Concerto Grosso in F Major **A66**
HWV 320   Concerto Grosso in F Major **A66**
HWV 325   Concerto Grosso in B-flat Major **A673**
HWV 328   Concerto Grosso in D Minor **A66**
HWV 432   Suite no. 16 **S138**
HWV 342   Suite in F Major **A184**
HWV 351   Music for the Royal Fireworks **A66**
HWV 433   Suite in F Minor **A66**
HWV 442   Chaccone in G Major, Var. 2 **A345**
Suite no. 8 Courante **A548**

Franz Joseph Haydn (1732–1809)
Kaiserhymne **A786**
Hob. I: 44   Symphony no. 44 in E Minor **A110**
Hob. I: 55   Symphony no. 55 in E-flat Major **A33**
Hob. I: 58   Symphony no. 58 in F Major **A33**
Hob. I: 73   Symphony no. 73 in D Major **D29**
Hob. I: 78   Symphony no. 78 in C Minor **A66**
Hob. I: 82   Symphony no. 82 in C Major **D29**
Hob. I: 83   Symphony no. 83 in G Minor **A66, D14, D29,**
Hob. I: 84   Symphony no. 84 in E-flat Major **D29**
Hob. I: 85   Symphony no. 85 B-flat Major **D29**
Hob. I: 86   Symphony no. 86 in D Major **D29**
Hob. I: 87   Symphony no. 87 in A Major **D29**
Hob. I: 88   Symphony no. 88 in G Major **D29**
Hob. I: 89   Symphony no. 89 in F Major **D29**
Hob. I: 90   Symphony no. 90 in C Major **A66, D29**
Hob. I: 91   Symphony no. 91 in E-flat Major **D29**
Hob. I: 92   Symphony no. 92 in G Major **D29**

Hob. I: 93	Symphony no. 93 in D Major **A66**
Hob. I: 98	Symphony no, 98 in B-flat Major **A427**
Hob. I: 99	Symphony no. 99 in E-flat Major **A352, D14**
Hob. I: 100	Symphony no. 100 in G Major **D14**
Hob. I: 101	Symphony no. 101 in D Major **A427, A451**
Hob. I: 103	Symphony no. 103 in E-flat Major **D36**
Hob. I: 104	Symphony no. 104 in D Major **A427, A609**
Hob. II: 46	St. Antoni Chorale **A836**
Hob. III: 19	Quartet no. 12 in C Major **D167**
Hob. III: 32	Quartet no. 25 in C Major **A605, D167**
Hob. III: 39	Quartet no. 32 in C Major **D167**
Hob. III: 63	Quartet no. 53 in D Major **A605**
Hob. III: 77	Quartet no. 62 in C Major **S143, A530**
Hob. III: 80	Quartet no. 65 in E-flat Major **A672**
Hob. XVI: 20	Sonata no. 36 in C Minor **B43**
Hob. XVI: 34	Sonata no. 39 in E Minor **A673**
Hob. XVI: 35	Sonata no. X in C Major **S138**
Hob. XVI: 36	Sonata no. 32 in C-sharp Minor **A538**
Hob. XVI: 37	Sonata no. 33 in D Major **B8**
Hob. XVI: 38	Sonata no. 34 in E-flat Major **A210**
Hob. XVI: 44	Sonata no. 18 in G Minor **B21**
Hob. XVI: 46	Sonata no. 16 in A-flat **A330**
Hob. XVI: 49	Sonata in E-flat Major **S149**
Hob. XVI: 50	Sonata no. 46 in C Major **A427**
Hob. XVI: 52:	Sonata no. 45 in E-flat Major **A137**
Hob. XVII: 6	*Andante con Variazioni* in F Minor **A690**
Hob. XX: 1	*Seven Last Words* **A63**
Hob. XXI: 2	*The Creation* **S147, A270, A367, D14**
Hob. XXII: 14	*Harmonienmesse* **A453**

Jimi Hendrix (1942–70)
Little Wing **A99**

Paul Hindemith (1865–1963)
Trombone Sonata **D67**	
1942	Interlude in B Flat from *Ludus Tonalis* **A192**
1942	Fugue in C from *Ludus Tonalis* **A387**
1942	Fuga undecima in B from *Ludus Tonalis* **B90**
1936	Sonata no. 1 **B43**
1936	Sonata no. 3 **D127**

Alan Hovhaness (1911–94)
Quadruple Fugue **D127**

Heinrich Isaac (1450–1517)
Instrumental Canzona, HAM 88 **A544**
Innsbruch, ich muß dich lassen **A357**
Missa Carminum **A713**

Charles Ives (1874–1954)
1898–1908   Symphony no.1 **D75**
                    Symphony no. 3 **D75**
1912–8   Symphony no. 4 **D127, D75**
1912   The Fourth of July **A598**

Leos Janácek (1854–1928)
Late chamber music **D227**

John of Damascus
Hymn for the consecration of the church **B43**

Kirnberger, Johann Philipp (1721–1783)
Fugue in E Minor **A690**

Josquin Des Prez (1440–1521)
Missa Pange Lingua **A357, A713**
Missa Gaudeamus **A507**
Huc me sydereo **A713**
Ave Maria . . . virgo serena **A494, A713**
Missa de Beata Virgine **A713**
Sancti dei omnes **A357**
In illo tempore **A357**
Miserere mei, Deus **A357**
Missa Mater patris **A357**

Orlando di Lasso (1532–1594)
Prelude to *Prophitae Sybillarum* **A712**

John Lennon (1940–80) and Paul McCartney (b. 1942)
She's Leaving Home **A435**
Strawberry Fields Forever **A463**
Julia **A463**

Franz Liszt (1811–86)
Héroïde Funébre **A159**
1835–56   Piano Concerto no. 1 **A155**
1837–8   *Annees de Pelerinage* II **D169**

1837–8	*Vallée d'Obermann* **A433**
1838	*Die Trauer-Gondel* I, **A461, D169**
1849–55	*Les Preludes* **A110**
1851	*Chasse-Niege* from *Etudes d'exécution trancendante* **A92**
1853	Sonata in B Minor **A433**
1854	*Blum und Duft* **A117, A259, A576, A569**
1858	*Hamlet* **A110**
1861	*Faust* Symphony **A110, A259, A461, A671**
1868	*La Marquise de Blocqueville* **A68**
1872	Impromptu in F **A824**
1880–1	Mephisto Waltzes **D94**
1885	Batelle ohne Tonart **A671**

Sonetto 104 del Petrarca **A461, A531, A633**
Spozalizio **A461**

Witold Lutosławski (1913–1994)
Symphony no. 4 **A12**
Livre per orchestre **A12**

Gustav Mahler (1860–1911)

1893	Symphony no. 3 **D47**
1896	*Lieder eines fahrenden Gesellen* **D80**
1899	Symphony no. 4 **D162**
1901	Symphony no. 5 **A512**
1904	Symphony no. 6 **A110, A128, A671, A817, D231**
	Symphony no. 7 **A128, A486**
1911	Symphony no. 10 **A608**
1911	*Das Lied von der Erde* **A95, A128**

Donald Martino (b. 1931)
Pianississimo **A620**

Felix Mendelssohn (1809–1847)

Op. 19/1	Song without Words in E Minor **A818**
Op. 26	*Hebrides* Overture **D14**
Op. 44	Quartet in E Minor **A741**
Op. 56	Symphony no. 3 **A330**
Op. 90	Symphony no. 4 **D14**
Op. 62/1	Song without Words in G Major **A189, A323, B8**
Op. 67/4	Song without Words in C Major **B43**
Op. 85/1	Song without Words in F Major **A323**
Op. 102/4	Song without Words in G Minor **A451**

Nikolai Medtner (1880–1951)
Märchen op. 26/3 **A20**

Darius Milhaud (1892–1974)
Op. 269   "Midi" from *Une Journée* **B90**

Thelonius Monk (1917–82)
Thinspace **D144**
Round Midnight **D144**

Claudio Monteverdi (1567–1643)
Ohimé dov'é il mio ben **A438**
Ohimé, se tanto amate **A549**

Wolfgang Amadeus Mozart (1756–1791)

K. 2	Menuet in F Major **B43**
K. 67–9	*Epistle* Sonatas **D168**
K. 279	Sonata no. 1 in C Major **A709**
K. 280	Sonata no. 2 in F Major **A198, A321, A525, D50**
K. 283	Sonata no. 5 in G Major **A321, A673, A709**
K. 284	Sonata no. 6 in D Major **A709, D50**
K. 309	Sonata no. 7 in C Major **D50**
K. 310	Sonata no. 8 in A Minor **S130, A39, A321, A430, A673, A707, B94**
K. 311	Sonata no. 9 in D Major **A311**
K. 330	Sonata no. 10 in C Major **A333, A526, A628, A818, B43**
K. 331	Sonata no. 11 in A Major **A150, A371, A515 A651, B21**
K. 332	Sonata no. 12 in F Major **A198, A333, A525**
K. 333	Sonata no. 13 in B-flat Major **A65, A66 A333, A350, A525, D29, D237**
K. 338	Symphony no. 34 in C Major **A40**
K. 339	Vesprae solennes de confressore **A94**
K. 366	*Idomeneo* **A110, A614**
K. 370	Quartet in F Major for Oboe, Violin, Viola, and Violoncello **A597**
K. 378	Violin Sonata **A451**
K. 384	*Die Entführung aus dem Serail* **A309, A558**
K. 385	Symphony no. 35 in D Major "Haffner" **A40**
K. 387	Quartet no. 14 in G Major **A40, A311, A483**
K. 399	Suite in C for Keyboard **A66**
K. 421	Quartet in E-flat Major **A707**
K. 421	Quartet no. 15 in D Minor "Haydn" **A396**

K. 425   Symphony no. 36 in C Major "Linz" **A330**
K. 428   Quartet no. 16 in E-flat Major "Haydn" **A396**
K. 448   Sonata in D for Two Pianos **A273**
K. 449   Piano Concerto in E-flat Major **A161**
K. 452   Quintet for Piano and Winds **A443, A785**
K. 453   Piano Concerto in G Major **A161,**
K. 457   Sonata in C Minor **A321, A389, A589, A673, B8**
K. 458   Quartet no. 17 in B Flat Major "Haydn" **A396**
K. 459   Piano Concerto in F Major **A65**
K. 464   Quartet no. 18 in A Major "Haydn" **A396**
K. 465   Quartet no. 19 in C Major "Haydn" **A396**
K. 466   Piano Concerto in D Minor **A589**
K. 467   Piano Concerto in C Major **A161**
K. 475   Fantasia in C Minor **A471**
K. 476   *Das Veilchen* **A385**
K. 481   Sonata in E Flat for Violin **A471**
K. 491   Piano Concerto in C Minor **A352, A360**
K. 492   *Le nozze di Figaro* **A453**
K. 494   Rondo in F **A726**
K. 499   Quartet no. 20 in D Major "Hoffmeister" **A451**
K. 504   Symphony no. 38 in D Major "Prague" **A40**
K. 511   Rondo in A Minor **A612, A707**
K. 516   Quintet in G Minor **A335, D143**
K. 525   *Eine kleine Nachtmusik* **A451, A579**
K. 527   *Don Giovanni* **A311, A335, A471**
K. 533   Sonata in F **A709, A795**
K. 540   Sonata **A335**
K. 543   Symphony no. 39 in E-flat Major **A335, A359, A459,**
                A484
K. 545   Sonata in C Major **S138, A24, A176, A314, A321, A505,**
                A662, A673, A709, B43
K. 550   Symphony no. 40 in G Minor **S148, A264, A303, A589,**
                A679, A824, D14,
K. 551   Symphony no. 41 in C Major "Jupiter" **A310, A673**
K. 563   Divertimento in E Flat **A65, A621**
K. 570   Sonata in B-flat Major **A709**
K. 574   Gigue in G **A260**
K. 575   Quartet no. 21 in D Major "Prussian" **D143**
K. 576   Sonata in D **A548**
K. 576b   Minuet in D Major **A644, A654**
K. 581   Quintet in A Major for Clarinet and Strings **A632, D98**
K. 589   Quartet no. 22 in B-flat Major "Prussian" **D143**
K. 590   Quartet no. 23 in F Major "Prussian" **A526, A451, D143**

K. 593   Quintet in D Major **D143**
K. 595   Concerto in B Flat **A359**
K. 614   Quintet in E Flat **A64, D143**
K. 620   *Die Zauberflöte* **A294, A336, A690, D251,**
K. 626   Requiem **A451, A827**
Motet: *Laboravi clamans* **A690**

Modest Mussorgsky (1839–1881)
"S njanej," from *Detskaja* **A351**
"Skucay" from *Bez solnca* **A160**
Pictures at an Exhibition: *Catacombae* **A347**

Pauline Oliveros (b. 1932)
1961   *Sound patterns* **D55**
1968   *O Ha Ah* **D55**
1966   *I of IV* **D55**

Petrus de Cruce (1240–98)
Motets from the Montpellier Codex **D134**

Cole Porter (1891–1964)
Night and Day **A44, A59**

Sergei Prokofiev (1891–1953)
Op. 80   Violin Sonata **D142**
Op. 92   Second Quartet **D142**
Op. 94   Flute Sonata **D142**
Op. 119   Violoncello Sonata **D142**

Robert of Valois
Venis sancta spiritus **B43**

Sergei Rachmaninov (1873–1943)
Op. 32/8   Prelude **D24**
Op. 32/10   Prelude **D24**
Op. 32/13   Prelude **D24**
Op. 33   Etude in E Flat **D24**
Op. 39/1   Etude in C Minor **D24**
Op. 39/5   Etude in E-flat Minor **D24**
Op. 39/6   Etude in A Minor **D24**
Op. 39/7   Etude in C Minor **D24**
Op. 39/8   Etude in D Minor **D24**
Op. 42   *Variations on a Theme of Corelli* **D24**

Jean-Phillipe Rameau (1683–1794)
1722   Motet: *Laboravi clamans* **A690**

Maurice Ravel (1875–1937)
1901   *Jeux d'eau* **D164**
1913   *Trois Poemes de Stephane Mallarme* **D164**

Max Reger (1873–1916)
Op. 45/5   Intermezzo **D151**
Op. 81   Variations and Fugue on a Theme of Bach **S147, A723**
Op. 143/1   *Larghetto* **D151**

Rodgers, Richard (1902–79), and Lorenz Hart (1895–1943)
Have You Met Miss Jones **A243**

Alessandro Scarlatti (1660–1725)
Attilio Regolo **A509**

Domenico Scarlatti (1685–1757)
Kr. 9 Sonata in D Minor **S1146**
Kr. 13 Sonata in G Major **S146**
Kr. 78 Sonata **A451**
Kr. 471 Sonata **A548**
Kr. 545 Sonata **A673**

Arnold Schoenberg (1874–1951)
Ca. 1896   *Mein Herz, das ist ein tiefer Schacht* **A343**
Ca. 1912   *Gurre-Lieder* **D242, B96**
Op. 2/2   *Schenk mir deinen goldenen Kamm* **A824**
Op. 4   Verklärte Nacht **B96**
Op. 7   String Quartet no. 1 **A134**
Op. 10   String Quartet no. 2 **A110, A291, B96, B31, D159**
Op. 11/1   Piano Piece **A535, D34**
Op. 11/2   Piano Piece **A230**
Op. 12/2   *Der verlorene Haufen* **A652**
Op. 14/2   *In diesen Wintertagen* **A508**
Op. 15/1   Book of the Hanging Gardens **D152**
Op. 15/2   **A441**
Op. 19   Piano Pieces **A319, D152**
Op. 19/1   Piano Piece **A535, A691**
Op. 19/2   Piano Piece **A731**
Op. 19/3   Piano Piece **A535, A583**

Op. 19/6	Piano Piece **D34**
Op. 21	*Pierrot Lunaire* **A535, D106**
Op. 22	Lieder **A200**
Op. 24	Serenade **D229**
Op. 33b	Piano piece **A16**
Op. 37	Quartet no. 4 **D242**
Op. 47	Phantasy for Violin with Piano Accompaniment **B90**

Franz Peter Schubert (1797–1828)

D. 118	*Gretchen am Spinnrade* **S140, A45**
D. 138	*Rastlose Liebe* **A149**
D. 216	*Meeresstille* **A148, A149**
D. 226	*Erster Verlust* **A673**
D. 233	*Geist der Liebe* **A149**
D. 257	*Heidenröslein* **B43**
D. 279	Piano Sonata in C Major **D194**
D. 300	*Der Jüngling an der Quelle* **A552**
D. 328	*Erlkönig* **A628**
D. 334	Sonata **A45**
D. 365	Waltz **A245**
D. 478	Harfenspieler I **A149**
D. 524	*Der Alpenjäger* **A593**
D. 531	*Der Tod und Das Mädchen* **A552, B43**
D. 544	*Ganymed* **A593**
D. 545	*Der Jüngling und der Tod* **A593**
D. 576	Variations on a theme of Hüttenbrenner **A609**
D. 664	Sonata in A Major **D162**
D. 667	Quintet **A170**
D. 703	Quartettensatz **A110**
D. 751	*Die Liebe hat Gelogen* **A149**
D. 759	Symphony no. 8 "Unfinished" **A72, D14, D128**
D. 768	*Wanderers Nachtlied* **A451, B8**
D. 775	*Dass sie hier gewesen* **A552**
D. 776	*Du bist die Ruh* **A65, B43**
D. 779/13	Valse Sentimentale **A827**
D. 779/2	Valse Sentimentale **A446**
D. 780/1	Moment Musicaux **A648, A653, A656, A658, A659**
D. 780/2	Moment Musicaux **B8**
D. 780/3	Moment Musicaux in F Minor **S143, A577**
D. 780/6	Moment Musicaux in A Flat Major **A208, D194**
D. 795/1	*Das Wandern* **A374, A609**
D. 795/4	*Wohin* **A165**

D. 795/5	*Die Liebe farbe* **A65**
D. 795/6	*Die Neugierige* **A69, A149**
D. 795/7	*Ungeduld* **B43**
D. 795/10	*Tränenregen* **A149**
D. 795/12	*Pause* **A65, A341**
D. 803	Octet **D62**
D. 810	Quartet in D Minor **D62**
D. 814	Quartet **A741**
D. 827	*Nacht und Träume* **A552**
D. 840	Sonata **D248**
D. 845	Sonata **A453, A673**
D. 845	Sonata in A Minor **D194**
D. 849	*Der Wanderer* **A148**
D. 887	String Quartet in G Major **D194**
D. 890	Hippolits Lied **A149**
D. 894	Sonata **A451**
D. 898	Piano Trio in B-flat Major **A208**
D. 899/3	Impromptu in G Flat **S143, A17, A17ᴿ, A150**
D. 899/4	Impromptu **D70**
D. 911/1	*Gute Nacht* **D131**
D. 911/5	*Der Lindenbaum* **D131**
D. 911/7	*Auf dem Fluße* **A46, A352, A582**
D. 911/11	*Frühlingstraum* **D131**
D. 911/12	*Einsamkeit* **A332, D131**
D. 911/19	*Täuschung* **D131**
D. 911/20	*Der Wegweiser* **A332, A366, A451, D131**
D. 929	Piano Trio in E Flat **D62**
D. 929	Piano Trio in E-flat Major **D194**
D. 935/2	Impromptu in A Flat **A208, D194**
D. 940	Four-Hand Fantasy in F Minor **D194**
D. 944	C Major Symphony "Great" **A208**
D. 946	Klavierstück in Eb Major **D194**
D. 947	Lebensstürme **A208, D194**
D. 956	String Quintet in C Major **D194**
D. 957/9	*Ihr Bild* **S135, A28, A58, A738**
D. 957/11	*Die Stadt* **A671**
D. 957/12	*Am Meer* **A671**
D. 957/13	Der Dopplgänger **B43**
D. 958	Piano Sonata in C Minor **D194**
D. 960	Piano Sonata in B-flat Major **D62, D194, D175**

Robert Alexander Schumann (1810–1856)

Op. 6/1	Davidsbündlertänze **A451**

Op. 12/8	*Ende vom Lied* **A350**
Op. 13	Symphonic Etudes **D105**
Op. 15/1	Kinderszenen "Vom fremden Länder und Menschen" **S143**
Op. 15/9	Kinderszenen "Träumerei" **S143**
Op. 24	*Liederkreis* **D135**
Op. 24/4	*Lieb' Liebchen* **B8**
Op. 28/2	Romance in F-sharp **B43**
Op. 39	Liederkreis **D15, D135**
Op. 39/1	*In der Fremde* **A673**
Op. 39/5	*Mondnacht* **A322**
Op. 39/6	*Schöne Fremde* **A322**
Op. 39/9	*Wehmut* **A65, A651**
Op. 42/1	*Seit ich ihn gesehen* **A253**
Op. 45/2	*Frühlingsfahrt* **A625**
Op. 48	Dichterliebe **D108**
Op. 48/1	*Im wunderschönen Monat mai* **A342**
Op. 48/2	*Aus meinen Thränen sprießen* **A330, A342, A374, A522, A585**
Op. 48/7	*Ich grolle nicht* **A342, A630**
Op. 48/9	*Das ist ein Flöten und Geigen* **A342**
Op. 68/12	*Erster verlust* **B43**
Op. 99/5	Albumblatt **A189**

Alexander Scriabin (1872–1915)
Op. 68 Sonata no. 9 **D48**
Op. 33/2 **A607**
Op. 45/1 **A607**
Op. 45/3 **A607**
Op. 49/1 **A607**
Op. 56/1 **A607**
Op. 52/1 **A671**
Op. 78/4 **A16**
Prelude in F Minor **A535**
Enigme **A524**

Ruth Crawford Seeger (1901–53)
Five Songs **D52**
Suite no. 2 **D52**
Three Chants **D52**

Jean Sibelius (1865–1957)
Op. 63   Symphony no. 4 **A45, A110, D141**
Op. 39   Symphony no. 1 **D141**

Op. 105   Symphony no. 7 **D141**
Op. 104   Symphony no. 6 **D57**

Paul Simon (b. 1941)
Still Crazy After All These Years **A104**
I Do It for Your Love **A104**
Jonah **A104**

Richard Strauss (1864–1949)
Op. 24 *Tod und Verklärung* **D231**
Metamorphoses **A85**

Igor Stravinsky (1882–1971)
The Dove Descending **A157**
1948   *Mass* **A363**
1909   *Petrouchka* **B90, B96**
1910   The Firebird **B96**
1911   The Rite of Spring **A16, A535, A745, B96**
1923   Octet **B96**
1920   Symphonies of Wind Instruments **A535**
1921   Les Noces **B96**
1924   Piano Concerto **A21, A671**
Larghetto from *Five Fingers* **B90**

Karol Szymanowskiego (1882–1931)
Pentezilea **A833**

Pyotr Ilyitch Tchaikovsky (1840–93)
Op. 36   Symphony no. 4 **A177**
Op. 64   Symphony no. 5 **A177**
Op. 74   Symphony no. 6 **D231, A177**

Georg Phillip Telemann (1681–1767)
TWV 55   *Musique de table* **A822**
Zwanzig kleine Fugen **A213**

Theodoros Studites
Hymn in remembrance of St. Euphrosyne **B43**

Theophanes
Hymn for the raising of the cross **B43**

Giuseppe Verdi (1813–1901)
Don Carlos **A673**
Il Trovatore **A572**
Un Ballo in Maschera **A545**
Simon Boccanegra **A500**

Felix-Eberhard von Cube (1903–87)
Urworte, orphisch **B43**
Op. 17 Quintet for Saxophone and Strings **B43**

Richard Wagner (1813–83)

WWV 90	*Tristan und Isolde* **A73, A79, A232, A290, A543, A528, A629, A725, A824, B96, B43**
WWV 91	*Wesendonck*-Lieder **A629, D254**
WWV 96	*Die Meistersinger von Nürnberg* **B96**
WWV 86a	*Das Rheingold* **A327, B96**
WWV 86b	*Die Walküre* **B96**
WWV 86c	*Siegfried* **A543**
WWV 86d	*Götterdämmerung* **A383, A303, A543**
WWV 111	*Parsifal* **A543, B96,**
WWV 103	*Siegfrie-Idyl* **A131**

William Walton (1902–83)
Concertos **D178**

Carl Maria von Weber (1786–1826)
Op. 12 *Momento cappricioso* **B43**

Anton von Webern (1883–1945)
Op. 5/4 Five Movements **A610**
Op. 9
Six Bagatelles for String Quartet **A535**
Op. 10/1 Five Pieces **A535**
Op. 10/5 Five Pieces **A535**
Op. 27 Piano Variations **A731, A739**

Hugo Wolf (1860–1903)
Seufzen **A415**
Herr, was trägt den Boden hier **A415**
Sonne der Schlummerlosen **A415**
Das verlassene Mägdlein **A469**
Italienisches Liederbuch **D38**

Wir haben beide lange Zeit geschwiegen **D54**
Sterb' Ich **A556**
Gesang Weylas **A556**

Yatsuhashi
Midare **A670**

Victor Young (1900–56)
Stella by Starlight **A111**

Benjamin McKay Ayotte completed a bachelor of arts *cum laude* from Eastern Michigan University (Ypsilanti, Michigan) in 1995, where he studied Schenkerian analysis with Sylvan Kalib. In 1997 he entered into the master's degree program at Bowling Green State University (Bowling Green, Ohio), where he completed coursework in musicology and music theory. He is currently enrolled in the Ph.D. program in music theory at Michigan State University, where his dissertation will be an analytical study of Schenker's *Lieder* for solo voice and piano. Mr. Ayotte's music bibliography on Schenker is his first publication with Routledge. Ayotte is a member of the Society for Music Theory, The College Music Society, and the American Musicological Society.